American Volunteer Police

Mobilizing for Security

American Volunteer Police

Mobilizing for Security

Martin Alan Greenberg

CRC Press
Taylor & Francis Group
Boca Raton London New York

CRC Press is an imprint of the
Taylor & Francis Group, an **informa** business

CRC Press
Taylor & Francis Group
6000 Broken Sound Parkway NW, Suite 300
Boca Raton, FL 33487-2742

First issued in paperback 2020

© 2015 by Taylor & Francis Group, LLC
CRC Press is an imprint of Taylor & Francis Group, an Informa business

No claim to original U.S. Government works

ISBN-13: 978-1-4822-3254-7 (hbk)
ISBN-13: 978-0-367-66917-1 (pbk)

Library of Congress Cataloging-in-Publication Data

Greenberg, Martin Alan.
  American volunteer police : mobilizing for security / Martin Alan Greenberg.
    pages cm
  Includes bibliographical references and index.
  ISBN 978-1-4822-3254-7 (hardcover : alk. paper) 1. Auxiliary police--United States.
  2. Volunteer workers in law enforcement--United States. 3. Crime prevention--United
  States. I. Title.

  HV8139.G74 2015
  363.2--dc23
                                                                        2014033185

**Visit the Taylor & Francis Web site at
http://www.taylorandfrancis.com**

**and the CRC Press Web site at
http://www.crcpress.com**

This book is dedicated to

the memories of

Gwen Elliott and John T. Gobble Jr.

Gwendolyn J. "Gwen" Elliott was a trailblazing champion for the rights of women, children, the elderly, minorities, and crime victims in her role as a Pittsburgh police commander. In the early 1970s, she was among the group of mothers who founded the Center for Victims of Violence and Crime. In 2002, the year she retired from the Pittsburgh force after 26 years, she founded Gwen's Girls, the first county nonprofit organization dedicated solely to the needs of at-risk girls aged 8–18 years.

John T. Gobble Jr. was the founding director of Point Park University's criminal justice programs and a remarkably gifted educator, mentor, and friend who motivated hundreds of students to succeed because of his caring attitude.

Both John and Gwen were visionaries who worked hard to make Pittsburgh a better place to live and to work.

Contents

Section I
OVERVIEW OF VOLUNTEER POLICING

1 Introduction   3

2 Mobilizing for Security   25

Section II
SPECIAL ISSUES IN VOLUNTEER POLICING

8 Youth Involvement in Police Work   199

9 Youth Involvement in Public Safety and Security at the Federal Level   235

Preface

According to the Federal Bureau of Investigation's *Uniform Crime Reports*, although the violent crime rate has been falling since 1992, it is still more than twice as great as it was in 1960. At the same time that the complexity and burden of police work have been evolving, agency budgets have failed to keep pace with such developments. However, there has been a fascinating trend with respect to the use of police volunteers. Since the end of World War I, the use of mostly unpaid volunteers in sworn or non-sworn capacities has become standard practice in many police departments, including in those of New York City, Washington, D.C., Detroit, and Los Angeles.

Three states lead the nation with respect to the total number of volunteer police officers: Ohio, Florida, and California. Over the years, training for these volunteers has vastly improved, and thorough background investigations are conducted for candidates. For example, all new California reserve police officers are required to attend a basic police academy as mandated by the California State Commission on Peace Officer Standards and Training (POST). The training requirement is the same academy program required of all regular full-time officers. Furthermore, in agencies that meet the standards of the Commission on Accreditation for Law Enforcement Agencies (CALEA), sworn volunteer police officers are required to receive the same training as regular police officers. The intent of this book is to document these trends.

A search on the Web can reveal much about the current status of many of these units. I hope that readers will want to learn more about the augmentation of first responder organizations through the recruitment and training of volunteers and will browse the Web to keep abreast of developments. Various Web sites are cited throughout the book. Readers should keep in mind that these online addresses were only current during the preparation of this book.

This work seeks to introduce the reader to the most current and relevant materials concerning modern units of volunteer police. It highlights what average Americans have done and are currently doing to safeguard their communities. The contributions of volunteers at all levels of government are presented. The materials should be of value to volunteer first responders, youth workers, educators, public officials, organizations, institutions, or private individuals concerned about contemporary public safety issues. In particular, students, urban planners, and emergency public safety administrators should discover within the book essential information about the past, present, and future roles of citizen participation in public safety.

In addition to describing a wide range of contemporary activities performed by volunteer police, this book also offers several recommendations toward utilizing qualified citizens in the following new roles: (1) serving as educators and supplemental staff for the prevention of human trafficking and worker exploitation; (2) serving as language interpreters to assist both documented and undocumented immigrants; (3) leading rescue teams to assist the homeless; (4) aiding youth and other users of community centers; (5) assisting school resource officers; (6) delivering crime prevention presentations to diverse community groups, especially in urban neighborhoods; and (7) augmenting border patrol security in a new federal auxiliary program.

This book is designed to serve as either a reference work or a textbook for courses dealing with public safety and security issues. Given the new responsibilities of the nation's law enforcement establishment, the need for augmenting police services through the use of qualified volunteers has never been greater.

Acknowledgments

Every book involves the assistance of a number of persons. I have had the very capable assistance of Joselyn Banks-Kyle, who served as the book's project coordinator, and Carolyn Spence, the acquisitions editor at CRC Press, a Taylor & Francis Company. In addition, I am very grateful for the permission to reprint Sections 16.3 and 16.4 from the Standards for Law Enforcement Agencies along with the manual's definition of "Reserve" and "Auxiliary" found in Appendix A of this book. The Commission on Accreditation for Law Enforcement Agencies, Inc. (CALEA®) is the registered copyright holder of the materials republished in Appendix A. The materials in this appendix are from *Standards for Law Enforcement Agencies* (©2006, update 5.17 from August 2013; all rights reserved).

I have been able to reach out to a number of law enforcement professionals, activists, historical societies, and scholars for assistance with this book. The following individuals were especially helpful in permitting the use of the various photographs included in this book: Officer Scott L. Harris, Public Information Officer/Explorer Post Advisor, Visalia Office of the California Highway Patrol; Donna Conley, Westbrook (Maine) Historical Society; Dave Griffin, president, Maynard (Massachusetts) Historical Society; Roberta Weintraub, founder of the Los Angeles Police Academy Magnet Schools and founder/executive director, Police Orientation Preparation Program; Michael Kovacsev, Acting Assistant Chief, St. Petersburg Police Department, Investigative Services Bureau; Ken and Patricia Driscoll and their creative and invaluable Web site located at BaltimoreCityPoliceHistory.com; Lt. Joseph Gruver, Cheltenham (Pennsylvania) Township Police Department; Auxiliary Colonel Arthur Wilson, Ohio State Highway Patrol Auxiliary; Michael Suess, chief, Oshkosh (Wisconsin) Auxiliary Police; Zachary Feder, New York City Parks and Recreation; Mark A. Elkins, president, New York City Parks Auxiliary Mounted Unit; and Russ Malone, City Clerk and Clerk of the Waltham City Council in Massachusetts.

For specific textual materials, special thanks are due to: Erick Hoffman, Glenn J. Kearney, president, New York State Association of Auxiliary Police, Inc. (NYSAAP); Philip Franckel, counsel, NYSAAP; James D. Brown, associate director, CALEA; and Bonnie Bucqueroux, Michigan State University. Bucqueroux was the associate director of the National Center for Community Policing at Michigan State University's School of Criminal Justice and currently teaches at Michigan State University's School of Journalism.

Author

Martin Alan Greenberg is the director of research and education for the New York State Association of Auxiliary Police, Inc. He was formerly a professor and administrator of several different criminal justice and law enforcement programs at a variety of colleges and universities including: Virginia Union University, Point Park University (Pittsburgh, Pennsylvania), the University of Hawaii at Hilo, Arkansas State University, and the State University of New York at Ulster. He holds four graduate degrees in criminal justice and law, including a PhD from the City University of New York and a JD from New York Law School. He is the past chair of the Security and Crime Prevention Section of the Academy of Criminal Justice Sciences and holds lifetime board certification in security management. His experiences also include service as senior court officer, probation officer, campus security assistant, and judicial clerk. He is the author of four books and received an honorable discharge recognizing 12 years of service in the New York City Auxiliary Police Force, having obtained the volunteer rank of auxiliary deputy inspector.

Overview of
Volunteer Policing

I

Introduction

1

The fall of Rome occurred over 300 years. That is longer than any democracy, including our own, has survived. As wondrous as it is, we can never take our democracy for granted. It can only survive as long as we, its citizens, are willing to nurture, to defend, and to tend it.

—Bob Schieffer
CBS News, Chief Washington Correspondent, The Citadel,
Corps of Cadets, Commencement Address, May 8, 2010

One of the most pressing crises facing America is the need to balance the various protections offered by the U.S. Constitution concerning individual freedom with public safety. This book is premised on the idea that the unending march of a wide variety of daily crime incidents and continuing threats to national security require the attention of full-time practitioners and qualified members of the general public. Both groups need to contend with these problems by adhering to the rule of law.

The combination of public servants and qualified citizens is needed to address such issues as: guarding borders in order to prevent the entry of illegal aliens, illicit drugs, and possible terrorists; reducing the carnage on our nation's highways; delivering antigun violence programs; supplementing the efforts to enforce "quality of life" laws and ordinances; curtailing human trafficking; and preparing for the radiological "dirty bomb" that could kill thousands. Other potential threats include: the explosion of tank cars carrying chlorine and phosgene gas and the release of plague bacteria in an American city or in Mexico City, resulting in a flood of refugees into the United States.

Nearly 30,000 American lives are lost to gun violence each year—a number far higher than in any other developed country. Since 1963, more Americans have died by gunfire than those perished in combat during the whole of the twentieth century. Gun violence reaches across borders and jurisdictions and compromises the safety of everyone along the way (IACP and Joyce Foundation 2008). No community or person in America is immune. According to Ronald C. Ruecker, the former president of the International Association of Chiefs of Police (IACP) and currently the assistant director of the Federal Bureau of Investigation's (FBI) Office of Law Enforcement Coordination (OLEC), "Every citizen in this country must stop accepting outrageous levels of gun violence in our streets, our schools, and our homes, and we must work with our fellow citizens as well as law enforcement and elected officials to put an end to this continuing tragedy" (Ruecker 2008, 6). These actual and potential threats should be of great importance to all Americans.

This chapter reviews current threats to national security and the need for volunteer preparedness. It also considers highlights in the development of citizen-based law enforcement officers in the United Kingdom and the United States. A brief overview of the office of sheriff is included. A final section summarizes the contents of the remaining chapters of this book.

National Security and Preparedness

About 100 years ago, a now famous poster first appeared on the cover of *Leslie's Weekly*. An illustration of Uncle Sam (as seen in Figure 1.1) appears with a pointed finger and he is declaring "I want you …." In subsequent

Figure 1.1 Illustration of Uncle Sam.

times of crisis, similar posters were designed again featuring Uncle Sam or depicting uniformed soldiers or citizens who had answered their nation's call for service. The need for everyday Americans to answer the call for service remains, although the types of threats have changed.

During the wars of the twentieth century, individuals who were not eligible for military service were encouraged (sometimes pressured) to participate in some type of civilian defense work (fire auxiliary, air raid wardens, auxiliary police, communications, etc.). By the time of the Korean War and the advent of the Cold War, our forebears were constructing and stocking bomb shelters in their backyards and basements. At the same time, children practiced ducking under their desks at school. This was family life in the new era of the A-bomb. This was the homeland defense of yesteryear.

Members of al-Qaeda first attacked the World Trade Center in 1993. The more recent events of September 11, 2001, should encourage all Americans to reconsider their own safety and security. Today, it is not fear of an atomic attack from a superpower that is driving the U.S. foreign and domestic security policy but the fear of a suitcase dirty bomb or some other stealth weapon of mass destruction. Although "al Qaeda has suffered a confusing mix of setbacks and advances ... it's worth reflecting on the many advances al Qaeda has made since 9/11, and on its impressive resilience" (Byman 2011).

Following the September 11 attacks, the federal government focused its energies on providing new measures to protect the nation from future terrorist attacks. The attacks led to a series of government actions aimed at countering the new threat of large-scale terrorism, including the establishment of a cabinet-level Department of Homeland Security. The FBI was not merged into the new department, but it has been reorganized in view of several instances of faulty intelligence gathering. For example, Coleen Rowley, the former chief legal adviser in the FBI's Minneapolis field office, wrote a 13-page letter to the director of the FBI that said that FBI headquarters stymied her efforts in the summer of 2001 to investigate Zacarias Moussaoui, who was eventually charged and convicted as a conspirator in the September 11 attacks. She testified before a Senate panel in June 2002 regarding her concerns. In addition, a memo from an agent in the bureau's Phoenix office came to light. The memo was prepared in July 2001, but it was never acted upon. It had urged FBI headquarters to investigate a group of Middle Eastern men training at U.S. flight schools.

Rowley's letter, a copy of which was also sent to key congressional leaders, was made public when lawmakers began grappling with the question of why the nation's vaunted intelligence apparatus was unable to "connect the dots." Some believed the clues dated back nearly a decade. In 1994, for example, a "test bomb" was detonated aboard a Philippine Airlines jet, which exposed an al-Qaeda plot to blow up more than a dozen jets over the Pacific. In 2000, the Central Intelligence Agency (CIA) began noting increased signs of terrorist activities abroad. In the spring of 2001, specific threats were received by the White House from intelligence sources that said a Middle Eastern terrorist group could potentially attack U.S. interests overseas. Subsequently, U.S. troops were deployed to Afghanistan and then to Iraq. Both interventions took more than double the length of time U.S. forces fought in World War II. The long-term nature of these overseas deployments and possible future ones has raised valid questions about the need for more resources for homeland defense.

Although many American citizens may be unaware or simply complacent about a new kind of war, one in which they may be combatants and targets, U.S. governmental efforts to protect citizens are moving forward. In April 2005, an antiterrorism drill was conducted involving hundreds of people in Canada, the United Kingdom, and the United States. The Canadian component of the simulation was titled "Exercise Triple Play," while the United States conducted "TOPOFF 3." The fictional scenario included the release of a pneumonic plague in New Jersey by a terrorist group and a chemical explosion in Connecticut. Canadian authorities were called upon to deal with victims and perpetrators heading into their country. In the scenario, a fictional senior official requested a plan to restrict the movement of people in New Brunswick, where a luxury ship was carrying victims of the New Jersey incident. The drill revealed a major logistical error—the request was ignored, and no contingency planning occurred!

Although this particular drill revealed significant glitches with antiterrorism planning, it provided a much-needed learning experience for our nation and one of its closest allies. It clearly demonstrated the fact that the United States and Canada need to create a revised civil defense program. Both nations need to ascertain the best ways to become mobilized to defend themselves against internal and external threats.

The events of September 11 have led to some concern about the relative responsibilities of individuals, localities, states, and the federal government to fund and implement protective and recovery programs. Moreover, the havoc of hurricanes, such as Katrina and Sandy, has renewed discussions in this regard. For the most part, the concept of disaster preparedness or even the need for the sharing of "self-help" defense methods has been a very low profile affair. Nonetheless, one of the easiest ways to tap the American citizenry's willingness to serve in the aftermath of September 11 is the formation of block watch and community emergency response teams (CERT).[1] Citizen volunteers can help their community's public safety by serving as the eyes and ears of their local police. In addition, the very presence of such teams will also help to decrease physical and social disorder.

It must be appreciated that although homeland defense recruitment efforts can garner publicity when calls for participation are made by high-ranking officials, local defense relies mostly on local initiatives. The general public should be participating in its own defense. However, the goal of recruiting Americans by the millions to assist with homeland defense has not been accomplished. According to Amitai Etzioni (professor at George Washington University), the problem has been twofold: "The Citizen Corps has only two problems: its name and its size. The name means nothing. It could be about getting people to vote, serve on juries, or remember to renew their passports. For some reason, the obvious title—Homeland Protection Corps—has been avoided....Overall, the Citizen Corps has not caught the eye or imagination of the public and is largely unknown...." (Etzioni 2002, 9).

Nonetheless, since Professor Etzioni's opinion article was published, the Web site pages for the Citizen Corps have been revised and new features have appeared. A new "Ready" campaign has been launched and a host of free independent study courses have been posted. (Information about the courses can be found at: http://www.ready.gov/citizen-corpstraining/ fema-independent-study-courses.) Moreover, materials about new partner and affiliate programs have been posted providing a clearer pathway for learning about the existence of various types of volunteer opportunities. (Links to 11 of these opportunities can be found at: http://www.ready.gov/ volunteer.)

Many citizen law enforcement officers are already serving in unsung units of volunteer police throughout the United States. They are our neighbors, friends, and relatives. They may be bankers, construction workers, teachers, clerks, physicians, and from many other occupations. They fly aircraft and operate boats as part of their duties. They patrol the streets of our eastern cities, the open spaces of the West, and protect our natural resources.[2] Citizens perform law enforcement duties in many countries. There are volunteer citizen peace officers in Canada, Finland, Germany, Holland, Hong Kong, Russia, Israel, South Africa, Singapore, Switzerland, Malaysia, and the United Kingdom (England, Wales, Scotland and Northern Ireland) (Hoffman 2014).

The term "reserve" includes many types of law enforcement officers. Typically, reserve or auxiliary police officers receive their authority for law enforcement by virtue of common law, case law, or statute. They may be entirely volunteer (unpaid) or part-time salaried officers. They may work intermittently for several hours a month or for 40 hours a week for a few months of the year. A number of shore communities on the U.S. East Coast use seasonal peace officers or non-sworn security rangers who work during the summer months.[3] The important distinction between reserve and career law enforcement officers (also called "regular officers") is that the reserve or auxiliary officer's employment, if paid, is not the person's primary source of income; rather such officers (if paid) are usually compensated on a per diem basis. Moreover, these part-time officers are usually not provided with health insurance or pension benefits (Hoffman 2014).

The titles of citizen police officers are varied. Titles include: auxiliary, reserve, special, part-time, supernumerary, and seasonal. In many instances, reserves are not distinguished by any title. One example is the title of "constable." Constables serve in numerous localities throughout the United States. Many constables are not full-time employees and do not receive health benefits or pensions. In Pennsylvania, constables work on a fee basis (collect fees for serving eviction orders, etc.). Many police departments and sheriff offices use paid part-time officers, but there is no difference in the title from a career officer (Hoffman 2014).

Special Constables in the United Kingdom

Citizen law enforcement officers were deployed long before the concept of modern policing took hold in the mid- to late nineteenth century. In these earlier times, such officers were known by a variety of titles, and they had an interesting array of duties and responsibilities. Depending on the era, all adult males were at one time required to keep the peace. For example, they raised a "hue and cry" when there was danger. "In the event of a crime, every man had to join in the 'hue and cry'—summoning aid and joining the pursuit of anyone who resisted arrest or escaped from custody" (Levy 1999, 136). One early group as far back as the tenth century in Britain was known as *constabulus* or count of the stable. Although at first they had a military role, their duties evolved into what today would be considered police duties. Some of these early police or "constables of the manor" were unpaid peace officers who were appointed by the manor court (i.e., selected by the local lord who owned the largest estate). They kept the king's peace, executed warrants, transported prisoners, removed "vagabonds," and set up procedures so that a "hue and cry" could be raised when necessary. Such procedures evolved into the use of villagers who acted as watchmen during the evening hours. Some of the more unpleasant duties of the manor constables were punishing lawbreakers (many were punished for not attending church!) by executing sentences such as dunking in the village pond and whipping. As Britain became more populated, the manor constable evolved into the parish constable. Manor constables as well as parish constables were unpaid peace officers. In addition, the parish constable worked with the justice of the peace (Hoffman 2014).

The unpaid parish constable still exists in Great Britain to this day. They are now called "special constables" and serve in all 43 police forces in Great Britain and Wales. The office of special constable has existed for more than 180 years, since the Special Constable Act of 1831. The act allowed the justice of the peace to "conscript men to combat riot and social unrest." This act was updated in 1914, 1923, and 1964. Special constables played an important role in protecting the public during the Blitz (bombing of Britain) during World War II. Many died in the line of duty (Hoffman 2014). The special constabulary is a voluntary body drawn mainly from the community served by each local force. Specials have full police powers and carry out a range of police work under the supervision and support of regular officers. Specials give a few hours of service each week, typically evenings and weekends. The specials have a key role in the reduction of crime and fear of crime and make a vital contribution to addressing local policing problems. They are volunteer police officers who work with regular police colleagues and other police staff, making an important contribution to the work of the wider police family.

Important new regulations for the special constables came into being in August 2012 and can be viewed at: http://www.legislation.gov.uk/uksi/2012/1961/contents/made. They amend the Special Constables Regulations of 1965 by inserting provisions about: the biometric vetting of candidates for appointment as special constables; the testing of special constables and candidates for substance misuse; and the notification and approval of business interests held by special constables, candidates, and their relatives. The new provisions are effectively identical to those applicable to regular police officers. In recent years, the number of special constables in England and Wales has increased. In 2012, there were more than 20,000 special constables in Home Office forces in England and Wales. This represented a 10.4% increase on the previous year's figures and an important indication of the value of special constables in supporting their regular colleagues in policing (College of Policing 2014).

Overview of Police History in the United States

The history of regular policing in the United States can be roughly divided into four different periods based on the dominance of a particular strategy of policing. In 1805, New Orleans inaugurated a distinctive paramilitary model of policing, and this style was duplicated in "Deep South cities with large slave concentrations" (Rousey 1997, 4). During the first few decades of the nineteenth century, military style policing was in vogue in New Orleans, Richmond, Mobile, Savannah, and Charleston (Rousey 1997, 11–39). The southern military model can be said to represent the first era of modern policing. Rousey (1997, 39) concluded that the military style of policing was used in the South because "policemen who looked like soldiers probably helped ameliorate the deep anxieties many whites harbored about the dangers of slave crime and revolt." The second period consisted of the ending of the Deep South military model and the beginning of the adoption of a civil style of urban policing during the 1840s, continuing through the Progressive Period, and ending after the first third of the twentieth century.

The third period took place from the 1930s through the late 1970s. The years since the latter period comprise the fourth era. Kelling and Moore (1988) have referred to eras two, three, and four as: (1) the political era; (2) the reform era; and (3) the community problem solving or community policing era, respectively. The political era was so named because of the existence of close ties between police and politics. The reform era resulted in reaction to the first era. The reform era has now given way to a period emphasizing community policing strategies (Hartmann 1988).

Office of the Sheriff

The position of sheriff evolved from the "shire-reeve" or headman of the shire, which means county. These officers worked primarily for the king serving "writs" (civil papers and warrants) and collecting tax. They were appointed by the king and, in many instances, it was a very lucrative occupation. Persons either bought or inherited the office of sheriff. They kept a portion of the taxes collected. They also were the direct representative of the king and wielded enormous power. They had very little to do with the day-to-day peacekeeping in the villages and towns. The sheriffs in early British history were viewed by the common people as "oppressors" rather than as "protectors." The sheriff could raise a posse under the common law concept known as *posse commitatus* or "power of the county" (not to be confused with the law in the United States entitled the Posse Commitatus Act of 1878, which generally prohibits the use of the military for direct enforcement of civilian law). The British common law allowed the sheriff to call on citizens to act as volunteer peace officers. They helped keep the peace in times of unrest and apprehended fleeing lawbreakers (Hoffman 2014). About "midway through the sixteenth century until the present time, the office of sheriff in England has had little political clout or government importance compared to the wealth of power that it once had during medieval times. The position of justice of the peace had relieved the last vestiges of the position's former judicial duties" (Buffardi 1998, 17).

The office of the sheriff is the oldest office under the system of common law in the United States and is an integral part of government in all states. In New York State, the office of sheriff is the oldest constitutional law enforcement officer of the county. In addition, the sheriff is charged with maintaining the peace in all municipalities, villages, and townships within his jurisdiction and the care and custody of persons pending court action. The sheriff also serves as the chief executive officer of the courts in some counties. The powers and the duties of the sheriff are embodied in the constitution of each state. There are more than 3,000 sheriffs in the United States who are elected officials; typically, the term of office is four years, and sheriffs are expected to be devoted to their duties full-time and to not hold any other public office. President Grover Cleveland began his political career as the sheriff of Erie County, New York, in 1871. He went on to become mayor of the city of Buffalo, governor of the state of New York, and then president (Erie County Sheriff's Office 2014).[4]

Overview of Volunteer Police History in the United States

The history of volunteer policing may be divided into slightly more diverse periods than those provided for regular policing. The epochs have some degree of overlap. They include: (1) the lay justice period, consisting of the Native American military societies, the militia (including slave patrols), and the constable and watch systems of the colonial settlements, which extended up until the establishment of unified day and night watches in the 1840s; (2) the vigilant era, consisting of the detective societies and posses (including slave patrols) of the nineteenth century as well as the rise of a score of anti-vice societies during the last quarter of the nineteenth century; (3) the spy era (including operatives from the Anti-Saloon League and the American Protective League, as well as charity workers) during the Progressive Era and World War I; (4) the transformation era between 1920 and 1941 (when special purpose units evolved into general purpose police reserve units); and finally, (5) the assimilation era, when civil defense and other varieties of volunteer police became integrated parts of the community policing strategy of many police departments (Greenberg 2005).

The offices of constable and sheriff were imported to the United States during colonial times. In 1651, the colony of Virginia provided for the selection of a sheriff who could summon a posse. The American colonies also had constables. Most were volunteer peace officers appointed by village leaders. Like their British counterparts, they were responsible for keeping the peace and arresting lawbreakers who were then brought before the local justices of the peace. In 1634, in Plymouth, Massachusetts, the constables were responsible for weights and measures, land surveys, and announcing marriages. During the War of 1812, a Maryland posse arrested several British soldiers for disorderly conduct and placed them in the custody of the sheriff. The leader of the posse was captured by the British and imprisoned beneath the decks of a British warship. One of the negotiators for his release was Francis Scott Key. The first peace officer to be killed in the line of duty was Constable Darius Quimby of New York. Constable Quimby was gunned down in 1791 (Hoffman 2014).

As America expanded westward, so did the use of citizens for peace officer work. There were posses of volunteer peace officers that worked for the sheriff. They were per diem part-time deputies, constables, and marshals.

It was not unusual for a person to get a one-day appointment as a deputy sheriff, constable, or marshal to find a lawbreaker and bring him to justice. In the late 1800s, Theodore Roosevelt served as a part-time deputy sheriff. There were also special U.S. Deputy Marshals, appointed by the U.S. Marshal. Special deputy marshals worked for a pittance and sometimes for nothing to protect the citizens in the territories (which were not yet states) from roving bands of outlaws and to administer justice for the federal district courts. Some of these volunteers and part-time lawmen died in the line of duty (Hoffman 2014).

In the 1940s, during World War II, many communities across the United States created auxiliary police units for civil defense purposes (see Chapter 4). Some counties and municipalities authorized their auxiliary units to provide law enforcement services. This happened in those communities that had lost manpower to the military and that needed extra protection at strategic facilities. The 1950s, 1960s, and 1970s saw a growth in citizen law enforcement in the United States. Membership in volunteer police units reflected the composition of each jurisdiction's population. In America's segregated regions, even volunteer organizations formed for the public good reflected social and cultural biases (e.g., see photos of the two squads of Baltimore Auxiliary Police in Figures 1.2 and 1.3).

Figure 1.2 In the city of Baltimore, the auxiliary police were first organized in 1941. However, integration within the Baltimore Police Department did not take place until 1966. Thus, two separate auxiliary police units were maintained for about 25 years. Photo, ca. 1960. (Photo used with permission of Retired Detective Ken Driscoll at BaltimoreCityPoliceHistory.com.)

Figure 1.3 Baltimore Auxiliary Police segregated unit. Photo, ca. 1960. (Photo used with permission of Retired Detective Ken Driscoll at BaltimoreCityPoliceHistory.com.)

By the 1980s, the use of the "civil defense" banner was replaced by the title of "emergency management."[5] However, in the 1980s, there was a decline in the number of programs and volunteer officers due to economic, social, and political changes. After the events of September 11, 2001, there was, at least briefly, a renewed interest in volunteer law enforcement (Hoffman 2014). Although homeland security has become an important national topic and many people would like to become involved, the necessity of maintaining at least two streams of income from both husband and wife can impede participation. In order to encourage recruitment of public safety volunteers, the IACP has hosted a federally funded Web site that features the activities of many citizen law enforcement units. Registration at this site is entirely voluntary. The IACP plans to upgrade their online services in 2014.

The legal authority of citizen police widely varies inasmuch as there are thousands of law enforcement agencies in the United States (see Chapter 10). The training ranges from the same that career peace officers receive (which is usually four to seven months of full-time instruction) to a few hours per week. Some volunteer officers are armed and some are not. Some have the same law enforcement arrest powers as career peace officers; some have limited arrest powers (Hoffman 2014).

Volunteer police serve at all levels of government. However, those at the federal level tend to be in youth programs (such as Explorer posts), seasonal workers, or in such semi-military organizations as the Civil Air Patrol and the Coast Guard Auxiliary. At the local and county levels, volunteer officers are an established part of law enforcement. In recent years, the police agencies in Los Angeles, California; Phoenix, Arizona; and Dallas, Texas, have expanded their reserve programs. In some states, many local municipalities have only part-time police. In a few states, there are reserve state conservation and game enforcement officers as well as auxiliary state police and reserve highway patrol officers. There are even college and university reserve police. One example of reserve law enforcement at the federal level is the use of seasonal U.S. park rangers (Hoffman 2014).

Although the future of reserve law enforcement is unknown, across the nation and the globe, law enforcement agencies are using volunteers to supplement regular police services. Moreover, the need for citizen participation in the fight against terror and crime has increased.

New Developments in Volunteer Policing

In April 2007, a two-day national firearm violence summit was held in Chicago. It was designed and sponsored by the IACP and the Joyce Foundation. The summit had 120 participants. An ad hoc advisory group composed of law enforcement, community health, and academic experts guided the planning and the preparation for the summit. The efforts of the attendees and advisory group led to the development of a comprehensive firearm violence reduction strategy. The final summit report presented a total of 39 recommendations, grouped into three major policy areas: keeping communities safe, preventing and solving gun crime, and keeping police officers safe. A summary of the report was published in *The Police Chief* magazine in April 2008. The report is entitled: "Taking a Stand: Reducing Gun Violence in Our Communities" (see IACP and Joyce Foundation 2008).

Recommendations 2, 3, and 4 of the final summit report are most appropriate for involving members of volunteer police units. Recommendation 2 states: "Law enforcement agencies and their partners should work to identify and implement effective education and prevention programs focused on youth at risk of gun violence" (see IACP and Joyce Foundation 2007, 11). The third recommendation states: "Law enforcement agencies and their partners should work to develop and implement education campaigns targeted at gun owners" (see IACP and Joyce Foundation 2007, 11). The fourth recommendation states: "Law enforcement leaders should devote resources and personnel to establishing and sustaining partnerships with community leaders to combat gun violence" (see IACP and Joyce Foundation 2007, 12). Together these three recommendations appear to represent a clear mandate for including qualified volunteer police in the delivery of a variety of educational programs to reduce the risk of gun violence.

The members of volunteer police units consist of thousands of citizen "partners" who have already made a major commitment in their lives to assist law enforcement and who stand ready to engage in further efforts to promote public safety.

Another important development is the new Commission on Accreditation for Law Enforcement Agencies, Inc. (CALEA) standards concerning the use of volunteer police. CALEA Standard 16.4.1 requires that agencies seeking the commission's national accreditation must have a written directive that establishes and describes the agency's auxiliary program, which includes a statement that auxiliaries are not sworn officers and a description of the duties of auxiliaries, including their role and scope in authority. Standard 16.4.3 states that "If auxiliaries wear uniforms, the uniforms clearly distinguish them from sworn officers." As part of the accreditation process, the CALEA standards also specify that every member of a volunteer or paid reserve force must complete the same training as a full-time certified police officer. Thus far, only 4% of the 18,000 non-federal law enforcement agencies in the United States have earned CALEA accreditation (Carder 2013). These standards are quite relevant to the future of volunteer policing because they demonstrate a distinction between the two major types of contemporary volunteer police: auxiliaries and reserves. Moreover, in several jurisdictions (Kansas City, Connecticut State Police, etc.), these particular new national training standards for police department accreditation have been used as the principal justifications for phasing out the use of existing volunteer police units. On the contrary, in addition to enlisting the services of volunteer police in antigun violence campaigns, police agencies seeking national accreditation and those interested in maintaining either type of volunteer police program should consider the programs proposed in Chapters 2, 11, and 12 of this book.

A third important development in the field of volunteer policing concerns the youth enrolled in Law Enforcement Explorer units. Since 1998, Explorer programs have been a cooperative venture with Learning for Life, an association affiliated with the Boy Scouts of America (BSA). Over the past few decades, hundreds of police agencies have established Explorer posts designed to give young men and women between the ages of 14 and 21, a chance to develop leadership skills and to learn about the wide range of law enforcement careers. In fact, according to John Anthony, national director of Learning for Life, there are more than 2,000 law enforcement posts across the country with 35,000 members (Steinhauer 2009). A new certification program exists for Law Enforcement Explorer posts. On a voluntary basis, each police agency or related organization now has an opportunity to have its Explorer basic or advance training programs recognized by the national office of the Explorer program (see Chapter 8 for more details). The new Explorer training standards are bound to promote a greater pool of qualified candidates for regular and volunteer police units.

Furthermore, these police candidates could also be tapped for assistance with antigun violence campaigns.

A fourth factor that is an encouraging development despite some very early criticism was the creation of the Citizen Corps itself. In January 2002, the president of the United States launched Citizen Corps to capture the spirit of service that emerged throughout our communities following the terrorist attacks of September 11, 2001. Citizen Corps was created to assist in coordinating volunteer activities to help communities better prepare to respond to any emergency situation. It provides opportunities for people to participate in a range of measures to make their families, their homes, and their communities safer from the threats of crime, terrorism, and disasters of all kinds. Citizen Corps is coordinated nationally by the Department of Homeland Security's Federal Emergency Management Agency. A few of its various initiatives have been indicated here.

In this day and age, there maybe a few reasons for not favoring the establishment and expansion of more volunteer police units. Perhaps the main one is that volunteers might replace regular full-time first responders. Police leadership can do much to dispel this type of fear. It is also critical that police officials in charge of their agencies and desirous of having effective volunteer police units know how to work with people, especially in groups (King 1960). With about 4,500 auxiliary police officers in New York City and perhaps as many as 200,000 or more nationwide, it is appropriate that qualified units of volunteer police play a significant role on behalf of homeland security and related concerns. Throughout this book, the term "volunteer police" is used to refer to authorized permanent groups that perform one or more police functions in an overt manner for little or no salary (Greenberg 2001).[6]

Chapter Overviews

Chapter 2 addresses the present-day need for citizen mobilization to enhance public safety related to national security as well as local quality of life concerns. It includes materials about local and national organizations. Historical information about militia forces is discussed. At the national level, the roles of the Corporation for National and Community Service (CNCS) and the Federal Emergency Management Agency (FEMA) Corps are outlined.

Chapter 3 presents an overview of the early history of volunteer police involving such groups as Native American military societies; militia units; slave patrols; the watch and ward; the posse and anti-horse thief society members; vice-suppression societies; boy police; and early volunteer caseworkers. In addition, this chapter presents materials concerning the largest volunteer domestic spy organization in the nation's history—the American Protective League.

Chapter 4 examines seven different auxiliary and reserve volunteer police units. They have distinctive names, but a lack of consistency in the use of unit titles makes it difficult to ascribe specific characteristics to each category. Nevertheless, a trend appears to have developed with respect to the use of titles in certain parts of the United States, especially within several New England states and in California. The seven units discussed are: the Buffalo (New York) Police Reserve; Brentwood (California) Reserve Police; the Cheltenham Township (Pennsylvania) Auxiliary Police; the Los Angeles (California) Reserve Police; the New York City Auxiliary Police; the New York City Parks Mounted Auxiliary Unit; and the Albemarle County (Virginia) Auxiliary Police.

Chapter 5 reviews the origins of several state police agencies as well as events associated with the development of auxiliary or reserve state police units to supplement the strength of their parent organization. The agencies examined are those of Alabama, Arizona, Connecticut, Florida, New Hampshire, Ohio, South Carolina, and Vermont. In addition, the events associated with the sudden demise of one historic regional volunteer police group are presented. This happened in 2005, when the Pennsylvania House of Representatives voted 198–0 to repeal the charter of a 133-year-old volunteer police unit known as the "State Police of Crawford and Erie Counties." The unit was established by legislation passed in 1872. The initial law set up a volunteer force to arrest horse thieves during a time when the nearest organized police force was across the state in Philadelphia, hundreds of miles to the east. The group provided traffic and crowd control at community events in the two counties. In the year prior to its ending, the organization had 100 active members and provided more than 4,000 hours of volunteer service.

Chapter 6 highlights the following national (nonprofit) and federal organizations: the Metropolitan Police Reserve Corps, the Civil Air Patrol, the U.S. Power Squadrons, the U.S. Coast Guard Auxiliary, and the FEMA Reserves. In addition, a proposal to consider the establishment of a Border Patrol Auxiliary is considered. The chapter begins with background materials about the nature of the federal government and some historical aspects related to a federal role in public safety.

Chapter 7 describes the nature and purpose of a variety of non-sworn or non-peace officer roles and involvement in groups such as: chaplains; Citizens Assisting Pasadena Police (CAPP Patrol); equestrians; Community Response to Eradicate and Deter Identity Theft (CREDIT); Missing Persons Unit (MPU); Pawn Detail; Criminal Investigations Division's Victim Assistance; records and traffic sections; general volunteers; and the Youth Accountability Board. In addition, brief reviews of a variety of adult citizen police academy programs are presented as well as their advantages and disadvantages. Following this information, a new role is proposed for qualified members of volunteer police units to serve as "neighborhood police academy" instructors.

Chapter 8 focuses on the establishment of various prominent local youth programs: youth (junior) police academies; junior police programs (e.g., P.A.L., Explorers, and cadets); school safety patrols; police academy magnet schools; and youth courts. The origins and purposes of the various programs are described, and recommendations concerning future trends are discussed. One of the newest models for the delivery of police education and training for youth, the Police Orientation and Preparation Program (POPP), is reviewed. This chapter also addresses the topics of liability and insurance as well as youth protection from abuse. Reportedly, many law enforcement officers serving at the federal, state, county, and local levels have been motivated to undertake their careers due to their experiences as Explorers.

Chapter 9 also deals with the development and activities of youth involvement with law enforcement work but focuses on the national level. The following current federal law enforcement or military related youth initiatives are reviewed: Senior (college level) Reserve Officer Training Corps (ROTC) units; the Coast Guard's College Student Pre-commissioning Initiative (CSPI) program; Junior ROTC units; FEMA Corps; U.S. Navy Sea Cadets; and the Civil Air Patrol Cadet Program. The nature of the federal Law Enforcement Explorer Leadership academies and Explorer posts are examined. For historical perspective, the civilian military training camps of past generations are described. In addition, a few federal internship programs are reviewed.

Chapter 10 considers the wide range of legal rights and responsibilities associated with volunteer police work as well as a discussion regarding the nature, problems, and issues associated with the creation of police/citizen partnerships. In particular, the following topics are covered: the status and authority of volunteer police; sovereign immunity and the public duty doctrines; indemnification in claims of negligence; the Law Enforcement Officers Safety Act of 2004 (LEOSA); The Volunteer Protection Act; and the impact of CALEA standards on volunteer policing. Chapter 12 also continues the discussion of CALEA standards.

Chapter 11 considers the important role that volunteer police and other concerned individuals may play in the prevention of human trafficking and worker exploitation. Human trafficking is considered to be one of the fastest growing criminal industries in the world. This chapter indicates the various types of existing human slavery (contract, chattel, etc.) and describes a citizen's role in the prevention of human trafficking. In addition, the purposes of the Trafficking Victims Protection Act of 2000 and the definition for human trafficking established by the Palermo Protocol are provided.

Chapter 12 concludes the book's discussions regarding America's volunteer police by reviewing a few of the emerging trends for citizens willing to undertake the duties of part-time volunteer police. Several new roles for volunteer police are identified involving school safety, the protection of the homeless, and immigration issues. Qualified unit members should also be able to conduct a variety of school-based crime prevention educational programs such as Drug Abuse Resistance Education (D.A.R.E.), Gang Resistance Education and Training (G.R.E.A.T.), or antiviolence and bullying classes. They can also conduct workshops devoted to the prevention of carjacking and to how to respond in the event of active shooters. In addition, a new program is proposed with a focus on training college students to be fully certified reserve police officers in conjunction with their undergraduate studies.

Summary

Volunteer police can serve many roles—for example, protecting against the illegal entry of terrorists, reducing highway fatalities, delivering antigun violence programs, curtailing human trafficking, enforcing quality of life statutes, and limiting the damages caused by the potential use of a weapon of mass destruction. With respect to national security and preparedness, the events of September 11, 2001, have led to new concerns about the relative responsibilities of individuals, localities, states, and the federal government to fund and implement protective and recovery programs. Ongoing threats relating to natural disasters require advance planning. The availability of cadres of CERT units and other types of volunteers is essential for aiding in the immediate aftermath of hurricanes, floods, and tornadoes.

The titles of citizen police officers are varied. They include auxiliary, reserve, special, part-time, supernumerary, and seasonal. In the United Kingdom, the volunteer police are known as "special constables." Important new rules governing the appointment of special constables have been established, and these are effectively identical to those applicable to regular police officers. There are about 20,000 specials performing routine patrol duties alongside regular constables in the United Kingdom. In the United States, the terms "reserves" or "auxiliaries" refer to citizen volunteer police officers. They became prominent when organized into various units during World War I and World War II, although unpaid "posse" members had been recruited in frontier towns during the nineteenth century. The offices of constable and sheriff were imported to the United States during colonial times. In the United States, the modern position of sheriff is an adaptation of the earlier role of the shire-reeve or sheriff in the United Kingdom. Sheriffs are still authorized to summon "the power of the county" (i.e., those able-bodied people who may be needed in times of distress).

The history of volunteer police can be divided into five epochs having some degree of overlap, including from earliest to latest: the lay justice period featuring the Native American military societies, the militia, and so forth; the vigilant era consisting of the detective societies and posses; the spy era during the Progressive Era and World War I; the transformation era between 1920 and 1941; and the assimilation era when civil defense and other varieties of volunteer police become an integrated part of the community policing strategy of many police departments. Volunteer police serve at all levels of government. However, those at the federal level tend to serve in youth programs, such as Explorer posts, or in such semi-military organizations as the Civil Air Patrol and the Coast Guard Auxiliary. There are also an interesting range of seasonal positions at the federal level.

There have been several important developments in the field of volunteer policing in recent years. The first has to do with new opportunities for volunteer police to participate as coequals with regular police in the initiation and delivery of antigun violence programs. This can be inferred from several recommendations found in the report prepared by the IACP and the Joyce Foundation. However, whether this will take place in any community is at the discretion of police administrators. A second opportunity is presented by the new CALEA standards concerning the use of volunteer police. These standards can be used to upgrade the training of volunteer police, and they can also serve as a catalyst for police agencies to assign new responsibilities to members of their volunteer police units. However, several agencies have thus far demonstrated an unwillingness to take this opportunity to enhance their sworn volunteer programs and have instead opted to eliminate them on fiscal grounds. Third, a new national certification program has been instituted to recognize those Law Enforcement Explorer programs that are adhering to specific guidelines with respect to their basic or advance training programs.

Review Questions

1. Identify at least four activities that citizens can undertake to assist in the improvement of public safety.
2. Search online for recent articles concerning al-Qaeda. State your findings.
3. Distinguish between volunteer reserve and career law enforcement officers.
4. Indicate several highlights regarding the history of volunteer policing.
5. Discuss the evolution of the position of sheriff in the United Kingdom.
6. Search online to find any examples of volunteer police being used for the activities you identified in response to question one. Present your findings.
7. Contrast the historical periods associated with the development of volunteer policing with those of regular policing.
8. Important new rules governing the appointment of special constables have been established in the United Kingdom. What is the nature or purpose of these rules?

9. State the author's definition of volunteer police. Is it appropriate? Discuss.
10. Search the Citizen Corps Web page (at: http://www.ready.gov/ volunteer). Use the links at this Web page to browse various homeland defense volunteer opportunities and discuss at least two programs that caught your attention.

Notes

1. There are more than 2,200 official CERT programs registered at: http://www. citizencorps.fema.gov/cc/CertRegWizard.do. "The Community Emergency Response Team (CERT) Program educates people about disaster preparedness for hazards that may impact their area and trains them in basic disaster response skills, such as fire safety, light search and rescue, team organization, and disaster medical operations. Using the training learned in the classroom and during exercises, CERT members can assist others in their neighborhood or workplace following an event when professional responders are not immediately available to help. CERT members also are encouraged to support emergency response agencies by taking a more active role in emergency preparedness projects in their community" (CERT 2014).
2. In 1981, the U.S. Congress authorized the Natural Resources Conservation Service (NRCS), formerly the Soil Conservation Service, to accept volunteers aged 14 and above to increase soil and water conservation efforts and to do this by working closely with Soil and Water Conservation Districts. Referred to as the "Earth Team," volunteers work side by side with professionals from NRCS, helping to protect and conserve the Earth's natural resources. A list of the types of jobs volunteers do is located at: http://www.nrcs.usda.gov/wps/ portal/nrcs/main/sc/people/volunteers/
3. For example, the New York State Park Police hire seasonal State Park and Recreation Public Safety Rangers (PSR). PSRs provide general public safety services throughout the state in support of the state park police. This is a seasonal-only position, generally from late May to Labor Day. PSRs are subject to the provisions of the Security Guard Act of 1993, are unarmed, and have neither peace nor police officer status. PSRs are assigned to patrol park facilities and grounds, maintain order, enforce park ordinances/regulations, and answer questions from park patrons. On a situational basis, incumbents may also assist with search and rescue operations and marine patrol. For more information, go to: http://nysparks.com/employment/park-police/default. aspx
4. An interesting U.S. Supreme Court Case involving whether a county sheriff is representing the state or the county when he acts in a law enforcement capacity was decided in *McMillian v. Monroe County*, AL, 520 U.S. 781 (1997). Petitioner McMillian sued Monroe County, AL, under 42 U.S.C. § 1983 for allegedly unconstitutional actions taken by the Monroe County sheriff. If the sheriff's actions constituted county "policy," then the county is liable for them. The parties agreed that the sheriff is a "policymaker" for § 1983 purposes, but

they disagreed about whether he is a policymaker for Monroe County or for the state of Alabama. In affirming the Court of Appeals for the Eleventh Circuit's dismissal of petitioner's § 1983 claims against Monroe County, the court held as to the actions involved in this case that the sheriff represented the state of Alabama and is therefore not a county policymaker. An important factor in the court's decision was the fact that the Alabama's Constitution, adopted in 1901, states that "the executive department shall consist of a governor, lieutenant governor, attorney general, state auditor, secretary of state, state treasurer, superintendent of education, commissioner of agriculture and industries, and a sheriff for each county" (Article V, Section 12, 520 U.S. 787). Moreover, the Alabama Supreme Court had already declared "unequivocally that sheriffs are state officers, and that tort claims brought against sheriffs based on their officials [sic] acts therefore constitute suits against the State, not suits against the sheriff's county" (520 U.S. 789). The court also used a historical analysis in coming to its conclusion. Chief Justice Rehnquist declared: "[The] petitioner's disagreement with the concept that 'county sheriffs' may actually be state officials is simply a disagreement with the ancient understanding of what it has meant to be a sheriff" (520 U.S. 795). The *McMillian* decision involved a 5–4 vote with Justices Stevens, Souter, Ginsburg, and Breyer dissenting.

5. The most significant and earliest instance of federal involvement in disaster relief occurred in 1803 when a series of fires swept through the port city of Portsmouth, NH. In response to the disaster, Congress passed legislation that provided relief for Portsmouth merchants, the Congressional Act of 1803. In the decades to follow, until the middle of the twentieth century, Congress dealt with each new disaster with special legislation adopted on a case-by-case basis. During the 1930s, the federal government incorporated disaster relief as part of its wide-reaching legislation to rebuild the U.S. economy. By the middle of the decade, laws were in place that provided federal funds for the reconstruction of public facilities, highways, and bridges damaged by natural disasters. During the 1950s, emergency management was dominated by wartime civil defense activities that the government believed would prepare the nation for a possible nuclear attack. A series of massive hurricanes and earthquakes during the 1960s and early 1970s served to focus public attention on natural disaster relief. In 1974, the Disaster Relief Act was enacted, establishing a process for presidential declarations of national disasters (Origins 2014).

Despite these changes, emergency and disaster activities remained fragmented. More than 100 federal agencies were involved in some aspect of these efforts, while state and local governments had many parallel programs and policies. The need to centralize federal emergency functions was made even more acute by the much publicized Three Mile Island nuclear power plant accident in 1978. In 1979, President Jimmy Carter signed an executive order to create FEMA. FEMA absorbed a host of disaster-related agencies, including the Federal Insurance Administration, the National Fire Prevention and Control Administration, the National Weather Service Community Preparedness Program, and the Federal Disaster Assistance Administration. It also assumed responsibility for civil defense (Origins 2014). Hence, the civil defense banner gave way to the new umbrella branding provided by the phrase: "emergency management."

In March 2003, FEMA joined 22 other federal agencies, programs, and offices in becoming the U.S. Department of Homeland Security. The new department brought a coordinated approach to national security from emergencies and disasters—natural and manmade. In 2006, President George W. Bush signed into law the Post-Katrina Emergency Reform Act. The act significantly reorganized FEMA, providing it with substantial new authority to remedy gaps that became apparent in the response to Hurricane Katrina in August 2005, the most devastating natural disaster in U.S. history, and included a more robust preparedness mission for FEMA (FEMA 2014).

6. This definition is not as robust as the one the author used in a previous work, but it is offered here for the sake of brevity. In the longer version, volunteer police are defined as: "Individuals who are members of a permanent organization (or one established during wartime mobilization) authorized by either governmental or societal action for the purpose of performing one or more functions of policing in an overt manner (i.e., functions that go beyond surveillance or communications work) for minimal or no salary" (Greenberg 2005, 14).

References

Buffardi, H. S. (1998). History of the office of the sheriff. Retrieved January 27, 2014 from http://www.co.ulster.ny.us/sheriff/admin/history/toc.htm

Byman, D. L. (2011). The history of al Qaeda. Retrieved January 26, 2014 from http://www.brookings.edu/research/opinions/2011/09/01-al-qaeda-history-byman

Carder, D. (2013, October 30). Police disband reserve force. Retrieved June 22, 2014 from http://ottawaherald.com/news/103113reserve

CERT. (2014). Community Emergency Response Teams. Retrieved January 26, 2014 from http://www.fema.gov/community-emergency-response-teams

College of Policing. (2014). Special Constabulary. Retrieved January 26, 2014 from http://www.college.police.uk/en/10040.htm

Erie County Sheriff's Office. (2014). History. Retrieved January 27, 2014 from http://www2.erie.gov/sheriff/index.php?q = history

Etzioni, A. (2002, July 25). Mobilize America's foot soldiers. *The Christian Science Monitor*, p. 9.

FEMA. (2014). About the agency: History. Retrieved January 28, 2014 from http://www.fema.gov/about-agency

Greenberg, M. A. (2005). *Citizens defending America: From colonial times to the age of terrorism*. Pittsburgh, PA: University of Pittsburgh Press.

Greenberg, M. A. (2001). *The evolution of volunteer police in America*. Ph.D. diss., City University of New York/John day College of Criminal Justice.

Hartmann, F. X. (1988). *Debating the evolution of American policing* (Perspectives on Policing, No. 5). Washington, DC: U.S. Government Printing Office.

Hoffman, E. (2014). A history of reserve law enforcement. Retrieved January 26, 2014 from http://www.reservepolice.org/History_of_Reserves.htm

IACP and Joyce Foundation. (2008). IACP and Joyce Foundation summit and report: Taking a stand: Reducing gun violence in our communities. *The Police Chief,* 75(4), 26–34.

IACP and Joyce Foundation. (2007). Taking a stand: Reducing gun violence in our
    communities; A report from the International Association of Chiefs of Police
    2007 Great Lakes Summit on Gun Violence. Retrieved June 22, 2014 from
    http://research.policyarchive.org/96387.pdf

Kelling, G., and Moore, M. (1988). *The evolving strategy of policing* (Perspectives on
    Policing, No. 4). Washington, DC: National Institute of Justice and Harvard
    University.

King, E. M. (1960). *The auxiliary police unit.* Springfield, IL: Charles C. Thomas.

Levy, L. W. (1999). *Origins of the bill of rights.* New Haven, CT: Yale University Press.

Origins. (2014). Origins of U.S. emergency management. Retrieved January 28, 2014
    from http://online.annamaria.edu/emergencymanagementhistory.asp

Rousey, D. C. (1997). *Policing the southern city: New Orleans, 1805–1889.* Baton
    Rouge, LA: Louisiana State University Press.

Ruecker, R. C. (2008). President's message: The need to take a stand against gun
    violence. *The Police Chief, 75*(4), 6.

Steinhauer, J. (2009, May 14). Scouts train to fight terrorists, and more. *New York
    Times*, p. A1.

Mobilizing for Security

2

> The ordinary, loyal, and decent citizens are themselves a priceless asset in combating terrorism if only they can be mobilized to help the government and security forces.
> —**Paul Wilkinson**
> *(1986, 25)*

We live in an age where catastrophic events often seem to be inevitable. As if worldwide wars of aggression and episodes of massive genocides were not enough during the twentieth century, the twenty-first century has already witnessed a wide range of manmade disasters because of terrorist actions. In addition, scores of floods, tsunamis, tornadoes, and other climatic events have produced mass casualties. In the United States, many disasters and mass casualty events are generally handled at the local level. At such times, the first few hours of response by the affected community will be critical. In brief, communities must look to themselves and adjoining communities for survival assistance. The formal agencies of response will be needed as well as those at the "grassroots" level. The latter consists of "community groups, such as civic organizations, religious groups, Boy/Girl Scout troops, and high school sport teams, among others. These groups provide ... social support for participation in the planning and response effort that will help individuals stay engaged over time, even during times of perceived 'low risk' when apathy about preparedness can become pervasive" (Joint Commission 2005, v).

It is a human desire to want to be safe and feel secure in everyday activities. In the United States, such a sense of security also includes being safe from the fear of arbitrary government intrusion or the intrusion of others. Under the U.S. system of justice, the police are the guardians of not only our safety but also our freedom. Today, most Americans feel it is altogether appropriate to rely on police agencies and their full-time sworn officers to effectively deal with any wrongdoers within the parameters set out by the criminal justice system. Americans trust that the police will be able to enforce the law and at the same time be respectful of the rights of the accused.

Fire departments have long depended on volunteers to accomplish their missions, but the duties and capacities of volunteer police are not generally known. However, since the end of World War II, the use of unpaid volunteers in sworn or non-sworn capacities has become standard practice in many police departments, including those in New York City, Washington, DC, Detroit,[1] and Los Angeles. This chapter explores why such volunteers are needed to enhance public safety for national security as well as for local quality of life concerns. It includes materials about local and national organizations. At the national level, the roles of the Corporation for National and Community Service, the Civil Air Patrol (CAP), and the Coast Guard are briefly considered. Greater details about federal and volunteer police relationships are presented in Chapter 6.

Militia

The U.S. Army traces the military organization we know today as the National Guard to a declaration made on December 13, 1636. On this date, the Massachusetts General Court in Salem, for the first time in the history of the North American continent, established that all able-bodied men between the ages of 16 and 60 were required to join the militia. The North, South, and East Regiments were established (Boehm 2012).

Every American colony except Pennsylvania organized a militia system during the seventeenth century. Generally, militia companies consisted of all free adult white males. Militia members were required to provide their own weapons, to keep them in good order, and to attend regular drills. The power to muster militia units was given to local militia officers because "the threat of surprise attack and the isolation of many localities made that power essential" (Cress 1982, 4). Militia officers were either elected by militia members, local assemblies or officials, and/or appointed by the colonial governor. By the middle of the eighteenth century, the militia had ceased to be a viable citizen army that could be mustered for frontier defense or other military requirements. According to Cress (1982, 7), "instead of a citizen army, colonists relied on special fighting forces manned by draftees and volunteers and officered by British regulars or American colonists holding commissions outside the militia establishment." However, in the North, the militia registry was used for the purpose of organizing night watch duty among community members (Cress 1982). During times of public disorder, units of the militia were called upon. In the North and the South, the militia was used to maintain the institution of slavery (Cress 1982).

In South Carolina, the repression of African Americans was codified between 1690 and 1740. These codes restricted almost all aspects of life including freedom of movement, religious worship, and work habits. They were enforced by the sheriff, the constable, and the slave patrol (Henderson 1976). For a complete review of the topic of slave patrols, Sally Hadden's book entitled *Slave Patrols: Law and Violence in Virginia and the Carolinas* (Harvard University Press 2001) is recommended.

Militia members not only helped to fill the ranks of the night watch and slave patrols but militia membership also provided a sense of affiliation and identification with one's settlement, town, and county. In general, this was of critical importance not only for general peacekeeping but also for survival. However, in the indigenous region (backcountry) of South Carolina, the lack of sufficient means for mobilization or even a court system contributed to the rise of a vigilante organization known as the "Regulators." In the mid-1700s, due to wilderness conditions, an area that was only 30–40 miles away from a population center—such as Charleston—was referred to as the backcountry. The Regulators were "a group of law-abiding citizens who organized patrols and tried members of criminal bands and others deemed to have committed crimes" (Johnson and Wolfe 1996, 121). In 1769, with the passage of the Circuit Court Act, the Regulator movement faded into history (Regulators 2014). There was also a "Regulator" movement in North Carolina that tried to effect governmental changes in the 1760s due to the abuse of local officials. After the American colonies obtained independence, various national militia laws were adopted—the first in 1792. The greatest reforms took place in 1903 and 1908. These laws repealed the Militia Act of 1792 and divided the militia into two groups: the Reserve Militia, defined as all able-bodied men between 18 and 45, and the Organized Militia, defined as state units receiving federal support. The latter became the National Guard of today (Donnelly 2001). Additional materials about the history of the militia and vigilantes are presented in Chapter 3.

Slavery divided the nation until the conclusion of the Civil War. But it was replaced by Jim Crow laws that fostered segregation and second class citizenship for black Americans that continued until new national civil rights laws were enforced. "Jim Crow was the name of the racial caste system which operated primarily, but not exclusively in southern and border states, between 1877 and the mid-1960s. Jim Crow was more than a series of rigid anti-black laws. It was a way of life. Under Jim Crow, African Americans were relegated to the status of second class citizens. Jim Crow represented the legitimization of anti-black racism" (Pilgrim 2012). In 1896, the U.S. Supreme Court affirmed a segregation law in Louisiana in the case of *Plessy v. Ferguson*. "Plessy gave Jim Crow states a legal way to ignore their constitutional obligations to their black citizens" (Pilgrim 2012). The *Plessy* decision set the precedent that "separate" facilities for blacks and whites were constitutional as long as they were "equal." The "separate but equal" doctrine was quickly extended to cover many areas of public life, such as restaurants, theaters, restrooms, and public schools. The doctrine was a fiction because facilities for blacks were always inferior to those for whites. Not until 1954, in the equally important Supreme Court decision of *Brown v. Board of Education of Topeka*, would the "separate but equal" doctrine be struck down.

Civil Defense

During World War II, the most ubiquitous form of volunteer police were the members of various civilian defense units. For example, volunteers in the War Emergency Radio Service were able to transform the basic automobile radio of that era into a shortwave War Emergency Radio Service set, permitting the auxiliary police communications officers to maintain constant two-way contact with their control centers. Thousands of volunteers also served in the Air Raid Protective Service and the Auxiliary Police Service. The members of these services played a unique role in guarding the various points where saboteurs might hope to operate, especially around gas tanks, power houses, telephone exchanges, and water works.

Although the end of World War II was greeted with spontaneous celebrations, especially after the defeat of Nazi Germany, America's reliance on atomic weaponry to end the war with Japan was to cast a mushroom cloud over all Americans and the rest of the world. As a result of the Cold War, American citizens had to face the fact that any hope of survival would be dependent upon some degree of luck and their own survival skills and degree of preparations. In case of nuclear attack, many Americans would not only become targets but also combatants. It was the Federal Civil Defense Administration's job to encourage citizens to adapt to their nuclear present and future. Many of the same types of civilian defense services established during World War II were resurrected for this new era.

Since 1959, during the time of the Cold War, there has been an auxiliary police force in Oshkosh, Wisconsin (see Figure 2.1). It began as an auxiliary police/civil defense organization to assist the Oshkosh Police Department at all public functions involving large numbers of people, as well as to assist in

Figure 2.1 The Oshkosh (Wisconsin) Auxiliary Police Color Guard was established in May 2000. Color Guard unit coordinator Auxiliary Captain Scott Footit appears at the far left. Various services are provided by the auxiliary police. For example, during the school year, they deploy a radar speed trailer at school zones throughout Oshkosh. The first class of recruits graduated from their academy in April 1959. There are currently 40 members in the volunteer police force, and there have been more than 380 auxiliary officers in the group. Nine members have become police officers in the Oshkosh Police Department. (Courtesy of the Oshkosh Auxiliary Police, Wisconsin and used with permission.)

any disasters or emergency situations within the city. The primary function at that time was a civil defense role. During the 1960s—at the height of the Cold War era, unit membership was as high as 70–80 members. All association with the civil defense function was eliminated in the 1970s as the auxiliary police organization's role evolved (Oshkosh Auxiliary Police 2011).

Today, a sudden and potentially devastating incident may arise due to terrorist actions. During World War I and World War II, and during the era of the Cold War (about 1947 to 1991), Americans were also beset by threats to homeland security. These concerns became even weightier after the Soviets acquired atomic capabilities in 1949. The fears expressed since 1945—that the next war might result in the end of civilization—seemed to be coming closer to reality. This new threat ushered in the Cold War and the reinstitution of civil defense planning efforts. Posters and pamphlets advocated parental readiness, and children were taught to "duck and cover" by the cartoon character Bert the Turtle (as seen in Figure 2.2).

In 1956, a 16-minute film produced by the Radio-Keith-Orpheum (RKO) Corporation for the Federal Civil Defense Administration (FCDA) highlighted the main threat to American safety and security during the Cold War—nuclear attack. The film discusses how the United States was built on the spirit of neighborliness and cooperation. The narrator explains that cooperation is required for survival of a nuclear attack and the key to survival is to be organized through civil defense. The film provides a brief view of the National Civil Defense Administration, headquartered in Battle Creek, Michigan, and then explores the volunteer work that has to be done at the local level to accomplish the goals of civil defense. In this film, the Berks County Civil Defense unit (which includes the city of Reading, Pennsylvania) is presented as a model program for other communities. In the aftermath of an attack, armed auxiliary police officers would maintain order.

Figure 2.2 "Bert the Turtle" illustration from 1951 pamphlet published by the U.S. Federal Civil Defense Administration.

"The people of Reading work together in a remarkable display of patriotism, public spirit, community pride, personal responsibility, and mutual assistance" (Oakes 1995, 4). The film is entitled *Alert Today—Alive Tomorrow*. A 9-minute clip from this film is available online at: http://www.youtube.com/watch?v=c3ZnNsVyWMA.

Quality of Life Matters

The threat of nuclear attack has greatly diminished since the collapse of the Soviet Union in 1991. Today, many law enforcement agencies are facing a variety of new responsibilities relating to gun violence, human trafficking, cybercrimes, homeland security, domestic abuse, and immigration enforcement. Moreover, the public is expecting excellence in all areas of service, including public nuisances. The term "quality of life offenses" is generally used to describe conduct that demoralizes community residents and business people because it involves acts that create physical disorder (e.g., graffiti or vandalism) or that reflect social decay (e.g., prostitution). These behaviors may be merely minor annoyances to some people, but they can be major problems for the community. These acts may also be accompanied by nuisances that affect the community's health and safety, such as noise and public urination. Although they are generally not serious enough to result in felony charges or to be the focus of large-scale enforcement operations, these misdemeanors and violations cause a great deal of misery to community residents. Such offenders need to be held accountable, but it is also important to offer them the assistance they need to avoid further criminal conduct.

As a response, police patrols have been directed toward many quality of life matters, such as prostitution and vandalism, and less than 15% of police time is being devoted to more serious law enforcement initiatives (Manning 1995). For example, in 2013, Jeffrey Blackwell was appointed chief of police in Cincinnati, Ohio. (Blackwell had been the deputy chief of police in Columbus and had 26 years of service experience.) His main concerns were to reduce crime and the fear of crime. Based on the findings of the community-oriented policing model, he announced plans to focus on quality of life issues, such as lighting in alleys, abandoned needles, graffiti, trash, loud noise, and teenage problems (Smith 2013). Police Chief Blackwell pointed out that police "have to get to know folks in their community by name—and not just the bad ones" (Smith 2013). Quality of life concerns the public, and members of the public are needed to relate information to the police about suspicious behavior.

Using volunteers to help supplement sworn staff is a possible way for law enforcement agencies to continue to enhance the safety of the community when police agencies are losing manpower. Community safety is promoted by having additional resources available to contend with quality of life matters, to increase the efficiency of sworn personnel, and to strengthen linkages between citizens and police. The North Miami Beach Police Department Neighborhood Services and Inspections (NSI) unit has taken volunteerism to a new level by using police recruits from local academies to volunteer their time to gain experience in the field. The NSI Community Policing Cadet Program allows "these cadets [to] patrol the city for quality of life issues, offering a valuable service—providing free services to the agency" (Alqadi 2011). Subsequently, in May 2012, Detroit's police chief announced an "Enhanced Police Reserve Program." The program made it a requirement that any person who applies to become a Detroit police officer must first serve as an active reservist. At the time, Police Chief Ralph Godbee said the department had about 240 reserve officers, but the goal was to recruit 200–250 more (Hackney 2012).[1]

In a paper concerning the design of a restorative community justice model, Bonnie Bucqueroux (2004) presents a three-phase plan. The first phase involves the synthesis of the diverse reform pieces of the existing justice systems. The second requires the branches and agencies within the justice apparatus to transform themselves by becoming learning labs or organizations, willing to change their nature from "an expert, command-and-control model to participatory management where managers act as coaches who nurture a climate that promotes innovation" (Bucqueroux 2004). The third phase focuses on the community "so that they become full partners in the process of merging formal and informal social control into a unified, community-based approach. Agencies and organizations also need to embrace the model of collaboration, open communication, and participatory management that they want communities to mirror" (Bucqueroux 2004). The third phase calls for the engagement of community participants in order that America's rate of incarceration (the highest in the world) and its crime rates can be reduced. The full utilization of the energies and talents of the American populous should be employed by the agencies of the justice system. For many years, this resource has been neglected, and communities continue to suffer. Box 2.1 reveals an episode of such neglect, but it also indicates how it might be overcome.

Volunteer Police Mobilization at the Local Level

Fortunately, since the end of World War I, the use of unpaid volunteers in sworn or non-sworn capacities has become standard practice in many police departments, including those in New York City; Washington, DC; Detroit; and Los Angeles. However, greater participation is still needed. The resources for planning and responding to natural disasters, potential terrorist attacks, and quality of life matters can be greatly enhanced through the recruitment,

BOX 2.1   A REALITY CHECK

The importance of involving the community in all phases of decision making cannot be overstated. I well remember the time a community resident, let's call her "Mary," stopped a meeting with local police dead in its tracks. "I have been coming to these meetings for months now. And I appreciate all your hard work. But I still see the same problem outside my window each day at noon." What Mary saw each day during the summer was a 12-year-old prostitute plying her trade.

The young girl would ride her bike in a circle in the intersection of the quiet residential neighborhood where Mary had lived for many decades. The girl's adult male pimp would sit on the curb, waiting to negotiate with customers. Mary would watch businessmen come by during their lunch hour. They would pay the girl's pimp, the girl would climb into the man's car, from which she would emerge a few minutes later. Mary often called police, but even when patrol cars arrived quickly, the girl and her pimp would always spot them coming and disappear.

Not only did Mary's story underscore the importance of dealing with the community's priorities, it also reminds us that the system alone can never have all the answers. Police, prosecutors, and courts can play a role in arresting and prosecuting the girl's pimp. Clearly, she and her family also need professional interventions and services. But there are important roles that the community can play in saving at-risk kids. This can mean recruiting neighborhood residents into a community patrol that can intervene when the girl and her pimp show up, with the police as protector. Saving kids one by one could also mean finding new ways for women in the community to play the role of formal and informal advisors and mentors, again with the system playing a role in setting up opportunities for old and young to form supportive relationships.

Engaging the community is not just a nice thing to do, it is the most effective way of addressing the underlying conditions that allow problems like child prostitution to persist. Given sufficient structure, support, and funding, our communities can function as learning labs, a place where professionals and community residents can work together to make the most of collaborative strategies.

Source: Bucqueroux, B., 2004, Restorative community justice: A comprehensive approach to reducing crime and violence in our culture. Available at: http://www.policing.com/articles/rcj.html. With permission.

selection, and training of qualified volunteer police. Opportunities currently exist and should be made more widely available to permit auxiliary and reserve volunteer police to perform a wide range of quality of life crime prevention and enforcement activities.

In a number of jurisdictions, auxiliary police are not authorized or trained to conduct quality of life enforcement duties or are not even able to issue summonses for parking violations. For example, New York City auxiliary police officers may only engage in traffic control, beat patrols, and provide security at public events. A few youthful auxiliaries may work in plainclothes under direct supervision of vice enforcement or precinct conditions unit supervisors. They are trained to attempt to purchase alcohol, box cutters, and other items that are not permitted to be displayed or sold to minors in licensed premises. Such undercover operations take place at restaurants, bars, and liquor and grocery stores based on community complaints. Relevant summonses are issued by borough vice and precinct conditions units using such auxiliary police (Kelly et al. 2008). Clearly, deciding to add responsibilities for volunteers requires imagination on the part of police leadership. However, this is a characteristic that Drucker (1990) warns can become suppressed in volunteer organizations.

On the contrary, due to shrinking budgets, various police officials have found that volunteers are indispensable in dealing with low-level offenses because they allow their full-time sworn officers to focus on more pressing crimes and more violent criminals. For example, Fresno's police chief, Jerry Dyer, whose department has lost more than 300 employees in recent years, has stated: "We had the option to either stop handling those calls or do it in a different manner ... I've always operated under the premise of no risk, no success. And in this instance, I felt we really didn't have very much to lose" (McKinley 2011). The Fresno, California, volunteers handle nonviolent crimes such as petty theft, stolen vehicles, and vandalism that is not gang-related.

Other chiefs facing budget problems are also using volunteers. In Mesa, Arizona, a Phoenix suburb, 10 volunteers have been trained to process crime scenes, dust for fingerprints, and even swab for DNA. In addition, volunteers supplement Mesa's sworn police force by on-scene processing of subjects who have been arrested for drunk driving. This processing includes fingerprinting and photographing the suspect and taking blood and urine samples. Volunteers work out of a specially equipped van, which responds to the location of the arrest for the processing. Program supervisor Sgt. Bill Peters stated: "I only have eight police officers for DUIs in a city of 440,000 people. If it weren't for the volunteers, I'd have to pull officers off the road to do the things the volunteers do. The volunteers are just as responsible as officers in keeping citizens safe from drunk drivers" (Worton 2003, 13). In Pasadena, California, a team of retirees is working to reduce identity theft. According to

Officer Celestine Ratliff, the volunteer liaison for the Charlotte-Mecklenburg Police Department in North Carolina, "citizens are more receptive to our volunteers than to our officers" (McKinley 2011).

Volunteer Police Mobilization at the National Level

In addition, volunteers are also needed to perform important law enforcement–related functions at the federal level. For example, the U.S. Coast Guard lacks the personnel and resources to fill critical gaps in its safety and security missions without help from its volunteer arm, the Coast Guard Auxiliary. It is for this reason that Homeland Security and Coast Guard leaders have become dependent on the Auxiliary to achieve a number of Coast Guard missions, a reliance that has become more tenuous because Auxiliary membership has dropped about 21% since 2003 to the current 28,635. This trend is in sharp contrast to membership trends in other large volunteer groups in the United States. For example, Dooris (2008) indicated that Coast Guard Auxiliary membership is declining even though membership in the CAP is rising.

Notwithstanding the decrease in enrollments in the Coast Guard Auxiliary, Americans are volunteering at record numbers; although there has been a moderate decline since 2005 (Dooris 2008). In 2011, an estimated 64.3 million Americans (more than one in four adults) volunteered through a formal organization, an increase of 1.5 million from 2010. The 7.9 billion hours these individuals volunteered is valued at $171 billion. Among citizens who volunteered through an organization, the top activities included fundraising or selling items to raise money (26.2%); collecting, preparing, distributing, or serving food (23.6%); engaging in general labor or transportation (20.3%); or tutoring or teaching (18.2%) (Volunteering 2013).

At one time, America's leading national civilian voluntary program was the Civilian Conservation Corps (locations of work camps are indicated in Figure 2.3). Formed in March 1933, the Civilian Conservation Corps (CCC) was one of the first New Deal programs. It was a public works project intended to promote environmental conservation and to build good citizens through vigorous, disciplined outdoor labor. President Franklin Roosevelt believed that this civilian "tree army" would relieve the rural unemployed and keep youth "off the city street corners." The CCC operated under the supervision of the U.S. Army. Camp commanders had disciplinary powers, and corpsmen were required to address superiors as "sir." By September 1935, more than 500,000 young men had lived in CCC camps, most staying from six months to a year. In all, nearly 3 million young men participated in the CCC (Foner and Garraty 1991).

Today, individuals aged 14 and above can still volunteer for conservation purposes. Volunteer positions are available within the Natural Resources

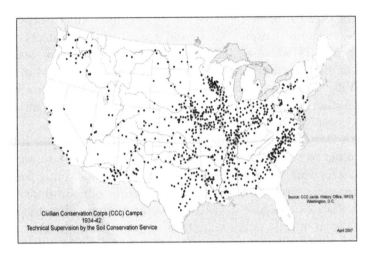

Figure 2.3 Location of Civilian Conservation Corps Camps, 1934–1942.

Conservation Service (NRCS), a division of the U.S. Department of Agriculture. NRCS partners with conservation groups and others to ensure private lands are conserved, restored, and more resilient to environmental challenges such as climate change. Working side-by-side with farmers and ranchers, the NRCS identifies natural resource concerns, such as soil erosion and water quality issues, and develops unique conservation plans for restoring and protecting resources. There are more than 19,000 volunteers who are considered an integral part of the NRCS agency, and they serve in every state (USDA Volunteers 2014).

Today, the leading federal agency devoted to encouraging Americans to volunteer is the Corporation for National and Community Service (CNCS). It is the nation's largest grant maker for service and volunteering, playing a critical role in strengthening America's nonprofit sector. CNCS's board of directors and chief executive officer are appointed by the president and confirmed by the senate. The chief executive officer oversees the agency, which includes about 600 employees operating throughout the United States and its territories (About CNCS 2013). Established in 1993, the CNCS has engaged more than 5 million Americans in service through its four core programs: Senior Corps, AmeriCorps, Federal Emergency Management (FEMA) Corps, and the Social Innovation Fund. AmeriCorps is often referred to as "the domestic Peace Corps." AmeriCorps and the Peace Corps are committed to service, and both offer challenging and rewarding full-time opportunities. Peace Corps assignments are all overseas, and AmeriCorps members serve only in the United States. Although Peace Corps volunteers serve for two years, assignments in AmeriCorps usually last 10 months to one year. Unlike the Peace Corps, some AmeriCorps projects may have part-time opportunities (FAQs 2013).

AmeriCorps has several service tracks including: AmeriCorps National Civilian Community Corps (NCCC) and AmeriCorps Volunteers in Service to America (VISTA). AmeriCorps NCCC is a residential, team-based, national service program that engages young adults aged 18–24 in full-time service. VISTA is the national service program designed specifically to fight poverty. Authorized in 1964 and founded in 1965, VISTA was incorporated into the AmeriCorps network of programs in 1993 (FAQs 2013).

FEMA Corps is a service track within AmeriCorps NCCC. It began in 2012 in order to strengthen the nation's ability to respond to and recover from disasters while expanding career opportunities for young people aged 18–24. Appendix B presents a modern era time line of nonmilitary national service initiatives. Because a specific federal program directly involving America's local or state police volunteers does not exist, the time line does not include any information about the rise of such volunteers since the World War II era. Nevertheless, the International Association of Chiefs of Police (IACP) has found a vast increase in the number of volunteers that are being used by American law enforcement agencies to perform police duties since 2004. A recent estimate of the number of police volunteers is well above 200,000. In fact, numerous U.S. police agencies have some type of volunteer worker. There are more than 2,000 such volunteers according to the IACP (U.S. Department of Justice 2011). The U.S. Bureau of Justice Assistance, under its Local Law Enforcement Block Grant Program, has awarded grants to police agencies for projects involving partnerships between community organizations and local law enforcement agencies to prevent crime in business districts, on school grounds, and around high-risk areas such as abortion clinics; for hiring additional police officers and purchasing necessary equipment to increase the effectiveness of police departments; for partnerships between social agencies and local law enforcement that combat domestic violence and child abuse; and for the development of computer systems that allow fingerprint identification, the maintenance of criminal history records, and so forth.[2] (Interested persons can search http://Grants. gov for federal grants by keywords or by more specific criteria. All discretionary grants offered by the 26 federal grant-making agencies can be found on this Web site.) Perhaps the best opportunity for a governmental agency or non profit organization to obtain funding related to a volunteer police project is through the AmeriCorps State and National Grant Competitions.

Civilianization

Clearly, the establishment of full-time police forces has not abated the need for supplemental volunteers and paid personnel. Most local and state police agencies in the United States recruit and train salaried civilian employees.

These efforts shift some of the duties typically reserved for sworn staff to civilian employees as a means of cost savings. The term civilianization generally refers to a law enforcement agency's hiring of non-sworn personnel in order to replace or supplement its current sworn staff (Forst 2000). By utilizing civilians to perform duties typically undertaken by sworn staff, police departments are able to save money primarily through lower pay, reduced training requirements, and smaller overhead requirements. According to one study, entitled *The Privatization and Civilization of Policing*, estimates from New York City indicate the average cost of a civilian employee is about one-third to one-half that of a sworn officer, even when they are performing the same functions (Forst 2000). In Oklahoma City, civilians working as part-time police ambassadors take on some of the light duties formally performed by police, such as giving directions or working special events (Loren 2010). The Mesa, Arizona, Police Department has begun using civilians for everything from crime scene processing to fraud investigations. They created a team of nine civilian investigators who are paid 30–40% less than an officer. In 2010, the unit handled about 50% of all burglary calls (Adams 2011).

In addition, since America's entry into World War II, the use of unpaid volunteers in sworn or non-sworn capacities has become a standard practice in many police departments. The titles of such volunteers varied throughout the twentieth century but, by the second half of the century, there emerged two distinctive categories for unpaid or low-paid volunteers: *auxiliary* and *reserve*. The titles *reserve deputy sheriff*, *reserve posse member*, and *reserve officer* are more common throughout the western and mid-western regions of the United States, while the designation *auxiliary police officer* appears to be in common usage in the eastern regions.

Irrespective of the specific title in use, there are volunteer units in every state. However, three states lead the nation with respect to the total number of sworn volunteer police officers: Ohio, Florida, and California. Over the years, training for these volunteers has vastly improved, and complete background investigations are usually conducted for candidates. For example, all new California reserve police officers are required to attend a basic police academy, as mandated by the California State Commission on Peace Officer Standards and Training (POST). Significantly, the training requirement for full-service volunteer reserve police officers in California is the same academy program required of all regular full-time officers.[3]

It is therefore somewhat surprising, given their numbers, that only one well known and national initiative has been undertaken to help recruit and otherwise publicize the existence of local volunteer police in the United States. The Volunteers in Police Service (VIPS) program is managed by the IACP with financial support from the Bureau of Justice Assistance. The goal of the VIPS Program is to enhance the capacity of state and local law enforcement to use volunteers. A variety of volunteer management tools can be found on a newly revised VIPS Web site. Citizens who wish to volunteer their time and skills with a law enforcement agency can find Information for contacting program coordinators.

More federal initiatives are needed to coordinate or at least assist in the training of additional police volunteers in case of a national, regional, or state emergency.[4] In fact, only a handful of states have initiated volunteer state police units. Yet assuming sufficient numbers, carefully trained and screened volunteer police could be deployed to reduce the yearly slaughter due to traffic accidents; to help secure homeless shelters and aid America's homeless population; to present antibullying and antiviolence programs to increase school safety and security[5]; to control human trafficking; and to tend to a host of matters involving everyday quality of life concerns. Several of these initiatives and recommendations are addressed in Chapters 11 and 12. It is again important to state that in this book, the terms "volunteer police" or "police volunteer" are used to refer to authorized permanent groups that undertake one or more police functions in an overt manner for little or no salary. In most cases, volunteer police are unpaid, and they pay for their own uniforms and personal equipment.

Counterterrorism Planning

Since the catastrophic events of September 11, federal and local authorities have been very reluctant to mobilize the community in such a way that the United States could be said to possess a new security force—the people of America—aligned and prepared to stop terrorists before they strike. Preferences in this regard still emphasize the military or semi-military establishment.

Guarding against future acts of domestic terrorism should be a number one concern of all Americans. By the end of the 1990s, President Clinton was urging the country "to get the very best ideas we can to try to strengthen this country's hand against terrorism" (quoted in Purdum 1996). At that time, several experts in the field commented that the problem of countering terrorism is complicated by the nature of America's open society, its large and diverse population, and the simmering hostility and anger felt by some groups in our society. Jeff Beatty, a terrorism expert who worked on security planning for the Olympic Games in Los Angeles in 1984 and in Barcelona in 1992, observed: "In the counterterrorism business, if you're investigating, you've already lost the battle. The key is stopping an attack beforehand. Terrorists build practice bombs and conduct casing and rehearsal activity that may be suspicious. Citizens need to chip in with additional eyes and ears to report suspicious activity. To win the war, we need an organization and tools designed from the ground up to beat terrorism worldwide" (Greenberg and Cooper 1996). A similar view was offered by Robbie Friedmann, another

Olympic security consultant, who stated: "The community should be called on to help law enforcement do their job. It's common sense. There are more of them than security personnel" (Greenberg and Cooper 1996).

At the federal level, the United States has two major volunteer organizations that could be given a greater role in the prevention of terrorism—the CAP and the Coast Guard Auxiliary. The CAP (as seen in Figures 2.4 and 2.5) was conceived in the late 1930s by legendary New Jersey aviation advocate Gill Robb Wilson, who foresaw aviation's role in war and general aviation's potential to supplement America's military operations. With the help of Fiorello La Guardia, the Mayor of New York, the new CAP was

Figure 2.4 Students of the Incident Command System School, Civil Air Patrol National Emergency Services Academy (NESA) conduct a tabletop exercise on search and rescue response and operations planning at Camp Atterbury, Edinburgh, Indiana, July 25, 2013. The Incident Command System School of NESA covers the skills required to be a leader and operate in a command post and operations management role. (Courtesy of Ashley Roy, Atterbury-Muscatatuck Public Affairs, Edinburgh, Indiana.)

Figure 2.5 Civil Air Patrol Master Sgt. Nathan Baker (left), CAP Staff Sgt. Troy Henson (center), and U.S. Air Force Staff Sgt. Angelito Cooper (right) pose with informational brochures following the CAP Clovis High Plains Composite Squadron change of command, May 28, 2013. The CAP organization was established as the official auxiliary of the Air Force in 1948 and was charged with three primary mission areas: aerospace education, cadet programs, and emergency services. (Courtesy of U.S. Air Force photo/Senior Airman Whitney Tucker.)

established on December 1, 1941, just days before the Japanese attacked Pearl Harbor. During World War II, the civilian group's mission expanded when German submarines began to prey on American ships off the U.S. coast and CAP planes began carrying bombs and depth charges. The CAP coastal patrol flew 24 million miles, found 173 submarines, attacked 57, hit 10, and sank two. By presidential executive order, CAP became an auxiliary of the Army Air Forces in 1943. A German commander later confirmed that coastal U-boat operations were withdrawn from the United States "because of those damned little red and yellow airplanes" (Congressional Record 2012). In all, CAP flew a half-million hours during the war, and 64 CAP aviators lost their lives in the line of duty. The U.S. Air Force was created as an independent armed service in 1947, and CAP was designated as its official civilian auxiliary the following year. CAP currently has 60,000 members and three main missions: to develop its cadets, to educate Americans on the importance of aviation and space, and to perform lifesaving humanitarian missions (History of Civil Air Patrol 2014).

Since its creation by Congress in 1939, the U.S. Coast Guard Auxiliary has served as the civilian, nonmilitary component of the Coast Guard. Today, more than 28,000 volunteer men and women of the Auxiliary are active on the waterways and in classrooms in more than 2,000 cities and towns across the nation. Each year, its members save nearly 500 lives, assist some 15,000 boaters in distress, conduct more than 150,000 courtesy safety examinations of recreational vessels, and teach more than 500,000 students in boating and water safety courses (Membership 2014).

The traditional roles of police include law enforcement, crime prevention, order maintenance, delivery of services, and the protection of civil liberties and rights. Terrorism involves the commission of a violent act for the purpose of making some kind of political statement. The most important role that local volunteer police can provide to help prevent terrorism is engaging in routine community safety and security patrols. Various experts have asserted that the U.S. Justice Department has neither the power nor the resources to effectively prevent terrorism. Moreover, even with stricter controls, surveillance, and other security measures in confined spaces such as buildings and airports, a particular act of terrorism may be impossible to stop. Philip Stern, a New York-based terrorism expert, has noted that Israel has survived because it has mobilized its citizens into a variety of professional and volunteer protective services (Greenberg and Cooper 1996). Alertness for suspicious behavior and objects and the reporting of such suspicions are critical to thwarting terrorist attacks. Appendix C provides a list prepared by the Federal Bureau of Investigation (FBI) of suspicious activities that should be reported. See Box 2.2 for a list of volunteer opportunities involving citizens in the prevention of terrorism.

**BOX 2.2   CITIZEN PARTICIPATION
OPPORTUNITIES IN TERRORISM PREVENTION**

- Citizen Corps Councils, which help drive local citizen participation by coordinating Citizen Corps programs, developing
community action plans, assessing possible threats, and identifying local resources
- The Community Emergency Response Team (CERT), which is
a training program that prepares people in neighborhoods, the
workplace, and schools to take a more active role in emergency
management planning and to prepare themselves and others
for disasters
- An expanded Neighborhood Watch Program, which incorpo-
rates terrorism prevention and education into its existing crime
prevention mission
- Volunteers in Police Service, who provide support for resource-
constrained police departments by using civilian volunteers to
free up more law enforcement professionals for frontline duty
- The Medical Reserve Corps, which coordinates volunteer
health professionals during large-scale emergencies to assist
emergency response teams, provide care to victims with less
serious injuries, and to remove other burdens that inhibit the
effectiveness of physicians and nurses in a major crisis

Since 1996, the State and Local Anti-Terrorism Training (SLATT) program has been funded by the U.S. Department of Justice, Bureau of Justice
Assistance. It has trained more than 120,000 state, local, and tribal law
enforcement officers in classes designed to help recognize and prevent terrorist attacks. Both on-site and online instruction is provided. The SLATT
program provides specialized multiagency antiterrorism detection, investigation, and interdiction training and related services at no cost to U.S. law
enforcement officers (SLATT 2014).

In the United States, the police and the citizens they serve must realize
that their combined efforts are needed to combat terrorism. The resulting
synergism can accomplish much more than their isolated individual efforts.
Citizens need to be included in governmental planning to combat terrorism. Their additional eyes and ears could help to report suspicious behavior.
Remember again Beatty's observation that, in the realm of terrorism, if you
are reacting to an emergency, such as a bombing, you have already lost the
battle—and maybe the war.

However, the idea of calling upon the community for assistance is often seen as a last resort, and when the call has gone out it is typically limited to asking citizens to respond to a toll-free hotline or to an e-mail address. Not surprisingly, the police may receive numerous calls that have little validity or value. Furthermore, although reserves and auxiliary units have been recruited by many police agencies, they are sometimes viewed as competitors because patrol officers feel that their jobs are threatened by unpaid volunteers.

Despite such drawbacks, there are several ways in which auxiliary police or reserves could be used in a day-to-day way for the purpose of promoting counterterrorism. For starters, the federal government could officially recognize the potential contributions of volunteer police by establishing a special training division at one or more of its training centers. Such centers would teach appropriate reporting techniques, crime prevention, and surveillance skills. Further, state governments could establish and train auxiliary police units for the specific purpose of screening employees in sabotage-prone industries, such as transportation workers and those working in ports and in fuel depots. Auxiliaries with appropriate training also could be assigned to teach crime prevention skills to the general public at Citizen Police Academies.

The armed forces including the National Guard are vital to U.S. security, but so much needs to be done. America needs to consider a new composite security force of qualified citizens, organized into largely civilian-based units such as CAP, the Coast Guard Auxiliary, and state and local auxiliary/reserve police units. The establishment of a fully trained volunteer Border Patrol reserve should also be implemented. The regular use of this new force would appear to be a natural type of counterterrorism strategy. Chapter 6 provides additional details regarding a proposal to establish a U.S. Border Patrol Auxiliary. If governments were to recognize their potential, the current forces marshaled against terrorism could be greatly enlarged. Moreover, this new combination of the American people and governmental organizations should be able to accomplish what they could not have achieved alone—establishing a much safer America with full regard to the dignity and freedom of all. Herman Melville once wrote: "We cannot live for ourselves alone. Our lives are connected by a thousand invisible threads, and along these sympathetic fibers, our actions run as causes and return to us as results" (Joint Commission 2005, 1). "The invisible threads that connect individuals, as described by Melville, must be pulled together to create a surviving community fabric" (Joint Commission 2005, 1).

Thus far, American planning has refrained from drawing upon the types of organizational structure developed as a result of its civilian mobilization during the World War II and Cold War eras. Nonetheless, it has maintained and, in some cases, enhanced the duties and responsibilities of existing volunteer units. America's reluctance to mobilize all of its citizen resources may be due to the fact that the creation of previous civil defense programs not only disrupted the lives of most Americans but produced new dilemmas about the degree to which civilian society should be militarized to defend itself against internal and external threats. Conflicts arose about the relative responsibilities of states and citizens to fund and implement home front security programs. The federal government had attempted to popularize and privatize military preparedness. The doctrine of "self-help" defense demanded that citizens become autonomous rather than rely on the federal government for protection. In many ways, during these earlier eras, families were expected to reconstitute themselves as paramilitary units that could quash subversion from within and absorb attack from without (McEnaney 2000).

Despite a considerable amount of planning at various levels of government, there still appears to be a lot more to do to mobilize the nation. Throughout the history of the United States, various conflicts have arisen regarding the use of average Americans as resources for community safety. Some of the earliest efforts in this regard are chronicled in the following chapter.

Summary

In colonial America, the militia served as a source of personnel for the earliest night watches as well as for southern slave patrols. A Regulator movement developed in the 1760s in South Carolina involving groups interested in establishing law and order. Slavery divided the nation until the conclusion of the Civil War. But it was replaced by Jim Crow laws that fostered segregation and second class citizenship for black Americans that continued until new national civil rights laws were enforced. New national laws in 1903 and 1908 created the Organized Militia, which became known as the National Guard.

This chapter also presented several ways volunteer police may be used for the purpose of countering terrorism and advancing public safety. For example, at the time of disasters, the efforts of both formal and informal agencies of response will be needed. The latter consists of community groups, such as civic organizations, religious groups, and Boy/Girl Scout troops. At such times, the CERT and volunteer police units will play important roles.

Carefully trained and screened volunteer police can also be deployed to deal with everyday problems. They can help to reduce the yearly slaughter due to traffic accidents, help to keep homeless shelters safe, present antibullying and violence programs to increase school safety and security, control human trafficking, and tend to a host of matters involving everyday quality of life concerns.

Guarding against future acts of domestic terrorism should be the number one concern of all Americans. At the federal level, the United States has two major volunteer organizations that could be given a greater role in the prevention of terrorism: the CAP and the Coast Guard Auxiliary. In addition, the federal government could officially recognize the potential contributions of volunteer police by establishing a special training division at one or more of its training centers. At the local level, states and police departments could allow auxiliaries with appropriate training to teach crime prevention skills to the general public at Citizen Police Academies. Moreover, federal and state agencies could establish and train auxiliary police units for the specific purpose of screening employees in sabotage-prone industries, such as ports, passenger transportation hubs, and fuel depots.

Review Questions

1. View the 9-min. clip from the film entitled *Alert Today—Alive Tomorrow*. Discuss whether any aspects of this film might be considered relevant today.
2. Provide at least two examples of "quality of life" crimes or problems.
3. Do you believe it is appropriate to require police academy cadets to engage in active street patrols in their free time or for police applicants to be required to serve as reserve officers? Discuss.
4. Discuss the pros and cons of using volunteer police to enforce low-level or misdemeanor crimes.
5. Visit the Web site for the Corporation for National and Community Service (CNCS) and determine if any of its four core programs have any new announcements. Describe your findings.
6. What do the CCC camps of the 1930s and today's NRCS volunteers have in common?
7. What do paid civilian police employees have in common with volunteer police officers?
8. The SLATT program provides an on-site training schedule and online training modules at no charge to law enforcement officers. Discuss the pros and cons of having this training available to volunteer police.
9. State at least two ways the federal government could augment the capacity of auxiliary police or reserves for the purpose of promoting counterterrorism.
10. Explain the role of the Civil Air Patrol during World War II.
11. Indicate the three main tasks of today's Civil Air Patrol.
12. Discuss why Americans were instructed at the height of the Cold War to prepare for possible roles as combatants.
13. Read the full article on the building of a Restorative Community Justice model by Bonnie Bucqueroux (2004). Based on your reading, discuss the value of creating "learning organizations."

Notes

1. The program also will allow retired officers to serve as reservists. Those officers would be able to maintain their state law enforcement certification, which expires after two years of inactivity. Reserve officers are volunteers who are trained and uniformed and who carry weapons and have full power to make arrests under the direction of a sworn Detroit police officer. Chief Godbee said the reserve officers will be used for special events where foot patrols are necessary and to help in various precincts. "We acknowledge challenges in public safety relative to resources, and this is a huge untapped resource," Godbee said. "We have a ready pool of people who have expressed a desire to be a Detroit police officer, but at times when we're not hiring, we need to leverage that energy and that desire, and it also gives us an assessment period to see if they really will fit in with our Police Department" (Hackney 2012).

2. A major exception was the funding of the VIPS Web site under the management of the IACP. In addition, the federal government has funded numerous initiatives involving local crime prevention programs. Grants have been available to police agencies since 1966 through the Office of Justice Programs. Typically, this funding has been accomplished through "block grants" that have been allotted to states or local governments such as counties and municipalities. Block grants are widely applied for by police agencies because of the low match (10%), accessibility, and diversity of the grants. These have been an important channel for funding some local volunteer police efforts. Sometimes these programs may have assisted in the establishment of volunteer police units. The Department of Justice usually dispenses these local law enforcement block grants; in past years, the focus has been on adding new officers to the rosters of agencies. In turn, these officers are now available to train and supervise volunteer police. The CERT Program is federally supported. In recent years, death benefits for the families of volunteer police officers killed in the line of duty have also been provided as well as programs to protect women from violence under the sponsorship of nonprofit organizations. Police departments are receiving federal aid for school resource officers, Drug Abuse Resistance Education (DARE) programs, driving under the influence (DUI) awareness and enforcement programs, and many others (Van Etten 1996). In the 1990s, due to the advent of new computer technology, many departments applied for block grants to equip their squad cars with new laptops. For example, the Pacifica (CA) Police Department obtained state block grants to replace older dispatch and communication systems. The older systems had required such long searches that officers were either unable to use them or spent excessive time on the computer rather than on their beat. Laptop computers were mounted in each vehicle to allow officers to make electronic reports from their vehicles while maintaining their presence in the community. In addition, a radar warning trailer was purchased and used on streets throughout the city to educate and warn citizens of the speed at which they were traveling (Pacifica 2014).

3. In addition to satisfying state POST standards, police agencies seeking recognition for excellence may apply to the Commission on Accreditation for Law Enforcement Agencies, Inc. (CALEA). Significantly, under their standards, sworn volunteer police officers must receive the same training as regular police officers.

In 1973, the first recommended standards for reserve officers appeared in the *Report on Police* presented by the National Advisory Commission on Criminal Justice Standards and Goals. The National Advisory Commission recommended that every state immediately establish minimum standards for reserve officer training and selection. In particular, the commission urged that reserve training programs meet or exceed state standards that regulate the training of regular, part-time, or reserve officers. Significantly, standards for auxiliaries were omitted. Yet, the fact remains that in some jurisdictions, auxiliary police officers may still be used the same as reserves. Presently, however, progress appears to be in the direction of both auxiliaries and reserves achieving sworn status and training parity with regular police, thus making the two titles equivalent. An example of this trend has occurred in the state of Virginia. Virginia State Code 15.2-1731 provides for the use of auxiliary officers. Consequently, the city of Williamsburg, VA, has declared that the term "auxiliary" is synonymous with "reserve" for compliance with CALEA Standards (see Rosenberg 1998).

4. In a state emergency, it is customary for the governor of the state to call upon the state's National Guard. This happens during hurricanes, wildfires, floods, and numerous other disasters. If necessary, missions will be prioritized and other state's National Guard and Department of Defense resources for special capability may be called upon. However, in any emergency, speed means life. The availability of volunteer police for similar purposes could be increased if the existing federal Reserve Officer Training Corps (ROTC) programs were authorized to accept not only potential military officer candidates but also reserve police officer candidates. This could be done with the cooperation of county sheriff agencies. In essence, after a certain amount of ROTC training, qualified college students could move into a law enforcement track conducted by the local office of the sheriff.

5. A recent national study released by Brown University reveals that large numbers of students are still being seriously hurt while on school grounds. Each year more than 90,000 schoolchildren suffer "intentional" injuries severe enough to land them in the emergency room. According to Patrick Tolan, a professor at the University of Virginia, part of the solution may be increased monitoring of the students (Carroll 2014).

References

About CNCS. (2013). About us: Who we are. Retrieved October 9, 2013 from http://www.nationalservice.gov/about/who-we-are

Adams, P. (2011, April 5). Arizona police force turns to civilian investigators. *BBC News.* Retrieved January 20, 2014 from www.bbc.co.uk/news/world-us-canada-12754776

Alqadi, N. (2011, October). Building relationships and solving problems in North Miami. *Community Policing Dispatch, 4*(10). Retrieved from http://www.cops.usdoj.gov/html/ dispatch/10-2011/North-Miami-Beach.asp.

Boehm, B. (2012). National Guard celebrates 376th birthday. Retrieved January 21, 2014 from http://www.army.mil/article/92912/

Bucqueroux, B. (2004, March). Restorative community justice: A comprehensive approach to reducing crime and violence in our culture. Retrieved January 27, 2014 from http://www.policing.com/articles/rcj.html

Carroll, L. (2014). School violence lands more than 90,000 a year in the ER, study finds. Retrieved January 13, 2014 from http://www.nbcnews.com/health/school-violence-lands-more-90-000-year-er-study-finds-2D11898820

Congressional Record. (2012, May 10). Awarding a Congressing gold medal to members of the Civil Air Patrol. Retrieved June 23, 2014 from http://www.gpo.gov/fdsys/pkg/CREC-2012-05-10/pdf/CREC-2012-05-10-pt1-PgS3071.pdf#page=1

Cress, L. D. (1982). *Citizens in arms: The army and the militia in American society to the War of 1812*. Chapel Hill, NC: University of North Carolina Press.

Donnelly, W. M. (2001). The Root reforms and the National Guard. Retrieved January 21, 2014 from http://www.history.army.mil/documents/1901/Root-NG.htm

Dooris, M. D. (2008). Enhancing recruitment and retention of volunteers in the U.S. Coast Guard Auxiliary. Master's thesis, Naval Postgraduate School.

Drucker, P. F. (1990). *Managing the nonprofit organization: Principles and practices.* New York: HarperCollins.

FAQs. (2013). Frequently asked questions (FAQs). Retrieved October 9, 2013 from http://www.nationalservice.gov/about/frequently-asked-questions-faqs#12454

Foner, E., and Garraty, J. A. (1991). *The reader's companion to American history.* New York: Houghton Mifflin Harcourt.

Forst, B. (2000). The privatization and civilization of policing. In C. M. Friel (Ed.), *Boundary changes in criminal justice organizations: Criminal justice 2000* (pp. 19–79). Vol. 2. Washington, DC: National Institute of Justice. NCJ 182409.

Greenberg, M., and Cooper, K. (1996, November 15). Unused secret weapon against terrorism. *Law Enforcement News.* Retrieved January 20, 2014 from http://www.lib.jjay.cuny.edu/len/96/15nov/html/forum.html

Hackney, S. (2012, May 11). Millage, volunteer police part of Detroit's public safety plan. *Detroit Free Press.* Retrieved January 21, 2014 from http://www.freep.com/article/20120511/NEWS01/205110438/Millage-volunteer-police-officers-part-of-Detroit-s-public-safety-plan?odyssey=nav|head

Henderson, W. C. (1976). The slave court system in Spartanburg County. In *The proceedings of the South Carolina Historical Association* (pp. 24–38). Columbia, SC.

History of Civil Air Patrol. (2014). Retrieved January 20, 2014 from http://vawg.cap.gov/history.html

Johnson, H. A., and Wolfe, N. T. (1996). *History of criminal justice.* (Rev. ed.). Cincinnati, OH: Anderson.

Joint Commission. (2005). *Standing together: An emergency planning guide for America's communities.* Oakbrook Terrace, IL: Joint Commission on Accreditation of Healthcare Organizations.

Kelly, R. W., Grasso, G. A., Esposito, J. J., Giannelli, R. J., and Maroulis, A. J. (2008, April). Auxiliary police program overview. Retrieved November 11, 2013 from http://www.nyc.gov/html/nypd/downloads/pdf/careers/nypd_auxiliary_police_overview_2008.pdf

Loren, J. (2010, February 3). Stimulus money used to save police jobs. *WorldNow and KWTV.* Retrieved June 23, 2014 from http://www.news9.com/story/11930579/stimulus-money-used-to-save-police-jobs

Manning, P. K. (1995). The police: Mandate, strategies, and appearances. In V. E. Kappeler (Ed.) *The police & society: Touchstone readings* (pp. 97–126). Mt. Prospect, IL: Waveland Press.

McEnaney, L. (2000). *Civil defense begins at home: Militarization meets everyday life in the fifties*. Princeton, NJ: Princeton University Press.

McKinley, J. (2011, March 1). Police department turn to volunteers. *New York Times*. Retrieved January 13, 2014 from http://www.nytimes.com/2011/03/02/us/02volunteers.html?pagewanted=all&_r=0

Membership. (2014). What is the Coast Guard Auxiliary? Retrieved January 20, 2014 from http://wow.uscgaux.info/content.php?unit = 092&category = units

Oakes, G. (1995). *The imaginary war: Civil defense and American Cold War culture*. New York: Oxford University Press.

Oshkosh Auxiliary Police. (2011). Program description. Retrieved January 31, 2014 from http://www.policevolunteers.org/programs/?fa = dis_pro_detail&id = 409

Pacifica. (2014). Pacifica police history. Retrieved January 20, 2014 from http://www.cityofpacifica.org/depts/police/history.asp

Pilgrim, D. (2012). What was Jim Crow? Retrieved January 21, 2014 from http://www.ferris.edu/jimcrow/what.htm

Purdum, T. S. (1996, July 30). Bomb at the Olympics: Legislation; bipartisan panel to frame an anti-terrorism package. Retrieved June 23, 2014 from http://www.nytimes.com/1996/07/30/us/bomb-olympics-legislation-bipartisan-panel-frame-anti-terrorism-package.html

Regulators. (2014). Lesson 8: The Regulators. Retrieved January 21, 2014 from http://www.scetv.org/education/emedia/guides/The%20Palmetto%20Special/lesson8.pdf

Rosenberg, P. (1998, March 7). Volunteer police force proposed. Retrieved June 23, 2014 from http://articles.dailypress.com/1998-03-07/news/9803070035_1_auxiliary-officers-volunteer-police-officers-police-leaders

SLATT. (2014). State and Local Anti-Terrorism Training Program (SLATT). Retrieved January 21, 2014 from http://www.iir.com/WhatWeDo/Criminal_Justice_Training/SLATT/

Smith, C. B. (2013, October 10). New chief's priorities fit with city's policing progress. Retrieved October 12, 2013 from http://news.cincinnati.com/article/20131011/NEWS01/310110048?gcheck=1&nclick_check=1

USDA Volunteers. (2014). Message from NRCS Chief Jason Weller. Retrieved January 21, 2014 from http://www.nrcs.usda.gov/wps/portal/nrcs/main/national/people/volunteers/

U.S. Air Force. (2014, May 19). Civil Air Patrol WWII members' gold medal journey new website tells their stories, describes their service. Retrieved June 23, 2014 from http://www.af.mil/News/ArticleDisplay/tabid/223/Article/484868/civil-air-patrol-wwii members-gold-medal-journey-new-website-tells-their-storie.aspx

U.S. Department of Justice. (2011, October). *The impact of the economic downturn on American police agencies*. Washington, DC: U.S. Department of Justice, Office of Community Oriented Policing Services.

Van Etten, J. (1996). The impact of grants on police agencies. Retrieved January 20, 2014 from http://www.fdle.state.fl.us/Content/getdoc/b34d43a0-b789-41e4-aad1-4ce6a61ac4df/VanEtten.aspx

Volunteering. (2013). Volunteering in America. Retrieved October 9, 2013 from http://www.nationalservice.gov/impact-our-nation/research-and-reports/volunteering-america

Wilkinson, P. (1986). Terrorism versus liberal democracy: The problems of response. In W. Gutteridge (Ed.), *The new terrorism* (pp. 3–28). London: Mansell Publishing.

Worton, S. (2003, September). *Volunteers in police work: A study of the benefits to law enforcement agencies.* An applied research project submitted as part of the School of Police Staff and Command Program, Eastern Michigan University. Retrieved January 20, 2014 from http://www.emich.edu/cerns/downloads/papers/PoliceStaff/Police%20Personnel%20(e.g.,%20Selection,%20%20Promotion)/Volunteers%20in%20Police%20Work.pdf

The Early History of Volunteer Police

3

Policing, like all professions, learns from experience. It follows then that as modern police executives search for more effective strategies of policing, they will be guided by the lessons of police history.

—**George L. Kelling and Mark H. Moore**
(1988)

In England, prior to 1829, law enforcement slowly evolved from the basic concept of preserving the "King's Peace" by mutual responsibility (Anglo-Saxon era, 550 to 1066) to the use of various constables and the keeping of a "watch and ward." The King's Peace refers to the general protection of persons and property secured in medieval times to large areas and later to the entire royal domain by the law administered by authority of the British monarch. In the ninth century, during the reign of King Alfred the Great, the office of "shire-reeve" was developed to maintain law and order within a shire (equivalent to a modern-day county).[1]

In 1066, the Norman conquest of England was led by William the Conqueror, Duke of Normandy. This was a pivotal event in English history. It largely removed the native ruling class, replacing it with a foreign, French-speaking monarchy, aristocracy, and clerical hierarchy. This, in turn, brought about a transformation of the English language and the culture of England in a new era often referred to as Norman England (Norman Conquest 2013). Every man in Norman England had to be part of a frank-pledge. In this system, every man belonged to a group of ten men who were responsible for the conduct of each member of the group. This was not only a system of law enforcement, but it was a system of mutual protection. "It was very important to belong somewhere and be protected by others, to be removed from this could be very dangerous indeed" (Sherwood Forest Archaeology Project 2014).

The office of constable and the keeping of a "watch and ward" were officially set forth in the Statute of Winchester of 1285 (Seth 1961). In the late 1600s, local justices of the peace were empowered to appoint additional or "special" parish constables (Critchley 1967; Leon 1991). Prior to the nineteenth century, it was generally considered an unpaid compulsory obligation to serve as a tithingman (a member of the frank-pledge who was elected to preside over the tithing), constable, or a member of the watch and ward (Prassel 1972). Today, approximately 14,000 "special constables" serve as unpaid volunteer police throughout the United Kingdom.[2]

Native American Societies

In America, the most dramatic advances in the utilization of volunteer police have taken place in recent times, but before the arrival of the first colonists to the New World, Native Americans were already engaged in maintaining order in their communities. One scholar has indicated that Native American societies maintained order through clearly defined customs "enforced by public opinion and religious sanctions" (Hagan 1966, 16). Nearly everyone knew and respected the customs and beliefs of their tribe. Such conformity was possible because the "tribes were homogeneous units—linguistically, religiously, economically, and politically" (Deloria and Lytle 1983, xi). By the time of the arrival of the European settlers, many tribes had founded numerous societies and cults to preserve order in camp and "to foster a military spirit among themselves and the rest of the tribe, since war was a matter of survival" (Mails 1973, 46). The Plains Indians instituted honorary military societies to police their annual reunion ceremonies and buffalo hunts. Similar societies were operated year-round by the Cheyenne and the Teton Sioux (Hagan 1966).

The Sioux maintained an organized system of volunteer police known as the *akicitas*. Various authors also refer to these groups as either "warrior societies," "policing societies," or "whip-bearers" (Humphrey 1942; Hassrick 1964; Hoxie 1986). Members lived in their own separate tents when the band was on the move, and they were supported by tribal contributions. Each band usually had several such societies that a young warrior could join. The *akicita* societies helped to ensure law and order. Members were selected by the tribal leader or a council of leaders at the spring gathering of the various Sioux bands. Because their authority was derived from a particular council or chief, bands were accountable to them. Their assignments could last just for the duration of the summer hunts or throughout the year. During the communal hunting activities, the members of these policing societies kept noise levels down, performed scouting missions to ensure security, repressed the tendency for some hunters to act overzealously, and helped prevent others from falling behind. Moreover, society members might also question individuals in order to learn the identity of trouble markers (Barker 1994).

Members of the Sioux volunteer policing societies could also be called upon by the tribal council to carry out various types of punishment but only as a last resort. Such punishments could involve the destruction of property (shelters, rifles, etc.), corporal punishment, and banishment (Barker 1994). When several societies were selected, the various duties of each group would be rotated to ensure that as many young warriors as possible could have an equal chance at performing the most important duties (Barker 1994).

Prior to 1838 (when they were forcibly moved to Oklahoma), the Cherokee Indians lived in what is now the state of Georgia.[3] They adopted many of the customs of their white neighbors—perhaps because of their location.

The Cherokees (one of the Five Civilized Tribes) were "admired and respected by the settlers because of their apparent willingness to acculturate" (Barker 1994, 40). In 1808, they instituted a system of appointed sheriffs and a group of quasi-police/militia they called the "lighthorse." These men enforced the first written legal code adopted by an Indian tribe (Hagan 1966). The lighthorse were small companies, each consisting of four privates and two officers who patrolled on horseback. Barker (1994, 36) referred to the Cherokee's lighthorsemen and the *akicitas* of the Sioux as "the first 'police departments' in America."

Watch and Ward

Volunteers served as America's first police officers as well as the organizers of the first police agencies (Garry 1980). Prior to American independence, justice in the colonies was administered by lay judges, community residents, militia and watch members, foreign soldiers, clergymen, constables, various administrative officers (e.g., governors, sheriffs, and constables), and by legislative assemblies. An important legacy of the colonial period was a system of petty courts manned by laymen (e.g., rural justices of the peace). In America's seaport towns, a constable was elected for each ward and a nighttime patrol called "the watch" was instituted. The earliest watch organizations relied on local citizen participation or on the use of paid substitutes.

During colonial times, "watch and ward committees" were established in New England, and they represented an early version of citizen patrols. The Dutch settlement of New Amsterdam, which later became New York, "created a burgher watch in 1643, one year after it was founded, but did not pay them until 1712" (Bayley 1985, 32). The governor of New Amsterdam, Peter Stuyvesant, also created the first American volunteer fire department in 1648. Eventually, either elected or appointed constables, sheriffs, marshals, and watches were established in every settlement (Bayley 1985). Initially, constable work was the communal responsibility of all adult males, and fines could be levied for refusing to assume this obligation (Walker 1998). In the South, during the colonial and antebellum periods, slave patrol laws were adopted. These patrols initially recruited militia members in order to maintain the institution of slavery.

The Militia

America's use of militias and town watches can be traced to thirteenth-century England and the reign of Henry III. He mandated that all his male subjects aged 15–50 own a weapon other than a knife so that they could stand guard to preserve the peace.

One of the earliest uses of an organized militia came in 1636 when militia companies were formed in the Massachusetts Bay Colony to protect against attacks by Native Americans. "Colonial militiamen defended the colonies and participated in expeditions against Indians and the French until the War of Independence" (Stentiford 2002, 6).

During the Revolutionary War, "militia augmented Washington's Continental Army, as well as enforced revolutionary discipline among the populace, clearly demonstrating the dual roles of militia during wartime of fighting the enemy and in stabilizing the homefront" (Stentiford 2002, 6). The existence of militia is referred to in the U.S. Constitution (see Article I, Article II, and the Second Amendment). It is of considerable importance that the framers of the Constitution "intended that the militia would be called into federal service when needed [since] Article II, section 3 established the president as the commander-in-chief of the militia when in federal service" (Stentiford 2002, 11).

The Militia Act of 1792 required most free white males between the ages of 18 and 45 to arm themselves and attend regular drills. However, "neither the federal government nor the states enforced the law....[and] in the years following the War of 1812, the militia as an institution fell into disuse. Few Americans, including Congressmen, saw any need for citizens to waste time drilling when no danger threatened and more profitable pursuits beckoned" (Stentiford 2002, 7).

At one time, George Washington served in a British militia unit and decades later Abraham Lincoln was chosen to lead a militia company during the Black Hawk War. When the famous French aristocrat Alexis de Tocqueville traveled in America (1831–1832), he was impressed by the fact that Americans had formed many voluntary associations. He noted that this ability to form self-help groups provided the basis and strength for maintaining democracy in America. Nevertheless, not all such organizations had egalitarian or noble purposes. In the South, slaves were controlled through a system of slave patrols that relied on the militia model to preserve the slave system.[4]

Changes in the militia's role of providing an external defense coincided with a need for internal protection of America's growing seaports and other centers of commerce. In general, the seaports needed increased security because of higher population and the transient nature of seaport life (Johnson and Wolfe 1996). In New York and in parts of New England, the militia was directly connected with the provision of police services as a result of the formation of the night watch. By statute, the militia was used "as the organizational base for distributing night-watch duty among the citizenry" (Cress 1982, 7). In addition, in times of emergency, the militia could be called upon to restore order in conjunction with the *posse comitatus*. In both the North and the South, the militia was used to maintain the institution of slavery, such as in 1741, when the New York City militia suppressed a slave revolt (Cress 1982).

Over time, the militia tradition developed into today's well-known concept of the "citizen soldier" who serves the nation in peacetime and in war as a volunteer member of the National Guard. Members of the New York Army National Guard were called to active duty after September 11, 2001, to provide security at airports, bridges, and train stations (Debnam 2003).

The New Police

During the two or three decades just prior to the Civil War, most eastern U.S. port cities abandoned the informal system of "watch and ward" (a system involving separate organizations for evening and day patrols). A wave of urban riots took place in this period, and many persons feared that America's experiment with democratic institutions was threatened. The establishment of the London Metropolitan Police Force in 1829 served as a convenient model for reform (Walker 1976).

However, the initial establishment of unified day and night salaried police departments did not result in any panacea for crime. It also did not serve as a guarantee that democratic traditions or that the rule of law would be respected, especially with regard to the protection of minority citizens and their rights. The new police forces excluded minority group members. Moreover, between 1882 and 1969, more than 4,700 people—mostly black—were lynched in the United States (Perloff 2000). Furthermore, a census bureau study conducted in 1973 found that in the five largest U.S. cities, "blacks were much more likely than whites to be the victims of robbery and burglary, in some cases by a ratio of nearly two to one" (Wilson 1975, 34). In the United States, the high point of this crisis was reached in the late 1960s when civil protests and riots erupted in more than 100 cities (Travis 1995). Ultimately only through the peaceful efforts of courageous civil rights leaders and demonstrators did it become possible for U.S. deputy marshals and National Guardsmen to be deployed in the South to enforce federal court orders for integration in schools and public accommodations, thereby initiating significant legal procedures to end the era of "Jim Crow."

The Posse

Due to a lack of records, it is not certain when the first American sheriff took office. However, various sources indicate that Captain William Stone was appointed sheriff in Virginia's Accomac Shire in 1634 (Buffardi 1998; Henry County Sheriff 2010; Scott 2013). Virginia's first counties were established that same year, and it is probable that one or more of these counties appointed a sheriff. In Maryland, the St. Mary's County Sheriff's Office can document that its first sheriff was appointed in 1637. In 1776, the position of sheriff became an elective office under Maryland's new constitution (St. Mary's County Sheriff 2013). By custom and law, one of the powers extended to a sheriff is the ability to select able-bodied individuals to help capture suspected criminals. The posse comitatus (or the "power of the county") refers to an ancient British common law right empowering sheriffs to summon the assistance of any citizen in time of civil disorder. In America, this right was put into statutory form and extended to other types of peace officers and to most magistrates (Prassel 1972). "Much of the philosophy of law regarding citizen's arrest powers are founded in the posse comitatus premise" (Buffardi 1998).

During the nineteenth century, the institution of the "posse" developed as America expanded to its Pacific Coast boundary. Klockars (1985, 22) refers to the use of the posse as a form of "obligatory avocational policing" because an individual could be arrested for failure to serve when called upon.

There are probably hundreds of interesting stories about the activities of posses. One of the earliest cases of note took place during the War of 1812. The sheriff's office of Prince George's County in Maryland was involved in an incident that resulted in the writing of the national anthem. "When the British army marched on Washington they passed through Upper Marlboro. The local residents cooperated with the invading army and the British Commander saw to it that no major damage was done to local property. After the battle of Bladensburg and the burning of Washington, the British army marched back through Upper Marlboro. This time some of the British soldiers looted local farms and were arrested by a Sheriff's Posse. The stragglers were placed in the county jail" (Oertly 2013). When the British commander learned of the arrests of his soldiers, he ordered the arrest of Dr. William Beam and other sheriff's posse members. They were taken aboard a British warship. Several notable officials of the U.S. Government were selected to negotiate their release, including a talented young lawyer. While the give and take of the bargaining was taking place over a period of a few days, the young lawyer, "Francis Scott Key witnessed an attack on Fort McHenry. Standing on the deck of an American ship, Key looked through a telescope and observed the fighting. Seeing that the American flag was still there meant that the British had failed in their attack on Baltimore. He was so overwhelmed by the sight that he was inspired to express his feelings in verse which was to become 'The Star Spangled Banner'" (Buffardi 1998).

The founder of the modern detective and security guard industry was also a posse member. In fact, the career of Allan Pinkerton and the eventual establishment of an entire new industry might be traced to the year 1847 when Pinkerton was searching on a tiny island for any wood he could use for his barrel-making business. His curiosity was aroused when he discovered the remains of a cooking fire. As a member of a sheriff's posse, Pinkerton later returned to the island to arrest a group of counterfeiters, and he engaged in the seizure of the evidence of their illegal activities. As a result of this event, Pinkerton's reputation led him to other local crime detective work. Eventually, he was appointed to a variety of law enforcement roles including deputy sheriff, becoming the first detective in Chicago, and being appointed as a special agent for the U.S. Postal Service. The latter position involved investigating thefts from post offices in Chicago. In 1861, Pinkerton safely escorted President-elect Abraham Lincoln to his first inauguration while Pinkerton's operatives protected the train route (Horan 1967).

Over time it became possible for posse members to be reimbursed for their services. For example, in the early spring of 1886, just as the ice was beginning to break up on the Little Missouri River in present-day North Dakota, three thieves stole a boat from its mooring at a local ranch and took it downriver. The boat belonged to a part-time deputy sheriff in Billings County. He chased after them with his ranch hands and made three arrests. Under the laws of the Dakota Territory, as a deputy sheriff, he received a fee for making the three arrests, and he was also compensated for the hundreds of miles traveled—a total of some $50. The rancher and deputy sheriff was Theodore Roosevelt (Roosevelt Pursues 2013). When President McKinley died from an assassin's bullet on September 14, 1901, Vice President Roosevelt—the former Dakota Territory cattle rancher—became president of the United States.

Today, most states still have laws that require the average citizen to come to the aid of a police officer when requested. During the nineteenth century, some northeastern and midwestern states passed laws authorizing the establishment of various protective, detective, or anti-horse thief associations. The charters of these groups provided for the preselection of posses to chase and apprehend wrongdoers. In addition, a number of societies were established to oversee the selection and distribution of private welfare aid.

The Volunteers

According to Stentiford (2002), a new institution arose in 1806 that supplanted the use of the militia during wartime. Known simply as "the Volunteers," these usually were companies and regiments recruited at the local level. "The men from each company elected their officers; the governor of the state appointed the regimental officers; and the regiment was then mustered into federal service for an agreed-upon period" (Stentiford 2002, 7–8). These types of voluntary military organizations existed throughout the nineteenth century and assisted state governments in strike breaking, riot control, and in disaster relief. Their existence obviated the need to enforce the Militia Act of 1792. In essence, they represented a body of self-selected men derived from the unorganized militia, who "formed or joined companies out of patriotism, from fear of slave uprisings ... or as a way of establishing social and political contacts, but not out of legal obligation" (Stentiford 2002, 8). Abraham Lincoln served in such a company during the Black Hawk War, and Theodore Roosevelt led his volunteer "Rough Riders" during the Spanish-American War.

Many volunteer companies were recruited during the Civil War and may have suffered high rates of loss because of their inexperience. Stentiford (2002, 11) notes that toward the end of the nineteenth century, "the resurgent organized militia—or as it was increasingly called, the National Guard—began to wrest from the Volunteers the official role as the nation's second line of defense. Unlike Volunteers, National Guard units trained during peacetime."

Friendly Visitors

During the nineteenth century, several types of specialized volunteer law enforcement organizations appeared in America. As early as the 1830s, Alexis de Tocqueville (1805–1859)—the French aristocrat who visited the United States to study its people and institutions—discerned a trend in American society for the establishment of a variety of voluntary associations. Many of these organizations were not solely of the amateur soldier variety but rather were concerned with the welfare of diverse immigrant groups. By 1878, in Philadelphia alone, "there were some 800 such groups of one kind or another in existence" (Trattner 1989, 85). The growth in their number created a need for the establishment of umbrella associations known as charity organization societies. They did not directly dispense relief but instead served as clear-inghouses for the registration, screening, and referral of applicants in need of charity. The largest organization of this type existed in New York City. Initially, the New York Charity Organization Society (COS) relied upon a corps of volunteers known as the "friendly visitors" to perform home visits (Trattner 1989). While they helped families contend with relief agencies, their intimate knowledge of family life could be used to ensure that families were conforming to the norms of the era (Katz 1996).

After a time, the New York COS was unable to recruit all the volunteers needed for its special type of charitable work. Initially, it created a Committee on Mendicancy, "which hired 'Special Agents' who were empowered by the city to arrest beggars" (Burrows and Wallace 1999, 1160). Eventually, additional agents were hired to conduct the everyday role of serving as "friendly visitors." Over time, the roles of the first social workers directly sprang from the nature of the duties of the field workers of the charity organization societies. Thus, by the second decade of the twentieth century, the caseworker was, in essence, "a trained, professional friendly visitor" (Katz 1996, 171).

Vigilantes

In the United States, various types of vigilante organizations were common in the nineteenth century. Richard Maxwell Brown, one of America's leading scholars on the subject, defined vigilantism as "organized, extralegal movements, the members of which take the law into their own hands" (Brown 1975, 95–66). Karmen (1990, 357) has clarified this classic statement by indicating that "vigilantes don't 'take' the law; they break the law. They don't act in self-defense, which is legal; they react aggressively, which is illegal." Historically, two of the most well-known episodes of vigilantism took place in California and Montana.

The San Francisco Committee of Vigilance (or simply "The San Francisco Vigilantes") was formed in 1851 in order to reduce government corruption and the extremely high crime rate during the California Gold Rush. The San Francisco Vigilantes were well-organized and forced several officials to resign on grounds of corruption. The Montana Vigilantes was a group of men who aimed to restore order in the small but lawless community of western Montana in 1860. These vigilante groups have been both praised and condemned. However, they were organized for the specific purpose of reducing crime and corruption.

Two of the most infamous types of vigilante organizations arose after the Civil War—the Ku Klux Klan and the White Caps. The Klan was formed to counter any efforts by southern blacks to achieve racial equality. The White Caps were concerned with the control of morality (wife beaters, prostitutes, drunkards, poor providers, etc.). Both groups wore masks. However, whereas the Klan was known for lynching, the White Caps relied on whipping to fulfill their goals (Brown 1971; Friedman 1993).

In numerous ways, the activities of extra legal vigilante groups represented the antithesis of the modern-day role of volunteer police. Generally, vigilante groups deviated from the traditional and contemporary democratic hallmarks of voluntary community service because they went about their business without regard to individual rights and liberties. Furthermore, these groups lacked any statutory authority when they engaged in punitive activities.

In contrast, the evolving role of volunteer police appears to be deeply rooted in the American democratic spirit. This spirit is best characterized by its concern for free speech, religious tolerance, universal suffrage, and other egalitarian concepts such as hiring and promotion based on merit. On the other hand, the evolution of volunteer police has had an undemocratic side, especially when it has been linked to other branches of government that have abused the rights of citizens. In particular, this occurred when slave patrols were used to control slaves in the South and later, during World War I, when the federal government condoned the use of thousands of volunteer citizen spies for the purposes of identifying draft evaders

Figure 3.1 In this photograph, 40,000 members of the Ku Klux Klan march down Pennsylvania Avenue on August 8, 1925. (Courtesy of Prints and Photographs Division, Library of Congress.)

and suspected anarchists. These volunteer spies were part of a giant civic organization known as the American Protective League (APL).

The first decades of the twentieth century saw a rebirth of the Ku Klux Klan after its having been dormant for 50 years. Although there was no actual connection with the original Ku Klux Klan of the post–Civil War Reconstruction period, the new organization (founded in 1915) adapted its rituals and dress (Slosson 1958, 308). It was not uncommon to see white-robed and masked figures in both southern and northern states (Sullivan 1939). On one occasion, Klan members marched down Pennsylvania Avenue in the heart of the nation's capital (as seen in Figure 3.1).

Boy Police

Since at least the time of World War I, there have been several types of law enforcement programs involving American youth. In the second decade of the twentieth century, various articles about the use of "junior police" or "boy police" appeared in such popular national periodicals as *The Literary Digest*, *The Survey*, and *The Outlook*. A few of the earliest programs were established in California, Iowa, Ohio, and New York. Figure 3.2 presents a page from an early twentieth-century catalog displaying a variety of school patrol

Figure 3.2 Early twentieth-century catalog page of student badges.

badges worn by students. The participants were encouraged to lead healthy lives and to engage in various projects related to community service. It is interesting to note that on some occasions arrests were made under the direction and initiative of members of the New York City Junior Police. For example, in 1914, a 13-year-old member of the junior police, Sergeant Louis Goldstein of the Fifteenth Precinct, caused the arrest of a storeowner who was charged with conducting an illegal lottery. Young Sergeant Goldstein provided testimony about the incident in the Court of Special Sessions of the city of New York. After the defendant realized the strength of the evidence against him, he pleaded guilty. Furthermore, this was not the first arrest in which Goldstein had participated. On a previous occasion, he encountered two men breaking into a display case. Each man received a jail sentence of six months. For this arrest, Goldstein was promoted to sergeant (Boy Police of New York 1915).

By the mid-1920s, some of these groups had been either transformed or replaced by school safety patrols and the establishment of Police Athletic Leagues (PALs). Junior police activities also morphed into the Law Enforcement Explorer program, administered on a national level by Learning for Life, an affiliate of the Boy Scouts of America. Law enforcement or police explorers are usually between the ages of 14 and 20.

The growth of youth safety patrols was triggered in the 1920s when the popularity of the automobile led to a rise in traffic fatalities among children aged 5–14. In 1926, the city fathers of Newark, New Jersey, took stock of their nine-year-old safety patrol program. They found that no serious injuries had taken place since its implementation (Rosseland 1926). In 1923, the Honolulu sheriff swore in 33 members of the Boy Scouts of America as "junior traffic police officers" (Honolulu Police Department 2000). By 1932, there were approximately 10,000 safety patrol units involving 200,000 boys in 1,800 cities and towns (Guarding Five Million Children 1932; Schoolboy Patrols Approved by the President 1933). Two future presidents of the United States, Jimmy Carter and Bill Clinton, were safety patrollers. In addition, Rudolph Giuliani, New York City's former Mayor, *Time Magazine's* "Person of the Year 2001," was also a safety patroller. Additional materials about youth involvement in public safety at both the local and national levels are presented in Chapters 8 and 9.

Vice and Alcohol Suppression Societies

There were also groups that were mainly concerned with the morals of the immigrants who were arriving daily from Europe during the latter part of the nineteenth century and the first two decades of the twentieth. Thousands of migrant, working class families settled in the largest U.S. cities, establishing densely packed ethnic neighborhoods. Conditions in these neighborhoods were often poor, with crowding and lack of proper sanitation compounding problems such as infant mortality, substance abuse, and crime. In Chicago, "improper sanitation led to high rates of disease, such as smallpox and tuberculosis. Working conditions were unsafe in the many 'sweatshops,' mills, and slaughterhouses where immigrant men and women sought employment" (Frances Willard 2013, 35). One of the earliest organizations of this type was the New York Society for the Suppression of Vice. Its agents identified and prosecuted vendors of pornography and birth control for more than 40 years (Hovey 1998).

Another group focused on the detection and prosecution of liquor law violators. The Anti-Saloon League (ASL) began operations in the 1890s. Its earliest agenda "was not to advocate prohibition in the broad sense, but was to rally the divided temperance forces for the more modest task of saloon suppression" (Timberlake 1963, 127). Private detectives were employed by the League and, by 1908, it had participated in more than 31,000 cases involving liquor law enforcement. Such groups worked in parallel with or in place of local police. The ASL-sponsored prosecutions and the use of private detectives in order to obtain evidence against local violators of temperance legislation. These actions were deemed necessary because of the laxity or disinterest of public officials in pursuing such offenders. Saloons were also associated with gambling and prostitution.

At the end of the nineteenth century, one national women's organization was particularly concerned with a reduction in the consumption of liquor as well as the curtailment of prostitution. The Women's Christian Temperance Union (WCTU) pursued its efforts under the banner of "home protection," perhaps in early recognition of the fact that the greatest threat to "homeland security" is the breakdown of the family. The WCTU's main accomplishment was in establishing "laws in every state compelling some form of Temperance Instruction in the public schools" (Gusfield 1963, 86). "Organizations like the WCTU faced a difficult challenge in their efforts to close down these drinking establishments. The city of Chicago, in the late 1800s, derived a significant portion of its revenues from the sale of liquor licenses, and the political establishment was committed to seeing that the saloons stayed open. Chicago politics during this period were often corrupt, and local ward bosses received payoffs from saloon owners in exchange for allowing them to operate on Sundays" (Frances Willard 2013, 34).

The American Protective League

The APL was active during U.S. involvement in World War I. Albert M. Briggs, a Chicago advertising executive, founded the APL. Briggs promised personnel and automobiles that could be used by the Justice Department at the discretion of the chief of its Bureau of Investigation (Jensen 1968). The Bureau of Investigation was the forerunner of the Federal Bureau of Investigation. This was a time when funds and departmental equipment were in short supply. Briggs made a persuasive case, and the APL was authorized by the U.S. Department of Justice to carry out the following duties: protection of property, reporting of disloyal or suspicious persons and activities, locating draft violators, assisting in the arrest of deserters, and enforcing vice and liquor law regulations in areas around naval and army bases. More than 200,000 citizens were recruited for this organization, and historians have acknowledged that the APL was the largest spy network ever authorized by the U.S. government. Numbered metal badges were sold by the League to help identify its members and to raise funds for the organization's administration. Their most notorious activities involved investigating and reporting

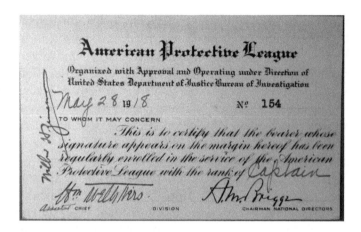

Figure 3.3 American Protective League membership card, ca. 1918.

"disloyal and seditious utterances" (Hough 1919, 120) and participating in raids where volunteer APL agents joined with police personnel in rounding up suspected draft evaders. Figure 3.3 displays an APL membership card.

Members of the APL were not sworn in as peace officers and did not have any powers beyond that of a private citizen. Membership also did not confer any special authorization to carry firearms beyond that extended to private citizens by local laws. Moreover, members were not exempted from Selective Service regulations, and they were instructed to avoid making any claims that they were government officers. However, they were permitted to state when conducting investigations that they were doing so "for the Department of Justice" (Hough 1919, 499). In addition, they were organized along a chain of command involving a local chief, an assistant chief, inspectors, captains, lieutenants, and general members (Hough 1919).

The tactics used by the APL to stifle dissent and members' participation in various raids to find draft evaders were condemned by liberal leaders, but in the main, their practices led to little public outcry. The Justice Department decided to disband the League at the end of World War I.

Citizen Home Defense Leagues, Home Guards, State Guards

At the time of World War I, many cities established citizen home defense leagues as well as state and home guard organizations to provide homeland security. State and home guard units were organized to fill the vacuum left when the National Guard was called upon for active military service; home or citizen defense leagues were instituted by some large city police chiefs concerned about both natural and man-made disasters. For example, in 1916 in New York City, nearly 21,000 citizens were recruited out of concern that the war in Europe would deplete police ranks and reduce the number of available personnel for guarding vital resources (i.e., reservoirs, bridges, transportation lines, etc.). The volunteers were asked to perform routine patrol duties and to participate in training programs. In 1918, New York City's Home Defense League was reorganized into a police reserve organization.

By 1917, various states (e.g., Massachusetts, Connecticut etc.) had established military state units to fill the void left by the induction of all or part of the National Guard into the regular army. Such units were named the "State Guard" to indicate the statewide obligation of the forces (Stentiford 2002, 23). They "provided needed services to their states during disasters, the 'Spanish Influenza' epidemic in 1918, and periods of civil unrest. By contrast, in the poorer and more rural Deep South, governors and state adjutants general reacted with indifference or hostility to locally created home guards. Lacking uniforms, support, or encouragement, southern home guardsmen contributed little service to the states" (Stentiford 2002, 23).

In Missouri, a state-directed Home Guard was also established. "At its peak, the Missouri Home Guard consisted of five regiments, six separate battalions, and sixteen separate companies.... The Home Guard contained six thousand men, mostly in the infantry" (Stentiford 2002, 37). The recruitment of such a force was facilitated by the existence of the Missouri Militia Act of 1908. This foresighted state law specifically authorized the governor to create a replacement militia for the National Guard when it left the state. One regiment of the Missouri Guard based in Kansas City was successful in controlling labor unrest during a general strike of workers that lasted six days. Between emergency the units of the Home Guard engaged in training exercises.

The municipality-based citizen defense leagues should not be confused with home and state guard organizations. According to Stentiford (2002, xi–xii), the home guard is "an organized militia of a town, city, county, or state, without a federal obligation. These units are usually liable for service within the jurisdiction of the government that recruited them." The units of the state guard were usually forces that "had a statewide obligation and depended on the local and state resources rather than federal..." (Stentiford 2002, xi–xii). Stentiford notes that such terms may have slightly different meanings depending on context and year.

Summary

Generally, Native American military societies, constables, watch members, and slave patrollers share the following attributes membership in a permanent organization or one established during wartime mobilization organized by governmental or societal action undertaking one or more police functions and serving in an overt manner for minimal or no salary.

The early constables and watch members were looked upon as part of a permanent organization for the purpose of maintaining the order and safety of a city's inhabitants. They were selected through governmental procedures (initially from the ranks of the local militia) and eventually were rewarded by being able to receive fees or a minimal salary for their services. In a similar fashion, the members of the southern slave patrols also were selected and were provided with small stipends. Finally, the Native American military societies were permanent organizations until they were required to disband by congressional mandate. They performed a wide range of peacekeeping and tribal functions. Because these groups could also punish violators for tribal custom transgressions, they performed a necessary role involving the use of proactive enforcement methods. Their members shared in the communal ownership of property and sometimes received extra gifts for their services. All three groups carried out their protective functions in an overt manner.

In colonial America, the duties of watchmen and constables were numerous; in the absence of any other frontline support groups, they were the primary law enforcers of their era. Their duties expanded and became more difficult as towns grew and when crime became a more frequent concern. Peak (1997) has noted that when their increased responsibilities became more demanding, many began to evade their duties whenever possible.

The advent of slavery gave rise to the creation of slave patrols whose members did not hesitate to use punitive means to carry out their duties. Yanochik (1997) has pointed out that the slave patrollers were merely one variety of a growing band of "specialists" that included salaried sheriffs and constables. He implies that what was important was not so much the nature of the "specific" duties being performed, but rather that the population at large was no longer being looked to for order maintenance. A differentiation in roles between the ordinary citizen and officers of the law had now begun.

Thus, prior to America's independence, justice was administered on the Great Plains by Native American military societies. In the eastern and coastal colonies, justice was administered by various combinations of lay judges, community residents (e.g., regulators or posse members), militia, slave patrols, foreign soldiers, clergymen, constables, watch members, various administrative officers (e.g., governors, sheriffs), and by legislative assemblies. An important legacy of the colonial period was a system of petty courts manned by laymen (e.g., rural justices of the peace). Town courts are a major feature of the modern American justice system.

During the late nineteenth century, several organizations were established to halt the distribution of pornography and birth control information (e.g., the New York Society for the Suppression of Vice). A substantial part of the history of the ASL and its volunteer police had to do with the phenomenon of American saloon life. "In the five or six decades before 1920, the saloon was an almost ubiquitous structure on the American landscape" (Engelmann 1979, 3). The ASL's attorneys and private investigators, although privately retained, performed the essential police functions of surveillance, investigation, arrest, and prosecution. Members volunteered for their assignments and, after arrests were made, their activities were publicized when the attorneys and their private investigators had to appear in court.

Charity organization societies used a system of "friendly visitors" who were middle- and upper-class women with leisure time who would visit aid recipients to help them achieve independence as quickly as possible. The societies that recruited these volunteers did not dispense any relief but rather coordinated its dispensation through cooperating churches and private associations.

Several pioneering youth programs were developed at the start of the twentieth century. In general, the junior police and safety patrollers engaged in a limited number of service-oriented projects, such as serving as school crossing guards, performing crowd control at special events, and working as security escorts. If a crime occurred in their presence, their duty was to call for assistance.

At the outset of World War I, various home defense leagues were established by police departments in such cities as New York, Chicago, and Berkeley, California. The largest of these was in New York City. Its chief purpose was to serve as a source of additional police workers during any emergency. In addition, the APL was founded by Albert M. Briggs, an outdoor advertising executive. Briggs was able to convince the head of the U.S. Department of Justice's Chicago office about the League's value. He offered a volunteer solution to the problem of investigating suspected German agents at a time when funds and departmental equipment were in short supply. Briggs promised personnel and automobiles that could be used by the Justice Department at the discretion of the chief of its Bureau of Investigation (Jensen 1968). Unlike many of the members of the ASL, all of the APL members involved in law enforcement activities were unpaid volunteers. However, both groups were proactive or aggressive in their approach to their assignments, and they performed a variety of special purpose police functions. Members of the APL conducted investigations for various federal agencies, especially the U.S. Department of Justice.

Unlike their volunteer specialist counterparts, the regular urban police of the post–Civil War era were preoccupied with maintaining their political appointments as well as performing a variety of non-law enforcement roles including supervision of elections, censoring of movies, operation of lodging homes in the basements of police stations, provision of emergency ambulances, disposal of confiscated liquor, and the inspection of boilers, tenements, markets, and factories (Fogelson 1977). These responsibilities and concerns no doubt contributed to the ability of the ASL and APL operatives to undertake specific law enforcement functions.

Review Questions

1. Discuss how Native Americans engaged in maintaining order in their communities.
2. The Sioux maintained an organized system of volunteer police known as the *akicitas*. Describe their role.
3. List who administered justice in the colonies prior to America's independence.
4. State the origin of the use of militias and town watches in America.
5. Explain why the militia as an institution fell into disuse after the War of 1812.
6. Identify the modern version of the militia.
7. Who and which made it possible for U.S. deputy marshals and National Guardsman to be deployed in the South to enforce federal court orders for integration of schools and public accommodations?
8. Describe the origin of caseworkers or social workers.
9. Identify two pre–Civil War and two post–Civil War vigilante groups.
10. Do you believe that 15-year-olds should be able to make arrests as part of a youth police group? Discuss.
11. What fact or facts contributed to the rise of youth safety patrols?
12. What were some of the issues that affected working class, urban families in the late 1800s?
13. Describe the activities of the Anti-Saloon League.
14. List the types of duties that the APL was authorized by the U.S. Department of Justice to carry out.
15. What activities preoccupied the urban police so that ASL and APL operatives were needed to carry out specific law enforcement functions?

Notes

1. "In early England, the land was divided into geographic areas between a few individual kings—these geographic areas were called shires. Within each shire there was an individual called a reeve, which meant guardian. This individual was originally selected by the serfs to be their informal social and governmental leader. The kings observed how influential this individual was within the serf community and soon incorporated that position into the governmental structure. The reeve soon became the King's appointed representative to protect the King's interest and act as mediator with people of his

particular shire. Through time and usage the words shire and reeve came together to be shire-reeve, guardian of the shire and eventually the word sheriff, as we know it today" (Scott 2013).

2. In the United Kingdom, the role of special constables has evolved from the performance of limited service on special occasions (especially during national emergencies) to routine neighborhood patrol assignments. In addition, the police force of the city of London and the Metropolitan Police use specials to conduct neighborhood self-defense classes. In Wiltshire, specials coordinate the neighborhood watch program. In 1986, there were more than 16,000 special constables in England and Wales, just under a third of whom were women (Conference on Special Constables 1987).

3. In 2013, a memorial wall to honor members of the Cherokee Nation who were forcibly removed from their native homeland was dedicated at the Cherokee Removal Memorial Park in Birchwood, TN. The location was selected because it is along the "Trail of Tears." Here, 9,000 Native Americans crossed a river and, at this stage of their journey, "they knew their homeland was gone forever" (Phipps 2013). Nancy Williams, park manager for the Cherokee Removal Memorial Park, said the Trail of Tears was much more brutal than people would like to think. Native Americans were forced to march in the worst winter on record in Tennessee (Phipps 2013).

4. Important treatments of slave patrols are found in several doctoral dissertations. Henry (1968) studied patrols in South Carolina from their origins in the late 1600s until 1860. He discusses the legal status and punishment of slaves, the role of the overseer, the patrol system, slave insurrections, and a variety of other aspects related to the lives of southern slaves, runaway slaves, and freed slaves. Hadden's study (1993) is divided into six parts including the origins of slave patrols, organization and administration, methods of appointment and compensation, routine functions of slave patrols, responses in time of crisis, and facts related to patrols during the Civil War and at the war's conclusion. In her discussion of the reasons for the formation of the original patrol groups, Hadden draws upon Henry's discussion of the origins of slave patrols in the late seventeenth and eighteenth centuries. Her dissertation includes an interesting epilogue concerning the legacy of patrols with respect to the establishment of regular police systems as well as the founding of the Ku Klux Klan. Subsequently, Hadden's dissertation was revised and published as *Slave Patrols: Law and Violence in Virginia and the Carolinas*. Currently, this volume is the most definitive work on this subject. Yanochik (1997) presents three essays regarding the economics of slavery. His second essay examines the economic effects of the slave patrol system. He considers some of the legal aspects of patrols as well as the personal characteristics of the individuals serving on them. He concludes that slave patrols acted as a subsidy to slave owners and that this served to lower the cost of using slave labor. Slavery served as a profitable mode of labor utilization in the South, in part due to the fact that the costs of maintaining slave labor would have been higher for the slave owner if the full cost of policing slaves had fallen on them. Green (1997) explores the relationship between slave patrols in South Carolina and the police in northern industrial centers. He notes the similarity in their features as well as the reasons for their existence. He found that "each law enforcement apparatus acted to protect the interests of the dominant economic class" (Green 1997, 121).

References

Barker, M. L. (1994). *American Indian tribal police: An overview and case study.* Unpublished doctoral dissertation, State University of New York, Albany.

Bayley, D. H. (1985). *Patterns of policing: A comparative international analysis.* New Brunswick, NJ: Rutgers University Press.

Boy Police of New York. (1915, July 28). *The Outlook*, pp. 706–708.

Brown, R. M. (1971). Legal and behavioral perspectives on American vigilantism. In D. Fleming and B. Bailyn (Eds.), *Perspectives in American history Vol. 5* (pp. 95–144). Cambridge, NY: Charles Warren Center for Studies in American History, Harvard University.

Brown, R. M. (1975). *Strain of violence: Historical studies of American violence and vigilantism.* New York: Oxford University Press.

Buffardi, H. C. (1998). The history of the office of sheriff. Retrieved November 9, 2013 from http://www.correctionhistory.org/html/chronicl/sheriff/ch10.htm

Burrows, E., and Wallace, M. (1999). *A history of New York City to 1898.* New York: Oxford University Press.

Conference on Special Constables. (1987). *Report of the conference on special constables.* London: Home Department.

Critchley, T. (1967). *A history of police in England and Wales.* London: Constable & Co.

Cress, L. D. (1982). *Citizens in arms: The army and the militia in American society to the war of 1812.* Chapel Hill, NC: University of North Carolina Press.

Debnam, B. (2003, June 29). Minutemen and the Declaration: Citizen soldiers. *TV Plus-The Sunday Gazette Supplement*, pp. 21–24.

Deloria, V., Jr., and Lytle, C. (1983). *American Indian, American justice.* Austin, TX: University of Texas Press.

Engelmann, L. (1979). *Intemperance: The lost war against liquor.* New York: Free Press.

Fogelson, R. (1977). *Big-city police.* Cambridge, MA: Harvard University Press.

Friedman, L. M. (1993). *Crime and punishment in American history.* New York: Basic Books.

Garry, E. (1980). *Volunteers in the criminal justice system: A literature review and selected bibliography.* Washington, DC: U.S. Department of Justice, National Institute of Justice.

Green, E. (1997). *Origins of American policing: Slave patrols in South Carolina from colonial times to 1865.* Unpublished doctoral dissertation, Howard University, Washington, DC.

Guarding Five Million Children. (1932, September). *School Life*, pp. 7 & 18.

Gusfield, J. R. (1963). *Symbolic crusade: Status politics and the American temperance movement.* Urbana, IL: University of Illinois Press.

Hadden, S. E. (1993). *Law enforcement in a new nation: Slave patrols and public authority in the old south, 1700–1865.* Unpublished doctoral dissertation, Harvard University, Cambridge, MA.

Hadden, S. E. (2001). *Slave patrols: Law and violence in Virginia and the Carolinas.* Cambridge, MA: Harvard University Press.

Hagan, W. (1966). *Indian police and judges: Experiments in acculturation and control.* New Haven, CT: Yale University Press.

Hassrick, R. (1964). *The Sioux: Life and customs of a warrior society.* Norman, OK: University of Oklahoma Press.

Henry, M. A. (1968). *The police control of the slave in South Carolina.* New York: Negro Universities Press. (Original work presented as a doctoral dissertation to Vanderbilt University in 1913).

Henry County Sheriff. (2010). A brief history of the office of sheriff. Retrieved November 9, 2013 from http://www.henrycountysheriff.net/SheriffsofHenry County/HistoryoftheOfficeoftheSheriff/tabid/208/Default.aspx

Honolulu Police Department. (2000). Junior police officers. Retrieved July 30, 2000 from http://www.honolulupd.org/history/museum/mu15.htm

Horan, J. D. (1967). *The Pinkertons: The detective dynasty that made history.* New York: Crown.

Hough, E. (1919). *The web.* Chicago: Reilly & Lee.

Hovey, E. B. (1998). *Stamping out smut: The enforcement of obscenity laws, 1872–1915.* Unpublished doctoral dissertation, Columbia University, New York.

Hoxie, F. (1986). Towards a new North American Indian legal history. *American Journal of Legal History, 30,* 351–352.

Humphrey, N. (1942). Police and tribal welfare in Plains and Indian culture. *Journal of Criminal Law and Criminology, 33,* 147–161.

Jensen, J. M. (1968). *The price of vigilance.* Chicago: Rand McNally.

Johnson, H. A., and Wolfe, N. T. (1996). *History of criminal justice* (Rev. ed.). Cincinnati, OH: Anderson.

Karmen, A. (1990). *Crime victims: An introduction to victimology* (Rev. ed.). Pacific Grove, CA: Brooks/Cole.

Katz, M. B. (1996). *In the shadow of the poorhouse: A social history of welfare in America* (Rev. ed.). New York: Basic Books.

Kelling, G. L., and Moore, M. H. (1988). *The evolving strategy of policing.* Washington, DC: U.S. Department of Justice, National Institute of Justice. Retrieved February 28, 2014 from https://ncjrs.gov/pdffiles1/nij/114213.pdf

Klockars, C. (1985). *The idea of police.* Beverly Hills, CA: Sage.

Leon, C. K. (1991). *Special constables: An historical and contemporary survey.* Unpublished doctoral dissertation, University of Bath, Bath, UK.

Mails, T. (1973). *Dog soldiers, bear men and buffalo women: A study of the societies and cults of the Plains Indians.* Upper Saddle River, NJ: Galahad Books.

Norman Conquest. (2013). Norman conquest of England. Retrieved November 9, 2013 from https://www.princeton.edu/~achaney/tmve/wiki100k/docs/Norman_ conquest_of_England.html

Oertly, L. (2013). The fascinating history of the office of the sheriff, 1696–1996. Retrieved November 9, 2013 from http://www.pghistory.org/PG/PG300/sherifhist. html

Peak, K. J. (1997). *Policing America: Methods, issues, challenges* (2nd ed.). Upper Saddle River, NJ: Prentice Hall.

Perloff, R. (2000, January 16). The horror that was lynching. *New York Sunday Times,* sec. 4, p. 16.

Phipps, S. (2013, October 23). Dedication of Cherokee Removal Memorial Wall concludes 25-year project. Retrieved November 6, 2013 from http://www.nooga. com/163965/dedication-of-cherokee-removal-memorial-wall-concludes-25- year-project/

Prassel, F. (1972). *The western peace officer.* Norman: The University of Oklahoma Press.

Roosevelt Pursues. (2013). Roosevelt pursues the boat thieves. Retrieved November 8, 2013 from http://www.nps.gov/thro/historyculture/roosevelt-pursues-boat-thieves.htm

Rosseland, F. M. (1926, November). Nine years without an injury to children on their way to or from school. *American City*, p. 684.

Schoolboy Patrols Approved by the President. (1933, October). *American City*, p. 70.

Scott, R. (2013). 'ROOTS': An historical perspective of the office of sheriff. Retrieved November 9, 2013 from http://www.sheriffs.org/content/office-sheriff

Seth, R. (1961). *The specials: The story of the special constabulary in England, Wales and Scotland.* London: Victor Gollancz.

Sherwood Forest Archaeology Project. (2014). Outlaws. Retrieved June 23, 2014 from http://sherwoodforesthistory.blogspot.com/p/outlaws-villains.html

Slosson, P. (1958). *The great crusade and after: 1914–1928.* Chicago: Quadrangle Paperbacks. (Original work published in 1930).

Stentiford, B. M. (2002). *The American Home Guard: The state militia in the twentieth century.* College Station, TX: Texas A & M University Press.

St. Mary's County Sheriff. (2013). Sheriffs' office history. Retrieved November 9, 2013 from http://www.firstsheriff.com/sheriffofficehistory.asp

Sullivan, M. (1939). *Our times 1900–1925.* New York: Charles Scribner's Sons.

Timberlake, J. H. (1963). *Prohibition and the progressive movement 1900–1920.* Cambridge, MA: Harvard University Press.

Trattner, W. I. (1989). *From poor law to welfare state: A history of social welfare in America* (4th ed.). New York: The Free Press.

Travis, L. F. (1995). *Introduction to criminal justice* (2nd ed.). Cincinnati, OH: Anderson.

Walker, S. (1976). The urban police in American history: A review of the literature. *Journal of Police Science and Administration, 4*(3), 252.

Walker, S. (1998). *Popular justice: A history of American criminal justice* (Rev. ed.). New York: Oxford University Press.

Willard, F. (2013). Frances Willard and the Woman's Christian Temperance Union, 1874–1898. Retrieved November 8, 2013 from http://www.franceswillardhouse.org/uploads/HST391-Project-2-finished_-_printer.pdf

Wilson, J. Q. (1975). *Thinking about crime.* New York: Basic Books.

Yanochik, M. A. (1997). *Essays on the economics of slavery.* Unpublished doctoral dissertation, Auburn University, Alabama.

Auxiliaries and Reserves
Volunteer Police Generalists

4

> Volunteering is the ultimate exercise in Democracy. In an election, you vote once—when you volunteer, you vote for your community every day.

—Deputy Inspector Phylis S. Byrne
Commanding Officer, New York City Police Department Patrol Service Bureau's Auxiliary Police Section (NYC Press Release 2012)

The International Association of Police Chiefs (IAPC) has listed more than 2,000 volunteer programs involving more than 200,000 citizens helping to augment police services (U.S. Department of Justice 2011). The existence of so many programs and participants is reminiscent of earlier times in U.S. history when citizen support and participation in community activities, such as the justice system, was viewed as a necessity in a democratic society. In those earlier times, it was commonplace for community residents to look after one another. Since the entry of the United States into World War II, there has been a resurgence of interest in civic participation. For example, many community residents throughout the United States are policing themselves through the establishment of "neighborhood watch" groups. They are selecting block captains, engaging in neighborhood surveillance, holding regularly scheduled safety meetings, and sometimes engaging in organized patrols. Local and national organizations concerned with public safety have benefitted from this renewed spirit of civic engagement. For example, at the national level, the all-volunteer Civil Air Patrol (CAP) has resources that are almost unparalleled by any other civilian search and rescue organization in the world today, including America's largest privately owned fleet of single engine aircraft and the world's largest privately owned shortwave radio network. Within six months of the Cadet CAP Program's inception in 1942, more than 20,000 youth had joined across the country (Blascovich 2013). In more recent years, new groups known as Community Emergency Response Team (CERT) volunteers have been recruited and trained at the local level. CERT teams support their local communities by assisting in emergency preparedness and response and by educating their communities about emergency preparedness. New York City (NYC) has more than 1,500 active CERT volunteers, and there are more than 3,500 CERT programs in the United States (NYC Press Release 2012).[1]

This chapter looks at seven different auxiliary and reserve volunteer police units. They have distinctive names, but a lack of consistency in the use of unit titles makes it difficult to ascribe specific characteristics to each category. Nevertheless, a trend appears to have developed with respect to the use of titles in certain parts of the United States, especially within several New England states and in California. The seven units discussed are: the Buffalo (New York) Police Reserve; the Brentwood (California) Reserve Police; the Cheltenham Township (Pennsylvania) Auxiliary Police; the Los Angeles (California) Reserve Police; the NYC Auxiliary Police; the NYC Parks Department Mounted Auxiliary Unit, Inc.; and the Albemarle County (Virginia) Auxiliary Police. According to Judge George Edwards, without such support, "the police tend to become an alien force imposing its power on a resentful population" (Greenberg 1984, 47). In addition, some details regarding the city of Miami's volunteer police are presented because its police department houses both auxiliary and reserve police units. However, tenuous, some distinctions, mostly regional in nature with respect to the two most common titles—reserve and auxiliary—can be discerned by examining aspects of volunteer law enforcement programs.

The Origins of Auxiliary and Reserve Police

The first white settlement in New York took place at the southern end of the island of Manhattan in about 1610. The area was known as Fort Amsterdam and was controlled by the Dutch East India Company. The Dutch settlement of New Amsterdam "created a burgher watch in 1643, one year after it was founded, but did not pay them until 1712" (Bayley 1985, 32). The English took possession of this region in 1664 and renamed it New York in honor of the Duke of York. Eventually, either elected or appointed constables, marshals, or watches were established in every settlement (Bayley 1985, 32).

Before whistles and radios, law enforcement used wooden rattles and their distinct noise to signal for help, even into the nineteenth century (Early Days 2012). The watchmen patrolled using their wooden rattles to warn people of threats or fires. The patrols also carried green lanterns from sunset until dawn. They hung their lanterns on a hook by the front door of the watch house to show they were on the job. Today, green lights are still placed outside the entrances of some police stations as a symbol that the "watch" is present and vigilant. In the decades between the American Revolution and the Civil War, the growth of population and industrialization eventually led to the unification of day and night watches to form municipal police departments. Philadelphia had accomplished such a unification in 1833, and by 1845, NYC had merged its two police forces. At the same time, London's new Metropolitan Police (established in 1829) served as a model for the effectiveness of a centralized and preventive type of police force.

Nonetheless, the establishment of such full-time police forces has not diminished the need for supplemental personnel, especially in rural areas where the only available police may be faraway. Today, most local and state police agencies in the United States recruit and train civilian employees. In addition, since the end of World War I, the use of unpaid volunteers in sworn or non-sworn capacities has become a standard practice in many police departments. Some of the titles of such volunteers have included special deputy, reserve deputy sheriff, reserve posse member, supernumerary, and reserve officer. However, by the second half of the twentieth century, there emerged two distinctive categories for unpaid or minimally paid volunteers: auxiliary and reserve. In some ways, these volunteer police may remind us of the old watch and ward committees that existed in the early settlements of New England.

Generally, the "auxiliary police officer" is an individual who wears a police uniform but does not possess regular police authority. The "reserve police officer" wears a police uniform and usually does possess regular police officer powers while in uniform and on duty. Some very clear exceptions exist to this general conclusion, and a few of these are considered here. Auxiliaries and reserves are required to conform to departmental rules and regulations, to undergo recruit and in-service training, and to participate in prescribed activities on a regular basis in order to maintain their positions. In most jurisdictions, they are uncompensated except for a clothing allowance and participation in state workmen's compensation programs. Their primary job is to serve as a deterrent to crime. It is generally believed that if a person bent on crime spots a uniformed officer on the street, he or she will think twice about committing a crime. If auxiliaries spot something wrong, they are instructed to call the stationhouse or use their walkie-talkies to call for immediate help.

The Miami (Florida) Police Department recruits and deploys both reserve and auxiliary officers. Candidates for positions as auxiliary or reserve police officers have different selection and training requirements. For example, auxiliaries must successfully complete a minimum of 272 hours of training consisting of a prerequisite course, which includes the 48-hour Medical First Responder Training Course; a weapons course; and various defensive tactics and high-liability training courses. There is also an optional 32-hour Vehicle Operations Training Course that may be required. On the contrary, reserve officers must satisfy all of the eligibility requirements established for full-time police officers as well as the minimum departmental requirements established by Florida's Criminal Justice Standards and Training Commission. The auxiliary serves without compensation assisting full-time or part-time officers and may—under the direct supervision of a full-time law enforcement officer—arrest and perform law enforcement functions. Reserve police officers have enhanced authority and are is considered part-time law enforcement officers Miami's reserve officers may be employed or appointed less than full-time, with or without compensation with the authority to bear arms and make arrests and whose primary responsibility is the prevention and detection of crime or the enforcement of penal, criminal, traffic, or highway laws of the state. At the Miami Police Department, both auxiliary police officers and reserve police officers are required to receive training on the use of force and to successfully complete annual firearms qualifications (Miami PD 2014).

In an odd twist of fate, an existing auxiliary police force in Los Angeles was upgraded to a reserve police program at the end of World War II. However, in NYC, a reserve force active in the 1920s was disbanded about a decade prior to America's entry into World War II. During World War II, NYC established a short-lived organization of volunteer police known as the "City Patrol Corps." Later, it created its present-day auxiliary program. During the wartime period, when enlistment in the armed forces acutely depleted the ranks of qualified full-time police recruits, many cities and towns throughout the United States turned to local residents to supplement the shortage of full-time police officers. Throughout the country, tens of thousands of citizens volunteered their services as civilian defense auxiliary police and as air raid wardens.

Today, NYC's auxiliary program involves approximately 4,500 auxiliary police officers. Their most distinctive feature is the star-shaped badge they have been issued since the late 1960s. This huge force, the largest of its kind in the United States, is trained to use radios to call for help. They receive about 64 hours of classroom instruction stretched over several months. They are armed only with a police nightstick but face the same risks as any regular full-time police officer. According to James Mitts, the volunteer commanding officer of the 125-member auxiliary unit at the 109th Precinct in Flushing, Queens, "We tell our people, 'Don't get into foot pursuits to apprehend somebody'" (Barron and Kilgannon 2007, p. 5). NYC auxiliary officers are repeatedly told that they are not police officers, only private citizens who act as "the eyes and ears" of the police department. On the contrary, Los Angeles's 700 police reserve officers receive hundreds of hours of instruction, and their volunteer police officers are armed and given additional instruction in order to carry out police duties that include making felony arrests.

NYC and Buffalo

Prior to America's entry into World War I, long-standing suspicions about the need for a standing army contributed to debate about the need for troop and equipment buildups. Many residents of the rural South and West opposed military expansion. However, a compromise was accepted by President Wilson that resulted in the passage of the National Defense

Act of 1916[2] (Tindall and Shi 2007). Although the U.S. Congress debated the need for such legislation, New York State and several cities led the way for protection on the home front.

The city of Buffalo, New York, was incorporated in 1832. By the time of World War I, it had a population of about 450,000 and a police force of about 800 regular officers that were assigned to 15 police stations. In place of the muddy roads of earlier days, Buffalo now had more than 600 miles of paved streets with about 30,000 automobiles. Seventeen different railroads, 13 of them trunk lines, entered the city. It had 2,500 manufacturing plants. Buffalo also had easy access to water transportation (being located at the foot of Lake Erie and the terminus of the state's barge canal transport system); it ranked high on the nation's list of industrial cities. It also had 66 public and 40 parochial schools, three colleges and the University of Buffalo, 19 hospitals, and six English daily newspapers. In short, Buffalo was an American city with critical infrastructure that was important to protect during wartime (Sweeney 1920).

On April 2, 1917, President Woodrow Wilson appeared before a joint session of the U.S. Congress to request a declaration of war against Germany. Wilson cited Germany's violation of its pledge to suspend unrestricted submarine warfare in the North Atlantic and the Mediterranean and its attempts to entice Mexico into an alliance against the United States as his reasons for declaring war.[3] On April 4, 1917, the U.S. Senate voted in support of the measure. The House concurred two days later. The United States later declared war on Austria-Hungary on December 7, 1917 (Office of the Historian 2014).

Many people in the United States had not been inclined to go to war with Germany, but state and local governments in many parts of the nation abruptly took steps to mobilize for the war effort upon learning of Wilson's war message. Thus, 12 days after Congress approved President Wilson's request, Mayor Louis P. Fuhrmann called for the creation of a reserve police force for the protection of life and property within the city of Buffalo. He asked for citizens "to act as volunteer policemen, so that in case of extreme emergencies, where a large number of policemen were needed, the reserve would be ready and willing to offer their services as special policemen" (Sweeney 1920, 430).

The reserve force received no compensation from the city of Buffalo. Members were issued a badge, baton, and patrol box keys. They "were organized and existed purely for the patriotic purpose of serving their city in case of riots or uprising, and when the members of the Police Department were detailed to protect the great water front which contained hundreds of storehouses and grain elevators, the Police Reserve after daily toil in banks, offices, and in the shops, patrolled the streets of the city in the absence of the regular police. The Police Reserve was a very active organization until long after the signing of the Armistice. They assisted the Department in disposing of a great many Liberty Bonds and War Savings Stamps, assisted the Red Cross to keep order at parades, and helped with election day and registration day details.... They were required to attend meetings at the station house once each week for the purpose of being instructed in the proper method of performing police duties, and observing rules and regulations, laws and ordinances. They were drilled in the military drills of the U.S. Army, received lectures from the training school instructor, and were ready to give efficient service when called upon, as was proven by the many meritorious arrests made by their members" (Sweeney 1920, 430). During the 1950s and 1960s, the Buffalo Police Department coordinated a civil defense auxiliary police program.[4] A successor organization now exists in the city of Buffalo, and it consists of a small group of uncompensated volunteers (about 45) who routinely maintain security at more than 40 events a year. Some of these events include: Winterfest at Delaware Park, the Shamrock Run, the fourth of July celebration at Riverside Park, and National Night Out. The events the "Buffalo Police Reserves" attend are first cleared through the city's police commissioner and then voted on by its membership before being accepted as an event or function to perform (Buffalo Police Reserves 2014a). A nonrefundable application fee is paid by potential members. Membership requirements include U.S. citizenship; being at least 20 years of age; the possession of a New York State driver's license; and satisfactory criminal history, drug testing, and physician physical fitness reports (Buffalo Police Reserves 2014b).

At the same time that the first Buffalo Police Reserve was being organized, Mayor Fuhrmann instituted a separate organization known as the Volunteer Patrol League. Members of the League were required to furnish their automobiles for patrol purposes in the city's residential districts. Also as a consequence of wartime preparation, in New York State, each county (pursuant to directives from New York's governor and the state's adjutant general) was required to establish a Home Defense Committee. These county committees formed additional committees to carry out their responsibilities, one of which was to organize and equip a Home Defense Corps. In due course, Erie County succeeded in establishing such an organization consisting of 12 companies in Buffalo and one each in the communities of Tonawanda, Kenmore, Depew, and East Aurora. The average number of men in a company was 80, making a total of 1,280. It was soon renamed the Home Defense Reserve. Officers for each company were selected based on prior military organization experience. In general, membership was composed of individuals who were either beyond draft age or too young to be conscripted. The companies participated in drills and helped with Liberty Loan campaigns. Over time, many members who remained on the home front joined the state militia or the state guard (Sweeney 1920).

By May 1916, 8,000 citizens in NYC had been enrolled into a "Citizens Home Defense League," Within two additional months that number had reached 21,000. It was also during this period when an early forerunner to today's Law Enforcement Explorer Posts and Police Athletic Leagues was established in NYC. It was known as the "junior police." At its peak, NYC's junior police program had enrolled approximately 6,000 boys between the ages of 11 and 15. By 1919, the "Citizens Home Defense League" had become a reserve force, and a state law was passed in 1920 that reorganized this group into a permanent adjunct to the police force with full police powers when on active duty. These assignments were curtailed in the late 1920s, and the reserves were formally abolished by order of the city's police commissioner in 1934 (Greenberg 1984).

When the United States entered World War II, Mayor Fiorello LaGuardia created a new type of auxiliary police force, the "City Patrol Corps." By 1942, this emergency auxiliary police force was in full operation, and by 1943, it had 32 companies with a total of nearly 4,500 volunteers. Its last patrol was on August 30, 1945; one month later it was officially demobilized. The corps helped to preserve the city's infrastructure and prevented crime during a significant period of world upheaval (Greenberg 1984).

Figure 4.1 is a photo of the front and rear covers of a 1942 "Civil Defense Index" booklet. Its pages offered information to civilians on the home front. Survival-related advice was given for air raids, blackouts, bombs, poison gas, as well as first aid situations. The rear cover (right side as seen in Figure 4.1)

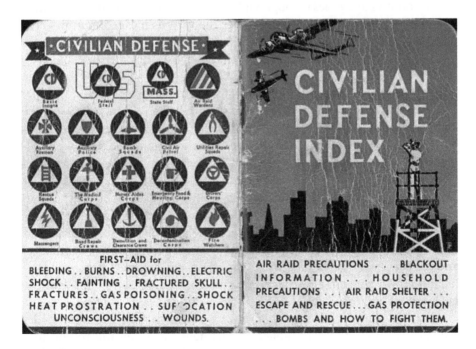

Figure 4.1 Photo of the front and rear covers of a 1942 *Civil Defense Index* booklet.

indicates the various units of civilian defense in which Americans were urged to enroll.

At the start of the Korean War, Congress passed Public Law No. 920 (entitled The Civil Defense Act of 1950), which authorized a Federal Civil Defense Program. This law provided a plan for the protection of life and property in the United States in the event of a national emergency, such as a nuclear attack. The responsibility for civil defense was vested in the states and their political subdivisions. The New York State Legislature followed the recommendations of the federal government and, in 1951, enacted the New York State Defense Emergency Act, which empowered the city of New York to create a civil defense program. This act, which is still in force, requires cities in New York State to recruit, train, and equip volunteers who will act as an adjunct to the regular police departments in the event of a civil defense emergency or natural disaster. In the final organization chart, NYC's defenses were divided into five volunteer divisions: police emergency, fire, public works, health, and emergency welfare. Currently, auxiliaries through- out the state function by virtue of the 1951 statute, and their routine patrols and assignments are officially considered training exercises (Greenberg 1984). However, as can be observed from the foregoing discussion, the origin of NYC's present-day auxiliary police program can be traced to several ear- lier volunteer defense groups.

In counties and cities throughout New York State during the 1950s, units of auxiliary police were organized under the various local community civil defense units, which were each headed by a local volunteer director. Nassau County is immediately east of NYC, within the New York metropolitan area. After World War II, training for auxiliaries in Nassau County consisted largely of an inspector from the Nassau County Police Department (NCPD) occasionally stopping by at an auxiliary police meeting. In the 1960s, the NCPD took responsibility for the program by detailing a deputy inspector to the county civil defense agency to serve as the head of the county's auxil- iary program. Later, the county's commissioner of police ordered that each auxiliary police officer attend an approved 23-session Nassau County Police Department Basic Training Course. Eventually, the NCPD took over respon- sibility for county-level oversight and direction. In the 1970s, their duties changed, reflecting concerns about safety. The auxiliary police were used as "eyes and ears" against crime. They were also used for various community- and county-sponsored events. They assisted the police department with traf- fic and crowd control, allowing regular police to devote more attention to emergencies and other duties.[5]

In 1967, John V. Lindsay, the Mayor of NYC, signed Executive Order #51. In that order, the NYC Police Department was given full responsibil- ity for the city's auxiliary police. Executive Order No. 38 (August 29, 1975) continued this responsibility. The second order was sparked by a period of turmoil in the ranks of regular and volunteer police. Throughout much of the 1980s, the auxiliary program moved along with little fanfare or further controversy. On occasion, however, there was enlightening press coverage. For example, in 1988, the *New York Times* reported that the "auxiliaries span the city's social order, from Wall Street professionals to high-school dropouts. They are held up by Police Commissioner Benjamin Ward and other police officials as an example of what civilians can do to help maintain order" (Hays 1988, p. 30). Members must be between the ages of 17 and 63 in order to patrol; persons over 63 may apply for administrative duties. (See Box 4.1 for the current requirements for membership.)

A Housing Auxiliary Police program was started in 1992 as a pilot project. Subsequently, this program expanded to the residents of the housing developments throughout the city. Auxiliaries patrol in each of nine Housing

---

BOX 4.1   NEW YORK CITY AUXILIARY
POLICE MEMBERSHIP REQUIREMENTS

- At least age 17
- Be in good health
- Proof of good character and satisfactory background
- Must comply with zero tolerance department drug policy
- Able to read and write English
- Be a U.S. citizen, lawful permanent resident, or authorized to work in the United States
- Live in New York City or live in one of the six authorized surrounding counties (Nassau, Suffolk, Westchester, Rockland, Orange, and Putnam) and work within New York City
- Must possess a valid New York State driver's license or New York State identification card
- A minimum of 144 hours of duty per fiscal year is required. Must comply with zero tolerance Department drug policy (Careers 2014)
- Never been convicted of a felony or have a previous arrest record that would prevent acceptance (Careers 2014; Kelly et al. 2008, 2, 5)

Source: Careers, 2014, Careers – Auxiliary police, available at: http://www. nyc.gov/html/nypd/html/careers/auxiliary_police.shtml; Kelly, R. W. et al., 2008, Auxiliary police program overview, available at: http://www. nyc.gov/html/nypd/downloads/pdf/careers/nypd_auxiliary_police_ overview_2008.pdf

Police Service Areas and are used for crime prevention, community events, and administrative functions. They attend tenant association and youth meetings to coordinate perimeter and lobby patrols and to address such specific concerns as gang-related activity.

The NYC Transit District auxiliary police crime deterrent program started in 2000, also as a pilot project in one area. In July 2005, this program expanded to include all 12 Transit Districts. Auxiliaries assigned to transit (subway) patrols center their activities at the entrances and exits, stairs leading to and from stations, mezzanine areas, and in street areas in the immediate vicinity of subway stations. This initiative was related to the 2005 London transit bombings. If medically qualified, transit auxiliaries may respond to common medical emergency calls in the transit system if they are near to the transit location. The main functions of the Transit auxiliary police primarily remain within the subway system.

NYC auxiliaries are also assigned to harbor, highway, headquarters, and special task units. In all of these units as well as in each of the city's 76 patrol precincts, members are supervised by officers of the regular police as well as superiors within the auxiliary police ranks.

Auxiliary police officers in NYC, unlike many of their counterparts in upstate New York, are not permitted to carry a sidearm on duty, even if independently licensed to carry a firearm. This restriction may have contributed to a major tragedy that occurred more than halfway into the first decade of the twenty-first century. Sixth Precinct Auxiliary Police Officers Eugene Marshalik (age 19) and Nicholas T. Pekearo (age 28) were killed in March 2007 by a gunman who had first fired upon and killed a pizzeria employee in Greenwich Village. The gunman then shot the two on-duty auxiliaries at close range. They were the seventh and eighth NYC auxiliary officers killed while on duty in the auxiliary force's modern-day history (which commenced during the Korean War era). Their deaths alone were tragic enough, but the matter became more heartbreaking with an initial decision by the federal government to deny death benefits for their families under the Public Safety Officers Benefits (PSOB) program. The federal government's representatives claimed that although the officers were killed in the line of duty, their lack of peace officer status when they were killed made them ineligible. The federal government came under heavy criticism for denying the benefits, and NYC Police Commissioner Raymond Kelly and U.S. Senator Charles Schumer made personal appeals to the Department of Justice on behalf of the stricken families. In a NYC Police Department (NYPD) press release, Kelly stated: "The City of New York has already awarded the death benefits available to Auxiliary Police Officers. It only makes sense that the Department of Justice follow suit and recognize Eugene and Nicholas as public safety officers within the meaning of the law. This was a wrong-headed decision. It needs to be reversed" (NYPD 2008). In March 2008, Kelly testified before an administrative hearing judge. At the appeal hearing, Commissioner Kelly stated that the killer had "made the calculated decision to specifically target Officers Pekearo and Marshalik because of their affiliation with the NYPD. It was the officers' willingness to continue to be the eyes and ears of the NYPD that led to these tragic results" (Gendar et al. 2008, p. 6). With respect to the U. S. Justice Department's reasoning in its original decision denying benefits, Kelly stated: "It's a hyper technical interpretation. Every citizen has arrest powers. You can arrest for a felony in any crime that takes place in your presence" (Gendar et al. 2008, p. 6). Finally, after much additional publicity, U.S. Attorney General Michael Mukasey reversed the original ruling and approved the death benefits.[6]

Two years later and more than 16 years after another NYPD auxiliary officer was slain trying to apprehend a gunman in the Bronx, the government granted a line-of-duty death benefit to the family of Milton Clarke. The Justice Department had repeatedly refused to grant the monetary award under the PSOB program to the Clarke family because auxiliaries are not considered peace officers. Clarke was off duty, working in his auto repair shop on December 1, 1993, when he heard the nearby sound of shots fired; he retrieved his licensed handgun. A 47-year-old father of five, Clarke ran in the direction of the gunfire and was immediately shot in the chest by a gunman who had wounded another man (Marzulli 2010). The precedent of the earlier award of benefits no doubt led to the payment of the claim instituted by the Clarke family.

In March 2007, less than two weeks after the unarmed volunteers were killed, Mayor Bloomberg vowed to provide bulletproof vests to each of the city's 4,500 auxiliaries.[7] In addition, a committee was selected to review the auxiliary program at the request of Commissioner Kelly. The report was supposed to be completed in 90 days.[8] About a year later, a report was released by the NYPD. The report began with these statements: "The Department has made it clear that the Auxiliary Police Program is one of the best vehicles offered for involving the citizenry and community in promoting public safety through their personal participation. Ranking superior officers of the NYPD have favorably evaluated the Auxiliary Police Program. Commanding Officers are encouraged to fully utilize this valuable personnel resource" (Kelly et al. 2008, 2).

The review report revealed some information that was not generally known to the public. For example, some auxiliaries participate in "quality of life" enforcement initiatives. The participants must be between the ages of 18 and 20½ and are given specialized training at the auxiliary police headquarters by members of the Organized Crime Control Bureau (OCCB) Vice Enforcement Unit and auxiliary police headquarters staff in safety, tactics, and integrity. They work in plainclothes under the direct supervision of the vice enforcement or precinct conditions unit supervisor. They are trained to attempt to purchase alcohol, box cutters, and other items that are not permitted to be displayed or sold to minors in licensed premises. Acting on community complaints, such undercover operations take place at restaurants, bars, and liquor and grocery stores. Each year summonses are issued by borough vice and precinct conditions units using auxiliary police (Kelly et al. 2008, 8, 17).

For a number of years, there were opportunities to participate in bicycle units in various commands. The bicycles were obtained through community donations or from the Community Policing Unit. Candidates for this assignment attended the department's bicycle training course conducted by the Police Academy Driver Training Unit at Floyd Bennett Field (Kelly et al. 2008). In 2011, apparently as a result of an unfavorable New York State Department of Labor investigation concerning the city's auxiliary program, the Auxiliary Bike Patrol Program was suspended. At that time, there was concern that an auxiliary officer's wooden nightstick might get stuck in bicycle wheels as volunteer police pedaled (Auer 2011).

Many auxiliaries would like to receive training in the use of pepper spray, to have peace officer status, and to see a state law passed to make it a felony to assault an auxiliary officer. In addition, just a few weeks after the March 2007 deaths of the auxiliary officers, City Councilman David Weprin created a ten-point plan—with the help of auxiliary officers—to improve the program. One of the points included the "full restoration of the Auxiliary Emergency Service Unit (AESU) name and function in order to allow auxiliary officers to properly serve as the auxiliary arm/adjunct of the NYPD Emergencies Services Unit as was originally mandated upon its creation in 1950" (Auxiliary Officers Assistance Plan 2007).[9]

A useful summary of NYC's Auxiliary Police program can be found at: http://cttfauxiliary.com/page5. This Web page indicates that, in 2010, funding for protective vests (Level IIIA vests, the same used by full-time officers) for the auxiliaries was no longer available in the NYPD budget. However, every Police Precinct, Housing Police Service Area, and Transit District had a pool of "loaner" vests for new auxiliary officers to use while on patrol.

There has been some confusion over the "peace officer" status of NYC auxiliaries. However, a 2008 program review report prepared by the leadership of the NYPD clearly states: "Auxiliary Police Officers are neither Police Officers nor Peace Officers (except during an emergency under 2.20 Criminal Procedure Law). They do not carry firearms and [have] no power of arrest beyond that of a private citizen" (Kelly et al. 2008, 2). In addition, the report also explains that: "In the event of an emergency, legislation exists which enables the Police Commissioner, Mayor, and/or New York State Legislature to confer Peace Officer status upon Auxiliary Police. Pursuant to Section 2.20 of the Criminal Procedure Law, Auxiliary Officers may be given Peace Officer status. This limited authority is only valid during a period of imminent or actual attack by enemy forces, or during official duties. The principal function that Auxiliaries would perform during this period would be to direct and control traffic" (Kelly et al. 2008, 3). Yet, several unofficial New York auxiliary police Web sites state that these volunteers are "NYS certified peace officers." Some of these sites refer to the fact that NYC auxiliaries are registered as "part-time peace officers" with a state agency. It needs to be understood that the New York State Division of Criminal Justice Services does not certify police or peace officers but merely maintains a database of employed officers and their training records.

Los Angeles Police Reserve Corps

California has many reserve police programs, and one of the most significant is the Los Angeles Police Reserve Corps. It is the state's largest volunteer police program with approximately 700 members. Its roots extend deep into the history of California and include meeting the need to recruit civil defense auxiliary police during World War II. During the post-war years, after the program's formal establishment by the Los Angeles (LA) City Council in 1947, its membership reached nearly 2,500. At that time, the reserve force paid for their own equipment and uniforms, much like the NYC auxiliaries. Today, police equipment and uniforms are provided. Unlike their NYC counterparts, the LA reserves' physical and medical membership qualifications were upgraded to be equivalent to that of regular LA police officers. Gradually, training requirements were also expanded so that the standards required by the California Commission on Peace Officer Standards and Training (POST) were met. Training classes are held evenings and weekends. Today, the LA police reserves are divided into three levels of membership.

Level III Reserve Officers are assigned duties at the front desk, with area detectives, and in community relations. Level III Reserve Officers receive approximately 240 hours of professional classroom instruction and must be at least 18 at the time of application for membership. Level III Reserve Officers also receive approximately 26 hours of basic self-defense training including wrist locks, twist locks, kicks, and other techniques at the lower end of the department's use-of-force scale. Physical fitness exercises are used to prepare recruits for self-defense training. Level III members are not eligible to carry firearms until their twenty-first birthday (Reserve Police Officer Program 2013).

Level I and II Reserve Officers receive additional training and must be at least 21 at the time of application. Level II Reserve Officers receive approximately 250 hours of professional classroom instruction. Level I Reserve Officers receive approximately 340 hours of professional classroom instruction. They receive approximately 72 hours of self-defense training. This training includes techniques available within the higher end of the department's use-of-force scale. Physical training includes weight training, calisthenics, and running. The additional hours of training are needed because Level I and II Reserve Officers perform the same functions as regular, full-time police officers. They are armed, uniformed peace officers who work in police vehicles along with full-time police officers (Reserve Police Officer Program 2013). After graduating from the academy, Level I and II Reserve Officers are required to work a minimum of 32 hours every two 28-day deployment periods, and they must attend mandatory monthly reserve officer meetings.

Today, the LA reserves tend to be older than new regular police recruits, and they come from all walks of life. During the day, they may be attorneys, small business owners, government employees, homemakers, retirees, or even city council members. Moreover, like most reserves and auxiliaries located elsewhere, their primary reasons for joining stem from their desire to make the community a better and safer place to live. All reserve officers undergo an exhaustive selection process, including a detailed background check, and are held to the high standards set by the department. As a result, they are looked upon favorably by full-time officers who often ask to work with reservists. One of the first acts performed by Charlie Beck when he became the new Los Angeles Police Department (LAPD) chief of police was to recognize volunteers who serve the community as members of the police reserves. As part of the LAPD's Financial Counseling Team, Attorney Doug Neistat was among those honored for their service. Neistat serves as a specialist reserve officer, working with departmental employees and their families and providing free legal assistance—especially in the areas of bankruptcy and insolvency. Volunteer Police Officer Neistat has served as an LAPD reserve officer since 1998 (Of Counsel 2010).

Like their full-time officer counterparts, LA reserves wear the same badge and have the same gun and the same uniform. They may progress to greater levels of responsibility by meeting additional training requirements. However, although NYC city auxiliaries wear the same uniform as regular officers, their star-shaped badges can distinguish them and none are permitted to carry a firearm while performing their duties. There is a promotional system for NYC auxiliaries, but it does not include the ability to carry out routine law enforcement duties. Some of the youngest auxiliaries may be assigned to undercover operations in order to make underage beverage or cigarette purchases, but it is a very small number. An entry-level LA reservist must work alongside a full-time officer and participate in special events such as festivals and art walks. LA volunteer officers with special qualifications have the opportunity to use their skills for the benefit of the public. For example, an individual with years of legal experience may be assigned as a reserve detective to help the LAPD investigate white-collar crime (Hillard 2011). On the contrary, NYC auxiliaries seldom have opportunities to work alongside full-time officers unless they have reached the higher ranks, such as captain and above.[10] In such cases, these auxiliaries will work closely with their regular precinct auxiliary coordinators in order to help in administrative matters. NYC auxiliary members seeking promotion to ranks of sergeant and above must complete additional training courses.

Brentwood Reserve Police

The city of Brentwood lies 325 miles north of Los Angeles and 32 miles east of Oakland, California. Brentwood has long been known for its crops of cherries, apricots, plums, peaches, and corn; however, the city has become more of a residential community in the last few decades. The Brentwood Police Department was established in 1948 and services an area of approximately 14 square miles. Prior to its establishment, an elected constable held law and order responsibility. The city is comprised of about 52,000 residents and is divided into four separate patrol beats. With a starting salary of approximately $75,000, the department currently has 62 sworn police officers and another 17 civilian support staff. In addition to its permanent staff, there are approximately 20 police volunteer citizens (Brentwood Police Department 2013). The Brentwood Police Department is in the process of reestablishing a reserve police unit. The department had a strong reserve police program dating back to the 1960s, providing the community with an auxiliary unit of trained and competent volunteer police officers. These officers were used to supplement the department's regular personnel and historically were used for special events, prisoner transports, and in emergencies. In June 2013, the city council voted to recruit a maximum of 10 reserve officers to assist with prisoner transports, traffic control, and public event security under the supervision of sworn officers (Szymanski 2013).

The new reserves will have to satisfy all the hiring qualifications and standards of full-time police officers. They would be expected to work a minimum of 20 hours a month after completing three training modules at the Contra Costa County Regional Police Academy. As Level II volunteer police, they would have the same authority as sworn officers. The city had an active force in the 1980s when the number of reserves outnumbered the full-time police. However, the population of this bedroom community has steadily grown, and the reserves are needed to transport prisoners and cover the local jail, especially on busy Friday nights. In return for their service, volunteers will be provided with all necessary equipment, a $25 monthly uniform cleaning allowance, $100 per court appearance, and an additional $100 for every weekend they agree to be on-call to transport arrestees to the Contra Costa County Detention Facility in Martinez. The program is expected to cost the city an estimated $153,000 a year (Szymanski 2013).

During the 1980s and 1990s, Brentwood had an average of 15 reserve officers, but attrition, retirements, and a lack of qualified candidates are said to have caused the program to be disbanded in 2006. Recently, law enforcement agencies, including the Contra Costa Office of the Sheriff, have started to recruit or create new reserve units (Szymanski 2013).

New York City Park Volunteer Units

In various western and midwestern states, volunteers who own their own horses and are interested in policing or participating in ceremonial events have become members of sheriff posse mounted units. Many of these units often appear wearing their distinctive regalia in various parades, such as the annual Tournament of Roses parade held in Pasadena, California. NYC's Central Park is patrolled by the NYPD's 22nd Precinct (also known as the Central Park Precinct) and the NYC Parks Enforcement Patrol (PEP) unit. Central Park was designed in 1858 by Fredrick Law Olmstead and Calvert Vaux, and it became the nation's first man-made public park. The park is made up of approximately 840 acres, 150 acres of water and 690 acres of land. It is 2.5 miles long and 0.5 mile wide. There are 58 miles of pedestrian paths, six miles of vehicle drives, and almost five miles of bridle paths. Two different volunteer auxiliaries in mounted units have performed public safety patrols in Central Park since the early 1950s. The first mounted auxiliary patrols were under the supervision of the NYPD, but in recent years, a different organizational unit has been under the command of the city's Parks Department.

In 1955, the Central Park Auxiliary Police unit had 75 members, and 50 of them carried pistols as part of their participation in the unit's gun club. The majority of these auxiliaries patrolled on foot or drove their own cars and motorcycles in order to police the park from 8 p.m. to midnight. In those days, members who choose to patrol on horseback provided their own horses or rented them from a nearby stable for two dollars a tour (Hudson 1955). In a 1974 interview, Auxiliary Inspector Joseph Siegel, an original member of the auxiliary mounted troop, indicated that during World War II he patrolled on horseback in Central Park as a member of the City Patrol Corps. He was instrumental in starting an auxiliary police mounted unit when the city's current auxiliary police force was organized during the Korean War era (Carmody 1974). In 1973, this unit was given added strength when 26 new members—including a night club singer, an economist, a computer programmer, several lawyers and business executives, and Michael Burke, the president of Madison Square Garden—completed the NYPD's riding school in Pelham Bay Park (City's First Auxiliary 1973). By the following year, the unit had grown and was patrolling in various city parks including Manhattan's theater district. In addition, a small uniform allowance became available to help with the cost of uniforms and equipment, but all mounts were provided by the NYPD. However, by the 1980s, unit members were again providing their own mounts (Buder 1980).

In September 1980, the Parks Department established its own full time professional and salaried unit of mounted riders that began park patrols in NYC; they were known as mounted rangers. This contingent joined a new paid urban park ranger force that had been created the previous year to patrol on foot and in vehicles. The mounted rangers were only assigned to daylight patrols (Goodman 1980).

Less well-known is the volunteer mounted auxiliary unit of the NYC Parks Department, which deploys experienced riders to conduct patrols to educate the public and to enforce park rules in Central Park in Manhattan, in Van Cortlandt Park in the Bronx, and in other parks throughout the city (as seen in Figures 4.2 through 4.4). The auxiliary unit serves to deter, identify, and report illegal or unsafe activities and is an informational resource for the public. It raises sufficient funds to pay for itself (Auxiliary Mounted 2013; Karni 2011). In this way, they supplement the services of the full-time, salaried, mounted PEP officers (Z. Feder, personal communication, February 5, 2014).

The mounted volunteers of the city's Parks Department help with crowd control during parades, shut down illegal barbecues, find lost children, and

Figure 4.2 Members of the NYC Parks Department Mounted Auxiliary Unit on patrol, ca. 2013. (Used with the permission of the NYC Parks Department Mounted Auxiliary Unit, Inc.)

Figure 4.3 Member of the NYC Parks, Department Mounted Auxiliary Unit on patrol in winter, ca. 2013. (Used with the permission of the NYC Parks Department Mounted Auxiliary Unit, Inc.)

Figure 4.4 Member of the NYC Parks Department Mounted Auxiliary Unit, ca. 2013. (Used with the permission of the NYC Parks Department Mounted Auxiliary Unit, Inc.)

report crime to police. For these purposes, the city's Parks Department owns four 1,800-pound Clydesdales and currently has 50 volunteers on its roster, all of whom are required to serve a minimum of 48 hours per year, including a minimum of six patrols and at least one special event. According to Mark Elkins, the president of the unit since 2006, "Central Park is an interesting beat. To the south, it's mostly interacting with tourists and making them feel more secure. To the north, there are areas that are heavily wooded and impenetrable except by horse" (Karni 2011).

The Parks Department auxiliary unit was founded in 1996. After being tested on riding skills, potential members are rigorously trained on policies, procedures, and communications before going out on patrol. Riding instruction is not provided. Members assist the PEP officers of the city's Department of Parks and Recreation. PEP officers are certified New York State Peace Officers and NYC Special Patrolmen. The NYC Parks Department Mounted Auxiliary volunteers serve as "eyes and ears" for the Parks Department, patrolling on horseback in areas inaccessible by vehicles, to ensure the safety of park patrons and the preservation of animals, plants, and natural resources. They also advise the public on park rules, provide directions and information, and assist those who are injured, lost, or victims of crime (Auxiliary Mounted 2013).

Cheltenham Township Auxiliary Police

Cheltenham Township covers an area of just over 9 square miles in eastern Pennsylvania. Cheltenham Township, as it exists today, is the product of more than 300 years of history and is known as Philadelphia's first suburb. The township is about 13 miles due north of Philadelphia and is governed by a board of commissioners who appoint the township's manager. The township's police department is located in Elkins Park. Its surrounding areas were developed around early mill establishments located next to a creek. Tookany Creek provided industrial opportunities for early settlers and entrepreneurs. As the mills prospered, small villages containing workers' housing and supporting businesses grew up around them. By the early twentieth century, most of the mills had been abandoned and demolished, but they had been the original reason for the settlement of the region (Cheltenham 2014d).

According to the 2010 U.S. Census, slightly more than half of the township's population is white and a quarter black. Their median age is 40, and more than half of the adult population have earned a bachelor's degree or higher. According to the 2000 U.S. Census, about 80% of its labor force is engaged in white-collar occupations and about 60% of all of the township's workers had an annual income exceeding $50,000 (Cheltenham 2014c).

The Township Board of Commissioners created the Cheltenham Police Department in February 1903, with an authorized strength of one police chief and "not more than seven officers." In those days, duties included patrolling the small villages, large estates, and open countryside comprising the township. Today, the Cheltenham Township Police Department is the third largest police department in Montgomery County, Pennsylvania. The department serves a population of approximately 37,000 residents and responded to more than 25,000 calls for service in 2008. The 84-member Cheltenham Township Police Department maintains round-the-clock street patrols, investigates crimes and serious accidents, conducts traffic studies, maintains special situation units, and offers safety education and crime prevention programs for community groups (e.g., the Drug Abuse Resistance Education, or DARE, officers teach school children about substance abuse avoidance). A mobile mini-station van and bicycle patrols are among the tools used by the agency's Community Policing Unit (Cheltenham 2014a).

In addition to its regular sworn police officers, the Cheltenham Township Police Department is assisted by volunteers who comprise an Auxiliary Police unit that assists at the scenes of serious accidents, fires, other emergencies and special events; they volunteer hundreds of hours of crowd and traffic control service each year (as seen in Figures 4.5 and 4.6). There is a Student Intern Program, a volunteer Chaplain's Program, and a volunteer residential Town Watch, equipped with cellular phones. The Town Watch members conduct mobile patrols of their neighborhoods and are alert for suspicious activity, functioning as additional trained "eyes and ears" for the police department (Cheltenham 2014a).

Figure 4.5 Auxiliary officer on traffic post at a special event. (Used with the permission of the Cheltenham (PA) Township Police Department.)

Figure 4.6 Auxiliary officer providing assistance to transit system bus driver at a special event. (Used with the permission of the Cheltenham (PA) Township Police Department.)

The Cheltenham Township Volunteer Auxiliary Police unit was formed in the mid-1950s. Auxiliary police officers are equipped with uniforms similar to those worn by regular officers. Though not armed, they are authorized to use police vehicles and police band radio communications equipment. The organization has assisted the police department with traffic and crowd control at various community events, such as the Community Harvest Festival and Sundays in the Park. By handling these responsibilities, auxiliary officers free Cheltenham police for regular patrol duties. Like other emergency services of the township, auxiliary police are available 24 hours a day. Training of the volunteer police is provided by members of the police department, supplemented by outside sources. Requirements for membership include being 18 years of age and a resident, for at least six months, of Cheltenham Township or any of 15 different other Montgomery County townships or boroughs (Cheltenham 2014b).

In February 2005, the Cheltenham Police Department introduced a Chaplain's Program to better serve the community and to help with difficult assignments. The program may strengthen relationships between the police and the community. It may also improve communication between police and local religious groups in the township. The program started with five local religious leaders representing various faiths and currently has seven volunteer chaplains active in the program. As trained counselors, the chaplains are available to offer support to residents in need, such as comforting grieving families during death notifications. Chaplains participate in ride-along shifts with regular police officers and may help to defuse potential problems that may arise. As a result of their close working relations with police, the volunteer police chaplains have developed a bond with agency personnel and are available to them as needed. In addition, the chaplains can help put residents in touch with representatives of many faiths if the need arises (Cheltenham 2014e).

Albemarle County (Virginia) Auxiliary Police

Albemarle County is in central Virginia and contains the homes of three of America's earliest presidents. Its 726 square miles rest at the foot of the Blue Ridge Mountains, situated approximately 110 miles southwest of Washington, D.C., and 70 miles west of Richmond. Its main city is Charlottesville, where the Monticello estate of Thomas Jefferson, America's third president, is located. Monticello annually attracts nearly 440,000 visitors. Charlottesville is an independent city enclave entirely surrounded by the county. Ash Lawn–Highland was the home of James Monroe, the fifth president of the United States and the author of the Monroe Doctrine; it is located two miles from Monticello. Montpelier, in Orange, Virginia, was the estate of James Madison, the fourth president of the United States and widely recognized as the "Father of the Constitution." When the Constitution was sent to the states for ratification, Madison (along with Alexander Hamilton and John Jay) wrote essays arguing in favor of the new form of government. First printed in New York newspapers, the essays were later published as *The Federalist*. The essays not only influenced the ratification debates but continue to influence legal thinking today.

The county currently employs 119 paid police officers, but in January 2014, it added six unpaid auxiliary officers and plans to recruit about a dozen more. The new unit was organized due to the initiative of the county's police chief, Col. Steve Sellers. He urged that it was a way to relieve the burden of some routine and administrative tasks of his regular officers. Sellers had been satisfied with the effort of the other police volunteers in his department and were aware that many other counties in Virginia have auxiliary forces.[11] In fact, all six members of the new unit had been members of the agency's Volunteers in Police Service (VIPS) program when they were selected to become auxiliary officers. Sellers said the new unit of auxiliary officers represents a cultural change to his department. He told the new volunteer officers that they would be "pioneers, ambassadors, and partners" in the department (Albemarle 2014).

Virginia's Department of Criminal Justice Services maintains standards for training volunteer police at three different levels, with the lowest level not trained in firearms. The two upper levels may be armed, with the highest level required to attend the 19-week police academy just like a paid officer.

The six new officers all entered their volunteer service at the lowest level. They will aid with tasks such as crime prevention programs, house safety checks, and traffic direction at special events. They are not armed with firearms and would rarely, if ever, respond to incidents such as robberies or domestic disputes without being accompanied by a full-time officer. Outfitting the first six auxiliary officers is costing $8,400, an amount that was included in the department's current fiscal year budget (Albemarle 2014).

Summary

This chapter has briefly highlighted seven units of volunteer police: the Albemarle County Auxiliary Police, the Buffalo Police Reserve, the Brentwood Reserve Police, the Cheltenham Township Auxiliary Police, the Los Angeles Reserve Police, the NYC Auxiliary Police, and the NYC Parks Department Mounted Auxiliary Unit.

It took many centuries for paid professional crime fighters to arrive on the scene in all regions of America. Therefore, some persons believe that returning to citizen involvement in policing, especially in urban areas, is a step backward rather than forward. America no longer needs to use citizen posses as it once did during the era of western lawlessness associated with the 1850s' Gold Rush. How can volunteers act as a "professional force" functioning 24 hours a day in order to deliver services and provide law and order?

The answer to this question can be traced to America's involvement in two world wars during the twentieth century. In those periods, many leaders and citizens believed that there was a profound need for additional security on the home front. Thereafter, the threat of nuclear attack spurred additional planning for citizen mobilization. Subsequently, urban and suburban police departments found value in maintaining their civil defense forces for crime prevention assignments. Regional distinctions appear to have arisen because the central and western regions of the United States were developed last and have had to cope with fewer public resources than the eastern third of the nation. The same can be said of some wilderness and mountainous regions of the East. These regions had to depend upon greater civilian involvement in peacekeeping for a longer time, and they tended to vest greater authority in their volunteer police. In the South, slave owners established slave patrols consisting of private citizens. The title of "auxiliary police" was part of the World War II and Korean War lexicons and remains in general use throughout the eastern half of the United States. In Virginia, the term "auxiliary police" dates back to at least the World War II era, but the title is not necessarily reflective of the broad scope of the powers of current members of volunteer police units who may progress through different classification levels. Moreover, citizen support of and participation in the justice system can take a variety of other forms nationwide: citizen watch member, VIPS administrative aide, CERT member, chaplain and just a few examples.

Reserve and auxiliary officers coexist in the Miami Police Department to assist the police force in the provision of emergency services and other functions. Both types of volunteer officers attend training opportunities and work alongside regular officers. However, the auxiliary is provided with somewhat less training and has less law enforcement responsibilities than reserve members. In particular, reserve officers must meet the same eligibility requirements and POST training standards as regular full-time officers.

During the 1950s and 1960s, the Buffalo Police Department coordinated a civil defense auxiliary police program. More recently, a "Buffalo Police Reserves" unit has been established with the approval of the city's police commissioner and mayor. It consists of a small group of uncompensated volunteers who routinely volunteer to maintain security at selected events of their own choosing and with the approval of Buffalo's police commissioner. At the time of America's entry into World War I, the city of Buffalo established its first Buffalo Police Reserve for the purpose of protecting the city in case of large disorders and when the members of the Police Department were detailed to protect the great water front which contained hundreds of storehouses and grain elevators.... They assisted the Department in disposing of a great many Liberty Bonds and War Savings Stamps, assisted the Red Cross to keep order at parades, and helped with election day and registration day details.... (Sweeney 1920, 430). They had the powers of special policemen and were assigned to each of the city's 15 precincts, but eventually the organization was phased out.

Today, most large urban police departments require huge budgets, the latest scientific aids, and the most up-to-date administrative techniques for the supervision of hundreds of employees. In the case of NYC, the police force is numbered in the tens of thousands. NYC volunteer and unsalaried police officers are unarmed, except for a straight nightstick. However, members of the volunteer force are exposed to the same dangers as regular officers. In 2007, auxiliary officers Marshalik and Pekearo of the 6th Precinct were shot to death in the line of duty. NYC auxiliaries are instructed to observe, report, and wait until full-fledged police officers arrive at the scene of a crime. Marshalik and Pekearo did not possess the necessary equipment to defend themselves when an armed and dangerous felon approached. In addition, it can be argued that the basic auxiliary training course of about 64 hours spread over a 16-week period is insufficient for the nature of their work.

The reserve police on America's West Coast (e.g., the LAPD Reserve) have quite a different set of training standards. They are provided with hundreds of hours of training. In the LAPD Reserves, volunteer police officers who go on patrol are Level II or I officers. Level II officers have approximately

460 hours of training, while Level I officers have approximately 800 hours of training. LAPD reserve officers are peace officers who have the same power and authority as full-time officers. Consequently, LAPD reserve officers are allowed to do certain things NYC auxiliary officers are not allowed to do, such as write tickets or make traffic stops.

The Brentwood Police Department is in the process of reestablishing its Reserve Police Officer Program. The police department had a strong Reserve Police Officer Program as far back as the 1960s, but it was demobilized in 2006. Due to a changed economic climate and an increase in population growth, there is renewed interest in reestablishing the program. It is planned that newly trained and qualified reserve officers will be assigned to provide support services such as prisoner transports, traffic control, and public event security.

The New York City Parks Department Mounted Auxiliary Unit, founded in 1996, is a group of private citizens who assist the PEP officers of the city's Department of Parks and Recreation. The full-time regular PEP officers are certified New York State Peace Officers and NYC Special Patrolmen. As non-sworn volunteers, the auxiliary officers serve as "eyes and ears" for the Parks Department, patrolling on horseback in areas inaccessible by vehicles to ensure the safety of park patrons and the preservation of animals, plants, and natural resources. Accepted mounted auxiliary unit candidates are trained in PEP policies and procedures, as well as park rules and regulations and the proper use of equipment.

The Cheltenham Township Volunteer Auxiliary Police unit was formed in the mid-1950s. Their auxiliary police officers are equipped with uniforms similar to those worn by regular officers. Though not armed, they are authorized to use police vehicles and police band radio communications equipment. The organization has assisted the police department with traffic and crowd control at various community events. The Cheltenham Police Department also conducts a Chaplain's Program to help with difficult assignments and to strengthen relationships between the police and the community.

The Albemarle County Auxiliary Police unit is the newest organization highlighted. The first group of their recruits will have limited police functions, but in the state of Virginia, it is possible for more highly trained volunteer police to assume the full range of law enforcement responsibilities. Its three different classifications of volunteer police appear to be comparable to the system used in California.

Currently, the "reserve police" title is more common in the western regions of the United States, and the "auxiliary" title is most common in the eastern half of the country. Nonetheless, in earlier times when the "reserve" title was used in the eastern region (e.g., during the 1920s in Buffalo and NYC), the volunteer officers had arrest authority comparable to regular officers. It is imperative that, irrespective of the type of auxiliary or reserve program established, it is essential that the unit's policies are consistent with the highest standards of human rights in order to preserve our nation's democratic heritage. Part II of this book discusses the various activities of volunteer youth police groups and critical issues, and it touches upon several new types of possible assignments. Volunteer police are capable of undertaking new roles, and they are in a unique position to augment the delivery of existing police functions and programs.

Review Questions

1. State a generalization about the authority of auxiliary and reserve police officers.
2. Provide at least one exception to the generalization you stated in response to the first question.
3. Why was there a need for volunteer police during WW II? Discuss.
4. Contrast the nature of the work of Buffalo's first Police Reserve Force with that of its second and ongoing "police reserves" force.
5. What was the "Volunteer Patrol League"?
6. Who comprised the membership of Buffalo's Home Defense Reserve, and how did it come into existence?
7. What historical events led up to the origin of NYC's present-day auxiliary police program?
8. At the time of the publication of this book, there was confusion among some online contributors about the exact nature of the "peace officer" status of NYC auxiliary police officers. The lack of "peace officer" status was the main reason for an initial refusal by the U.S. Department of Justice to award death benefits to the families of three slain auxiliaries. Research the current nature of these issues and discuss your findings.
9. State at least two advantages and two disadvantages concerning the assignment of volunteer police to work alongside regular officers.
10. This chapter indicated that one California police department was revising a reserve police program and one Virginia police department had recently instituted its first auxiliary police program. Do you believe that either of these types of programs will encounter resistance from regular police? In your discussion, consider the nature of these two programs.
11. Is there a volunteer police force in your hometown? If so, research and present information about the nature of the program.
12. The author of this book theorizes that there exist particular regional differences among volunteer police units in the United States. How could a study be designed to test this theory?

Notes

1. The Community Emergency Response Team (CERT) idea was first developed in 1985 by the city of Los Angeles Fire Department. It was established because citizens would probably have to work together during the early stages of a disaster. The Los Angeles CERT training proved to be so beneficial that the Federal Emergency Management Agency (FEMA) decided the program should be made available to communities across the United States. In 1994, FEMA and the Los Angeles Fire Department expanded the CERT curriculum. And, in 2003, FEMA's Citizen Corps Council adopted CERT as a primary way to encourage people to volunteer to make their communities safer, stronger, and better prepared to respond to emergencies. There are currently more than 3,500 active CERT programs in the United States. In January 2012, Deputy Inspector Byrne spoke at a graduation ceremony for more than 100 new (CERT) volunteers (NYC Press Release 2012).

2. "The National Defense Act of 1916 expanded the regular federal army from 90,000 to 175,000 and permitted gradual enlargement to 223,000. It also increased the National Guard to 440,000, made provision for training, and gave federal funds for summer training camps for civilians" (Tindall and Shi 2007, 941).

3. On January 19, 1917, British naval intelligence intercepted and decrypted a telegram sent by German Foreign Minister Arthur Zimmerman to the German Ambassador in Mexico City. The "Zimmerman Telegram" promised the Mexican government that Germany would help Mexico recover the territory it had ceded to the United States following the Mexican-American War. In return for this assistance, the Germans asked for Mexican support in the war. The British had initially not shared the news of the Zimmerman Telegram with U.S. officials because they did not want the Germans to discover that British code breakers had cracked the German code. However, following Germany's resumption of unrestricted submarine warfare in February, the British decided to use the note to help sway American official and public opinion about joining the war (Office of the Historian 2014).

4. The Cold War centered on the threat of a nuclear exchange between the Union of Soviet Socialist Republics (USSR) and the United States. It was the Federal Civil Defense Administration's job to encourage citizens to adapt to their nuclear present and future. Civil defense media showed fathers building bomb shelters and mothers stocking them while the children practiced ducking under their desks at school. This was family life in the new era of the A-bomb. This was civil defense, and it turned the front lawn into the front line. The reliance on atomic weaponry as a centerpiece of U.S. foreign policy cast a mushroom cloud over everyday life. American citizens now had to imagine a new kind of war, one in which they were both combatants and targets. According to McEnaney (2000), the creation of America's civil defense program produced new dilemmas about the degree to which civilian society should be militarized to defend itself against internal and external threats. Conflicts arose about the relative responsibilities of state and citizen to fund and implement a home front security program. Today's security conflicts center on the debate between gun control advocates and those who would defend the right of all law-abiding citizens to possess firearms.

5. An important case, *Fitzgibbons vs. The County of Nassau, et al.*, held that counties and cities in New York State were fully liable for the actions taken by their auxiliary police. Previously, the State's Defense Emergency Act gave blanket immunity for the auxiliary's actions.

6. It is also likely that a Justice Department report critical of how the department reviewed each claim for benefits greatly impacted the decision by the Justice Department to reverse its previous decision in the case. The 103-page report was prepared by the Inspector General's Office, which oversees the Justice Department. The report indicated that the claims filed by families of those seeking compensation were processed far too slowly and that Justice Department officials responsible for reviewing claims too "narrowly interpreted" terms of the act in at least 19 cases filed in the first year after the act went into effect (Parascandola 2008). Moreover, John Hyland, president of the Auxiliary Police Benevolent Association of the City of New York, Inc., had pointed out that there had been a prior precedent. In fact, the families of two on-duty NYC auxiliary officers killed by a drunken driver in the Bronx in 1989 were awarded benefits. Relatives of Sgts. Noel Faide and Larry Cohen were initially denied but won on appeal. Hyland stated: "It's been done before. It should almost be automatic" (Gendar et al. 2008, p. 6).

7. As of September 2010, the issuance of the vests remained an issue among the largest municipal volunteer police force in the United States. An initial complement of vests was received in February 2008, but many new volunteers were receiving ill-fitting loaner vests. Deputy Inspector Kim Royster, an NYPD spokeswoman, acknowledged that new members of the auxiliary force are no longer getting new vests. She stated that "all auxiliary officers wear vests while out on patrol. If they don't have a vest assigned to them, they must wear a loaner vest" (Weichselbaum 2010, p. 13). "A police source said each of the vests costs about $580 and that the NYPD hoped to one day return to issuing new vests to auxiliary cops. No timetable has been set" (Weichselbaum 2010, p. 13).

8. By early March 2008, no report was released. However, a high-ranking member of the NYPD, Assistant Chief Michael Collins, said the committee had handed down its recommendations within 90 days as required. He indicated that he did not know why the report was never presented to the city council but that all recommendations have been implemented, including centralization of training under the police academy, issuance of bullet resistant vests to nearly 2,000 auxiliaries, and requiring the NYPD recruitment office to take over recruiting tasks from the auxiliary division. John Hyland, president of the auxiliary union, indicated the training of auxiliary cops is improving, but more must be done. Marshalik and Pekearo never called for help on their radios after the shooter had first punched Marshalik. Instead, they tailed the gunman. According to Hyland, "You can't ask them, why didn't you make the call so you assume why; it's really scary when you think about it, and the radio is their lifeline…." (White 2008). Hyland also indicated that most auxiliary cops are discouraged from using their radios and are told by supervisors to use cell or pay phones (White 2008). The long awaited report was presented by the NYPD the following month and is available online at: http://www.nyc.gov/html/nypd/downloads/pdf/careers/nypd_auxiliary_police_overview_2008.pdf.

9. In addition to the restoration of the various units of the NYPD AESU, the plan proposed by City Councilmember David Weprin involved equipping NYC's auxiliary officers with: (1) bulletproof vests, (2) mace, (3) expandable nightsticks,

(4) protective masks, and (5) automatic external defibrillators for all AESUs who are already authorized by the NYPD for its use. Legislation for (1) increased penalties for attacking and/or injuring auxiliary police officers by granting auxiliary officers the status of "peace officer while on duty" (auxiliary members will be requalified as "NYC Special Patrolmen," a status that exists in the NYC Administrative Code and the NYS Criminal Procedure Law, such a change in status will automatically bring with it an increased range of penalties for injury to an auxiliary officer); (2) appropriate benefits for disabled auxiliary officers and their families; (3) mandated regular reporting by the NYPD to the city council on auxiliary program statistics such as equipment, vehicles, training, hours, and number of personnel; and (4) improved and increased training and self-defense classes for auxiliary officers to be administered by police academy instructors (Auxiliary Officers Assistance Plan 2007).

10. During times of disaster, auxiliaries have played and can play major roles in search and rescue efforts as well as a variety of other assignments. Such efforts require close cooperation between full-time first responders as well as part-time first responders, such as volunteer police. "Most disasters and mass casualty events are experienced locally; in this country, incidents are generally handled at the lowest possible jurisdictional level. When significant events occur, the 'intrusive reality' is that small, rural, and suburban communities in the United States may be on their own for 24 to 72 hours before help arrives from regional, state, and federal sources" (Joint Commission 2005, 1). The New York State Association of Auxiliary Police, Inc., published a special tenth anniversary issue of their newsletter devoted to the contributions of auxiliary police during the aftermath of the collapse of the World Trade Center Towers on September 11, 2001. The issue is available at: http://www.auxiliary-police.org/newsletter.pdf.

11. For example, the Chesterfield County (VA) Auxiliary Police program began as part of the civil defense program during the 1950s. Its 22 members exercise full police powers, perform patrols with regular department officers, and provide assistance in cases of civil unrest, natural disasters, or missing person's searches. They perform traffic enforcement measures, respond to crimes, maintain security at crime scenes, and investigate citizen complaints. This valuable unit also patrols assigned areas during public events, such as the annual Chesterfield County Fair, and during the holiday season at shopping centers and business areas. In 2008, Chesterfield auxiliary officers made 384 arrests, worked 42 special assignments, and served a plethora of summonses. Chesterfield police estimate that auxiliary volunteers donate 11,105 hours each year, saving the county $224,876 annually. Participants are provided the same training that regular police recruits receive. However, it is stretched over a longer period of time because the auxiliary recruits are volunteers who attend part-time; the regular recruits attend full-time (Burchett 2010).

References

Albemarle. (2014, January 3). Albemarle swears in first auxiliary police officers. *The Daily Progress*. Retrieved January 18, 2014 from http://www.dailyprogress.com/news/local/albemarle-swears-in-first-auxiliary-police-officers/article_fe5a08c2-74e1-11e3-8331-001a4bcf6878.html

Auer, D. (2011, November 12). An auxiliary farce. *New York Post*. Retrieved November 11, 2013 from http://nypost.com/2011/11/12/an-auxiliary-farce/

Auxiliary Mounted. (2013). Who are we? Retrieved November 16, 2013 from http://www.auxparksmtd.org/faqs.html

Auxiliary Officers Assistance Plan. (2007, March 26). Retrieved November 14, 2013 from http://www.gothamgazette.com/index.php/open-government/3516-auxiliary-officers-assistance-plan

Barron, J. and Kilgannon, C. (2007, March 16). Rampage in Greenwich Village; auxiliary officers know the limitations, and the dangers, when they volunteer. *New York Times*, p. 5.

Bayley, D. H. (1985). *Patterns of policing: A comparative international analysis*. New Brunswick, NJ: Rutgers University Press.

Blascovich, L. (Ed.). (2013, April). Introduction the Civil Air Patrol. Retrieved January 17, 2014 from http://www.capmembers.com/media/cms/P050_005_C3E62FDD0BD80.pdf

Brentwood Police Department. (2013). About us. Retrieved November 15, 2013 from http://www.brentwoodca.gov/department/pd/index.cfm

Buder, L. (1980, December 28). Expanded auxiliary unit annoys city police union. *New York Times*, p. 36.

Buffalo Police Reserves. (2014a). Retrieved January 15, 2014 from http://buffalopolicereserves.com/information.htm

Buffalo Police Reserves. (2014b). Buffalo Police reserve requirement. Retrieved January 15, 2014 from http://buffalopolicereserves.com/apply.htm

Burchett, M. (2010, January 6). Auxiliary police help in Colonial Heights, Chesterfield. Retrieved January 20, 2014 from http://progress-index.com/news/auxiliary-police-help-in-colonial-heights-chesterfield-1.528186

Careers. (2014). Careers – Auxiliary police. Retrieved January 18, 2014 from http://www.nyc.gov/html/nypd/html/careers/auxiliary_police.shtml

Carmody, D. (1974, November 30). 100 volunteer mounties ride herd on park crime: 100 volunteer mounties in the parks organized in 1951. *New York Times*, pp. 33 & 49.

Cheltenham. (2014a). About us. Retrieved January 14, 2014 from http://www.cheltenhamtownship.org/pView.aspx?id = 3125&catid =29

Cheltenham. (2014b). Auxiliary police unit. Retrieved January 14, 2014 from http://www.cheltenhamtownship.org/pView.aspx?id = 3126&catid =29

Cheltenham. (2014c). Demographics. Retrieved January 14, 2014 from http://www.cheltenhamtownship.org/pView.aspx?id = 2448&catid =25

Cheltenham. (2014d). Early industrial development. Retrieved January 14, 2014 from http://www.cheltenhamtownship.org/pView.aspx?id = 3008&catid =25

Cheltenham. (2014e). Police chaplain. Retrieved January 14, 2014 from http://www.cheltenhamtownship.org/pview.aspx?id = 3094&catID =29

City's First Auxiliary. (1973, September 9). City's first auxiliary mounted policemen will help patrol parks: Took horsemanship course. *New York Times*, p. 57.

Early Days. (2012, April). The early days of American law enforcement: The watch. *Insider*, 4(4). Retrieved November 10, 2013 from http://www.nleomf.org/museum/news/newsletters/online-insider/2012/April-2012/early-days-american-law-enforcement-april-2012.html

Gendar, A., White, M. and Connor, T. (2008, March 27). Fed official shuns key evidence to gain benefits for slain auxiliary cops. *New York Daily News*, p. 6.

Goodman, G., Jr. (1980, September 13). Mounted rangers begin patrol of parks. *New York Times*, p. 25.

Greenberg, M. (1984). *Auxiliary police: The citizen's role in public safety*. Westport, CT: Greenwood Press.

Hays, C. L. (1988, August 20). Unpaid eyes and ears of the police. *New York Times*, p. 30.

Hillard, G. (2011, May 19). In tight times, L.A. relies on volunteer police. Retrieved January 12, 2012 from http://www.npr.org/2011/05/19/136436405/in-tight-times-l-a-relies-on-volunteer-police

Hudson, E. (1955, August 28). Volunteer force aids park police. *New York Times*, p. 60.

Joint Commission. (2005). *Standing together: An emergency planning guide for America's communities*. Oakbrook Terrace, IL: Joint Commission on Accreditation of Healthcare Organizations.

Karni, A. (2011, December 25). Mounting interest in civilian park patrol. *New York Post*. Retrieved November 13, 2013 from http://nypost.com/2011/12/25/mounting-interest-in-civilian-park-patrol/

Kelly, R. W., Grasso, G. A., Esposito, J. J., Giannelli, R. J. and Maroulis, A. J. (2008, April). Auxiliary police program overview. Retrieved November 11, 2013 from http://www.nyc.gov/html/nypd/downloads/pdf/careers/nypd_auxiliary_police_overview_2008.pdf

LAPD (2013). Reserve police officer program. Retrieved November 14, 2013 from http://www.lapdonline.org/join_the_team/content_basic_view/542

Marzulli, J. (2010, June 25). Justice Department grants benefits 17 years late for auxiliary cop Milton Clarke's family. *New York Daily News*, p. 26.

McEnaney, L. (2000). *Civil defense begins at home: Militarization meets everyday life in the fifties*. Princeton, NJ: Princeton University Press.

Miami PD. (2014). Community involvement. Retrieved January 15, 2014 from http://www.miami-police.org/COMMUNITY_INVOLVEMENT.HTML

NYC Press Release. (2012, January 12). Retrieved January 17, 2014 from http://www.nyc.gov/portal/site/nycgov/menuitem.c0935b9a57bb4ef3daf2f1c701c789a0/index.jsp?pageID = mayor_press_release&catID = 1194

NYPD (2008). New York City Police Commissioner Raymond W. Kelly and U.S. Senator Charles E. Schumer urge Department of Justice to approve death benefits for auxiliary police officers. NYPD Press Release No. 2008-11. Retrieved November 12, 2013 from http://www.nyc.gov/html/nypd/html/pr/pr_2008_011.shtml

Of Counsel. (2010, March 26). Of counsel Doug Neistat receives LAPD commendation. Retrieved June 15, 2010 from http://www.greenbass.com/newsdetail.aspx?id=6

Office of the Historian. (2014). Milestones: 1914–1920 – American entry into World War I, 1917. Retrieved January 16, 2014 from http://history.state.gov/milestones/1914-1920/wwi

Parascandola, R. (2008, April 1). Report may help death benefits case for auxiliary cops. Retrieved November 12, 2013 from http://www.newsday.com/long-island/report-may-help-death-benefits-case-for-auxiliary-cops-1.881568

Sweeney, D. J. (1920). *History of Buffalo and Erie County, 1914–1919*. Buffalo, NY: Committee of One Hundred.

Szymanski, K. (2013, July 4). Brentwood to bring back police reserves program. Retrieved November 15, 2013 from http://www.thepress.net/view/full_story/23045301/article-Brentwood-to-bring-back-police-reserves-program

Tindall, G. B. and Shi, D. E. (2007). *America: A narrative history, Vol. 2* (7th ed.). New York: W.W. Norton.

U.S. Department of Justice. (2011, October). *The impact of the economic downturn on American police agencies.* Washington, DC: U.S. Department of Justice, Office of Community Oriented Policing Services.

Weichselbaum, S. (2010, September 16). NYPD auxiliary officers at risk because they aren't getting best protection, say union officials. *New York Daily News,* p. 13.

White, M. (2008, March 9). Family blames lack of training for slain auxiliary cop tragedy 1 year ago. *New York Daily News,* p. 23.

Volunteer State Police

5

> It's not fair to require them to go through extensive training programs when
> they are not paid. It's not practical.
> **—Connecticut State Police Capt. Gregory Senick**
> *(quoted in Waldman 2001)*

Contemporary volunteer auxiliary and reserve police represent the epitome of "community policing" by serving to bridge the gap between local community residents and police agencies. Although the dominant amount of community policing activities has been conducted at the local level by town, city, and county police agencies, there are state police agencies that routinely assign their officers to act as "resident police" in communities without an established police force (Connecticut, Vermont, etc.). Moreover, given the recent string of major school tragedies from Columbine, Colorado, to Newtown, Connecticut, many state law enforcement agencies have begun to address how they can assist communities to ensure that all children and staff are safe in school. In many ways, community policing has represented a new paradigm in policing. Community policing has a profoundly different outlook regarding police–citizen relationships than traditional methods of policing. Under the community policing concept, the police are the public, and the public are the police! Police officers are merely those who are paid to give full-time attention to the duties of every citizen (Sparrow 1988). It is extremely noteworthy that this precise understanding of police was initially proclaimed nearly 200 years ago by the father of modern policing—Sir Robert Peel. Peel recognized that the community and its police department were linked; neither was able to function properly without the other.

The development and organizational arrangements of state police forces during the early part of the twentieth century are the quintessential models of the traditional methods of policing because they resembled a military force, complete with various troops housed in barracks throughout the state under a strong central command. Moreover, with an emphasis on highway safety enforcement and the investigation of serious crimes in rural areas, very few agencies are likely to have available additional resources for community policing initiatives (the conduct of Citizen Police Academies, sponsorship of police Explorer posts, etc.) or the inclination to lobby for such activities. Therefore, it is somewhat surprising to learn that a handful of states do, in fact, have statewide auxiliary/reserve units.

This chapter first considers a selected group of traditional state police agencies that have developed into full-service state agencies responsible for statewide law enforcement services, especially on highways and in rural areas. This is followed by a closer look at those state agencies that have opted to include an auxiliary or reserve volunteer police component to supplement the strength of their existing departments. Such agencies are located in Alabama, Arizona, Connecticut, Florida, New Hampshire, Ohio, and Vermont. A section of the chapter is devoted to the rise and gradual decline of the Connecticut State Police Auxiliary program.

Throughout this book, and in this chapter, various references have been made regarding the existence of the "Volunteers in Police Service (VIPS) online directory." The directory used for these references is no longer available, having been removed at the end of March 2014 and replaced by a new set of Web pages located at: http://www.theiacp.org/VIPS. Prior to its removal, over 2,200 volunteer programs had indicated their existence by being registered and briefly described in the former online directory. Established in 2002, the former VIPS Web site was extensively used by the author. The former Web site was designed to serve as a gateway to information for law enforcement agencies and citizens interested in law enforcement volunteer programs. The new Web site and directories (domestic and international) offer hundreds of opportunities to network with other law enforcement volunteer programs, and updated contact information is provided in the new directories.

Origins of State Police Forces

Everyday policing in the eastern settlements of colonial America largely consisted of voluntary watch groups formed by citizens and a system of slave patrols in the south. The latter patrols were used to control slave populations and have been identified by historians as the first formal police agencies in America. During the first half of the nineteenth century, a unique force was created in the region known as Texas, which was first claimed by Spain and then by Mexico after its independence. Spain encouraged immigration to Texas beginning in 1820. Spain expected the new settlers in this region to spur its economic development and to discourage any interference by such Native Americans as the Comanche and Kiowa nations. In 1821, Mexico continued the Spanish colonization plan after its independence from Spain by granting contracts to *empresarios* (a type of land agent) who would help to settle and supervise new immigrants (Henson 2013). Stephen Fuller Austin (1793–1836) was the eldest son of Moses Austin. The elder Austin had been granted various land contracts as an empresario and his son inherited these tracts. By 1834, near the end of the empresario system, Stephen Austin had helped to settle nearly 1,000 families. As the leading empresario in Texas and without an available set of established Mexican laws, Austin had administrative and judicial authority for his colony (Henson 2013).

"In 1823, only two years after Anglo-American colonization formally began in Texas, empresario Stephen F. Austin hired ten experienced frontiersmen as 'rangers' for a punitive expedition against a band of Indians" (Procter 2013). "During Austin's day, companies of men volunteered and disbanded as needed. Some served for days and others for many months. The official records show that these companies were called by many names: ranging companies, mounted gunmen, mounted volunteers, minutemen, spies, scouts, and mounted rifle companies" (Cox 2013). Late in the 1835, Texas lawmakers instituted a specific force known as a "Corps of Rangers" in order "to protect the frontier from hostile Indians. For the first time, their pay was officially set at $1.25 a day and they were to elect their own officers. They were also required to furnish their own arms, mounts, and equipment" (Cox 2013). During the war between the United States and Mexico (1846–1848), the Rangers achieved worldwide fame as scouts and as a fighting force. Later, having been organized into several companies, the Rangers were periodically called upon to contend with outlaws as well attacks from Mexican citizens and occasional threats from Indians. During various periods throughout the nineteenth century, when the Rangers did their job with such effectiveness, the need for their services was diminished, their numbers were reduced and for the most part the organization went into an inactive status. Between 1914 and 1919, "Regular rangers, along with hundreds of special rangers appointed by Texas governors, killed approximately 5,000 Hispanics…, a source of scandal and embarrassment" (Procter 2014).

In 1935, a new governor won office on a platform of better law enforcement, and the legislature established the Texas Department of Public Safety (DPS). The new agency was organized into three basic units: the Texas Rangers, the Highway Patrol, and a scientific crime laboratory and detection center known as the Headquarters Division. In 1938, with the appointment of Colonel Homer Garrison Jr. (1901–1968), as its new director, the Rangers regained much of their lost status. Over the next 30 years, "The Rangers became the plainclothesmen of the DPS: they were the detectives, and the Highway Patrol officers were the uniformed state police" (Procter 2014). Thus, the Rangers have had a long evolving history beginning in the days of Anglo settlement in Texas and are often recognized as the oldest law enforcement agency with statewide jurisdiction in North America. However, most of their earliest activities had been more military than law enforcing in nature. This tradition continued even after Texas was officially inducted into the United States on December 29, 1845, when Rangers served as scouts and as a fighting force during the war between the United States and Mexico. Two other related agencies were established in the American West primarily for border protection. The Arizona Rangers were established in 1901, and the New Mexico Mounted Police came into being in 1905 (Lyman 2005).

The first regional law enforcement effort in Arizona occurred in 1901 when the territorial governor organized the Arizona Rangers. This small force made a strong impact on the rustling and smuggling problems of the time but was disbanded in 1909, three years before Arizona achieved statehood. Twenty-two years later, because of concern regarding the growing number of accidents and unlicensed vehicles on its highways, the Arizona Highway Patrol was instituted as a branch of the Arizona Highway Department. In 1931, the initial force was limited to a superintendent, 14 patrolmen (one authorized for each county), and one desk sergeant. In 1967, the Arizona Governor's Crime Commission recommended creation of a department to "assemble state-level law enforcement activities into a single, effective governmental unit" (Arizona DPS 2013a). Two years later, on July 1, 1969, the Arizona Department of Public Safety was officially established. It consolidated the functions and responsibilities of the Arizona Highway Patrol, the Enforcement Division of the Department of Liquor Licenses and Control, and the Narcotics Division of the Arizona Department of Law. Since 1969, the department has been charged with additional responsibilities and has developed into a modern, comprehensive law enforcement agency. The department enforces state laws with primary responsibility in the areas of traffic, narcotics, organized crime/racketeering, liquor, and specific regulatory functions (Arizona DPS 2013a).

Meanwhile, in the last half of the nineteenth century, the field of American municipal policing learned about and drew upon the experience of Sir Robert Peel's London Metropolitan Police. However, political considerations trumped true reforms and consistently controlled the shaping of the American policing establishment for many years. At times, some state legislatures assumed control over big city police forces due to struggles for control over police during the late nineteenth century and even into the twentieth century (Walker 1977). For example, beginning in 1857 and for a period of 13 years, the New York State Legislature took control over the New York City force. In other states as well, legislatures intervened in the administration of municipal agencies, seeking a political advantage or because of dissatisfaction "for the way city police were or were not enforcing liquor and vice laws" (Lyman 2005, 41). However, prior to the twentieth century, the institutions that most closely resembled what would become state police were state militia forces and posses composed of citizen volunteers. Militia could be summoned by state governors, although posses were usually organized by a local official, such as a county sheriff. In time of need, sheriffs have a legal prerogative derived from older traditions to call upon the able-bodied men of their counties for assistance. In the United States, the sheriff typically is an elected office, like the office of governor.

By the early 1900s, the first state police forces were established in the eastern half of the United States to enforce the laws governing prohibition, vice, and labor disputes. Often local constables or sheriffs either could not, or would not, enforce these laws fairly. Initially, the formation of the Connecticut State Police was directly related to the problems associated with alcoholic beverage enforcement. "The roots of state law enforcement in Connecticut began in 1895 with the creation of the Law and Order League of Connecticut" (History of CSP 2013). A new state law empowered the state's governor to appoint four "agents" to enforce state liquor and vice laws, which at the time were being ignored by local authorities. The Law and Order League served until it and other versions of it were abolished in 1903. In 1903, Governor Abiram Chamberlain signed a new law establishing the creation of the Connecticut State Police and their very first responsibilities included enforcement of state liquor and gaming statutes (History of CSP 2013). In this way, the rise of the Connecticut State Police was related to concerns over illegal liquor manufacturing, its distribution, and the general public's clamor over vice enforcement (Seeley 2013).

By about the middle of the twentieth century, all of the contiguous mainland states had developed statewide law enforcement agencies.[1] (Online links to all 50 state police, state highway patrol, or public safety departments can be found at: http://www.scdps.gov/schp/links.asp. A full set of multiple links for finding information about each state police agency can also be found at: http://www.statetroopersdirectory.com/#SC.)

In the early decades of the twentieth century, the new state police agencies arose not only out of concern for improved vice and liquor law enforcement. Historically, industrial labor strife in coal and iron regions and the inadequacy of the sheriff–constable system in rural areas were contributing factors. Moreover, the rise of the automobile industry necessitated the development of highway patrol units to regulate motor vehicles and motorists (Smith 1940). Highway policing in the early years of the twentieth century was a taxing affair for troopers. "When patrolling by car and motorcycle became possible, there still was no radio system. Officers on patrol maintained contact with the barracks by telephone. When the desk officer needed to contact a patrolling trooper, he would make a phone call to one of several stores or gas stations on the man's patrol. The proprietor would raise a small flag, and the officer would call in when he saw it.... Troopers rode in all kinds of weather, and stuffed their uniforms with newspaper for insulation" (Seeley 2013).

In 1905, two years after the establishment of the Connecticut State Police, the Pennsylvania State Constabulary was created. Labor conflict appears to have been the chief catalyst for its inception. The agency focused its earliest attention on controlling strikes because business leaders believed that local police and the militia were unreliable for this purpose. "Organized labor bitterly attacked the Constabulary, denouncing its officers as 'Cossacks'" (Walker and Katz 2011, 37). A major characteristic of this force was the robust executive power granted to its superintendent who was only responsible to the governor.

Its other major characteristics included widely distributed substations for policing rural and semirural areas and its use of mounted and uniformed troops (Smith 1940). For a time, subsequent state efforts to establish similar agencies met with opposition from labor interests. For example, the legislation establishing a New York State Police force passed by only a single vote. Less controversial were those state police agencies limited to highway traffic enforcement.

An instance of the birth of a statewide highway enforcement agency took place in 1921 when the Illinois General Assembly authorized the Department of Public Works and Buildings to hire a "sufficient number of State Highway Patrol Officers to enforce the provisions of the Motor Vehicle Laws." Subsequently, the Illinois State Police was officially created in 1922. Today, it is comprised of full-time sworn personnel and civilians totaling more than 3,000 persons (Illinois State Police 2013). In 1995, the Illinois State Police had approximately 40 individuals serving as volunteers in various non-sworn roles. In 2013, 22 different local auxiliary/reserve police units were registered in the discontinued VIPS online directory for the state of Illinois, and there were more than 70 other types of local police volunteer programs listed. In recent years, however, a controversy arose regarding the unauthorized use of independent auxiliary/reserve police organizations. Most of them were operating in the Chicago metropolitan area.[2] (A 19-page copy of the Illinois Attorney General's opinion on this matter, dated December 30, 2010, can be found at http://www.ptb.state.il.us/pdf/AuxOfficersOpinion/ILAGOpinion12-31-10.pdf.)

The need for the New Jersey State Police arose when that state was making a limited effort to provide protection for its rural inhabitants. This effort was wholly dependent upon the county sheriff and his constables. Based on a political system of election and appointment, some elected officials were more competent than others. Demands for a well-trained rural police force increased in direct proportion to an increasing population and crime rate. Legislation for this purpose was first introduced in 1914 and for several years thereafter. There was opposition to this legislation from those who feared the creation of a "police state" and their possible use as strikebreakers. A wave of public sentiment surged against the proposal. However, by the beginning of the 1920s, a discernible "state police movement" had appeared in the United States and 13 states had organized such a force. Moreover, the state's chamber of commerce and the New Jersey Grange worked on behalf of the necessary legislation. The measure passed in the spring of 1921. On July 1, 1921, Herbert Norman Schwarzkopf, a graduate of the U.S. Army Military Academy at West Point, was appointed as the first superintendent. Before the year ended, 81 men successfully completed the initial three-month training program. In a severe snowstorm, they started out on horseback and motorcycle toward their posts throughout the state. Their "first modes of transportation consisted of sixty-one horses, twenty motorcycles, one car, and one truck. The horse remained the principal means of transportation throughout the twenties" (New Jersey State Police 2013). The initial success of the New Jersey State Police has been attributed to the theories adopted by Colonel Schwarzkopf who believed that the agency was not only an enforcement agency but that prevention, education, and service were equally important for the achievement of its goals (New Jersey State Police 2013).

In 2013, the state of New Jersey had about 27 local auxiliary/reserve police units registered with the former online VIPS directory and more than 50 additional types of police volunteer programs. The state police are served by about 200 non-sworn police volunteers (Volunteers in Police Service 2013). In addition, 70 volunteers serve in the New Jersey Search and Rescue (NJSAR), a volunteer emergency service organization that assists the New Jersey State Park Police. The NJSAR unit also assists with various departmental activities at the request of the park police (NJSAR 2013). Throughout most of the twentieth century, responsibilities for law enforcement in those townships without their own police departments have been carried out by the New Jersey State Police.[3]

The establishment of the New York State Police (NYSP) had a grassroots origin. Often overlooked in introductory textbooks is the fact that the NYSP was created, in large part, as a result of the lobbying efforts of two women. Although the women never actually enrolled in a volunteer police capacity, their pioneering achievement is a classic example of the importance of community-based initiatives. Their perseverance is illustrative of the type of community spirit that undoubtedly helped to motivate many persons to participate in volunteer police units between the two world wars and throughout the remainder of the twentieth century. In 1913, a construction foreman named Sam Howell was murdered during a payroll robbery in Westchester County, New York. At that time, Westchester County was a rural area with very limited police services, and Howell's murderers escaped, even though he identified them before he died. This vicious crime spurred Howell's employer, Moyca Newell, and her friend, Katherine Mayo, to initiate a movement to form a state police department to serve in rural areas. Mayo, a writer, researcher, and historian, authored a book about the value of the Pennsylvania State Police and how it could be a useful model for the state of New York.[4] In addition, New York Governor Charles Whitman urged that the shortage of National Guard recruits could be alleviated by the adoption of this act because members of the Guard would no longer be required to perform domestic police duties. In the past, these duties had taken guardsmen away from their families and regular employment, resulting in substantial inconvenience and personal financial loss. The final bill was passed in 1917. It contained the following clause to help its passage: the use of state police shall be prohibited "within the limits of any city to suppress rioting and disorder except by the direction of the Governor or upon the request of the Mayor of the city with the approval of the Governor" (Greenberg 1984). The newly formed state police was given capable leadership by its first superintendent, George F. Chandler, a former army surgeon. Although it was not his intention, Chandler's early successes with the organization of the NYSP may have motivated political figures in New York City to develop their own style of volunteer quasi-military police—the New York (City) Police Reserves. In 2013, New York State had 31 auxiliary/reserve units registered with the IACP VIPS online directory, including New York City's auxiliary police force with more than 4,000 members.

Pennsylvania's Other State Police Force

In 1875, in the Erie, Pennsylvania, metropolitan area (in the most northwest corner of the state), an organization of nearly 1,000 members was authorized with the power of arrest and the right to carry weapons to provide policing assistance to a two-county area. This organization was known as "the State Police of Crawford and Erie Counties." It had 29 companies in the two-county area, organized along borough and township lines, and was commanded by elected captains and other officers. It was mobilized in 1877 (based on the records of the court of Crawford County).

However, its legislative origin can be traced to an 1872 statute that referred to the need to establish an organization for individuals to band together to form "a company for the recovery of stolen horses and other property, and for the detection of thieves." Residents within this region were concerned about interstate livestock rustling and requested that the state legislature permits the establishment of a public corporation to contend with the problem. "In 1872, the only police force in the Commonwealth of Pennsylvania was the Philadelphia Police Department, whose officers had statewide powers" (Neubert 1975, 1).

In the 1940s, the group had about 4,000 members and had several secretive aspects. At that time, members spoke in code and had secret handshakes, and anyone who applied for membership had to be voted in by at least 75% of the existing membership. The latter tradition was maintained till the organization was disbanded in 2005 when only 220 members remained (Simonich 2005).

This state-chartered organization was supported by donations. Local school districts were the main source of these donations because the members of the volunteer police often performed traffic control at school events. Additional traffic direction and patrol work took place at church services, community festivals and fairs, Memorial Day parades, Halloween night, and various picnics and open houses. A major concern was the provision of training for members. During the 1970s, after the passage of a state law mandating training for regular police, some efforts were made to see if a nearby college could provide such training because members would be unable to attend the full-time training programs established for municipal officers (Neubert 1975).

However, because there was also confusion over whether the new training requirements applied to such a volunteer organization, training on how and when to use force was provided by senior members, who had been schooled by companies that manufacture police equipment (Simonich 2005).

Members of the organization were recruited and deployed for a continuous period of well over a century until 2005, when the Pennsylvania General Assembly revoked its authority through the wording of the Act of Jun. 30, 2005, P.L. 29, No. 8 Cl. 44: "The General Assembly of the Commonwealth of Pennsylvania hereby enacts as follows: Section 1. The act of April 3, 1872 (1873 P.L.1061, No.1109), entitled 'An act to incorporate the State police of Crawford and Erie counties', is repealed. Section 2. This act shall take effect in 120 days." This was accomplished when officials of the Pennsylvania State Police convinced the legislature to repeal the 1872 law, dissolving the force despite the fact that the group had provided armed volunteer officers at festivals, dances, and games, sparing town governments and school districts the expense of hiring private security companies for many decades. If any organization members had to break up a fight at a festival or catch a pickpocket at a parade, their practice was to hold the individual until municipal or Pennsylvania State Police officers could arrive at the scene to take charge of the matter (Simonich 2005).

The statute repealing the volunteer Crawford/Erie police agency's charter was drafted by State Representative Ron Marsico. At the time, Marsico was concerned that the organization was "not answerable to any elected official or public body" (Simonich 2005). Marsico added that unionized members and administrators of the Pennsylvania State Police see the organization as a problem because of their spotty training and lack of any real police standards. Linette Quinn, public information coordinator of the Pennsylvania State Police, stated: "We've voiced our concerns about their existence for years" (Simonich 2005). On the other hand, Bob Merski, the Erie County sheriff, said he had worked in law enforcement for 25 years and never heard a complaint about the Crawford/Erie state police. In addition, the members of the group agreed to drop the words "state police" from their name (Simonich 2005). Nevertheless, lacking legislative support for their continued existence, the group has become only a remnant of history.

Origins and Activities of Volunteer State Police Forces

In 1942, the Ohio State Highway Patrol Auxiliary (OSHPA) was formed when many troopers began entering the armed forces, creating a shortage of personnel for the wartime needs of patrolling highways, airports, bridges, defense plants, and military installations. At that time, membership was limited to members of the Ohio American Legion. The Legion was largely made up of World War I veterans who were unlikely to be drafted into the military

(OSHP Auxiliary Reaches 1992). The recruitment of local Legionnaires for temporary volunteer police work had occurred since the end of World War I in several American cities. Many were deputized at the time of the Boston police strike in 1919. In that same year, local American Legion members also helped to preserve the peace during labor-related strikes in Denver, Colorado, and Youngstown, Ohio. However, at other times and in different jurisdictions, Legion members assisting local law enforcement engaged in violent confrontations with striking longshoremen and steelworkers (Dale 2011).

The first official meeting for the purpose of organization and enrollment in the OSHPA was held in February 1942. By April 1942, there were 2,650 Legion members attending weekly training classes. The members of the new OSHPA were assigned to assist in emergency calls and traffic control. One of the first disasters requiring their assistance occurred on May 31, 1942, when a huge wave from Lake Erie created a great deal of property damage in North Madison. Within an hour, most of the members of the Lake County Auxiliary unit of the OSHPA were at the scene to aid in rescue and recovery efforts. By 1945, the OSHPA had reached its peak strength of nearly 5,000 members. After the war, the Auxiliary became a critical component of Ohio's civil defense preparation (OSHP Auxiliary Reaches 1992).

Today, OSHP Auxiliary members contribute thousands of hours in an assortment of functions (see Figures 5.1 through 5.3). Each member is required to log a minimum of 120 hours per year to remain active. Membership is no

Figure 5.1 Highway Patrol Auxiliary Officer on traffic detail at Ohio State University football game. (Used with permission of the Ohio State Highway Patrol Auxiliary.)

Figure 5.2 Highway Patrol Auxiliary Officer participating at the yearly "Shop With A Cop" event. (Used with permission of the Ohio State Highway Patrol Auxiliary.)

Figure 5.3 Two Highway Patrol Auxiliary Officers participating at the yearly "Shop With A Cop" event. (Used with permission of the Ohio State Highway Patrol Auxiliary.)

longer limited to the members of the American Legion. The requirements to become a Highway Patrol Auxiliary in Ohio are indicated in Box 5.1.

There was a decline in active members in the OSHPA for a short period following World War II; however, as the fears related to the "Cold War" intensified, enrollment increased. During the 1950s, the OSHPA helped to conduct

**BOX 5.1   OHIO STATE HIGHWAY PATROL
AUXILIARY MEMBERSHIP REQUIREMENTS**

- U.S. citizen
- Ohio resident with valid Ohio driver license
- Good physical condition (pass a physician's exam at the applicant's expense)
- Between ages 21 and 55 (except for retired OSHP officers)
- No prior felony convictions
- Availability for training and service
- Submit to and pass a background investigation
- Ability to read and write, and convey thoughts in a clear and concise manner
- Weight proportionate to height (OSHP standard plus 10%)
- Submit to and pass a polygraph examination
- Pass written and physical tests
- Complete OSHP Auxiliary training
- Purchase a uniform
- E-mail OSPAux@dps.state.oh.us to apply

Source: Ohio State Highway Patrol (OSHP), http://statepatrol.ohio.gov/auxiliary.stm

nuclear disaster test alerts and other simulated exercises (e.g., evacuations). Throughout the 1950s and 1960s, the OSHPA also helped at crash scenes and with other highway traffic activities (OSHP Auxiliary Reaches 1992). In 1999, 160 men and women were serving in the OSHPA. They were engaged in a wide range of routine patrol duties. Their average age was 45, with eight years of service. Nearly half had one or more years of college. More than one-third were military veterans, and a dozen had been certified as emergency medical technicians (EMTs). About a dozen had completed the entire basic police academy (Profile of the Auxiliary 1999). Initial training requirements were 82 hours. An important state law concerning personal immunity from civil liability for damages and limitation of powers was adopted in 1998. Section 5503.11 (A) of the Ohio Revised Code specifically declares that "No member of the auxiliary unit shall have any power to arrest any person or to enforce any law of this state." A survey by Weinblatt (1993) indicated that the state of Ohio had the largest number of volunteer police officers, with more than 18,000 citizens performing a variety of police services, primarily at the local level of enforcement.

In 2011, 18 new OSHPA officers graduated from the OSHP Training Academy. It was the first auxiliary class since 2009, and the auxiliary candidates spent eight days in residence at the academy undergoing law enforcement training, which included firearms familiarization, traffic and criminal laws, self-defense, cultural sensitivity, and assisting in crash investigations (Auxiliary Officers Commissioned 2012).

Since 2008, OSHPA officers have been eligible for associate membership in the Ohio State Highway Patrol Retirees' Association (OSHPRA) if they meet the following definition: "Any person who was a member of the Ohio State Highway Patrol Auxiliary and left the Auxiliary in good standing. 'Good standing' is defined as leaving service in the Ohio State Highway Patrol or the Patrol Auxiliary under positive circumstances and not under the color of a criminal or administrative investigation for which he/she could have potentially been removed from his/her position had he/she not elected to leave" (OSHPRA Bylaws 2013, 3). (Additional information about the benefits of membership can be found at http://www.oshpretiree.org/OSHPRA_By-Laws.pdf.)

Auxiliary officers in Ohio volunteer their assistance for the annual "Buckeye Boys State Week," the largest Boys State program in the nation with a yearly attendance of 1,200 young men. Established in 1936, it is the single largest program of its type in the nation. Participants represent more than 500 high schools and also include home-schooled students. It has been held at Bowling Green State University since 1978 (American Legion 2013). Following this program, a "Junior Cadet Week" program is held at the Ohio state Highway Patrol Training Academy in Columbus, Ohio, for Boys State and Girls State graduates who are interested in learning about law enforcement.[5] In 2013, the state of Ohio had 53 auxiliary/reserve/citizen patrol units registered with the former VIPS online directory, including the Ohio Highway Patrol Auxiliary.

In 1956, the Arizona State Legislature created the Arizona Highway Patrol Reserves. In 1985, there were 100 unsalaried, fully certified reserve officers. The volunteers were assigned to each of the highway patrol's 13 regional districts on the basis of the district's needs and the residence of the volunteer. A full-time police officer provided logistical support in each district. The auxiliaries were required to serve a minimum of 16 hours per month and to obtain the same recertification that regular full-time officers needed. Basic equipment was provided as well as a prorated monthly uniform allowance. Reserve officers performed all the functions of a regular full-time highway patrol officer, except for the investigation of fatal accidents because of the extensive time commitment involved in such cases (Deitch and Thompson 1985). In 2013, throughout the state of Arizona, there were 21 auxiliary/reserve/posse units registered with the older version IACP VIPS online directory, not including its Highway Patrol Auxiliary. The current minimum requirements for selection as an Arizona reserve officer are indicated in Box 5.2.

In 2013, applicants for participation as an Arizona state police reserve officer had to pass the written examination with a minimum score of 75%. The physical fitness test was a pass/fail component of the overall selection

**BOX 5.2   ARIZONA STATE POLICE RESERVE
OFFICER MINIMUM REQUIREMENTS**

Complete an application

Be 21 years of age (or will be 21 prior to graduation from an approved
law enforcement training academy)

Possess high school diploma General Educational Development
(GED) certificate

Present birth certificate

Have a valid driver license and/or other form of identification

Pass a physical fitness test

Pass written examination

Pass extensive interview

Pass background investigation

Pass polygraph examination

Pass drug screening

Pass psychological and medical examinations

Be a U.S. citizen

Source: Arizona Department of Public Safety (AZDPS), http://www.
azdps.gov/careers/reserves

**BOX 5.3   ARIZONA STATE POLICE RESERVE
OFFICER MINIMUM REQUIREMENTS FOR
THE PHYSICAL FITNESS TESTS**

1.5-mile run within 16 minutes

300-meter run within 73.2 seconds

Push-ups—24 reps

Agility run in 21.8 seconds

Sit-ups—28 reps/min.

Source: Arizona Department of Public Safety (AZDPS), http://www.
azdps.gov/careers/reserves

process and consisted of five events: sit-ups, push-ups, 1.5-mile run, 300-
meter run, and agility run. Box 5.3 indicates each fitness event requirement.
Applicants receive either a passing or a failing score for each event. All applicants were also required to successfully complete each physical fitness test in
order to qualify for participation in the remaining components of the selection process (Arizona DPS 2013b).

An oral interview involving interpersonal skills and problem-solving
abilities was also required. In order to assist in preparation for this interview,

a Qualifications Appraisal Board (QAB) study plan is provided to each applicant. All aspects of the testing process are subject to verification based on a background investigation and polygraph examination. Finally, every Arizona reserve officer applicant has to complete a psychological evaluation to determine suitability as well as a comprehensive medical evaluation provided at no cost to the applicant (Arizona DPS 2013b).

Having been successfully screened, reserve officer candidates attend a Law Enforcement Training Academy. The training must be equivalent to that received by full-time officers (585 hours of training) and must be certified by the Arizona Peace Officer Standards and Training Board (AZPOST). The approved training academies are conducted at four different community colleges throughout the state. Classes are normally held during evenings and on weekends, and the entire training course can be completed in approximately 10–12 months[6] (Arizona DPS 2013b). The cost of the basic training academy, and certain associated equipment, is the responsibility of each reserve officer candidate. During academy attendance, the state police reserve officer candidates are designated as "reserve cadets." The Arizona DPS provides the following items to its reserve cadets and regular officers: (1) duty weapon (firearm), ammunition, holster and magazine pouch; (2) duty belt and related accessories (handcuffs and case, OC spray (oleoresin capsicum, also known as pepper spray) and case, police radio and holder); (3) reimbursement for body armor (up to $1,000); and (4) badges (wallet and breast) and police credentials. Other benefits may be available, and advanced officer training courses are available to the reserve officers. Within one year of academy graduation, all reserve officers are required to complete the field officer training program. Following completion of field training, reserve officers must contribute a minimum of 240 hours per calendar year. Continuing officer training is also required annually. All Arizona state police (full-time or reserve) are not permitted to have separate, full-authority peace officer employment/sponsorship with any other law enforcement agency, either in or outside the state of Arizona (Arizona DPS 2013b).

Arizona reserve volunteer police officers are not compensated for their services nor are they eligible for state employee benefits, except for those provided under the state's Workers' Compensation Law. They wear the same uniform and use the same equipment as full-time officers. Reserve officers purchase their own uniforms. However, they may qualify for a uniform allowance based upon satisfactory performance and by meeting the minimum work hour requirement. However, specialized equipment is provided at no cost to the officer (Arizona DPS 2013b).

In 1986, there were about 14,000 persons serving as volunteer police officers in various departments throughout the state of Florida. In Tallahassee, Florida's capital city, a reserve unit was established and members had to complete the same training as regular officers. Qualifications included citizenship;

a satisfactory background investigation; no criminal history; and two years of college credits. In addition, prospective reserves had to pass an oral interview, a polygraph exam, a medical exam, and psychological testing. Upon successful completion of the training requirements (a minimum of 360 hours in 1986), members were equipped with the same uniform and other equipment that was issued to regular officers. The volunteer police officers possessed the same police powers as regular officers (Berg and Doerner 1988). Berg and Doerner (1988) found that although some volunteer police joined for self-serving interests (maintaining or obtaining police certification), participants also derived an intrinsic sense of satisfaction through the fulfillment of their assignments.

The Florida Highway Patrol Auxiliary (FHPA) is an all-volunteer law enforcement organization dedicated to providing direct assistance and operational support to the Florida Highway Patrol and is authorized to so by Florida statutes. Founded in 1957, the FHPA has assisted the Florida Highway Patrol by patrolling the streets and highways of the state, providing timely assistance to disabled motorists, participating in vehicle equipment and license checkpoints, participating in specialized details, and responding to natural disasters and other emergency situations (About the FHPA 2013a). The total number of FHPA members is limited to five times the total number of regularly employed highway patrol officers authorized by law (sec. 321.24[3], Florida Statutes). Auxiliary trooper candidates undergo a rigorous hiring process and training similar to that of a full-time state trooper. They ride with a regular trooper to provide "second officer" backup. After additional experience and training, these volunteer police officers may be approved for "limited scope patrol" (LSP). LSP-certified officers patrol solo in a marked patrol unit to provide assistance to motorists and troopers (About the FHPA 2013a).

In Florida, the legal definition of an "auxiliary law enforcement officer" is "any person employed or appointed, with or without compensation, who aids or assists a full-time or part-time law enforcement officer and who, while under the direct supervision of a full-time or part-time law enforcement officer, has the authority to arrest and perform law enforcement functions" (sec. 943.10[8], Florida Statutes). In 2007, there were 428 members of the Florida FHPA, and 105 had 20 or more years of service. That same year, in recognition of the FHPA's service to the state of Florida, the legislature passed a new law providing the following benefits for 20-year retiring members of the FHPA: one complete uniform, the badge worn by the officer, the officer's service handgun, if one was issued as part of the officer's equipment, and an identification card marked "retired." The bill also removed the provision prohibiting compensation to individuals who volunteer for the FHPA (sec. 321.24[6]; sec.943.10[8], Florida Statutes).

While under the direct supervision of a Florida Highway Patrol Trooper, the auxiliary troopers have the authority to bear arms and the power to arrest violators. Florida law and the Florida Criminal Justice Standards and Training

Commission require that every member of the FHPA receive law enforcement training at a state-approved training center by state-certified instructors. In 2013, troopers needed to complete a minimum of 320 hours of training by approved instructors. Similar to the policies in place for Arizona basic law enforcement training, police academy programs are conducted locally at community colleges as well as from approved courses offered by the FHP. However, unlike the Arizona rule, in Florida, qualified FHPA candidates have all tuition expenses covered. In addition, Florida provides all equipment and uniforms needed for work as an auxiliary trooper (About the FHPA 2013a).

On average, it takes 12–24 months to have applications reviewed and for training to be completed to become certified as a Level II Auxiliary Trooper. Applicants must pass a basic abilities test (BAT) at a local testing center before application access is issued. In addition, there are preliminary tests for each applicant involving physical abilities, a polygraph examination, medical and eye examinations, a psychological examination, and a background investigation. Upon successful completion of the necessary academy instructional classes, FHPA officers have authority to carry a firearm, defensive spray (pepper spray), and the dart firing stun gun (known as the TASER) (About the FHPA 2013b; FHPA 2013). Law enforcement agencies use the TASER X26 and the ADVANCED TASER M26. These two devices are only available to law enforcement and are capable of recording data useful to officers in court (Tell Me About 2013).

As part of their training, qualified FHP auxiliaries ride with a full-time trooper for approximately one year. During that time, a defensive driving class and the LSP classes are taken. Forty hours of additional police vehicle instruction is then conducted by a field training officer. If all of these experiences are completed, the volunteer officer is designated a Level III Auxiliary Trooper and is authorized to drive a police vehicle to assist motorists on the freeway and to identify abandoned vehicles as well as for backing up other troopers. FHPA members must serve 24 hours per quarter or eight hours each month; however, very few, if any, volunteer police contribute only the minimum hours.

Level IV Auxiliary Trooper status may be obtained by Level III volunteers after patrolling for about one year. Auxiliary troopers so designated may complete an additional 200 hours of training and thereby qualify to respond to and investigate noncriminal crash scenes. These officers must commit to performing 16–24 or more patrol hours per week (About the FHPA 2013b).

In 2013, Florida had 111 auxiliary/reserve/citizen patrol units registered with the older version IACP VIPS directory, including the FHPA and a Florida Park Police reserve officer program. In 2011, the Florida Department of Environmental Protection's (DEP) Florida Park Police Reserve unit had 27 members. DEP Park Police reserve officers follow the same rules and training standards as full-time officers. However, reserve officers are unpaid volunteers. Upon completion of the field training officer (FTO) program, park police reserve officers may patrol alone with the same authority as a full-time officer. They are required to work at least 16 hours per month or 48 hours averaged over a three-month period. Park police reserve officers serve as a resource for augmenting the field responsibilities of regular park police officers within the Florida state park system and on other state lands. Florida state parks are some of the most beautiful in the world and may attract more than 20 million visitors each year (Florida DEP 2011).

According to the New Hampshire Revised Statutes Annotated, Chapter 106-B-19 entitled "Auxiliary State Police," "The director is authorized to recruit, train, and organize an auxiliary state police force for the purpose of providing emergency services throughout the state for peacetime or wartime emergencies or threatened emergencies and for augmenting the state police force in such manner as the director may deem appropriate. Notwithstanding other provisions the director may recruit such auxiliary force from retired state or local police." The New Hampshire State Police Auxiliary Troopers are considered part-time sworn troopers and are assigned throughout the state. They provide assistance at special events (Motorcycle Week, NASCAR, etc.) and in selected investigations as well as perform patrol work and traffic control. The minimum qualifications to become an auxiliary trooper are the same minimum qualifications to become a State Trooper I. The auxiliary troopers must also meet the same annual in-service and firearms training requirements as full-time troopers (Support Services 2013). Auxiliary troopers are required to volunteer 16 hours each month, which is usually accomplished by patrolling with a trooper and by attending firearms and in-service training. In 2006, auxiliary troopers volunteered more than 700 hours. These hours indicate that their ranks have been rather thin. In 2013, the now defunct IACP VIPS directory listings for New Hampshire had only one registered volunteer auxiliary program. However, several departments used citizen patrols.

In 2013, there were 31 Vermont auxiliary troopers assigned to the Marine/Snowmobile Division (Vermont State Police 2013b). Auxiliary troopers are paid part-time positions within the Vermont State Police. The minimum age is 19. Applicants need to reside within a 200-mile radius of departmental headquarters and must have been a resident of that geographical area for at least three years prior to applying. Living out of the residence area for educational purposes or military service was acceptable pending departmental review (Vermont State Police 2013a). All applicants must complete initial training requirements for law enforcement officers and annual training activities in order to maintain certification thereafter. (A list of the essential job functions for Vermont auxiliary troopers who are mostly assigned to the Marine Program and to the Snowmobile Enforcement Program with occasional duty to assist state troopers directing traffic at special events or in other nonroutine functions can be found at: http://vsp.vermont.gov/sites/vsp/files/Documents/VSP_Auxiliary%20Trooper%20Essential%20Job%20Functions.pdf.)

In 2013, the former VIPS online directory entry for the state of Vermont had only three programs described—none involving an auxiliary/reserve unit.

The Oregon Department of State Police was formally established in 1931 (Oregon Law 1931, Chapter 139) to serve as a rural patrol force and to provide assistance to local and county law enforcement. The Oregon State Police Reserves Board consists of retired Oregon State Police Reserves members. Board members are appointed from various regions around the state. The board meets as necessary to provide direction and oversight for the Oregon State Police Reserves program. This program has only consisted a pool of retired state police officers. (Oregon DSP 2011).

At the local level, Umpqua Community College offers a certificate of completion for the Police Reserve Academy. The academy is conducted in conjunction with the Douglas County Sheriff's Department; the Roseburg, Winston, Sutherlin, and Myrtle Creek police departments; and the Oregon State Police. This academy trains reserve officers and deputies for law enforcement agencies throughout southwest Oregon. Many full-time officers and deputies are hired from the reserve ranks. This rigorous course of study starts in mid-September and concludes in May of the following year. Classes are taught on Saturdays from 7:00 a.m. to 5:30 p.m. This is a 320-hour program designed to train police reserve officers to enter a career in law enforcement. Prospective academy students who have a letter of sponsorship from a law enforcement agency have first priority for admission into the program, and those who are not sponsored but have letters of recommendation from a law enforcement agency have second priority for admission into the program (Police Reserve Academy 2013).

The former VIPS directory entry for Oregon indicated 46 different auxiliary/reserve/citizen patrol units in 2013. For example, the city of Portland has a reserve officer program. It has the same minimum qualifications and hiring process as entry-level police officers with the exception of the college, military, or police certification requirements. Two years of service as a reserve police officer (after training and with at least of 500 hours of service rendered) satisfies the work experience requirement for entry into the full-time ranks. There are approximately 1,300 reserve officers throughout the state (Weisberg 2013). However, there was only one registered active citizen patrol group affiliated with the Oregon State Police in Florence, Oregon. The Florence Chapter of the Oregon State Police Volunteers was formed in 1994 to combat the rising number of auto break-ins. Volunteers contributed a minimum of 10 hours a month. Break-ins and thefts were reduced by more than 75% in the first year of operation. The group, which consisted of 21 members in 2013, patrols campgrounds and waysides of the central Oregon coastline providing a positive point of contact for visitors and serving as a deterrent to crime. The program is supported by grants and donations from the community and from concerned individuals. There is no state funding involved (Jarvis 2013).

South Carolina has had a system of volunteer state constables for many decades. It is unlike any of the other state auxiliary trooper or reserve units previously described. State constables are not agents of the South Carolina Law Enforcement Division (SLED), but they are regulated by that agency.[7] Depending on their specific constable commission category or class, they may be of assistance to a particular law enforcement agency. The Group III category appears to be the commission used by individuals who may be interested in a career in law enforcement or who are more settled in their respective careers and want to promote their community's safety. Generally, state constables are appointed by the South Carolina governor. Their commission type indicates whether they will be eligible upon request to assist law enforcement throughout the state. When performing such an assignment, they are not to be used to replace law enforcement in any agency. "The Chief of South Carolina Law Enforcement (SLED) advises the Governor about policies and regulations pertaining to State Constables; establishes training requirements, sets standards for conduct, prescribes limits for use of authority, determines suitability and fitness of applicants and enforces governing regulations. A South Carolina State Constable is not a stand-alone law enforcement department. It is the purpose of the Constable to assist and augment local law enforcement agency personnel efforts. A South Carolina State Constable is required under S.C. law to preserve and protect the citizens according to the laws of the state and is required to respond to any actions that result in a crime. A State Constable must protect and preserve a crime scene until a regular on-duty officer, with jurisdiction, arrives to take charge of the situation. A South Carolina State Constable is a certified law enforcement officer ... may carry a concealed weapon as outlined in the regulations within the State of South Carolina only after successfully completing an approved firearms qualifications course ... is not allowed to receive any compensation for services rendered; therefore Constables may not perform any private security work or private investigations. A South Carolina State Constable may not serve as a reserve police officer or any other position as a sworn law enforcement officer" (McCoy 2011).

There are a variety of reasons that will automatically disqualify individuals from holding a state constable's commission including owners or workers in the field of private security, bail bondsmen, law enforcement officers who presently are commissioned under other existing state statutes, having a criminal record, and so on. As noted previously, there exist specific standards governing issuance of any of the four categories of state constable commissions (Group I, II, III, and Advanced). For example, "The Group III state constable commission is available to qualified citizens who request such commissions for the purpose of assisting named law enforcement agencies, to employees of financial institutions whose primary job duties include investigation of criminal offenses and who have a need for inter-county authority, and to employees of utility companies deemed by the chief of SLED to be essential to public safety and security and who have a job-related need for inter-county law enforcement authority and whose primary duties include the security of utility company property and services" (SC State Constables 2012). All Group III candidates must attend an approved State Constable Basic Training School conducted by South Carolina Technical Education Colleges, complete at least 120 hours of voluntary service activity each year, and complete annual in-service training (SC State Constables 2012). Uniform costs and other expenses are the responsibility of each commissioned state constable. The cost for attending the basic training school at York Technical College, Rock Hill, South Carolina, was $560 in 2012. (The requirements for each of the various categories of state constable can be found at: http://www.sled.sc.gov/Constables.aspx?MenuID=Constables.)

The South Carolina Highway Patrol was formed in 1930 to enforce newly enacted laws governing the use of motor vehicles. It attempted to initiate an Auxiliary Trooper Program in 2006. The program was to be similar to the reserve officer program used by local law enforcement agencies, bolstering existing resources by using nonpaid volunteers to assist troopers at special events with traffic and crowd control and during times of natural disaster such as hurricanes. The auxiliary troopers were to be partnered with full-time state troopers. At that time, Russell F. Roark, former Highway Patrol Colonel, stated: "This model has worked well for local law enforcement agencies, and we are confident that it will be a plus for bolstering our presence in communities and on our roadways" (SC Highway Patrol 2006). According to Captain Jones Gamble of the South Carolina Highway Patrol, a few citizens received training, but the program was discontinued before anyone was assigned to actual duties due to budget cuts (personal communication, June 25, 2014).

In 1965, Col. C. W. Russell, a former state trooper, was appointed to direct the Alabama Department of Public Safety. Col. Russell established the Alabama State Trooper Reserve program to "serve side by side with state troopers throughout the state on routine assignments, as well as during natural disasters and other special details" (Alabama DPS 2013). In 1972, integration of the state trooper force was ordered by Judge Frank M. Johnson in what was to be known as the Paradise Case. In the federal court order, Judge Johnson ruled that public safety must hire one black trooper for each white hired until 25% of the force was black. It would be 1990 before a federal court consent decree was issued in the case.[8] As a result of another court case, height and weight standards for state trooper applicants were abolished because the requirements discriminated against women. U.S. District Judge Frank M. Johnson ordered that the standards be eliminated as part of the screening process for prospective state troopers in June 1976 (Alabama DPS 2013).

In 1978, the Alabama State Trooper Reserve program resumed functioning after more than a year's hiatus. The program was given a new start through the passage of a state law authorizing peace officer powers to active duty members. All former members who wanted to remain members were required to submit new applications. The program's new requirements included a 48-hour training course and the requirement that members work at least three shifts in every three-month period. All members would have to cover their own expenses. At the time of the announcement, Col. Meady L. Hilyer, the newly appointed director of the Alabama Department of Public Safety, stated: "Interested and qualified blacks are encouraged to apply for membership" (Reserve given service 1978, 13). In 2014, general information about the Alabama State Trooper Reserve program, a program manual, and an application were posted on the agency's Web site, but the word "closed" appeared at the top of the information site (see Alabama DPS 2014). However, there had been an effort to recruit additional members in 2009 when there were 80 reserve troopers in Alabama including three trooper reserve pilots (Kitchen 2009). At that time, applicants have been at least 21 years old and U.S. citizens. A background investigation was required, and applicants completed a training program consisting of firearms qualifications and a physical fitness test (Douglas and Jones 2009). The only specific information available at the time of the publication of this book was that the state's reserve trooper program had suspended recruitment efforts and that the active number of volunteer reserve troopers had fallen below 60. Figure 5.4 shows only a hat badge insignia. The absence of the hat might symbolize the current uncertainty surrounding the nature of this program.

Figure 5.4 Alabama State Trooper Reserve Highway Patrol hat badge.

The Rise and Fall of the Connecticut State Auxiliary Police

As noted previously, the Connecticut State Police was established in 1903. Its first five officers were assigned to enforce laws pertaining to intoxicating liquor and gaming violations. They received three dollars for each day of service. In 1941, concern about the need to protect the Connecticut shoreline against possible invasion was high; in a short time, the nation's entry into World War II solidified the need for an auxiliary program because there was a greatly diminished supply of men eligible for police assignments due to military call-ups. Many citizens responded for home front civil defense purposes, and before the war's end, about 1,200 auxiliary volunteers had been assigned to guard bridges, waterways, and other installations against possible sabotage. Connecticut auxiliary officers are still doing their job today but on a much smaller scale (History of CSP 2013). After the conclusions of World War II and the Korean War, many of the volunteers were absorbed by local police departments, but others were reassigned to work as volunteer troopers to help patrol highways, to assist disabled motorists, to direct traffic at accidents, to do courier work for barracks, and to back up the regular full-time troopers. These state volunteer police officers had no police arrest authority and did not respond to alarms, but they carried firearms for self-defense as they drove in marked state police cruisers (Leukhardt 1995). A state law adopted in 1951 and amended in 1963 regarding peacetime use authorized the commissioner of the Department of Public Safety "to recruit, train, and organize a volunteer police auxiliary force for the purpose of providing emergency services throughout the state" (see ch. 529, sec. 29–22, Connecticut statutes).

The year 1982 signaled the decline of both state and local auxiliary membership. In that year, a new state law required all municipal police officers to be trained and certified. The new training course consisted of 560 hours of instruction, while the basic state police auxiliary course consisted of 60 hours and two weekends of small arms training at the state police range. At first, because this law did not refer to the state auxiliary members, it impacted mostly local towns and cities. Many simply found it too expensive to try to certify their part-time volunteer officers and dissolved their units rather than risk the liability associated with having uncertified but armed and uniformed volunteers (Leukhardt 1995).

In 1986, there were about 400 auxiliary troopers, working out of the 12 state police barracks under the command of an auxiliary volunteer whose role was to be a liaison between the auxiliary force and the commanding officer of the barracks. When interviewed, Charles A. Morrison, the president of the Connecticut State Police Union, praised the auxiliary unit. "They perform a very valuable service for us and they perform a terrific assistance to regular troopers at the scene of accidents and crimes. They also free troopers for other duties" (Cavanaugh 1986, 2). Nevertheless, state police officials soon developed concerns about the need for training its auxiliary, especially because they were interested in obtaining Commission on Accreditation for Law Enforcement Agencies, Inc. (CALEA), accreditation. (The CALEA standards pertaining to volunteer police are found in Appendix A.) In 1986, when the Connecticut state police attained accreditation, the existing auxiliary force was "grandfathered in"—they could stay until their retirement (Youmans 2000). Thus it was decided that it would be best to phase out the program by not accepting new applicants, although one newspaper report indicated that hundreds of citizens were eager to join. By 1995, the trooper auxiliaries numbered 130 (Leukhardt 1995). As members reach the age of 70, they undertake administrative assignments and do not wear a uniform or carry a firearm.[9] By 2000, the auxiliaries had about 55 volunteers certified for patrol and 22 who did mostly administrative work. In addition, the minimum training hours had risen to 240 hours (Youmans 2000).

In 2003, upon the one hundredth anniversary of the Connecticut State Police, Governor John Rowland stated: "As the oldest law enforcement agency of its kind, the Connecticut State Police has survived countless societal changes and changes within its ranks—and throughout remained a steadfast bastion of security for all our citizens. Troopers and auxiliary troopers have selflessly given their lives in furtherance of this mission. It is upon the path these brave men and women have paved that the Connecticut State Police have met the challenges of the new millennium. All of the residents of our state should recognize the rich history of the Connecticut State Police and its essential role in our lives today" (Daley 2003). During its existence, 19 regular troopers and two auxiliary troopers have lost their lives while performing their duties in the Connecticut State Police (History of CSP 2013). The two volunteer troopers killed in the line of duty were Edward Truelove in 1992 and Philip Mingione in 1994 (Youmans 2000).

In 2012, the state legislative committee on public safety and security held a hearing regarding a proposed law dealing with state police staffing levels. The proposed legislation would have eliminated the mandated cap on the number of state police, which was set at 1,248. The bill also called for the elimination of the cap on the state police volunteer auxiliary force, which under current law could not exceed twice the number of state police officers. By law, the commissioner would be authorized to appoint and organize the volunteers to perform emergency services and to augment the force. The 1,248 minimum state police number had been imposed in 1998 due to an incident involving the death of a woman who had called 911 for police help but received no police response for about 20 minutes.[10] In 2012, Sgt. Andrew Matthews, an attorney and president of the state police union, spoke against the measure, fearing that an arbitrary number might be established reducing public safety. He also testified that he supported the work of the auxiliary force, which at that time consisted of 49 active patrol members and

16 performing administrative work (S.B. 32 Hearing 2012). As of May 2012, the proposal to eliminate the state police cap was considered to have "died in the Senate."

In press interviews, William Klein, the certification officer for the Police Officer Standards and Training Council (POST) in Connecticut, has indicated that the era of the auxiliary officer is ending, but in its place there has emerged a more professional and better trained police force. In addition, Jeff Matchett, president of the Connecticut Council of Police Unions, noted that if an auxiliary or part-time police officer is to carry a gun and have arrest powers, he or she must complete the same academy training as full-time police officers. In 2011, such preparation consisted of at least 818 hours of classroom and field training preceded by extensive background checks (Juliano 2011).

Nonetheless, at the local level there have been new developments in Connecticut involving volunteer police having limited authority. For example, the city of New Britain is willing to run some risk of liability and deploy volunteer auxiliary police who do not carry guns, have arrest powers and did not work regular shifts. New Britain disbanded its auxiliary force in the early 1980s but reinstituted a program in 1995 at the recommendation of its police chief and with the approval of its city council. At that time, it was noted that auxiliary officers generally fell into two categories: young people exploring law enforcement as a career and middle-aged people driven by community activism. The revival of the program was presented as a natural outgrowth of block watches and other community-based policing programs (Leukhardt 1995). However, in 2013, the now defunct VIPS online directory of registered programs indicated only four police departments having an auxiliary/reserve or citizen patrol unit. Neither New Britain nor the Connecticut state auxiliary police were listed. Yet, during 2012, seven members of the state auxiliary police unit assigned to Troop H in Hartford and their unit leader volunteered 451 days for a total of more than 4,200 hours of service. Their patrol hours were nearly four times that of any other volunteer unit. To achieve these numbers as a unit, they each had to work one 10-hour shift per week for the entire year, which is in addition to their regular full-time jobs. A unit citation was awarded attesting to their service (Auxiliary Troopers 2013b). Included among this group was Auxiliary Trooper Michael Tiernan (a member since 1965). He was named "the Connecticut State Police 2013 Auxiliary Trooper of the Year" for his many hours of dedicated service (Auxiliary Troopers 2013a). After 1995, the city of New Britain reorganized its auxiliary program, and it is now referred to as a "community service officer (CSO) Program." Members are unpaid and wear distinctive uniforms.[11] The CSO program is described "as an excellent opportunity for those interested in a career in law enforcement to gain valuable experience and for service-oriented individuals to contribute to the community" (CSO Program 2013).

Other State Police Volunteer Initiatives

The great majority of state police agencies do not have volunteer police units who possess peace officer status, but many do use the services of civilians in closely related roles. For example, the California Highway Patrol (CHP), established in 1929 by an act of the state legislature, has a senior volunteer program that provides support for the CHP's efforts to protect travelers on county and state highways and in educating the public concerning driver safety issues. Members in the program must be at least 55 and most volunteer for a six-hour shift once a week. Statewide, in 2012, there were more than 740 senior CHP volunteers. They perform patrols to deter speeders in marked CHP vehicles bearing a removable "volunteer" sign. They also help in deploying radar trailers, work in schools, direct traffic at special events, and have administrative duties. The volunteers complete tasks that enable officers to spend more time patrolling. While on patrol, they are not armed and do not enforce the law. The use of a cruiser's siren or the making of traffic stops is not permitted. All potential members undergo a background check and must have no prior felony convictions (Scroggin 2013). There is also an active Explorer Post at the Visalia office of the California Highway Patrol (see Figures 5.5 through 5.7). Additional details about Law Enforcement Exploring are provided in Chapter 8.

Another program involving unarmed and unsworn citizens was initiated in 2013. It began as a response to the Sandy Hook Elementary School shooting in Newtown, Connecticut. The program involves Oregon State Police volunteers who patrol either on foot or in marked vehicles in neighborhoods around public schools in Lincoln County. A random schedule is used. The Oregon State Police (OSP) has used citizen volunteers in Lincoln County for

Figure 5.5 Visalia Explorer Post 480 members engaged in training scenario. (Used with the permission of the California Highway Patrol, Visalia, California (CA).)

Figure 5.6 Visalia Explorer Post 480 members engaged in training scenario. (Used with the permission of the California Highway Patrol.)

Figure 5.7 Visalia Explorer Post 480 unit photo, ca. 2012. (Used with the permission of the California Highway Patrol.)

more than 25 years. However, this is the first time they have been specifically deployed for school safety. Volunteers qualify through background checks and training with the OSP. According to Sue Graves, the safety coordinator for Lincoln County schools, "Their role is not to intervene but to call 911 if there is a dangerous situation or if it's not an immediate danger, to call the school principal or the secretary to let them know what they're seeing so that the school principal can then take whatever action they deem is important" (Kellner 2013).

The state of Maryland has two prominent statewide volunteer police related programs: the Natural Resources Police Reserves (NRPR) and the Volunteers in Police Service (VIPS) program of the Maryland State Police. The former program was established in 1996 and the latter in 1986. In recent years, the NRPR has had about 200 members and the VIPS program has involved about 100 participants (Maryland NRP 2013; Maryland State Police VIPS 2013).

The Maryland Natural Resources Police (NRP) is a law enforcement agency with statewide jurisdiction that enforces the laws and regulations that protect Maryland's natural resources on a half million acres of land owned or controlled by the Maryland Department of Natural Resources and that ensures the enforcement of Maryland's recreational boating regulations and maritime homeland security. The NRP responds to approximately 2,400 maritime incidents a year on Maryland's Chesapeake Bay, tidal rivers, inland waters, and coastal waterways off the Atlantic Ocean (Maryland NRP 2013). Members of the NRP Reserves have assisted with radio/telephone communications, boating and hunting safety education, community and public relations, patrol with sworn NRP officers, search and rescue operations, vessel safety checks, traffic control, vehicle and vessel operations, and administrative matters (Maryland NRP Reserves 2013). In this manner, NRPR officers perform duties in the field other than law enforcement, which frees time for commissioned officers to deal with criminal matters.

The VIPS of the Maryland State Police (MSP) work in most barracks throughout the state and the human resources, forensic sciences, central records, medical, and police training divisions. In 2010, VIPS volunteers contributed more than 13,000 hours. The member of the VIPS program have been involved in fingerprinting, community service events, serving as adult advisors to Police Explorers, photographic work, role playing in live scenarios for trooper training, and a variety of administrative duties. The VIPS program also allows MSP personnel to devote more time to their direct law enforcement responsibilities (Maryland State Police VIPS 2013).

A related program involving police volunteers is conducted by the Virginia State Police (VSP). Almost any type of needed activity, except actual police work, is open to citizens over the age of 16 who can pass a background investigation. Examples of activities include computer maintenance, various administrative services (e.g., data entry, filing, typing, cataloging, and copying), radio repair and installation, telephone answering, translation, vehicle servicing, and warehousing. In 2013, the VSP advertised for volunteers to work at its sex offender registry at state police headquarters to assist with community mailings to child minding facilities, scanning documents into the registry, copying court cases, and similar activities. It also was seeking an individual with a background in insurance work for its insurance fraud and auto theft section within Division 1 Headquarters in Glen Allen, Virginia.

This volunteer would be assigned to assist with investigations and general office duties (Virginia SP 2013).

In the United States, the first Citizen Police Academy (CPA) was hosted by the Orlando (Florida) Police Department. Since that time, CPA programs have been formed by police agencies all over the country. CPAs are intended to open the lines of communication between the community and their local police and to help expand a police agency's community-based efforts. Such programs can help to alleviate some misunderstandings by providing citizens with a firsthand look at the operations, procedures, statutes, regulations, and policies that guide police in their daily duties.

In communities large and small, various state police agencies have instituted CPAs, often on an annual basis. Notable programs have been conducted by the Alaska State Troopers, Pennsylvania State Police, Kentucky State Police, Connecticut State Police, Delaware State Police, Rhode Island State Police, Utah Highway Patrol, and the Tennessee Highway Patrol. The Pennsylvania CPA has covered such topics as the history and structure of the state police, traffic law and crash investigation, executing a search warrant, defensive tactics, domestic violence issues, use of drug dogs, use of the polygraph, special emergency response teams, role of the patrol officer, criminal investigations, forensics, aviation, mounted police units, and the use of force. Ride-a-long and shooting range opportunities typically are provided. Most of the CPAs are open to a limited number of citizens above the age 18 or 21 who live or work in the jurisdiction of the agency. Many agencies also conduct background investigations of applicants (who must not have prior felony or serious misdemeanor convictions) and may even restrict participation to a select group of government, media, and community leaders. Candidates must be willing to attend weekly three-hour sessions, and the academies may last anywhere from six to ten weeks.

One typical academy is run annually by Troop P of the Pennsylvania State Police. It is open to all residents of the Troop P coverage area, which includes Bradford, Sullivan, Wyoming, and a portion of Luzerne County. The program is held on eight consecutive Wednesdays from 6 p.m. to 8 p.m. in a classroom setting. The participants receive instructions and demonstrations from various members of the Pennsylvania State Police. There is no cost to the participants. At the CPA's conclusion, a graduation is held and participants receive a certificate of participation and a class photo (Troop P Community Services Unit 2013).

Summary

Today, opportunities to engage in "community policing" activities are available not only at local police departments but also at state police agencies. In fact, a number of state police agencies have used the services of local citizens, especially since the World War II era. Initially, these activities were devoted to civil defense functions (e.g., protecting the infrastructure vital for defense), but as threats of invasion or sabotage abated, attention and the use of volunteer police shifted to the more routine or everyday needs of public safety (highway safety, crowd control, etc.). Since the wake-up call associated with the events of 9/11, there has existed a need to rethink how best to protect America's infrastructure, major landmarks, and places involving mass gatherings (shopping malls, stadiums, etc.). Throughout the latter half of the twentieth century and continuing into the present time, volunteer police have routinely supplemented police strength at special events.

In some respects, the formation of the Texas Rangers served as a prec-edent for the creation of later statewide law enforcement agencies. However, its first roles centered on the protection of frontier settlements from Indians and on attacks by Mexicans who had crossed into Texas territory. In the early decades of the twentieth century, the new state police agencies were called upon for vice and liquor law enforcement, peacekeeping in coal and iron regions due to labor unrest, the provision of rural police services, and high-way safety. In New York, an important justification for their establishment included less reliance on National Guard troops during emergencies. Details about the Arizona, Connecticut, Texas, Illinois, New Jersey, and New York state police agencies were presented as examples of how their origins stemmed from these specific needs. In Pennsylvania, interesting history of the vol-unteer state police of Crawford and Erie Counties was also examined. This organization was conceived in the 1870s to contend with livestock thieves but became a popular community resource for traffic and crowd control work during its last 50 years of existence.

In addition, information about each of the existing state volunteer police units was presented. These units and programs include the Alabama State Trooper Reserve, Arizona Highway Patrol Reserve, Connecticut State Auxiliary Police, Florida Highway Patrol Auxiliary, Florida Park Police Reserve, New Hampshire State Police Auxiliary, Oregon State Police Reserves, Ohio State Highway Patrol Auxiliary, South Carolina State Constable pro-gram, and Vermont Auxiliary Troopers.

An interesting feature of the work of the OSHP Auxiliary officers is the assistance they provide at both the annual "Buckeye Boys State Week" and "Junior Cadet Week" programs. The latter event is held for both Boys State and Girls State graduates who are interested in learning about law enforce-ment. After additional experience and training, FHP Auxiliary officers may be certified to patrol solo in a marked patrol unit to provide assistance to motorists and troopers. The paid part-time auxiliary troopers in Vermont are generally assigned to the marine/snowmobile division within the state police. Although their work is based on the seasons, they must complete the state's basic and annual law enforcement training requirements to remain eligible for assignments. In Oregon, many full-time officers and deputies are hired from the reserve ranks. A South Carolina State Constable's commission cannot be used for private security work. In order for the state constable program to provide maximum assistance, specific standards have been established for each of four different commission categories. The Alabama State Trooper Reserve announced the suspension of its recruitment efforts prior to the publication of this book.

The Connecticut State Auxiliary Police has been in a phasing out status since the mid-1980s. A major reason given for this decision is the state's fiscal inability to pay for the necessary enhanced training as a result of new state standards and/or CALEA requirements. However, another reason concerns an apparent disinterest in seeking qualified citizens who might be willing to pay for it themselves. It could also be due to reasons unknown by this author. In response to inquiries regarding the status of the Connecticut State Auxiliary Police program, Connecticut State Police Capt. Gregory Senick remarked: "It's not fair to require them to go through extensive training programs when they are not paid. It's not practical" (quoted in Waldman 2001). Nonetheless, many other states continue to maintain their programs and in most instances have endeavored to enhance their training and preparedness.

Moreover, volunteer programs involving unsworn positions appear to be making a comeback in a few local jurisdictions in Connecticut. For example, the city of New Britain has introduced a community service officer (CSO) program. CSOs are volunteers who receive no salary and who wear distinctive uniforms. The program is advertised as an excellent opportunity for those interested in a career in law enforcement to gain valuable experience and for service-oriented individuals to contribute to the community (CSO Program 2013). The events of September 11, 2001, and the tragedy that occurred at the Sandy Hook Elementary School in Newtown on December 15, 2012 (the nation's second-worst school shooting), surely indicate a need to develop more locally based and innovative public safety programs. In time, policy makers in Connecticut may decide to reconsider the need for their state's well-respected auxiliary trooper force.

Although the vast majority of state police agencies do not have volunteer state police units who possess peace officer status, many appear to use the services of civilians in a variety of roles ranging from citizen observer patrols to administrative assistance. In order to garner community support for their initiatives, a number of state police agencies have adopted the practice of conducting CPAs. Ride-a-long and shooting range opportunities are typically provided. Most of the CPAs are open to a limited number of applicants above the age 18 or 21 who live or work in the jurisdiction of the agency.

Review Questions

1. The new VIPS Web site directory is divided into various categories. Identify these categories by visiting the new Web site at: http://www. theiacp.org/VIPS

2. Make a case for arguing either for or against the proposition that the Texas Rangers were America's first state police agency.

3. Provide at least three reasons for the establishment of state police in the eastern half of the United States.

4. The Crawford/Erie state police was dissolved by the legislature even though the group agreed to change its name so it could not be confused with the Pennsylvania State Police and also agreed that it would strengthen its public accountability by inviting the Erie County sheriff and district attorney to serve on its advisory board. These changes did not overcome legislative opposition to the group. Discuss whether you think that the organization could have done more to save itself.

5. Read the online copy of the Illinois Attorney General's (AG) December 30, 2010, opinion dealing with independent auxiliary police contracts. Indicate the main opinion of the AG and the reasons for it. Discuss whether you agree or disagree.

6. Look up the history and present activities of the state police organization that serves your state. Identify and discuss at least two issues associated with such activities.

7. State at least one difference and one similarity between the Ohio State Highway Patrol Auxiliary (OSHPA) and the Florida Highway Patrol Auxiliary (FHPA).

8. Berg and Doerner (1988) found that some volunteer police joined for a self-serving interest. Identify at least one example of this type of interest and discuss why or why not your example(s) should disqualify an applicant.

9. Two of the volunteer state police agencies (i.e., Florida and Connecticut) limit the total number of volunteer police based on the total number of regularly employed state police. Discuss at least two possible explanations for this limitation.

10. Some state police agencies cover all initial training expenses for volunteer police while others do not. Should such expenses be covered? Discuss.

11. The bylaws of the Ohio State Highway Patrol Retirees' Association refer to the potential need for the services of the "Retired Trooper Reserve Auxiliary." Visit the Web site of this association and review its posted bylaws in order to determine the purpose of this organization and how it differs from the OSHP Auxiliary.

12. The state legislature of Connecticut has set a state police staffing level at 1,248. There has been an unsuccessful effort to eliminate this specific staffing level. Is there any possible connection between this staffing level requirement and the phasing out of the state's auxiliary trooper program? Discuss your views.

13. New Britain's CSO program is an example of how citizen volunteers can perform non-sworn (i.e., peace officer) functions such as providing transportation to stranded motorists, patrolling school grounds, and standing by at alarms. Present arguments for and against using volunteers for these types of activities.

14. Since the tragedy that occurred at the Sandy Hook Elementary School in 2012, various new strategies have been proposed to upgrade school security including the use of volunteer school resource officers. In 2013, the state of North Carolina passed a law to permit the sheriff of each county to recruit former police officers or military police officers to act in this capacity. Give reasons for and against instituting such a program. If regular citizen volunteers were to be used in such a program, would your reasoning change?

Notes

1. The state of Hawaii has four major police departments aligned with its four counties. Because this is an island state, these departments developed along rather partisan traditions and in relative isolation from each other. "With the creation of four counties in 1903, local police departments were developed, with each having an elected sheriff as its head. In the 1930s, counties created police commissions who had the power to appoint chiefs of police" (Hawaii DPS 2004, 8). For many years, marijuana growing and distribution has been a major underground factor in the economies of several of the state's island jurisdictions. A statewide agency would likely infringe on local law enforcement prerogatives with respect to this enterprise, which has four growing seasons in a single year. In Hawaii, every imaginable location is used to grow marijuana, from tree-tops to lava tubes. A county police department is the primary law enforcement agency on each island. A Department of Public Safety exists at the state level that includes Administration, Corrections, and Law Enforcement Divisions. The lattermost division is divided into two sections: Narcotics Enforcement and Sheriff. "The Narcotics Enforcement Division (NED) serves and protects the public by enforcing laws relating to controlled substances and regulated chemicals. They are responsible for the registration and control of the manufacture, distribution, prescription, and dispensing of controlled substances and precursor or essential chemicals within the State. The Sheriff Division carries out law enforcement services statewide. Its mission is to preserve the peace by protecting all persons and property within premises under the control of the Judiciary and all State facilities; providing process services and execution of court documents; handling detained persons; and providing secure transportation for persons in custody.

It also provides law enforcement services at the Honolulu International Airport" (Law Enforcement Division 2013). In Honolulu, the Sheriff Division has a very limited patrol function, primarily around the Honolulu International Airport. This role began in November 1999. The Sheriff unit also provides 24-hour services to the Civic Center complex as well as services to the Maui Memorial Hospital, Hawaii State Hospital, Waimano Training School and Hospital, and Fort Ruger at the Department of Defense. The Executive Protection staff protects the governor, lieutenant governor and, when requested, national and international dignitaries (Hawaii DPS 2004, 9). Overall, the Sheriff Division and Narcotics Enforcement Division (NED) do not appear to have the resources, trained manpower, or the support to perform the duties of a major state agency. Obviously, the establishment of a Narcotics unit was a nod to the existence of a marijuana problem. The Department of Public Safety has disclosed its problems in the narcotics enforcement field in its *Annual Report for 2004*. The report states: "Due to increases in requests for drug prevention services and investigative services needed at Hawaii's airports, prison facilities, state controlled areas on all islands and participation in federal drug taskforces, the Division needs additional personnel and resources to be able to adequately handle these current responsibilities. The Division is in critical need of a chemist and laboratory facility to conduct drug analysis that is generated from cases initiated by the department and outside agency referrals. NED is also experiencing a backlog in pharmaceutical diversion cases initiated on the neighbor islands due to a lack of presence on the islands of Maui, Kauai and Hawaii (Kona). The current law enforcement personnel complement of 12 staff members is inadequate to handle the overwhelming request for services received by the Division" (Hawaii DPS 2004, 15).

2. In 2011, the Illinois Law Enforcement Training and Standards Board, in cooperation with the U.S. Marshals Service (Northern District of Illinois), U.S. Department of Justice, and the Illinois State Police, began an investigation into nongovernmental, legally unrecognized, and unauthorized "auxiliary/reserve police organizations" offering "police assistance, services, and employees" to county and local police agencies. According to the Board, "certain illicit organizations have been successful in convincing law enforcement agencies that they are legitimate. These organizations have also attempted to create an appearance of authority through financial records and other 'legal' documents to avoid constitutional requirements establishing real law enforcement authority for the use of police powers" (Illinois Law Enforcement Training and Standards Board 2013).

3. For example, prior to 1968, when the first organized police department was established in Egg Harbor Township, the community relied heavily on the New Jersey State Police for patrol and related police duties. However, there also existed a corps of special officers that supplemented police duties within the township. In the 1960s, the uniform consisted of a blue shirt with the triangle patch on the arm sleeve. These officers wore badges issued with unique numbers, and this badge style would continue to be used for several years—including by the organized police department—before being replaced in the 1980s. Because this corps consisted of volunteers, they worked at various times on an as-needed basis (Egg Harbor Township Police 2013).

4. In 1910, Mayo "met M. Moyca Newell, a wealthy heiress. The two became life-long friends, with Newell providing the money necessary for Mayo's writing projects. The two women traveled the globe to research the facts for Mayo's reform books. Mayo began her first social reform book, *Justice For All*, in 1913 when a paymaster was murdered on Newell's estate in Bedford Hills, New York. The book was published in 1917, and was a historical look at the Pennsylvania State Police. The book was so influential that is crediting with helping to start the foundations of the New York State Police, and even Theodore Roosevelt contributed to the introduction of the book. Mayo also wrote two other books on the topic, *The Standard Bearers* (1918) and *Mounted Justice* (1922). Mayo then took on the YMCA in 1920, with the book *That Damn Y*. She followed in 1925 with *The Islands of Fear* which was published as a serial in the *New York Times*. Mayo had gone to the Philippines with Newell to research, and the book illustrated her opposition to the independence of the islands. This book set the tone for her most famous work, *Mother India*. Like her later work, the book was written in a sensationalized, almost muckraking style" (Frick 2006).

5. "Junior Cadet Week" is a joint program of the Ohio State Highway Patrol, Ohio American Legion, Buckeye Boys State, Ohio American Legion Auxiliary, Buckeye Girls State, and the Ohio State Highway Patrol Auxiliary. Each year, 20 young men at Buckeye Boys State interested in learning about law enforcement are chosen by the Ohio State Highway Patrol to spend five days following Boys State at the Ohio State Highway Patrol Academy in Columbus in an intense mini-training course on the operations of the Ohio State Highway Patrol that is called "Junior Cadet Week." During Junior Cadet Week, the 20 Boys State representatives join with 20 representatives from Buckeye Girls State who were similarly chosen plus sons and daughters of Ohio State Highway Patrol person-nel. The Ohio State Highway Patrol provides the training facilities, staff, and curriculum. The OSHPA covers the cost of food and housing plus program materials for each cadet. Funding for Junior Cadet Week is provided by the Ohio State Highway Patrol. Junior Cadet Week culminates in a formal graduation cer-emony attended by the superintendent of the Ohio State Highway Patrol, the Ohio American Legion department commander, the Buckeye Boys State presi-dent, the Buckeye Boys state director, the Buckeye Girls state director, and mem-bers of the OSHPA (Buckeye Boys State 2013).

6. Attendance at any of these community college academy programs is not limited to only Arizona state police "reserve cadets." Attendees can have sponsorship by other police departments or can apply under an "open enroll-ment" policy. The latter attendees are unsponsored (i.e., they are not affiliated with a law enforcement agency, but they desire to enroll in the academy). Such persons must complete a qualification process consisting of a background investigation, a polygraph test, and a medical examination. Such open enroll-ment cadets have to pay for this qualification process, which cost approxi-mately $650 in 2013. In 2013, the approximate two-semester cost (processing and tuition) for open enrollment at the Glendale Community College law enforcement training academy was $3,780 (not including necessary personal equipment). In addition, open enrollment applicants are required to partici-pate in a physical fitness assessment to determine their overall level of fitness. The physical fitness assessment is known as the "Cooper test" (1.5-mile run,

push-ups, sit-ups, and vertical jump), with a minimum of 40% set as the goal for the applicants to achieve (Open Enrollment 2013). Additional information about this process and printouts of various required forms (application, background questionnaire, consent, etc.) are available at: http://www. gc.maricopa.edu/justice/leo/files/oeprocess.html. At the conclusion of the academy, the recruits who are sponsored receive full peace officer certification. The open enrollment students await sponsorship or employment before full certification is achieved.

7. In the United States, there is no consistent use of the office of constable and use may vary even within a state. A constable may be an official responsible for service of process—such as summonses and subpoenas for people to appear in court in criminal and/or civil matters. Or, they may be fully empowered law enforcement officers. They may also have additional specialized duties unique to the office. In some states, a constable may be appointed by the judge of the court that he or she serves; in others, the constable is an elected or appointed position at the village, precinct, or township level of local government. In Alaska, a constable is an appointed official with limited police powers. The military police arm of the Alaska State Defense Force, a voluntary state defense group, is designated as the constabulary force of the state. This agency is empowered to act in a police capacity when called into service by the governor. Some official missions the constables have performed include port security after 9/11, disaster relief, and Alaska Pipeline patrols. In South Carolina, Group III state constables are urged to act only in instances of emergencies when police are not immediately available and when a threat to life is present. It is SLED policy that "except as necessary to preserve life, state constables should take only such actions as might be undertaken by a member of the public" (SC State Constables 2012, 7). Any handguns they carry must be concealed unless they are in a state approved uniform. South Carolina State Constable Group I can be uniformed police or investigators for a specifically designated state department (i.e., SC Department of Mental Health Public Safety, state universities, etc.). Group II are retired police in good standing that desire a state constable commission to continue to have authority and to carry a weapon as set forth by SLED. (For additional information and a state-by-state overview of the office of constable, see http://www.mobileconstable. com/constables-within-the-united-states.)

8. An immediate result of the consent decree was the promotion of 50 troopers to the rank of corporal. Promotions to other ranks soon followed. Pursuant to the consent decree, a detailed, formalized transfer and reassignment policy and expanded equal employment opportunity program were implemented as well as the development of new test summary information and evaluation procedures to establish promotional registers for each rank and the development of management training programs for sworn officers and civilians. In addition, new recruiting, testing, and hiring procedures for entry-level positions of state trooper trainees and cadets were developed and implemented, with the goal of minimal negative impact. Included was a statewide pre-sign-up publicity campaign designed to inform prospective applicants about the sign-up and testing process. During the weeklong sign-up period, an astounding number of cadet and trainee applicants—6,586, of which 39% represented minorities—made

application at 18 sites throughout the state. Applicants were required to view a videotape illustrating typical duties of a trooper and providing information about the video-driven test. They also were provided with study materials for the test, which was administered to some 3,400 applicants simultaneously in Huntsville, Montgomery, and Mobile. By the late summer of 1990, test scoring was continuing with the goal of producing a listing of the top 300–400 eligible candidates from which Public Safety planned to select for hire in early 1991 (Alabama DPS 2013).

9. Several members of the Connecticut State Police Auxiliary who have been performing administrative functions (i.e., clerical work) are well past the age of 70. For example, in 2009, auxiliary officer Alma Anderson, a New Britain native, was routinely reporting each Friday for duty at State Police Troop F Barracks. Her late husband had first become a sworn auxiliary officer in the 1950s by patrolling the waters looking for stolen boats. In 2009, she celebrated her 91st birthday and her 25th year of service with the Connecticut State Auxiliary Police Force (Vahl 2009).

10. On January 3, 1998, Heather Messenger was home with her husband, David, and her five-year-old son. When threatened by her husband, she barricaded herself in an upstairs bedroom with her son and called 911 as her husband used a cedar post to break into the bedroom, beating her to death while a state police dispatcher listened helplessly. A trooper arrived almost 20 minutes later. In 2001, a three-judge panel in Putnam Superior Court found David Messenger not guilty by reason of insanity, and he was sent to a secure psychiatric hospital for 20 years or until such time as he can prove he is no longer a danger to anyone (Summers 2001).

11. At the New Britain police Web site, the program is described under the title: "The Police Reserve: Community Service Officers." The site states that the program seeks "to recruit, train, and deploy a corps of community service officers to provide direct assistance to police officers and members of the community. Although community service officers (CSOs) do not perform law enforcement duties or have the power of arrest, they do perform functions which are currently the responsibility of sworn officers…. CSOs are deployed in pairs during the evening hours and the weekly commitment will be minimal" (CSO Program 2013). Some examples of CSO duties are providing assistance at accident scenes, completing reports in noncriminal cases, assisting in searches, providing transportation to stranded motorists, patrolling school grounds, and standing by at alarms (CSO Program 2013). Reference to the goal of patrolling school grounds may have been added as a result of the Sandy Hook Elementary School massacre, which took place in Newtown, CT, on December 14, 2012. The 911 recordings from the school massacre were released December 4, 2013, less than two weeks before the first anniversary of the tragedy, after state officials lost a fight to keep them under wraps. Prosecutors had argued that audio of seven calls placed from inside the school would cause anguish for the families of those slain and for the survivors. The recordings were released days after state law enforcement officials released a long-awaited report on the shooting and on gunman Adam Lanza, age 20. The report noted that Lanza was obsessed with school shootings and had carefully planned the rampage, but it did not uncover a clear motive (Connor 2013).

References

About the FHPA. (2013a). Retrieved November 30, 2013 from http://www. mytrooper.org/

About the FHPA. (2013b). Retrieved November 30, 2013 from http://www.mytrooper. org/faq.htm

Alabama DPS. (2013). Department of Public Safety history: 1935–1990. Retrieved December 3, 2013 http://dps.alabama.gov/Home/wfContent.aspx?ID = 0&PLH1 = plhInformation-History

Alabama DPS. (2014). Alabama Reserve Program (closed). Retrieved March 1, 2014 from http://www.dps.alabama.gov/Home/wfContent.aspx?ID=70&PLH1= plhInformation-EmploymentTrooperReserveProgram

American Legion. (2013). American Legion Buckeye Boys State. Retrieved December 1, 2013 from http://www.ohiobuckeyeboysstate.com/index.html

Arizona DPS. (2013a). History. Retrieved November 30, 2013 from http://www. azdps.gov/About/History/

Arizona DPS. (2013b). Reserve officer. Retrieved November 30, 2013 from http:// www.azdps.gov/careers/reserves/

Auxiliary Officers Commissioned. (2012). 18 new auxiliary officers commissioned. Applications for next class now being processed. Retrieved December 1, 2013 from http://statepatrol.ohio.gov/doc/SpareWheelSpring2012.pdf

Auxiliary Troopers. (2013a, June 6). Connecticut: Auxiliary troopers: Michael Tiernan, Troop H, Hartford. Retrieved December 5, 2013 from http://www. lexisnexis.com.libproxy.uml.edu/hottopics/lnacademic/?

Auxiliary Troopers. (2013b, June 6). Connecticut: Auxiliary troopers, Troop H, Hartford. Retrieved December 5, 2013 from http://www.lexisnexis.com. libproxy.uml.edu/hottopics/lnacademic/?

Berg, B. and W. Doerner. (1988). Volunteer police officers: An unexamined personnel dimension in law enforcement. *American Journal of Police, 7*(1), 81–89.

Buckeye Boys State. (2013). Junior cadet week. Retrieved December 1, 2013 from http://www.ohiobuckeyeboysstate.com/jr-cadet.html

Cavanaugh, J. (1986, September 28). Auxiliary state police: Peril without pay. *New York Times*, sec. 11CN, p. 2.

Connor, T. (2013). Sandy Hook shooting: 911 calls from Newtown massacre released. Retrieved December 5, 2013 from http://usnews.nbcnews.com/_ news/2013/12/04/21755185-sandy-hook-shooting-911-calls-from-newtown-massacre-released

Cox, M. (2013). A brief history of the Texas Rangers. Retrieved November 30, 2013 from http://www.texasranger.org/history/BriefHistory1.htm

CSO Program. (2013). The Police Reserve: Community service officers. Retrieved December 4, 2013 from http://www.newbritainpolice.org/cso-program

Dale, E. (2011). *Criminal justice in the United States, 1789–1939*. New York: Cambridge University Press.

Daley, J. J. (2003). Preview of Andy Thibault's new book on the history of the CT State Police. Retrieved December 4, 2013 from http://www.andythibault.com/ History%20of%20CT%20State%20Police.htm

Deitch, L. and L. Thompson. (1985). The reserve police officer: One alternative to the need for manpower. *The Police Chief, 52*(5), 59–61.

Douglas, A. and L. Jones. (2009, January). Join the reserve trooper program. Retrieved December 3, 2013 from http://www.fox10tv.com/news/jointhetrooperreserve-program

Egg Harbor Township Police. (2013). History of the Egg Harbor Township Police. Retrieved November 28, 2013 from http://www.ehtpd.com/about/history.html

FHPA. (2013). Florida Highway Patrol Auxiliary. Retrieved December 1, 2013 from http://fhpa.info/index.php/about-us/faq?showall = &start = 1

Florida DEP. (2011). Florida Department of Environmental Protection Division of Law Enforcement, Florida Park Police. Retrieved December 1, 2013 from http://www.policevolunteers.org/programs/index.cfm?fa = dis_pro_detail&id = 2858

Frick, K. (2006). Mayo, Katherine (Prence, Katherine). Retrieved November 29, 2013 from http://pabook.libraries.psu.edu/palitmap/bios/Mayo__Katherine.html

Greenberg, M. A. (1984). Auxiliary Police: The citizen's approach to public safety. Westport, CT: Greenwood Press.

Hawaii DPS. (2004). Retrieved January 30, 2014 from http://dps.hawaii.gov/wp-content/uploads/2012/10/PSD-AnnualReport-2004.pdf

Henson, M. S. (2013). Anglo-American colonization. In: *Handbook of Texas*. Texas State Historical Association. Retrieved November 30, 2013 from http://www.tshaonline.org/handbook/online/articles/uma01

History of CSP. (2013). Abbreviated history: A brief history of the Connecticut State Police. Retrieved December 4, 2013 from http://www.cspmuseum.org/CMSLite/default.asp?CMSLite_Page = 7&Info = History

Illinois Law Enforcement Training and Standards Board. (2013). Information on private auxiliary/reserve police organizations. Retrieved November 28, 2012 from http://www.ptb.state.il.us

Illinois State Police. (2013). History. Retrieved November 26, 2013 from http://www.isp.state.il.us/aboutisp/history.cfm

Jarvis, B. (2013). Oregon State Police Volunteers Florence Office. Retrieved December 30, 2013 from http://www.policevolunteers.org/programs/index.cfm?fa = dis_pro_detail&id = 2918

Juliano, F. (2011, March 5). Higher training standards, costs mean fewer part-time police. Retrieved December 4, 2013 from http://www.ctpost.com/local/article/Higher-training-standards-costs-mean-fewer-1043894.php#

Kellner, A. (2013, October 8). Oregon State Police Volunteers patrol Lincoln County school neighborhoods. Retrieved December 9, 2013 from http://klcc.org/post/oregon-state-police-volunteers-patrol-lincoln-county-school-neighborhoods

Kitchen, S. (2009, December 27).Troopers work to reduce road deaths amid budget worries. *Montgomery Advertiser*. Retrieved June 25, 2014 from http://www.lexisnexis.com.libproxy.uml.edu/hottopics/lnacademic/?

Law Enforcement Division. (2013). Retrieved November 27, 2013 from http://dps.hawaii.gov/about/divisions/law-enforcement-division/

Leukhardt, B. (1995, February 19). A city calls auxiliary police back to duty. Retrieved November 30, 2013 from http://articles.courant.com/1995-02-19/news/9502190210_1_auxiliary-professional-police-citizens-and-police

Lyman, M. D. (2005). *The police: An introduction* (3rd ed.). Upper Saddle River, NJ: Pearson Prentice Hall.

Maryland NRP. (2013). NRP history. Retrieved December 8, 2013 from http://www.mleo.info/maryland-natural-resources-police.html

Maryland NRP Reserves. (2013). About. General information. Retrieved December 8, 2013 from https://www.facebook.com/pages/Maryland-Natural-Resources-Police-Reserves/309503192401509?sk = info

Maryland State Police VIPS. (2013). Retrieved December 8, 2013 from http://www.policevolunteers.org/programs/index.cfm?fa = dis_pro_detail&id = 501

McCoy, D. (2011). About the South Carolina State Constables. Retrieved March 10, 2011 from http://www.police-writers.com/south_carolina_state_constables.html

Neubert, N. M. (1975). *The State Police of Crawford and Erie Counties*. Workshop in Political Theory and Policy Analysis. Police Services Study Fact Sheet No. 6. Bloomington, IN: Indiana University.

New Jersey State Police. (2013). Retrieved November 27, 2013 from http://www.njsp.org/about/20s.html

New York State Police. (1967). *The New York State Police: The first fifty years 1917–1967*. Albany, NY: New York State Police.

NJSAR. (2013). New Jersey Search and Rescue/NJ State Park Police. Retrieved November 28, 2013 from http://www.policevolunteers.org/programs/index.cfm?fa = dis_pro_detail&id = 3225

Open Enrollment. (2013). *Open enrollment*. Law Enforcement Training Academy, Glendale Community College. Retrieved December 2, 2013 from http://www.gc.maricopa.edu/justice/leo/files/oe.html

Oregon DSP. (2011, May). Oregon Department of State Police. Administrative overview. Retrieved December 3, 2013 from http://arcweb.sos.state.or.us/doc/recmgmt/sched/special/state/overview/2011statepoliceadminoverview.pdf

OSHP Auxiliary Reaches 50-Year Milestone. (1992). *Flying Wheel* (Published by the Ohio State Highway Patrol), *28*(1), 12–13.

OSHPRA Bylaws. (2013). Retrieved December 8, 2013 from http://www.oshpretiree.org/OSHPRA_By-Laws.pdf

Police Reserve Academy. (2013). Umpqua Regional Police Reserve Training Program. Retrieved December 3, 2013 from http://www.umpqua.edu/police-reserve-academy

Procter, B. H. (2014). Texas Rangers, Handbook of Texas Online. Retrieved June 24, 2014 from http://www.tshaonline.org/handbook/online/articles/met04

Profile of the Auxiliary. (1999, December). Profile of the auxiliary: Who are these people? *The Spare Wheel: An Ohio State Highway Patrol Publication*, pp. 1–2.

Reserve given service. (1978, September 23). Reserve given service go-ahead. *The Tuscaloosa News*, p. 13.

S.B. 32 Hearing. (2012, February 28). Public Safety and Security Committee hearing testimony. Retrieved December 4, 2013 from http://ct-n.com/ondemand.asp?ID = 7513

SC Highway Patrol. (2006, August 18). SC Highway Patrol recruiting for auxiliary trooper program. Retrieved December 3, 2013 from http://www.scdps.gov/oea/nr2006/081806.htm

Scroggin, S. Y. (2013). Senior volunteers big benefit to Highway Patrol. Retrieved December 8, 2013 from http://www.timespressrecorder.com/articles/2012/05/04/news/news03.txt

SC State Constables. (2012). Policies and procedures: Group III. Retrieved December 3, 2013 from http://www.sled.sc.gov/Documents/Constables/PoliciesProceduresSignedByChiefKeel.pdf

Seeley, T. (2013). Connecticut State Police: An unofficial website. Retrieved November 26, 2013 from http://www.cspmail.com/

Simonich, M. (2005, March 27). Legislator hopes to dissolve 'other' state police. Retrieved December 8, 2013 from http://www.post-gazette.com/frontpage/2005/03/27/Legislator-hopes-to-dissolve-other-state-police/stories/200503270240

Smith, B. (1940). *Police systems in the United States*. New York: Harper & Brothers.

Sparrow, M. K. (1988, November). *Perspectives on policing, monograph 9: Implementing community policing*. Washington, DC: National Institute of Justice & the Program in Criminal Justice Policy & Management, John F. Kennedy School of Government, Harvard University.

Summers, S. (2001, February 18). The last word of Heather Messenger. Retrieved December 5, 2013 from http://articles.courant.com/2001-02-18/news/0102202688_1_david-messenger-barracks-state-police

Support Services. (2013). Support Services Bureau: Auxiliary troopers. Retrieved November 26, 2013 from http://www.nh.gov/safety/divisions/nhsp/ssb/auxiliary/

Tell Me About. (2013). Tell me about TASER devices. Retrieved December 5, 2013 from http://www.womenonguard.com/how_work.htm

Troop P Community Services Unit. (2013). Troop P Citizens' Police Academy. Retrieved December 10, 2013 from http://www.portal.state.pa.us/portal/server.pt/community/troop_p/4596/community_services_unit/471833

Vahl, H. (2009, December 14). Woman still serving as auxiliary state police officer at 91. Retrieved November 1, 2013 from http://positiveleo.wordpress.com/tag/connecticut-state-police/

Vermont State Police. (2013a). Auxiliary trooper application Vermont State Police. Retrieved November 30, 2013 from http://vsp.vermont.gov/sites/vsp/files/Documents/Auxiliary%20Application.pdf

Vermont State Police. (2013b). Vermont State Police FY14 budget presentation to commissioner. Retrieved November 30, 2013 from http://www.leg.state.vt.us/jfo/appropriations/fy_2014/Public%20Safety%20-%20Strategic%20program%20information.pdf

Virginia SP. (2013). Retrieved December 9, 2013 from http://www.vsp.state.va.us/Employment_Volunteers.shtm

Volunteers in Police Service. (2013). Volunteers in police service programs in New Jersey. Retrieved November 27, 2013 from http://www.citizencorps.gov/cc/listPartner.do?partner = 3&state = NJ

Waldman, L. (2001, May 29). After 40 years, auxiliary trooper retires. *The Courant*. Retrieved February 2, 2014 from http://articles.courant.com/2001-05-29/news/0105291015_1_trooper-program-auxiliary-state-police

Walker, S. (1977). *A critical history of police reform: The emergence of professionalism*. Lexington, MA: Lexington Books.

Walker, S. and C. M. Katz. (2011). *The police in America: An introduction* (7th ed.). New York: McGraw-Hill.

Weinblatt, R. (1993). *Reserve law enforcement in the United States: A National study of state, county and city standards concerning the training and numbers of non-full-time police and sheriff's personnel.* Monmouth, NJ: New Jersey Auxiliary Police Officers Association and the Center for Reserve Law Enforcement.

Weisberg, B. (2013). Ore. City shooting highlights risks faced by reserve officers. Retrieved December 6, 2013 from http://www.koin.com/news/multnomah-county/ore-city-shooting-highlights-dangers-risks-faced-by-reserve-officers#. UnmHE5opkQU.facebook

Youmans, S. (2000, July 30). *Unit begun during WWII puts volunteer troopers on patrol.* The Associated Press State & Local Wire. Retrieved December 5, 2013 from http://www.lexisnexis.com.libproxy.uml.edu/hottopics/lnacademic/?

The Federal Government and Volunteer Policing

6

The citizen looks upon the fortune of the public as his own, and he labors for the good of the state ... participates in all that is done in his country ... obliged to defend whatever may be censured in it; for it is not only his country that is then attacked, it is himself.

—**Alexis de Tocqueville**
(1835/1990, 43–44)

Introduction

Citizen participation related to public safety is found at all governmental levels, although the vast amount of participation takes place at the community level. This was especially the case in 1831, when Alexis de Tocqueville (1805–1859), a French nobleman, came to the United States (Figure 6.1). Ostensibly, he was commissioned to investigate the U.S. penitentiary system. Before his trip, he had been appointed a judge-auditor at the tribunal of Versailles. He traveled to the United States with his friend and fellow judge, Gustave de Beaumont. Over a nine-month period he studied the methods of local, state, and national governments as well as the everyday activities of the American people. His multivolume, *Democracy in America*, is considered to be a masterpiece concerning the nature of American democracy prior to the Civil War. He discovered, with a degree of amazement, the numerous and varied types of "associations" formed to help others and for the general good of the community. During the early days of our nation, volunteerism was a trait born of necessity because community service was rooted in westward expansion. "There was no government to solve problems on the frontier, no rich people to invest in infrastructure. If settlers wanted a church or a barn or a town they had to join hands and build one" (Kadlec 2013).

In order to maintain the promise of American democracy and to counter any trends whereby individualism might cause citizens to refrain from meeting their civic duties, Alexis de Tocqueville recommended an independent and influential judiciary, a strong executive branch, local self-government, administrative decentralization, religion, well-educated women, freedom of association, and freedom of the press. Moreover, he considered jury service to be an important civic obligation because it helps citizens to think about other people's affairs and educates them in the use of their freedom (Alexis de Tocqueville 1835/1990).

Figure 6.1 Portrait of Alexis de Tocqueville in 1848.

Opportunities for citizen participation at the federal level became more prevalent during and after World War II. Today in the United States, citizens may do more than fulfilling such ordinary civic responsibilities as voting, calling authorities for help in emergencies, serving on juries, and participating in interest groups to influence federal policy. They can also identify, report, and enforce potential and alleged violations of various federal regulatory laws (e.g., by bringing citizen lawsuits against polluters for violations of environmental laws in the federal district courts). On an entirely unsalaried basis, citizens may also support national efforts for disaster relief by volunteering with the American Red Cross or by helping to rebuild a house in a natural disaster zone through Habitat for Humanity. In addition, opportunities to reduce the threats of terrorism by joining the U.S. Coast Guard Auxiliary (USCGA) or the Civil Air Patrol (CAP) also exist. On a temporary assignment and salaried basis, a citizen may apply to become a Federal Emergency Management Agency (FEMA) Reservist. FEMA Reservists are called upon when a national emergency is declared by the president. Interested citizens are selected and deployed on an as-needed basis. In addition, to promote the education of youth, qualified citizens can assist with such federal initiatives as Civil Air Patrol Cadets, the JROTC, and the Customs Border Protection Explorer programs. There are thousands of nonprofit organizations seeking volunteers in a variety of fields, many with local chapters. (To identify such organizations by type and location go to: http://www.volunteermatch.org or http://www.idealist.org.)

College students (undergraduate or graduate) have opportunities to serve in internships with a wide range of federal agencies. In general, requirements include U.S. citizenship or a valid work permit (for some agencies) and enrollment in an undergraduate or graduate studies program at an accredited school; there may be other requirements depending on the agency. Federal internships are often competitive because of the number of students who are interested in them. Interested students should consult their academic advisors and/or their campus office of career services.

Numerous volunteer opportunities exist at the federal level within homeland security, law enforcement, and disaster relief organizations. In addition, there are a variety of nonprofit organizations engaged in related work. It is difficult to narrow the list of agencies for inclusion in this chapter; however, the few selected include the following national (nonprofit) and federal organizations: the Metropolitan Police Reserve Corps, the CAP, the U.S. Power Squadrons (USPS), the USCGA, and the FEMA Reserves. Information about volunteer police in Puerto Rico, Guam, and the U.S. Virgin Islands is also presented. Finally, a proposal to establish a Border Patrol Auxiliary (BPA) is considered because of its relevance to national security and its potential as a provider of volunteer service opportunities (Hall et al. 2007). The chapter begins with background materials about the nature of the federal government and some historical aspects related to the federal role in public safety.

Historical Background

The U.S. Constitution was ratified by the last of the 13 original states in 1791. The original 13 states were the successors of the 13 colonies that rebelled against British rule. The constitution created the three branches of the federal government and granted certain powers and responsibilities to each. The legislative, judicial, and executive branches have different responsibilities that have kept the branches more or less equal. The executive branch has the widest range of responsibilities and employs most of the federal workforce.

The federal system in the United States is one that is based on enumerated powers specifically granted to it in the U.S. Constitution and its statues. The Tenth Amendment to the Constitution provides that powers not delegated to the federal government or prohibited to the states by the constitution are reserved for the states. Key federal powers include the collection of taxes and duties, payment of debts, and providing for welfare and the common defense. Other federal powers include regulating commerce among multiple states and foreign nations, establishing a militia, and protecting civil rights and liberties. The idea of shared powers between states and the national government is known as "federalism," and the specific reference to this concept is found in the Tenth Amendment. Because of federalism, the designation of what is considered a local or national disaster and who should direct an emergency response can be confusing. Therefore, it is best to check a state's emergency management statute in order to determine who may declare an emergency and the powers that are provided to the state's governor, and to find out what powers are given to officials at the local level.

During the nineteenth century, there were very few federal law enforcement agencies. A notable exception is the U.S. Marshals Service, which was established in 1789.[1] The Marshals have very broad jurisdiction and authority. For more than 200 years, U.S. Marshals and their deputies have served as the instruments of civil authority used by all three branches of government and have been involved in most of the major historical episodes in America's past. For most of their history, U.S. Marshals enjoyed a surprising degree of independence in performing their duties. Quite simply, no headquarters or central administration existed to supervise the work of the Marshals until the late 1950s (Calhoun 1991; Civilian Enforcers 2013). "As our young nation expanded westward, U.S. Marshals embodied the civilian power of the Federal Government to bring law and justice to the frontier. For every new territory, marshals were appointed to impose the law on the untamed wilderness" (History 2013). Throughout much of their history, "the Marshals struggled to balance the enforcement of federal laws against the feelings of the local populace" (Calhoun 1991; Civilian Enforcers 2013). Significantly, policing has been and remains mostly a local affair. "Unlike the London police, American police systems followed the style of local and municipal governments. City governments, created in the era of the 'common man' and democratic participation, were highly decentralized.... The police were an extension of different political factions, rather than an extension of city government. Police officers were recruited and selected by political leaders in a particular ward or precinct" (Uchida 2004, 10-11).

During most of the nineteenth century, federal government jobs were held at the pleasure of the president—a person could be fired at any time. The "spoils system" meant that jobs were used to support the influence of politicians and their parties. This was changed in incremental stages by the Pendleton Civil Service Reform Act of 1883 and subsequent laws. By 1909, almost two-thirds of the U.S. federal workforce was appointed based on merit, that is, qualifications measured by tests. In contemporary times, it is a common practice to fill a variety of top level federal service positions, including some heads of diplomatic missions and executive agencies, with political appointees. The Pendleton Act required federal government employees to be selected through competitive exams and on the basis of merit; it also prevented elected officials and political appointees from firing civil servants. However, the law did not apply to state and municipal governments. Nevertheless, today, in varying degrees, most state and local government entities have competitive civil service systems that are modeled on the national system. The U.S. Civil Service Commission was created by the Pendleton Civil Service Reform Act to administer the U.S. civil service system. Effective January 1, 1978, the commission was renamed the Office of Personnel Management (OPM) under the provisions of Reorganization Plan No. 2 of 1978 (43 F.R. 36037, 92 Stat. 3783) and the Civil Service Reform Act of 1978. The OPM is also responsible for a large part of the management of security clearances.

A controversial national organization, composed entirely of volunteers, arose during wartime. The advent of World War I, as well as politics and influence, contributed to the establishment of the semisecret organization named the American Protective League (APL). The APL was formed when there was a credible threat of subversive and seditious activity within the United States. Acts of sabotage and the notorious Zimmerman Telegram had fueled these fears. During its short lifespan, the APL was engaged in ferreting out spies, saboteurs, and seditious aliens. It received recognition from the U.S. Department of Justice, the U.S. Secret Service, and other governmental departments, although it had no governmental or legal status. Its official history was published in 1919 in a book entitled *The Web: The Authorized History of The American Protective League* by Emerson Hough (Figure 6.2).

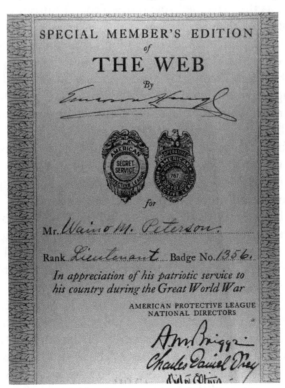

Figure 6.2 A page from *The Web,* signed by the author in a special edition in 1919.

Perhaps as many as 200,000 or more professionals, businessmen, and wage earners who were American citizens and willing to take a special oath became members.

Unlike many nations around the world, the United States has no national police force. Currently, there are more than 1,300 federal government agencies; more than 90 of these agencies carry out one or more specialized law enforcement functions.[2] Much of the growth in federal law enforcement is due to congressional legislation. For example, in 2002, the Department of Homeland Security (DHS) was established and now has more sworn federal law enforcement agents and officers than any other department of the U.S. government. An earlier and major contributing factor toward federal policing occurred within the executive branch when the Eighteenth Amendment became effective in 1920. The Eighteenth Amendment placed a ban on the sale, distribution, and manufacture of alcoholic beverages. This prohibition lasted until its repeal by the Twenty-First Amendment in 1933. The Department of Justice enforced prohibition, along with the Customs Service, Coast Guard, and Bureau of Internal Revenue. Over time, Americans have come to expect more from federal law enforcement than ever before. Its size, jurisdiction, and responsibilities continue to grow. Some growth is clearly justified, such as the expanded role of the Federal Bureau of Investigation (FBI) in counterterrorism.[3]

Federal strategies to enhance the nation's preparedness for disaster and attack have evolved over the course of the twentieth century and into the twenty-first. Highlights from this history include the air raid warning and plane-spotting activities of the Office of Civil Defense in the 1940s, the "duck and cover" filmstrips and backyard shelters of the 1950s, and today's all hazards preparedness programs led by the DHS.[4]

Even before September 11, 2001, when al-Qaeda terrorists struck the World Trade Center in New York City and the Pentagon near Washington, D.C., killing nearly 3,000 people federal authorities and Congress enlisted local law enforcement on behalf of federal law enforcement concerns. For example, the Illegal Immigration Reform and Immigrant Responsibility Act of 1996 encouraged state and local police agencies to enter into agreements with the U.S. Attorney General to train and deputize local immigration enforcement officers. The same statute also authorized the attorney general to enlist local forces during an immigration emergency.

Since the events of September 11, various federal initiatives have been undertaken to involve the nation's local police agencies in the war on terrorism. In order to strengthen the security of the nation's transportation systems, the U.S. Transportation Security Administration (TSA) was established with the passage of The Aviation and Transportation Security Act of 2001. The statute required the TSA: (1) to be responsible for security for all modes of transportation; (2) to recruit, assess, hire, train, and deploy security officers for 450 commercial airports from Guam to Alaska in 12 months; and (3) to provide 100% screening of all checked luggage for explosives by December 31, 2002. This was a mandate for the creation of one of the largest agencies in the history of the U.S. government.

But the most controversial action after September 11 was the passage of the USA PATRIOT Act (the acronym for Uniting and Strengthening America by Providing Appropriate Tools Required to Intercept and Obstruct Terrorism Act). Less controversial have been the ongoing contributions of community-minded men and women who participate in the CAP, USCGA, Community Emergency Response Teams, and in volunteer fire units.

In 2005, Hurricane Katrina caused severe destruction along much of the Gulf Coast, devastating New Orleans. In the same year, Congress adopted the Real ID Act, which set state standards for issuing drivers' licenses to immigrants. It also required states to regulate the activities of persons who are for any reason without status. Among its provisions is the need for each state to provide electronic access to information contained in its motor vehicle database to all other states. The law has been promoted primarily as an antiterrorism measure. In addition, the Vision 100—Century of Aviation Reauthorization Act of 2003 requires air carriers providing scheduled passenger air transportation to conduct basic security training for their flight and cabin crewmembers in order to prepare them for potential threat conditions that may occur onboard an aircraft. The act further requires the TSA to develop and make available to flight and cabin crewmembers an advanced self-defense training program that includes appropriate and effective responses for defending against an attacker.

Although most states have introduced civil service testing and other basic requirements for police officer selection, the actual day-to-day operations of police departments are determined by local officials and by the discretion exercised by officers on patrol. Policing in the United States is conducted by numerous types of agencies at many different levels. Every state has its own nomenclature for agencies, and their powers, responsibilities, and funding vary from state to state. In some states, there can be several hundred local police agencies. Each agency has its own chief and manual of procedures. At a crime or disaster scene affecting large numbers of people, multiple jurisdictions involving several police agencies may be deployed. Depending on the emergency, the response can be very problematic. A case in point was the Hurricane Katrina disaster where the basic emergency channels of communication were disrupted. In such a situation, one researcher has noted that even the "moral order of the police force itself was also called into question, as many remaining officers were troubled by those who abandoned their posts after the hurricane, wondering how they could ever trust those officers again" (Sims 2007, 115). Command in such situations remains a complex and sometimes contentious issue.

Today, federal law enforcement agencies are routinely asked to assist in local law enforcement matters. In many instances, such assistance has resulted in "cross-deputization." Cross-deputization is an agreement that allows police officers to cross borders and enforce the law outside their areas of jurisdiction. Deputization agreements give tribal, federal, state, or city law enforcement officials power to enforce laws outside their own jurisdictions regardless of the identity of the perpetrator, thus simplifying the exercise of criminal jurisdiction. These agreements may include the creation of police task forces involving more than one agency. Such joint federal, regional, state, and county task forces have become an important tool to contend with crimes involving gangs, drugs, guns, and human trafficking. These highly desired agreements enable task force members to be deputized in order to cross state lines and enforce federal laws. Moreover, such agreements also become a necessity due to the need to contend with the vastly increased problems of global crime, terrorism, cyberterrorism, and cyberwarfare.

On July 29, 2010, Congress enacted a much needed criminal reform known as the Tribal Law and Order Act (TLOA) for Indian country. "TLOA encourages cross-deputization. Tribal and state law enforcement agencies in Indian country receive incentives through grants and technical assistance to enter into cooperative law enforcement agreements to combat crime in and near tribal areas. At the federal level, TLOA enhances existing law to grant deputization to expand the authority of existing officers in Indian country to enforce federal laws normally outside their jurisdiction regardless of the perpetrator's identity. This measure simplifies the exercise of criminal jurisdiction and provides greater protection of Indian country from crime through increased enforcement" (Bulzomi 2012).[5]

In 2007, in testimony before the Subcommittee on Healthy Families and Communities, Congressman John P. Sarbanes stated: "Volunteers are a large part of what makes America such a great and strong nation. Throughout this country, volunteers fill in gaps where local, state, and federal governments are unable to effectively serve people. Further, the community-minded spirit fostered by volunteer activity benefits all people by strengthening the fabric of our nation" (Dooris 2008, 42).

Metropolitan Police Reserve Corps

The Metropolitan Police Department (MPD), founded in 1861, is the primary law enforcement agency for the District of Columbia; it is one of the ten largest local police agencies in the United States. According to its Web pages, the department uses the latest advances in evidence analysis and state-of-the-art information technology. These techniques are combined with a contemporary community policing philosophy, referred to as "customized community policing." Community policing bonds the police and residents in a working partnership designed to organize and mobilize residents, merchants, and professionals to improve the quality of life for all who live, work, and visit the nation's capital (About MPDC 2013).

From the 1920s until 1950, police officers traveled to Washington, D.C., from other jurisdictions (such as New York City and Philadelphia) to assist members of the MPD with crowd control during the Shriners convention and presidential inaugurations. Local residents also participated. They were issued a credential in the form of an auxiliary MPD badge. In time, an Auxiliary Division was created within the department. "In 1950 a number of auxiliary detectives and auxiliary detective sergeants were caught running a burglary ring. It became a major scandal since these officers were picked from the elite of Washington.... The police administration fired all of the Auxiliaries and formed the Metropolitan Police Reserves" (Blickensdorf 2014).

As in most American cities, during World War II, the police force in the nation's capital was also aided by units of civil defense. Civilian defense auxiliary police and other groups were organized in case of any attack on the nation's capital. After the war, although civil defense was no longer a top priority, it became apparent that a permanent reserve force could be of benefit to the regular police by assisting them in carrying out their everyday responsibilities (About the MPD 2013). The District of Columbia's auxiliary police that were associated with civil defense during World War II appear to be unrelated to the Auxiliary Division, which was mostly a political organization that "had more power then someone would have thought during that time period" (Blickensdorf 2014).

The Metropolitan Police Reserve Corps was established in November 1948. The organization was given greater recognition with the passage of a federal law in 1950 that gave authority to the chief of police to select, organize, train, and equip certain residents of the District and the metropolitan area in a special reserve unit known as the Metropolitan Police Reserve Corps (About the MPD 2013).

Members of the new Reserve Corps were first deployed on October 31, 1951, to guard fire alarm boxes to prevent the sounding of false alarms on Halloween night. In 1961, the Reserve Corps was called to duty and sworn in to assist with the inauguration of President John F. Kennedy. Throughout the 1960s, the Reserve Corps was frequently called upon to assist with civil demonstrations arising from national tragedies such as the assassinations of President Kennedy, his brother Senator Robert F. Kennedy, and Dr. Martin Luther King Jr. (About the MPD 2013). Figure 6.3 shows members of the Reserve Corps standing at attention outside the 6th Precinct station house.

In 1970, the chief of police prepared an order setting forth the policy, procedures, and responsibilities of the Reserve Corps. This general order was replaced in 2006 by a more comprehensive document, 26 pages in length.

Figure 6.3 Members of the Metropolitan Police Reserve Corps standing at attention outside the 6th Precinct stationhouse in the District of Columbia, ca. 1950s.

The revised general order provided sufficient clarifications so that the Reserve Corps was better prepared to render community service and to become an integral part of the MPD (About the MPD 2013). Prospective members must successfully complete the same entrance screening required of full-time officers: a written test (national police officer entrance exam), a background suitability investigation, and medical and psychological examinations. All basic training must be substantially the same as that completed by full-time sworn officers.

The members of the corps serve in different ways, depending upon individual experience and qualifications and upon the time commitment they are able to make. For example, a Reserve Officer Level I carries out the same duties as a regular officer under the regular officer's general supervision. A Reserve Officer Level II carries out assignments under close supervision and is not authorized to carry a department-issued firearm. Some reserve officers may work indoors in a patrol district, while others will work side-by-side with patrol officers performing frontline law enforcement activities. Significantly, while on duty, Reserve Corps members are authorized to exercise the full law enforcement authority of a sworn police officer except as restricted by the 2006 General Order or by the police chief. "When not on department duty, Reserve Corps members shall possess only such police powers as granted to a private citizen" (General Order 2006, 6). Reserve officers usually begin at Level II and must have had at least one year of good standing at Level II and at least 60 college credits or 960 hours of volunteer service, or an equivalent combination of education and experience, in order to move to Level I. There are several additional requirements, and these meet or exceed the requirements, established by the Commission on Accreditation for Law Enforcement Agencies (CALEA) (General Order 2006). Reserve Corps members who successfully compete to become regular sworn police officers can be credited with training already completed as a Reserve Officer. A person with law enforcement experience can enter the force directly as a Reserve Officer Level I if various criteria are satisfied and with the approval of the chief of police (General Order 2006).

In 2009, the Reserve Corps had more than 100 members contributing at least 16 hours a month, the department's minimum volunteer commitment. According to Richard Southby, the Reserve Corps' commanding officer (with more than 20 years of service), most volunteers offer much more of their time. By his estimate, Reserve Corps members contribute about 3,000 hours a month to the department. Southby, now in retirement, is a former George Washington University faculty member and administrator. As a result of his involvement with the Reserve Corps, he helped in setting up the police science program in the College of Professional Studies at George Washington University (Morse 2009). In March 2010, the MPD began deploying the Reserve Corps in teams in order to deter crime in various targeted areas (Williams 2010).

Civil Air Patrol

On December 1, 1941, CAP was officially established as a volunteer civilian defense organization, just one week before Japan attacked Pearl Harbor. During World War II, the CAP became famous for coastal patrol, where civilian volunteers used privately owned aircraft to spot enemy submarines along the Atlantic and Gulf Coasts. It was first placed under the control of the Office of Civilian Defense, but by April 1943, the organization was under the command of the Army Air Forces. CAP members became known as the "Minutemen" of World War II, performing many coastal patrol missions involving searching for enemy submarines and saving hundreds of crash victims (CAP History 2002). "Anti-submarine patrol for the Civil Air Patrol lasted from March 5, 1942, until August 31, 1943.... 26 CAP pilots and observers lost their lives and seven sustained serious injuries. In all, 90 aircraft were lost during that 18 months" (Burnham 1974, 28). CAP aircraft and pilots also were used for patrolling the U.S.–Mexican border to spot any unusual activities by enemy agents.

The CAP became an official auxiliary branch of the U.S. Air Force by an Act of Congress in May 1948 (Public Law 557). The Act provided that the CAP would have three major missions: aerospace education, emergency services, and a cadet program. The CAP's national headquarters is located at Maxwell Air Force Base in Montgomery, Alabama. The organization has nearly 53,000 members in 1,900 units. Applicants are screened by the FBI. Since 1986, the CAP has provided communications support to various federal and local law enforcement agencies engaged in counterdrug operations, especially in remote and sparsely populated areas. However, members cannot carry firearms or act as law enforcement officers (CAP Support to LEA 2002). Assessing natural disasters through aerial surveys and transporting vital supplies are among the many duties also performed by the CAP (Dooris 2008).

As an auxiliary of the U.S. Air Force, the CAP is organized along military lines. However, it is also classified as a nonprofit, 501(c) (3) corporation, allowing the organization to accept donations and to raise money for aircraft maintenance, fuel, and other costs and services (Dooris 2008). Its governing body is a national board whose members are elected except for the post of the senior air force advisor. The advisor's position is held by an active duty air force colonel who, in addition to serving in this critical advisory role, is also the CAP–U.S. Air Force commander. CAP is organized into eight geographic regions with a total of 52 wings. Each state, the District of Columbia, and the Commonwealth of Puerto Rico has a CAP wing. Each wing is headed by a CAP commander and has one or two retired U.S. Air Force members who perform liaison duties. The wings are subdivided into groups, squadrons, and flights depending on their size (CAP Organization 2002). In addition, there is a CAP National Staff College (NSC). The NSC offers a one-week executive management course that provides CAP officers with advanced leadership training (CAP News 2001).

The CAP provided the first direct aerial photos of the World Trade Center (WTC) disaster site in New York City. (Images can be found at http://www. Capnhq.gov.) On September 12, 2001, a day after the attack on the WTC, CAP planes began to fly over the disaster site in order to take high resolution digital images for study by the Graphic Information Program of the New York State Emergency Management Office. In addition, CAP volunteers transported cases of blood, needed medical supplies, and government officials; monitored airspace at many airports; and provided communications support to many state and local agencies (CAP News 2001).

The CAP implemented a security background check for all members in 1988. This resulted in a decrease in senior membership numbers for the next six years. CAP receives oversight from the Inspector General Program. "The CAP Inspector General Program ensures the integrity of the organization and provides CAP leadership the ability to identify and rectify program shortfalls for the purpose of bolstering efficiency.... Once every four years, the U.S. Air Force, working in conjunction with the CAP Inspector General, conducts quality assurance assessments of each of the 52 wings to streamline processes and detect and eliminate wasteful or fraudulent practices" (Dooris 2008, 47).

U.S. Power Squadrons

The U.S. Power Squadrons (USPS) was founded in 1914 and constitutes the only other major U.S. maritime volunteer organization in addition to the Coast Guard Auxiliary (CGA). The USPS is not associated with the military; rather, it is a self-sustaining, privately funded organization composed of nearly 40,000 members organized into more than 400 squadrons across the country and in some U.S. territories. The operational unit of the USPS is the "squadron." USPS members use squadrons to conduct meetings, training, social events, and other boating-related activities. The USPS works closely with organizations such as the U.S. Coast Guard (USCG), the U.S. Coast Guard Auxiliary (USCGA), and the National Ocean Services Division of the National Oceanic and Atmospheric Administration to promote boating safety, conduct courtesy vessel safety checks, update and correct nautical charts, and to assist with other community improvement projects. The USPS offers an array of educational courses to its members, as well as the boating public, and fellowship activities afloat and ashore. Successfully completing a USPS boating safety course meets the educational requirements for boat operation in all states. "USPS is America's largest non-profit boating organization and has been honored by three U.S. presidents for its civic contributions" (About USPS 2013).

Membership in the USPS can be advantageous. For example, in 2013, the navigation law for New York State was amended. The new law requires operators of mechanically propelled vessels in New York waters (who must be over 10 years old), born on or after May 1, 1996, to be holders of a boating safety education certificate. However, there are certain exceptions, including minors between 10 and 18 accompanied by an adult certificate holder, new boat owners (within a 120-day grace period), boating safety instructors, USPS members, USCGA members, licensed captains, or on-duty emergency service, rescue, and law enforcement personnel (Peconic Bay PS 2013).

U.S. Coast Guard Auxiliary

The USCG enforces a wide variety of laws, from halting the flow of illegal drugs, aliens, and contraband into the United States through maritime routes to preventing illegal fishing and suppressing violations of federal law in the maritime arena. Before receiving its current name in 1915, it had five predecessor agencies: the Revenue Cutter Service, the Life-Saving Service, the Lighthouse Service, the Bureau of Navigation, and the Steamboat Inspection Service.[6] Its civilian volunteer counterpart, the Coast Guard Auxiliary, was established in 1939 in response to the increasing number of recreational boating accidents.

The original name of the Coast Guard Auxiliary was the "Coast Guard Reserve." The 1939 federal law establishing it provided that members were not to hold military ranks, wear uniforms, receive military training, or "be vested with or exercise any right, privilege, power, or duty vested in or imposed upon the personnel of the Coast Guard" (Hall et al. 2007, 15). Nor were Coast Guard Reservists to be considered government employees. The Coast Guard Reserve lasted less than two years in its original form. On February 19, 1941, Congress restructured the Coast Guard Reserve, renaming the original organization the U.S. Coast Guard Auxiliary (USCGA) and establishing a new U.S. Coast Guard Reserve that would function as a source of wartime manpower, like the reserves of the other armed services (Hall et al. 2007). The CAP and the USCGA are the only military-sponsored volunteer (unsalaried) institutions in the United States (aside from ROTC and JROTC units).

The opportunities for service in the new Coast Guard Reserve included two categories—"regular reservists" and "temporary members of the reserve" (known as a "Coast Guard TR"). A Coast Guard TR was "a volunteer who served only in some designated geographic area (usually near his home or workplace) and less than full-time. Age limits for TRs were 17 and 64, and physical requirements were not stringent. Members of the Auxiliary were invited to enroll in the Reserve as TRs and bring their boats with them" (Tilley 2003, 3).

During World War II, "the character of the Auxiliary changed from an organization primarily designed to help pleasure boaters into a flexible work-force able and willing to step in wherever the USCG needed them" (Hall et al. 2007, 15). Volunteers, including movie stars such as Humphrey Bogart, as well as Arthur Fiedler, conductor of the Boston Pops Orchestra, patrolled for German U-boats. In addition, a unique Volunteer Port Security Force was established to prevent sabotage and subversive activities' on the nation's water-fronts. According to Tilley (2003, 4), "perhaps the Auxiliary's most important contribution to the war effort came in the form of the Volunteer Port Security Force.... The task of protecting the hundreds of warehouses, piers, and other facilities that kept the American shipping industry in business fell to the Coast Guard." Fortunately, the depleted forces of the Coast Guard were bolstered by its two-part Reserve system and its Auxiliary. Approximately 20,000 Reservists and Auxiliarists participated in the Volunteer Port Security Force (Tilley 2003). Generally, individuals assigned to the Port Security Force performed their unsalaried duties on shore. "As the war went on and the Coast Guard's resources were stretched thinner, Auxiliarists were called upon to fill gaps wherever active duty Coast Guardsmen left them. Auxiliarists' boats patrolled the waterfronts and inlets looking for saboteurs, enemy agents, and fires. Other Auxiliarists manned lookout and lifesaving stations near their homes, freeing regular Coast Guardsmen for sea duty. When a flood struck St. Louis in the spring of 1943, Coast Guard Auxiliarists evacuated 7,000 people and thousands of livestock. In addition, airplanes joined the Auxiliary and Auxiliarists began flying missions for the USCG (Hall et al. 2007).

(A five minute recruiting film for the Coast Guard Volunteer Port Security Force entitled "So's Your Old Man" may viewed online at: http://www.youtube.com/watch?v=x72rrOHohIC.)

One of the most challenging events in the history of the USCG was the "Mariel Boatlift." It began when Cuba suddenly announced it would permit a massive emigration through the Port of Mariel. For three weeks, a steady stream of small boats of every description, averaging 200–300 per day, made their way from Cuba to Florida. The USCG mobilized all of its resources in the area. Auxiliarists manned radios, performed search and rescue along the Florida coast, and stood watch at the stations in the Coast Guardsmen's absence (Hall et al. 2007).

Currently, the USCG is a division of the DHS. In recent years, its role in the suppression of drug trafficking has been significantly expanded. The USCG has about 35,000 active duty members and about 8,000 Reservists. More than 2,700 Reservists were called up to assist in antiterror efforts after the attacks on America's homeland on September 11, 2001. In addition, there may have been as many as 28,000 CGA members who were available for the performance of volunteer assignments during the emergency (Gilmore 2001).

Typically, many members of the Auxiliary operate their own boats to assist in marine safety programs. When so used, these craft are considered to be U.S. government property. Prior to September 11, the Auxiliary had three major missions: public education, the provision of courtesy marine inspections, and on-water operations (search and rescue, safety patrols, etc.) (Kastberg 1998).

According to Coast Guard Commander Chris Olin, Auxiliary members performed approximately 124,000 hours of volunteer duty between September 11 and December 7, 2001 (Olin 2001). By January 4, 2002, that number had reached 152,850 hours, an increase of approximately 45,040 hours over the previous year's hours in similar categories of effort (Operation Noble Eagle 2002). Hundreds of multimission waterside and shoreside patrols were conducted during this time frame (Olin 2001). Many of these patrols involved the protection of the nation's more than 360 ports, especially some 90 ports and waterway areas that had been designated as "security zones." In such zones, boat and ship traffic were prohibited. In New York City, there were eight such zones including areas near the United Nations and the WTC site. The auxiliary members augmented the work of the active duty Coast Guard personnel during the largest port security operation since World War II (Gilmore 2001).

On October 2, 2001, Viggo C. Bertelsen Jr. the volunteer national commodore of the USCGA announced that he had received a call from Admiral James M. Loy, the commandant of the Coast Guard. In the call, Loy expressed his appreciation for Auxiliary's service in providing critical assistance to the

Coast Guard's missions since the events of September 11. In particular, he said: "We couldn't have done it without you" (Bertelsen 2001).

Applicants for the CGA must be U.S. citizens at least 17 years of age. Members are eligible to take advance training courses in navigation, seamanship, communications, weather, patrols, and search and rescue procedures. The Auxiliary has members in all 50 states, Puerto Rico, the Virgin Islands, American Samoa, and Guam. Although under the authority of the commandant of the USCG, the Auxiliary is internally autonomous, operating on four organizational levels: flotilla, division, district, and national. At the national level, there are officers who are responsible, along with the commandant of the USCG, for the administration and policy making for the entire Auxiliary (Hall et al. 2007).

In the past, Auxiliarists have played limited roles in the law enforcement field; for example, providing vessels and crews for training Coast Guard members, engaging in port security, performing unobtrusive law enforcement observations, conducing safety checks by boarding recreational boats, providing transportation and platforms for Coast Guard boarding parties, rendering assistance in the validation process for Merchant Mariner credential applications, and carrying out other missions incorporated into programs such as America's Waterway Watch and Operation Patriot Readiness (Dooris 2008). However, in recent years, there have been efforts made to clarify the role of the Auxiliary in any law enforcement activities. In 2006, a policy directive was issued declaring the Auxiliary was to be restricted to the performance of only specific types of non-law enforcement missions. For example, "Auxiliary facilities may be used to conduct the newly renamed Maritime Observation Mission (MOM).... This is a non-law enforcement mission whose primary purpose is to provide increased maritime domain awareness by observing areas of interest and reporting findings to the operational commander while maintaining the safety of auxiliary personnel. Should Auxiliarists observe anything suspicious during the course of normal multi-mission patrols, they should record and report the same immediately ... but take no additional action" (Hall et al. 2007, 17). In particular, in accordance with operations policies, Auxiliarists cannot execute direct law enforcement missions, but they may support certain Coast Guard law enforcement activities. The key restriction is that no command can vest Auxiliarists with general police powers (e.g., power to search, seize, or arrest) or give them the authority to engage in any type of direct law enforcement or police action. In addition, Coast Guard Auxiliarists are prohibited from carrying weapons (Hall et al. 2007).

Dooris (2008) concluded that the USCG lacks the personnel and resources to fill critical gaps in its safety and security missions without help from its volunteer arm, the CGA. However, such a reliance has become more tenuous because Auxiliary membership has decreased by about 20% since 2003 to its current strength of 28,635. This trend is in sharp contrast to membership trends in other large volunteer groups in the United States. Furthermore, at its current strength, the Auxiliary is far from the 48,000-member goal declared, in a 1987 governmental report, as mission critical by 2000 (Dooris 2008).

The USCGA has not instituted any in-house youth program with appropriate standards for operation and, as of the present time, appears to have no interest in doing so. Nonetheless, on a limited basis, the USCGA has expanded its youth interaction by entering into participatory agreements with the Boy Scouts of America (BSA) and the U.S. Naval Sea Cadet Corps (NSCC) to provide shoreside and boating safety training opportunities to the interested youth of these organizations. However, in March 2011, the national commodore of the USCGA cautioned all subdivisions that before members undertake such training programs, "They must understand the risks involved including potential legal liability inherent in working with youth in our litigious society. Before engaging in such activities, interested members and units should first use their Chain of Leadership to obtain the consent of the District Commodore to engage in the activities; and, thereafter, consult with the District Legal Officer (DSO-LP) regarding all pertinent legal issues" (Vass 2011).

The absence of any youth division within the USCGA is in stark contrast to the youth training offered by the CAP, Police Explorers, and other organizations. The absence of a structured youth program is likely to forestall future membership of young adults in the organization.

Proposal for a U.S. BPA

Within the DHS is the U.S. Customs and Border Protection (CBP) division, which includes the U.S. Border Patrol (USBP) and the CBP Office of Air and Marine, the largest aviation/marine force in federal law enforcement.

In 2007, Christopher Hall, a captain in the USCG, and three other senior governmental and military officers proposed the creation of a "Border Patrol Auxiliary".[7] The BPA has been proposed as a professional organization of auxiliary members working side-by-side with Border Patrol agents in support of the Border Patrol mission. To guarantee the integrity and respectability of the Border Patrol, volunteers would be screened to ensure they have the characteristics essential for maintaining the high standards of the Border Patrol.

The mission of the proposed BPA would be "to assist the U.S. Border Patrol in accomplishing the mission of detecting, interdicting and apprehending those who attempt to illegally enter or smuggle people, including terrorists, or contraband, including weapons of mass destruction, across U.S. borders between official ports of entry" (Hall et al. 2007, 37). In order to maximize the effectiveness of the BPA, a two-tiered system would be developed. The primary purpose of tier one auxiliary members would be to improve the efficiency of the Border Patrol by relieving regular Border Patrol agents from administrative and support roles, which keep them from performing direct operational missions. The primary purpose for tier two auxiliary members would be to improve the effectiveness of the Border Patrol by increasing the number of agents along the border beyond the congressionally restricted number of 18,000 Border Patrol agents.

The actual strength of the BPA would reflect the needs of the Border Patrol, but the number authorized would be at least equal to the authorized agent strength for the Border Patrol. On this point, the proposers noted that the number of USCGA members outnumbers their active duty counterparts. After completion of an appropriate training program, tier one BPA members would be required to perform a minimum of 12 hours per month or 36 hours per quarter in order to maintain proficiency in an auxiliary member's functional area. They would make up approximately 80% of the members of the BPA. Tier two auxiliary members would be the elite members of the BPA making up the remainder of the force. They would be fully trained at the Border Patrol Academy to perform side-by-side with Border Patrol agents in all aspects of border security operations. In order to maintain good standing in the force, a minimum of 16 hours per month or 48 hours per quarter would be required. In addition, the members would have to complete the same annual training as regular full-time Border Patrol agents (Hall et al. 2007). The two-tier BPA proposal parallels to some extent the two-level MPD Reserve Corps program requirements.

With regard to finding sufficient volunteers for the new BPA, the proposers pointed out that other federal agencies such as the Coast Guard Auxiliary have found them and that the BPA should have the same appeal, namely, "patriotic duty and local community impact—with little geographic overlap to create competition between them" (Hall et al. 2007, 29). However, they also indicate that recruiting tier two members would be difficult because the ideal candidates would be those persons who already possessed a law enforcement or military service background. Criminal justice college graduates would also fall into this preferred category. In addition, finding qualified tier two volunteers for service in rural areas would also be a problem. In order to address this recruitment problem, the BPA proposal would be stronger if it followed the design of the Metropolitan PD Reserve Corps, which provides specific criteria for transitioning from a Level II to a Level I Reserve Officer.

In support of their BPA proposal, Hall and his associates (2007, 44) argue that "securing the border is the first step to controlling the influx of criminal activity and illegal immigration into the United States. By creating the U.S. BPA, the Border Patrol can increase the number of qualified agents on the border, which is a proven deterrent to illegal immigrants and criminals along the border while increasing their capability and capacity across the entire spectrum of operations. All of this can be accomplished at a fraction of the cost by using volunteers. It will also expand citizen involvement in a critical area of national security. Together the nation can once again overcome a direct threat to our national security through the cooperation of governance and the people."

The Commonwealth of Puerto Rico Auxiliary Police

The Puerto Rico Police Department (PRPD) is responsible for policing and carrying out essential public safety functions for the Commonwealth of Puerto Rico. The PRPD is the second-largest police department in the United States, second only to the New York City Police Department. The PRPD has over 17,000 police officers who serve the island's approximately 3.7 million residents (ACLU 2012, 2).

The Puerto Rico Police traces its history back to 1837, when the *La Guardia Civil de Puerto Rico* (Puerto Rico Civil Guard) was created to protect the lives and property of Puerto Ricans, who at the time were Spanish subjects. It provided police services to the entire island, although many municipalities maintained their own police force. Since taking possession of Puerto Rico in July 1898, as a result of the Spanish-American War, the United States has controlled the island as a U.S. Territory. In 1996, a substantial revision of the police organization took place by virtue of the Puerto Rico Police Act of 1996. This act included various provisions about an auxiliary police organization and indicated the following definition for an auxiliary police officer: "a volunteer citizen accredited by the police as such, subject to the norms established by the Superintendent. Through their services, they shall assist in the fight against crime and towards the welfare of the citizens. They shall receive no financial compensation whatsoever for their services" (Puerto Rico Police Act of 1996, 2012, 5).

Members of the auxiliary force have the same uniforms as regular members of the Puerto Rico Police. All pins, identification, and uniform accessories are also the same. Qualifications for membership include being an American citizen and resident of Puerto Rico The auxiliaries may render crime prevention services on routine patrol, in schools, parks, malls, urban train stations, and at other locations. They may also be assigned to provide support services at the offices of police superintendents, area command centers, districts, precincts, police detachments, and mini police stations. Auxiliary Police officers who have been trained in the proper use and safe handling of firearms and have complied with the provisions of law are authorized to use their firearms in the performance of their duties (Puerto Rico Police Act of 1996, 2012, 33–35).

U.S. Virgin Islands Police Auxiliary Service

The U.S. Virgin Islands are located in the eastern Caribbean, approximately 1,100 miles southeast of Miami, Florida. They are 40 to 50 miles east of Puerto Rico. During the seventeenth century, the archipelago was divided into two territorial units, one English and the other Danish. Sugarcane, produced by slave labor, drove the islands' economy during the eighteenth and early nineteenth centuries. In 1917, during World War I, the United States purchased the Danish portion for $25 million, which had been in economic decline since the abolition of slavery in 1848. The United States was concerned that Germany would capture Denmark, and Denmark was afraid that the United States would simply take them if that happened. Today tourism contributes majorly to the Islands' economy; many of the tourists visit on cruise ships.

During World War I, Congress passed the National Defense Act of 1916, which required the use of the term "National Guard" for the then existing state militias and further regulated them. Congress also authorized the states to maintain Home Guards, which were reserve forces separate from the National Guards. The Secretary of War was authorized to furnish these units with rifles, ammunition, and supplies (see Vol. 40, U.S. Statutes at Large 1917, 181). In 1940, with the onset of World War II, and as a result of its federalizing the National Guard, Congress amended the National Defense Act of 1916, and authorized the states to maintain "military forces other than National Guard" (see Vol. 54, U.S. Statutes at Large 1940, 1206). This law authorized the War Department to train and arm the new military forces that would come to be known as State Guards. Many states and U.S. Territories took advantage of this law and maintained distinctive local military forces throughout the war. Congress granted U.S. citizenship to Virgin Islanders in 1927. The governor was elected by popular vote for the first time in 1970; previously he had been appointed by the U.S. president. Residents of the islands substantially enjoy the same rights as those enjoyed by mainlanders, but they may not vote in presidential elections (U.S. Virgin Islands, 2014).

As a result of the Revised Organic Act of 1954, the governor of the Virgin Islands was required to reorganize and consolidate various island governmental agencies into the executive branch. Consequently, in 1955, island police agencies were merged to form a Department of Public Safety, as an executive department. Previously, the Organic Act of 1936 had divided the U.S. Virgin Islands into two municipalities, namely the Municipality of Saint Croix and the Municipality of Saint Thomas and Saint John. Each municipality had its own law enforcement agency known as the "Police and Prison Department." The new territory-wide Department of Public Safety included both a Police Division and a Fire Division. In addition to enforcing the laws relating to public safety, the Police Division supervised a Civilian Defense Program and the activities of the Home Guard. In 1967, Civil Defense was transferred from the

Department of Public Safety to the Office of the Governor and is presently under the Office of the Adjutant General of the Virgin Islands National Guard, having been renamed the Virgin Islands Territorial Emergency Management Agency (VITEMA). In the late 1970s, responsibilities for fire prevention and control were transferred to the Office of the Governor. In 1985, as a result of these changes and other duties being removed to other executive agencies, the Department of Public Safety was renamed the U.S. Virgin Islands Police Department (VIPD). Several years earlier, the Home Guards had been renamed the Virgin Islands Police Auxiliary (Lewis 2014).

Upon acceptance into the U.S. Virgin Islands Police Department Auxiliary Program, members are required to complete a police training academy for certification (VIPD 2014a). In May 2010, ten new volunteer police recruits completed the 22-week course alongside regular police recruits (Shea 2010). Police auxiliary members must work a minimum of 24 per month, unless otherwise ordered by the Police Commissioner. The members of the police auxiliary help with civic activities and a wide range of other duties, including partnering with a patrol officer to delivering a speech at a Neighborhood Watch meeting. The members of the volunteer police in the U.S. Virgin Island can achieve various ranks from auxiliary police corporal to captain. In times of natural disaster or other emergency, auxiliary police have been called upon to serve their communities under difficult circumstances (VIPD 2014a). During the passing of Hurricane Omar in October 2008, auxiliary officers helped to maintain public safety; protected life and property; assisted with emergency evacuation and provided security at designated shelters (VIPD 2014b).

The VIPD also sponsors a police cadet program that prepares young men and women for careers in police work and in partnership with the University of the Virgin Islands provides police cadets full scholarships if they are pursuing a degree in Criminal Justice. "Cadets work alongside police officers and during official police activities, such as funerals, police week activities or other similar programs" (VIPD 2014c).

Guam Police Department Civilian Volunteer Police Reserve

Guam, lying about 6,000 miles west of San Francisco, is an organized, unincorporated territory of the United States located in the western Pacific Ocean. After the Spanish-American War of 1898, Spain ceded Guam to the United States. It is one of five U.S. territories with an established civilian government. Guam is the southernmost and largest tropical island in the Mariana island chain and is also the largest island in Micronesia. By plane, Guam is approximately 3 hours flying distance to several major Asian cities, including Manila, Hong Kong, Tokyo, Seoul, Taipei, and Sydney.

Guam was probably explored by the Portuguese navigator Ferdinand Magellan (sailing for Spain) in 1521. The island was formally claimed by

Spain in 1565, and its people were forced into submission and conversion to Roman Catholicism beginning in 1668. For two years during World War II, the Japanese military occupied Guam until it was retaken by force in 1944. The people of Guam have been U.S. citizens since 1950. Since 1973, Guam has been represented in the U.S. Congress by a nonvoting delegate, but they do not participate in presidential elections. The people of the U.S. Virgin Islands also have a nonvoting representative in Congress. The executive branch includes a popularly elected governor, who serves a four-year term. It is home today to a relatively large U.S. military presence (Guam 2014).

Similar to the history of policing in the U.S. Virgin Islands, in 1985, Guam's Department of Public Safety was separated into two departments—the Guam Police Department and the Guam Fire Department. In 1952, the Department of Public Safety was established to replace the U.S. Navy's control over the Guam Insular Guard, a local police force dating back to 1905 (Torre 2011). Currently, the Territory of Guam has two volunteer police programs associated with its police department: the Guam Police Department's Community Assisted Policing Effort (CAPE) and the Guam Police Department's Civilian Volunteer Police Reserve composed of over 100 persons. The police reserves have peace officer authority, but the volunteers of the CAPE program are not peace officers. Regulations require that CAPE volunteers acknowledge that their services do not constitute employment for purposes of the Worker's Compensation Act and that they are not entitled to benefits under the act.

The general functions and duties of the Civilian Volunteer Police Reserve (CVPR) are to provide backup manpower for the suppression of crime, preservation of law and order, fight and control fires, and to assist in civil emergencies (Guam CVPR 2014).

In March 2012, 22 men and 11 women became members of the Guam Police Department's CVPR unit after graduating from their training academy course. Several of the volunteer police reservists had previously participated as members of the CAPE program. At the graduation event, Eddie Baza Calvo, Guam's Governor, stated: "You are putting yourself in the line of fire every day" (Taitano 2012). Indeed, in 1979, Reserve Officers Helen Lizama and Rudy Iglesias were killed when they responded to a burglary alarm at a business. They were both shot by a getaway driver as they exited their patrol car (ODMP 2014). In December 2012, an additional 25 persons completed the reserve academy that involved eight months of training (Sablan 2012). In January 2014, 29 more individuals were sworn in and among the graduates were a mother and her two children. The ceremony was held at the Sheraton Laguna Guam Resort, and the three family members took their oath of office from Guam's Lt. Governor Ray Tenorio (Reilly 2014).

In 2010, the successful recruitment, selection, and training of Guam Police Department's CVPR unit served as a role model for the passage of a law to establish a Civilian Volunteer Airport Police Reserve program within the Airport Police. The statute indicated that the authority of such new organizational personnel shall include when rendering assistance to police or fire service officers "the same powers, duties, rights (including coverage under the Worker's Compensation Act), privileges and immunities as if they were paid, full-time members of the Airport, *except* that they *shall* earn recruitment credit for services performed as volunteers" (Title 12, Chapter 1, §1112.3, Guam Code Annotated). Recruiting and training for the new Civilian Volunteer Airport Police Reserve program began in 2012.

FEMA Reserves

For more than 200 years, disaster response and recovery efforts were left to a haphazard approach with a succession of federal agencies being given responsibilities. However, a series of damaging hurricanes and earthquakes in the 1960s and early 1970s prompted a more comprehensive approach to federal disaster assistance. In addition, new concerns about public safety arose due to the advent of nuclear power plants and the transportation of hazardous substances. Although such congressional legislations as the National Flood Insurance Act of 1986 and the Disaster Relief Act of 1974 were enacted, emergency and disaster activities were still fragmented.

Finally, in 1979, the numerous and separate disaster-related agencies and programs were merged into the FEMA by presidential executive order. Among the agencies transferred to FEMA was the Defense Department's Defense Civil Preparedness Agency. Thus, civil defense responsibilities were also shifted to FEMA. Today, FEMA (a division of the DHS) coordinates the federal government's role in preparing for, preventing, mitigating the effects of, responding to, and recovering from all domestic disasters, whether natural or man-made, including acts of terror. After the experience of Hurricane Katrina in August 2005—where a final death toll of 1,836 people has been reported, making it the third deadliest hurricane in U.S. history (FAQs, Hurricane Katrina 2013)—the Post-Katrina Emergency Reform Act of 2006 was adopted to provide improved levels of preparedness, response, and recovery by FEMA (FEMA History 2013). By comparison, according the U.S. Geological Survey, the 1906 San Francisco earthquake took more than 3,000 lives (Calvan 2005). However, "by one incontestable measure Katrina stands out among this nation's historic natural disasters. In dollars and cents Katrina was the worst. The toll is estimated at $200 billion" (Forgues-Roy 2013).

In April 2012, a major transformation of the FEMA disaster workforce was announced involving the establishment of the FEMA Reservist Program. The members of the existing disaster workforce were offered the opportunity to seek new appointments in the Reservist Program by applying for specific incident management positions within the new FEMA program.

The transformation was to be completed within a year. Most importantly, the announcement declared that the FEMA Reservist Program was a national asset and served as America's "primary resource" for disaster response and recovery, comprising up to 80% of field office positions. In addition, a wage analysis was to be conducted to align pay and pay grade distribution with the knowledge and skills associated with the duties for each of the incident management positions. Moreover, upon first deployment in a new position, mobile communication and computing equipment would be assigned and retained by the reservist for future use. Finally, a reservist ombudsman program was also announced with new positions at headquarters to advocate at a senior level on behalf of reservists (Change and Opportunity 2012).

Reservists play a very important role in meeting the needs of disaster survivors. The work of a reservist can be exhausting, frustrating, challenging, and rewarding. The hours can be long, and the conditions are sometimes difficult. In general, in order to become a FEMA Reservist, a person must want to assist others in a disaster or an emergency, be willing to commit to being professional, keep the public trust, follow all FEMA/DHS rules and regulations, and must abide by the conditions of employment. Specific qualifications include U.S. citizenship, passing a background investigation, being approved for a government-issued travel card, being able to leave home on short notice, being able to be away from home for 30 days or more, and being able to travel to any state or U.S. territory (Requirements 2013).

The desired skills for membership in the FEMA Reserves include being highly motivated, a self-starter, capable of working with little supervision, computer literate, able to prioritize tasks, customer service focused, good at working under physical and mental stress, and being able to work on an as-needed basis with a flexible work schedule (Reservist Applicants 2013).

Summary

When America was still a very young country, Alexis de Tocqueville traveled to learn about the nation's new prison system.[8] During the course of a nine-month visit, he expanded his research, and his findings are considered an invaluable narrative about the nature of American democracy. In order for such a system to thrive, he recommended an independent and influential judiciary, a strong executive branch, local self-government, administrative decentralization, religion, well-educated women, freedom of association, and freedom of the press. Moreover, he considered jury service to be an important civic obligation because it helps citizens think about other people's affairs and educates them in the use of their freedom (Alexis de Tocqueville 1835/1990).

Alexis de Tocqueville discovered an American democracy heavily reliant on the civic activities of its citizens. Volunteers are most often engaged in community work, but they can also perform important law enforcement–related functions at the federal level. In times of peril, when most needed, civil defense volunteers and reserve or auxiliary police have been available. In particular, the CGA and CAP organizations have had long and successful histories in the field of homeland security. At the municipal level, the Reserve Corps of the MPD in Washington, D.C., represents an outstanding example of how ordinary citizens may serve as a supplemental force permitting full-time officers to handle more calls for service and other duties. The police powers that the Reserve Corps possess distinguish it from all of the other organizations discussed in this chapter.

The proliferation of local, state, and federal law enforcement agencies in the United States can result in overlapping jurisdiction. At a crime or disaster scene affecting large numbers of people, multiple jurisdictions and several police agencies may be involved. Command in such situations remains a complex and sometimes contentious issue. For example, Farber and Cen (2006) notes that Hurricane Katrina may have exposed a weakness in the federal system. Because of our federalized system, FEMA and the DHS are not in complete control. As a result of this shared power arrangement, there is no single authority to effectively prepare, respond, mitigate, and aid in recovery from disasters. The history of civil defense and homeland security in the United States has been one of frequent policy and organizational change.

The CAP was officially founded in December 1941, one week before Pearl Harbor, by citizens involved in aviation and concerned about the defense of America's coastlines. It was first placed under the control of the Office of Civilian Defense. By April 1943, the organization was under the command of the Army Air Forces. Its members became known as the "Minutemen" of World War II, performing many missions involving coastal patrol searching for enemy submarines and saving hundreds of crash victims (CAP History 2002). In 1948, a federal law was passed incorporating CAP as an official auxiliary of the newly created U.S. Air Force.

Since 1939, the USCG Auxiliary has had a history as an all-volunteer organization assisting the Coast Guard in times of war and peace. It is a proven success story that can be used as a model for any federal or state agency. Although the Auxiliary does not conduct direct law enforcement activities, Auxiliary members can man communications consoles, conduct search and rescue and safety patrols, and can provide administrative support enabling the USCG active duty forces to spend more time on maritime security and national defense. One scholar has indicated that the U.S. Coast Guard currently lacks personnel and resources and cannot fill critical gaps in its safety and security missions without help from its volunteer arm, the CGA (Dooris 2008).

This chapter also included information about volunteer police in U.S. Territories and establishing a civilian auxiliary within the Border Patrol to be known as the "U.S. Border Patrol Auxiliary." It would recruit and train two types of volunteers. Tier one auxiliary members would perform support functions. These functions would keep members from direct contact with suspects and away from the dangers involved in field operations. Tier one auxiliary members would comprise approximately 80% of the BPA. The primary purpose of these members would be to relieve Border Patrol agents from support jobs allowing them to return to performing field operations along the border. Tier two auxiliary members would be the elite members of the BPA who would attend training at the Border Patrol Academy to gain the knowledge and skills required to perform alongside Border Patrol agents in every facet of the Border Patrol mission. These members would comprise the other 20% of the BPA. Their primary mission would be to increase the number of people performing security operations along the border under the direct supervision of members of the Border Patrol. This two-tier system resembles that used by the volunteer reserve police officers in Washington, D.C., with the important distinction that its unarmed Level II officers are still available for assignments in the field. The parallel BPA volunteer is restricted to inside or clerical duties.

The USPS is a nonprofit, educational organization dedicated to making boating safer and more enjoyable by teaching classes in seamanship, navigation, and related subjects. It celebrated its hundredth anniversary in 2014.

President Carter's 1979 executive order merged many of the federal government's disaster-related responsibilities into the FEMA. In 2012, a major transformation of the FEMA disaster workforce was announced involving the establishment of the FEMA Reservist Program. The members of the existing disaster workforce were offered the opportunity to seek new appointments in the part-time salaried Reservist Program by applying for specific incident management positions within the new FEMA program. In addition, on a temporary assignment and salaried basis, citizens can apply to become a FEMA Reservist. Interested citizens who are available and qualified would be selected and deployed based on the needs of the agency.

Several ideas raised in this chapter concerned the possibility of establishing a BPA, increasing the number of Coast Guard Auxiliarists, and adding a youth program in the CGA. All three recommendations could help stem the tide of illegal border crossings, and drug smuggling, as well the overall capacity of the United States to contend with natural disasters and homeland security.

Review Questions

1. Who was Alexis de Tocqueville, and what did he discover about the nature of American democracy in the mid-1830s?
2. Identify a charitable organization using either volunteermatch.org or idealist.org. Describe the purpose or mission of the organization.
3. Use Internet-based research tools to find at least one instance in the history of the U.S. Marshals Service that involved an effort to

balance concern for popular feelings with the needs of federal law enforcement. Discuss your findings.

4. Provide at least one example of how, prior to September 11, 2001, Congress sought to obtain the aid of local law enforcement on behalf of federal law enforcement matters.

5. The Real ID Act was enacted in 2005 at the recommendation of the 9/11 Commission to verify the authenticity of every driver's license applicant. (This statute can be accessed online at http://www.dhs. gov/xlibrary/assets/real-id-act-text.pdf.) Read the statute and list at least three of its specific provisions.

6. Implementation of the Real ID Act was delayed on several occasions. Use Internet-based research to learn the reasons for the delays in implementation. Discuss whether these delays were justified.

7. Discuss the nature and benefits of deputization agreements.

8. Distinguish between Level I and Level II members of the Metropolitan Police Reserve Corps.

9. When was the Civil Air Patrol (CAP) founded, and what role did it play during World War II?

10. Identify and describe one of the Coast Guard Auxiliary's most important contributions during World War II.

11. List at least four of the activities Coast Guard Auxiliarists have engaged in that are related to the law enforcement field.

12. During the first decade of the twenty-first century, there was a significant decline in the membership of the Coast Guard Auxiliary. Conduct online research to determine possible reasons for this decline.

13. Should there be a youth division program within the U.S. Coast Guard Auxiliary? Discuss.

14. Discuss the pros and cons for the establishment of a Border Patrol Auxiliary.

15. Identify at least three of the qualifications and three of the desired skills established for FEMA Reservists.

16. Search the Web to find a U.S. police department that is unarmed. Hint: It is a U.S. Territory. In addition, discuss the pros and cons for arming volunteer police who are directly involved in state or federal law enforcement.

Notes

1. There is some prideful disagreement regarding the origins of federal policing and its first agencies. Some historians point to the creation of the federal judiciary and its use of marshals, while others recall the creation of the early forerunner to the U.S. Coast Guard—the Revenue Marine. Perhaps the oldest may be the Postal Inspection Service because it can trace its origins back to 1772. In that year,

the position of "surveyor" was created. Since 1737, the colonial postal system had been supervised by Postmaster General Benjamin Franklin. Franklin created the position of "surveyor" because he could no longer single-handedly regulate and audit post offices. In 1801, the title of surveyor was changed to "special agent." In 2011, there were more than 1,400 postal inspectors, about 700 postal police officers, and approximately 600 related support personnel (About the Chief 2011).

2. The jurisdiction of the majority of federal police is narrow in scope. For example, Congress and the United States Supreme Court have different police forces. There are three separate law enforcement agencies that report to Congress— Capitol Police, Government Printing Office Police, and the Library of Congress Police. If the three congressional agencies were consolidated, there would only be one chief of police, one set of hiring and training standards and policies, integrated communications systems, and therefore a reduction of bureaucracy. Since 1970, the Federal Law Enforcement Training Center (FLETC), now a component of the DHS, has been serving as America's foremost law enforcement training organization. It performs training for 90 federal agencies—63 in the executive branch, three in the legislative branch, two in the judicial branch, and 22 others (About FLETC 2011).

3. Indeed, the history of the development of the nation's federal law enforcement system has been checkered with the passage of numerous federal crimes and the establishment of a wide variety of federal agencies. This has taken place in accordance with changing congressional perceptions of "the crisis of the moment." Today, there are more than 3,000 federal crimes on the books. Many crimes, no matter how local in nature, appear to be within the reach of federal criminal jurisdiction, and the number of crimes deemed "federal" continues to increase. U.S. Postal Inspectors enforce more than 200 of these federal statutes. Their jurisdiction includes the investigation of crimes that may adversely affect U.S. mail, the postal system, or postal employees. For example, the protection of post office employees is an essential function of their responsibilities. Inspectors promptly investigate assaults and threats that occur while postal employees are performing official duties or as a result of their employment. In addition, postal inspectors invest significant resources into the investigation of mail theft by criminals.

4. For an excellent discussion of the U.S. national response system see: Davis, Lynn E., Jill Rough, Gary Cecchine, Agnes Gereben Schaefer, Laurinda L. Zeman (2007). *Hurricane Katrina Lessons for Army Planning and Operations*. Rand Corporation. Santa Monica, CA. See also the 36-page report entitled: *Civil Defense and Homeland Security: A Short History of National Preparedness Efforts* (2006, September), prepared by Department of Homeland Security: National Preparedness Task Force.

5. In general, the need for cross-deputization may have first arisen due to the overlapping jurisdictions associated with police work on Indian reservations and other tribal lands. For example, "Depending on the nature and location of the crime, and whether the offender of the victim were Indian or non-Indian, police officers of states, cities, and counties, tribes, the BIA or the FBI may be called upon when a crime occurs" (Barker and Mullen 1993, 157). The issue is made more complex due to the fact that 16 states have assumed jurisdiction for general law enforcement on various Indian reservations under the framework set forth in Public Law 280. In 1953, with the passage of Public Law 280,

"Congress transferred criminal jurisdiction in Indian country to six states. This federal law granted so-called mandatory states all criminal and civil jurisdiction over Indian land within their borders. The states affected by the legislation included California, Minnesota (except for the Red Lake Reservation), Nebraska, Oregon (excluding the Warm Springs Reservation), Wisconsin, and Alaska after it gained statehood (except for the Annette Islands Metlakatla Indians). This law effectively terminated all tribal criminal jurisdictions in the affected tribal area within these states. Public Law 280 also provides that any state (so-called optional states) wishing to assume jurisdiction over tribes within their borders may do so by state law or by amending the state constitution. Following passage of Public Law 280, 10 states chose to do so. In 1968, an amendment to Public Law 280 was passed requiring tribal consent before additional states could extend jurisdiction. Since 1968, no tribe has consented. In response to the skyrocketing crime rate and confusion with respect to jurisdiction in Indian country, Congress passed the Tribal Law and Order Act of 2010 (TLOA). It states that in cases of no referrals or declinations of criminal investigations in Indian country, "'Any federal department or agency shall coordinate' with their tribal counterparts. This requirement extends to the FBI; U.S. Attorneys Offices; Drug Enforcement Agency (DEA); Bureau of Alcohol, Tobacco, Firearms, and Explosives (ATF); and others conducting investigations in tribal land" (for more details, see Bulzomi 2012).

6. The Coast Guard is an amalgamation of five formerly distinct federal services. A useful timeline that considers the establishment of those services and when they became part of what is now the U.S. Coast Guard, as well as changes in the organizational structure of the Coast Guard itself, can be found at: http://www.uscg.mil/history/faqs/when.asp.

7. The content and discussion presented here regarding the BPA are entirely based on Christopher Hall, Gregg Schauerman, Robert Ewing, and Brian Brandner, *Securing the Borders: Creation of the Border Patrol Auxiliary*, National Security Program, Kennedy School of Government, Harvard University, May 5, 2007.

8. The focus of this book is on volunteer police work, but many additional opportunities exist throughout America for contributing to public safety, especially in the fields of prisoner rehabilitation and reentry work. The services and programs offered by the Federal Bureau of Prisons, as well as state and county correctional facilities, are routinely supplemented by citizen volunteers. Many volunteers currently work within prisons as tutors, recreational aides, chaplains, and vocational instructors. Interested individuals need only to contact their closest facility to learn about volunteer positions. For more information about volunteering within the federal prison system, visit: http://www.bop.gov/jobs/volunteer.jsp.

References

About FLETC. (2011). Retrieved August 17, 2011 from http://www.fletc.gov/about-fletc

About MPDC. (2013). Retrieved October 17, 2013 from http://mpdc.dc.gov/page/about-mpdc

About the Chief. (2011). About the chief postal inspector. Retrieved August 20, 2011 from https://postalinspectors.uspis.gov/aboutus/Chief.aspx

About the MPD. (2013). About the MPD Reserve Corps. Retrieved October 17, 2013 from http://mpdc.dc.gov/page/about-mpd-reserve-corps

About USPS. (2013). U.S. Power Squadrons. Retrieved October 16, 2013 from http://www.usps.org/newpublic2/about.html

ACLU (2012). Island of impunity: Puerto Rico's outlaw police force. Retrieved June 27, 2014 from http://www.aclu.org/files/assets/islandofimpunity_executivesummary_english_0.pdf

Barker, M. L. and Mullen, K. (1993). Cross-deputization in Indian country. *Police Studies: The International Review of Police Development, 16*, 157–166.

Bertelsen Jr., V. C. (2001). Thanks from the commandant. U.S. Coast Guard Auxiliary National Bridge Page. Retrieved January 1, 2002 from http://www.cgaux.org/cgauxweb/tbbridge.shtml

Blickensdorf, J. (2014). MPDC Auxiliary Police. Retrieved March 2, 2014 from http://www.dcmetropolicecollector.com/MPD-Reserve-Force.html

Bulzomi, M. J. (2012). Indian Country and the Tribal Law and Order Act of 2010. *FBI Law Enforcement Bulletin*. Retrieved October 15, 2013 from http://www.fbi.gov/stats-services/publications/law-enforcement-bulletin/may-2012/indian-country-and-the-tribal-law-and-order-act-of-2010

Burnham, F. A. (1974). *Hero next door*. Fallbrook, CA: Areo Publishers.

Calhoun, F. S. (1991). *The lawmen: United States marshals and their deputies: 1789–1989*. Penguin Books.

Calvan, B. C. (2005, February 27). San Francisco revises death toll for 1906 earthquake: Tally could exceed 3,400. Retrieved October 19, 2013 from http://www.boston.com/news/nation/articles/2005/02/27/san_francisco_revises_death_toll_for_1906_earthquake/?page = full

CAP History. (2002). Retrieved February 3, 2002 from http://www.capnhq.gov/nhq/pa/50-2/history.html

CAP News. (2001, September). Retrieved January 8, 2002 from http://www.capnhq.gov/nhq/capnews/01-09/news.htm

CAP Organization (2002). CAP organization. Retrieved January 8, 2002 from http://www.capnhq.gov/nhq/pa/50-2/organization.html

CAP Support to LEA. (2002). Retrieved January 8, 2002 from http://www.capnhq.gov/nhq/do/cd/leaspt.htm

Change and Opportunity. (2012). Change and opportunity in our disaster workforce. Memo to all FEMA employees from Richard Serino, Deputy Administrator, April 17, 2012. Retrieved October 9, 2013 from http://www.fema.gov/pdf/about/memo_change_opportunity_disaster_workforce_041712.pdf

Civilian Enforcers. (2013). History: Civilian enforcers. Retrieved October 14, 2013 from http://www.usmarshals.gov/history/civilian_enforcers.htm

Dooris, M. D. (2008, December). *Enhancing recruitment and retention of volunteers in the U.S. Coast Guard Auxiliary*. Master's thesis, Naval Postgraduate School, Monterey, CA.

FAQs, Hurricane Katrina. (2013). Retrieved October 19, 2013 from http://www.hurricanekatrinarelief.com/faqs.html

Farber, D. A. and Cen, J. (2006). *Disasters and the law*. New York: Aspen Publishers.

FEMA History. (2013). Retrieved October 9, 2013 from http://www.fema.gov/about-agency

Forgues-Roy, N. (2013). Was Katrina the biggest, the worst natural disaster in U.S. history? Retrieved October 19, 2013 from http://hnn.us/article/17193

General Order. (2006). General order 101.3: Organization, authority, and rules of the Metropolitan Police Department Reserve Corps, effective March 28, 2006. Retrieved October 17, 2013 from https://go.mpdconline.com/GO/GO_101_03.pdf

Gilmore, G. J. (2001, November 1). Coast guard on guard, to meet terrorism threat. *U.S. Department of Defense, American Forces Information Service.* Retrieved January 1, 2002 from http://www.defenselink.mil/news/Nov2001/n11012001_200111011.html

Guam. (2014). Territory of Guam. Retrieved July 1, 2014 from http://www.infoplease.com/country/guam.html

Guam CVPR. (2014). Civilian volunteer police reserve. Retrieved June 30, 2014 from http://www.guamcourts.org/compileroflaws/GCA/10gca/10gc066.PDF

Hall, C., Schauerman, G., Ewing, R. and Brandner, B. (2007, May 5). *Securing the borders: Creation of the Border Patrol Auxiliary.* National Security Program, Kennedy School of Government, Harvard University. Retrieved October 10, 2013 from http://www.dtic.mil/dtic/tr/fulltext/u2/a476945.pdf

History. (2013). U.S. Marshals Service. Retrieved October 14, 2013 from http://www.usmarshals.gov/history/index.html

Kadlec, D. (2013, September 19). Giving back: How retiring boomers get the rush they crave. Retrieved October 18, 2013 from http://business.time.com/2013/09/19/giving-back-how-retiring-boomers-get-the-rush-they-crave/

Kastberg, S. (1998, August 2). Watching the water. *The Times Union* (A Special Promotional Supplement), Albany, NY, p. 8.

Lewis. E. (2014). History. Retrieved June 30, 2014 from http://www.vipd.gov.vi/About_Us/History.aspx

Morse, J. (2009, May 19). Police Reserve Corps in Washington attracts a wide variety of talent. Retrieved October 17, 2013 from http://newsblaze.com/story/20090519081527tsop.nb/topstory.html

ODMP. (2014). ODMP remembers. Retrieved June 30, 2014 from http://www.odmp.org/officer/8190-reserve-officer-helen-kuulei-lizama#ixzz368UsHHsz

Olin, C. (2001, December 20). An approximate synopsis of multi-mission and overall volunteer effort as of 12/7/02. *U.S. Coast Guard Auxiliary National Bridge Page.* Retrieved January 1, 2002 from http://www.cgaux.org/cgauxweb/memtable.shtml

Operation Golden Eagle. (2002, January 4). Operation golden eagle tops 150,000 hours. Retrieved January 7, 2002 from http://www.cgaux.org/cgauxweb/memtable.shtml

Peconic Bay PS. (2013). Education – public courses. Retrieved October 16, 2013 from http://www.pbps.us/education/public/abc3.html

Puerto Rico Police Act of 1996. (2012). Puerto Rico Police Act of 1996 as amended; rev. May 9, 2012. Retrieved June 27, 2014 from http://www2.pr.gov/presupuestos/Budget_2012_2013/Aprobado2013Ingles/suppdocs/baselegal_ingles/040/040.pdf

Reilly, G. T. (2014, January 27). 29 police reserve officers graduate, total grows to 100. Retrieved June 30, 2014 from http://mvguam.com/local/news/33314-29-police-reserve-officers-graduate-total-grows-to-100.html

Requirements. (2013). Requirements to become a reservist. Retrieved October 17, 2013 from https://faq.fema.gov/app/answers/detail/a_id/1016/related/1

Reservist Applicants. (2013). Reservist applicants' desired skills. Retrieved October 17, 2013 from https://faq.fema.gov/app/answers/detail/a_id/1020/session/L3Rpb WUvMTM4MjA1MTYyNi9zaWQvQnhBYk0yRGw%3D

Sablan, J. (2012, December 31). 25 police reservists sworn in. Retrieved June 30, 2014 from http://www.guampdn.com/article/20121231/NEWS01/212310301/ 25-police-reservists-sworn-in

Shea, D. (2010, May 15). 32 new officers finish police academy. Retrieved June 30, 2014 from http://virginislandsdailynews.com/news/32-new-officers-finish-police-academy-1.790578

Sims, B. (2007). 'The day after the hurricane': Infrastructure, order, and the New Orleans Police Department's response to Hurricane Katrina. *Social Studies of Science, 37*(1), 111–118.

Taitano, Z. (2012, March 23). GPD swears in civilian volunteer police reservists. Retrieved June 30, 2014 from http://www.mvguam.com/local/news/22826-gpd-swears-in-civilian-volunteer-police-reservists.html

Tilley, J. (2003). *History of the U.S. Coast Guard Auxiliary*. Retrieved July 1, 2003 from http://www.cgaux.org/cgauxweb/news/auxhist.html

Tocqueville, A. D. (1835–1990). *Democracy in America: Volume I*. New York: Vintage Books.

Torre, M. (2011, October 28). A citizen-centric report for Guam Police Department. Retrieved June 30, 2014 from http://www.guamopa.org/docs/2010/official-citizen-centric-report/Guam%20Police%20Department%20(GPD)%20FY%20 2008-2010%20CCR.pdf

Uchida, C. D. (2004, December). The development of the American Police: An historical overview. Retrieved August 16, 2011 from http://www.globalcitizen.net/ Data/Pages/1418/Papers/2009042815114290.pdf

U.S. Virgin Islands. (2014). United States Virgin Islands. Retrieved July 1, 2014 from http://www.infoplease.com/country/us-virgin-islands.html

Vass, J. E. (2011, March 24). Youth policy. Retrieved October 17, 2003 from http:// bdept.cgaux.org/wp/wp-content/uploads/2012/11/Youth_Training_Letter.pdf

VIPD. (2014a). Police auxiliary service. Retrieved June 30, 2014 from http://www. vipd.gov.vi/Employment/Police_Auxiliary_Service.aspx

VIPD. (2014b). Police commissioner activates law enforcement personnel. Retrieved June 30, 2014 from http://www.vipd.gov.vi/Public_Interest/Press_Releases/ show_press_release_xml.aspx?id=2008-235&month=10

VIPD. (2014c). Connecting with youth. Retrieved June 30, 2014 from http://www. vipd.gov.vi/Libraries/PDF_Library/VIPD_Informant_Newsletter_v2_1_2012-2013.sflb.ashx

Williams, C. (2010, March 2). D.C. police call on reserves to boost community presence. Retrieved October 17, 2013 from http://voices.washingtonpost.com/ crime-scene/clarence-williams/dc-police-calling-on-their-res.html

Special Issues in Volunteer Policing

II

Non-Sworn Roles of Adults in Volunteer Policing

7

Congratulations graduates, I commend each of you for taking the time away from your schedules and families to participate in the Citizen Police Academy and for becoming a vital part of the police department!
—**Chief John M. Young Jr.**
Kerrville (Texas) PD, The 7th CPA Graduation, October 21, 2010

Introduction

During America's colonial period, there was a general understanding about significant values and norms because communities were small and composed of close-knit families. Most individuals adhered to the local rules of social order because snooping neighbors and members of the local church and clergy were ever-watchful for any deviance from societal customs. For the few who transgressed and were discovered, various shaming rituals were used to encourage conformity to societal rules (Walker 1998). Moreover, newly arrived families to New England were headed by men whose authority was reinforced by the divinely ordained hierarchy in which they believed (Norton 1996, 13). This earlier form of "morality policing" has given way to today's more formal and complicated system of social controls involving an array of institutions beyond the family, clergy, and curious neighbors. The most visible of these newer social institutions consist of the components of the criminal justice system, especially the uniformed members of local police agencies and the nearly 50,000 security officers employed by the federal Transportation Security Administration (TSA). The TSA workforce was recruited to help protect America's transportation infrastructure from terrorist attacks and to ensure freedom of movement for people and commerce (TSA 2014).

In September 2011, Eric Anderson, assistant city attorney for the city of Scottsdale, Arizona, appeared before his city's Parks and Recreation Commission. He was asked to comment on the fact that budget cuts had eliminated a police patrol unit that had been assigned to cover skate parks. He replied that the city's "legal responsibilities for a skate park are the same as they are for the regular parks; generally, the City is not a guarantor of safety just like having a Police Department is not a guarantor of no crime" (City of Scottsdale 2011). Due to America's falling tax revenues arising from a declining economy, it is likely that this same scenario has taken place in many communities. According to the U.S. Department of Justice, "Police agencies are some of the hardest hit by the current economic climate. Curtailing revenues nationwide have forced local governments to make cuts in spending across the board, which includes public safety operating budgets. While budget cuts threaten the jobs of law enforcement officers, the duties and responsibilities to ensure public safety remain" (Economic Downturn 2011, 3). The Major Cities Chiefs Association found that 52% of agencies surveyed had furloughed sworn officers (McFarland 2010). Agencies have used a number of techniques to reduce their personnel costs. Layoffs, mandatory furloughs, and loss of positions through attrition have taken place as the result of these budget reductions in many police agencies. Therefore, it is not surprising that the need for alternative resources is on the agenda of many governmental agencies.

More and more agencies are turning to technology to offset the lack of human resources. For example, certain technologies such as closed-circuit televisions (CCTVs) and light-based intervention systems (LBIS) can act as force multipliers through incident intervention and crime prevention, without requiring the immediate presence of an officer (Cordero 2011). Moreover, other technological breakthroughs are being used to increase officer effectiveness and efficiency such as reducing police response times to emergency calls. For example, the tactical automatic vehicle locator (TAC-AVL) indicates to police supervisors the locations of patrol cars with a real-time map of the city, allowing them to determine whether the vehicles are in the right place at the right time. TAC-AVL enables a supervisor to see the type of call to which an officer is responding, how long the officer has been on the call, the result of the call, and whether nearby zones are understaffed (Mayer 2009).

In addition to using new technology, alternative human resources are also being used by more and more police agencies. In many agencies, responsibilities that were once performed by sworn staff have been shifted to civilian personnel, and some agencies have even engaged citizen volunteers to help alleviate the strain on police workloads. Such approaches can provide sworn staff with more time to focus on pressing and time-sensitive issues that can only be successfully managed by a law enforcement officer. Chapter 2 provides additional information concerning civilianization in police agencies.

Furthermore, in order to fulfill their public safety mission, hundreds of police agencies in the United States have turned to the general public for help. Volunteers in Police Service (VIPS) is now a major program within the International Association of Chiefs of Police (IACP). It has become a common practice among many of the nation's law enforcement agencies to have civilians volunteering their time in a variety of roles inside and outside of station houses. A list of non-sworn roles involving public safety is presented in Box 7.1. Volunteers can be recruited for each of these positions.

> **BOX 7.1 TYPICAL CIVILIAN/NON-SWORN**
> **LAW ENFORCEMENT POSITIONS**
>
> Civilian Investigators
> Correctional Staff
> Crime Analysts
> Crime Prevention/Community Outreach
> Dispatchers/Call Takers
> Equipment/Fleet Management
> Forensic Technicians
> Information Technology Specialists
> Intelligence Analysts
> Planners/Researchers
> Property/Evidence Management
> Public Information Officers
> Records Management
> Victim Services Providers/Advocates
>
> *Source:* http://discoverpolicing.org/whats_like/?fa=civilian_alternatives

Due to ongoing technological advances in crime-fighting equipment such as in-car mobile data terminals (MDTs), computerized mapping, digital video, and wireless communication, there is a high demand for qualified information technology (IT) professionals and volunteers in police agencies.

This chapter describes a few of the non-sworn or non-peace officer roles that are currently being performed by volunteers. In addition, a brief review of a variety of adult Citizens' Police Academy (CPA) programs is presented as well as their advantages and disadvantages. Finally, a new role is described for existing members of volunteer police units as "neighborhood police academy" instructors.

Volunteers in Police Service

One of the hundreds of programs registered at the older IACP's VIPS program Web site is administered by the Pasadena (California) Police Department (PD). Pasadena is located 10 miles northeast of downtown Los Angeles. It is a richly diverse community. About 56% of Pasadena's approximately 140,000 residents are white, 33% are Latino, 13.4% are African American, and 12.7% are Asian. The word Pasadena literally means "valley" in the Ojibwa (Chippewa) Indian language (Pasadena Facts 2014). In addition to the deployment of reserve police officers (sworn positions), the Pasadena PD has recruited citizen volunteers since 1984. The use of volunteers is viewed as an integral part of the department's efforts to use the community policing model. The Pasadena PD has attempted to integrate volunteers into the Department's overall operations. A "Volunteer Services" office coordinates the various opportunities for service with the Department (Pasadena PD 2013).

The Pasadena PD volunteers contribute their time and efforts through the following areas of service: chaplains, Citizens Assisting Pasadena Police (CAPP) patrol, equestrians, Community Response to Eradicate and Deter Identity Theft (CREDIT), Missing Persons Unit (MPU), Pawn Detail, Criminal Investigations Division's Victim Assistance, Records and Traffic sections, general volunteers, and Youth Accountability Board (YAB). The agency also sponsors a Law Enforcement Explorer unit, which includes a 22-week Explorer Academy (Pasadena PD 2013).

In 2013, the Pasadena PD had approximately 200 active volunteers. Their responsibilities included patrolling streets and parklands; providing pastoral care for officers, staff, and related family; leading volunteer programs; assisting in the investigation of identity theft and missing persons; assisting with security for the annual Tournament of Roses Parade; participating in Police Activities League (PAL) programs; providing clerical assistance; providing guidance and support to first-time juvenile offenders; and working side-by-side with sworn and non-sworn staff whenever and however needed (Pasadena PD 2013). Today, about one million people come to Pasadena to watch the Tournament of Roses. The parade was first held in 1890 (Pasadena Facts 2014).

Volunteers are integrated into most areas of Pasadena's police operations. When volunteers have completed the application process and been accepted, they can immediately begin to participate in the general volunteer program as jobs become available. Other programs may have additional training and requirements for their participants. Police volunteers may serve in more than one program upon meeting the specific criteria for the additional program.

The following brief sections describe the various volunteer areas and activities involving non-sworn Pasadena police volunteers. The information is presented to illustrate the wide range of services that volunteers can provide without the requirement of attending a lengthy and costly law enforcement training academy program.

Volunteer Services Steering Committee

The Volunteer Services Steering Committee provides leadership in developing the department's volunteer programs and in coordinating the participants in each program. Committee members help to prepare an operations manual, volunteer handbook, and additional protocols and policies to enhance the delivery of volunteer services (Pasadena PD 2013).

Chaplain Corp

The chaplains group is made up of ordained clergy from established and recognized faiths within the community. The chaplains serve in situations that involve death, serious injuries, suicide, and domestic violence. The chaplains console family members and offer guidance and support while leaving the officer available to focus on the police investigation. The chaplains are on a prearranged "on call" schedule and are required to respond to emergency situations upon request (Pasadena PD 2013).

Citizens Assisting Pasadena Police

CAPP members are extra "eyes and ears" for the department. CAPP members drive designated white volunteer cars, wear department-approved uniforms, and must be able to communicate using a radio. Some of their duties are crime prevention, patrol, assisting at driving under the influence of drug (DUI) checkpoints; traffic control for requested incidents; 24-hour call out for emergencies; park safety; radar, stop sign, and red light surveys; quality of life issues; residential vacation checks; graffiti reporting; Safe Shopping Detail and Parade Watch during the holiday season; and many other activities. CAPP members are required to complete eight hours of service a month and to participate in their unit meetings and training (Pasadena PD 2013).

Safe Shopping Detail

The Safe Shopping Detail was established to patrol shopping areas from Thanksgiving to Christmas to reduce crime during the peak holiday season. Participants are given training, and then patrols are formed by having a general volunteer accompany a CAPP member on foot patrols of key shopping areas in Pasadena (Pasadena PD 2013).

Parade Watch

One of the department's most important activities is Parade Watch (which was established as a direct result of the terrorist attack of September 11, 2001) to enhance the overall safety of the annual Tournament of Roses Parade by using volunteers to contact all recreational vehicle owners staged along the parade route to solicit their assistance in reporting any suspicious activity or persons. Graduates of the department's CPA may sign up to participate in this annual event. Participants are given training and then go into the field in groups with active volunteers to contact all recreational vehicle drivers in the area surrounding the Rose Parade (Pasadena PD 2013).

Volunteer Equestrian (Mounted) Unit

The Equestrian Unit provides uniformed patrol and surveillance in the Arroyo Seco Recreation Area and in the foothills of Pasadena, providing high police visibility in an area largely secluded from public view. The unit reports violations and other circumstances that may be a threat to public safety. The Volunteer Mounted (Equestrian) Unit was originally formed to assist at the Rose Bowl in patrolling parking lots during the 1984 Olympics. It was formalized and adopted by the police department in 1985 when the department recognized the need for passive patrol in the remote hiking and riding trail areas not readily accessible by patrol units. Since then, Volunteer Mounted Unit members have donated thousands of hours creating a police presence and providing an important link between the department and the community that uses the parks. Requirements for participating in this volunteer activity include riding skills, access to a serviceably sound horse and tack (ownership not required), a background check, completion of the department's CPA, and certification in first aid/cardiopulmonary resuscitation (CPR). Volunteers are required to complete 12 hours of service a month and to participate in unit meetings and training. They must also be at least 21 years old and are required to satisfactorily complete 24 hours of patrol ride-along (Pasadena Mounted Unit 2013).

Missing Persons Unit

Volunteers in this unit assist the department's detectives by helping to conduct missing person's investigations (Pasadena PD 2013).

Community Response to Eradicate and Deter Identity Theft

In this program, volunteers assist victims of identity theft by conducting investigations in fraud, sending letters to various financial entities, contacting outside jurisdictions, and collecting evidence (Pasadena PD 2013).

General Volunteers

The general volunteers are individuals who desire to help the department in a variety of capacities but who prefer to work inside the department or for special events rather than going out on patrol. They are called on for clerical work, filing, staffing department and community events, participating in the Safe Shopping Detail and Parade Watch during the holiday season, participating in PAL activities, staffing the front desk, participating on disciplinary review boards (DRBs), and other activities (Pasadena PD 2013).

General volunteers may also assist with such special events as the Safe Shopping Detail over the Christmas holiday, car show, National Night Out, CPA classes, police awards luncheon, Take Your Child To Work Day, Truancy Programs, Park Watch, Traffic Rodeo, Helicopter Fly In, Neighborhood Watch events, crime prevention and service area meetings, and other special or community events. There are also opportunities to help with PAL activities and to participate on DRBs, oral boards, and promotion boards. By serving as members of these boards, citizens attend various hearings for the purpose of advising on matters concerning critical disciplinary and promotional decisions (City of Pasadena 2013).

Youth Accountability Board

YABs are made up of adult community volunteers that hear and resolve cases involving first-time offenders deemed most amenable to rehabilitative measures. The offenders volunteer to appear before the YAB and allow it to determine their "sentences," usually in the form of contracts for restitution and community service time. In exchange for successfully completing the program, the record of the offense is eliminated. If the youth fails to complete the commitment to the board, the case is referred back for normal processing through the juvenile court system. Once a volunteer is appointed to the YAB, he/she will receive training in basic legal concepts, juvenile justice issues, theories relating to youth accountability, and issues of confidentiality and liability. Boards are usually held during evening sessions, and various time commitments are required (Pasadena PD 2013).

Adult Police Academies

In the United States, the concept of the "Junior Police Academy" (see Chapter 8) might be considered to be the forerunner of the adult "Citizen Police Academy". However, several authors have attributed America's CPA initiatives to the efforts of the United Kingdom's Devon and Cornwall Constabulary when it created a "Police Night School" for the public in 1977. In the United States, the first adult CPA took place in 1985 when the Orlando (Florida) Police Department instituted such a program. In that same year, Missouri City, Texas, duplicated the effort. Subsequently, the practice has become a regular and featured program for educating citizens about police work throughout the nation (Ferguson 1985).

A CPA is an educational and informative program that allows citizens the opportunity to learn about the issues that face law enforcement efforts in their community. The program helps local residents better understand police work in their community, and it is also thought to promote stronger ties between communities and their respective police agencies. CPA programs do not train individuals to be reserve or auxiliary police officers, but they do produce better informed citizens. They may provide a forum in which community members and police officers are able to meet with one another to share mutual concerns. In such a setting, it is possible to forge stronger citizen–police relationships and to open new lines of communication. Information from citizens about crime problems and suspects is necessary in order to reduce crime.

Such citizen–police contacts and participation may expand community-based crime prevention efforts and offer police departments the opportunity to learn about the concerns of their communities (Breen and Johnson 2007; Brewster et al. 2005). However, it is more important for academy instructors to focus on crime prevention topics rather than public relations (Greenberg 1991).

Pasadena CPA

In Pasadena, the CPA is an informative, 12-week classroom series that gives an inside look at Pasadena police operations while discussing the principles of community policing. Its stated purpose is to promote a greater awareness and better understanding of local law enforcement's continuously changing role in the community. Accordingly, the class covers a wide variety of subject areas including police communications, criminal law and procedures (laws of arrest), street crime enforcement, investigations, field identification, weaponless defense training, youth programs, and more. The course concludes with a graduation dinner, where students receive a certificate of completion. Requirements for participation include: 18 years of age; live, work, or own property in Pasadena; no felony convictions; and no misdemeanor convictions within one year of application (Pasadena CPA 2013).

University of Kentucky CPA

The University of Kentucky's Police Department program is typical of many such programs. It is offered in seven or eight weekly three-hour classes, and participants take part in a formal graduation ceremony. There is no cost for participants (University of Kentucky PD 2012).

Buffalo Grove (Illinois) CPA

The village of Buffalo Grove (10 square miles, population 41,500) is located only 30 miles outside of downtown Chicago, in its northwest suburbs. O'Hare International Airport, one of the world's busiest, is a 25-minute drive from the village. Residents there have a median household income of $88,272 (Buffalo Grove 2012b). The Buffalo Grove Police Department began its CPA in 1997. For a period of eight weekly classes, the CPA covers the use of Radio Detection and Ranging (RADAR) and Light Detection and Ranging (LIDAR) units in speed enforcement, traffic crash investigation, crime scene processing, and crimes against property and person(s), and it provides an Emergency Dispatch Center tour, firearms safety, and so forth (Buffalo Grove 2012a). The Illinois Citizens Police Academy Association has published a quarterly newsletter since March 2007 (Web site at: http://www.illinoiscpaa.org/). The Web site has links for useful brochures, alumni association bylaws, class schedules, and application and waiver forms from local CPAs.[1]

Ponca City (Oklahoma) CPA

In Oklahoma, the city of Ponca City[2] holds an annual 13-week academy to acquaint participating citizens with all aspects of the work of its police department. Through an active alumni association, it offers CPA graduates opportunities to continue their interest and involvement in the department by volunteering in an "extra eyes" program. Such volunteers receive extra training and perform work that enables regular police officers to get back to the street more quickly, saving the taxpayers' money (City of Ponca City 2012).

Ponca City Police Foundation Trust

Many police departments have also involved citizens in the establishment of police foundations. Such foundations are independent fundraising nonprofit corporations. The Ponca City Police Foundation Trust was organized in 2000 to financially supplement and benefit the entire community and to help keep Ponca City safe and secure. The Ponca City Police Department was the first within the state of Oklahoma to have dedicated citizens develop a police foundation on the department's behalf. Following are a few of the foundation's goals that are typical of other police foundations: assist with special equipment needs that are outside the normal department budget; provide a financial death benefit to families of active members of the police department who pass away; provide scholarship opportunities for Ponca City police officers; provide scholarship opportunities for Ponca City youth interested in pursuing a career in law enforcement; support advanced law enforcement training opportunities; support police training for members of the community as well as paid members of the police department; support the CPA and related alumni events; and support the Youth Police Academy (City of Ponca City 2012).

Texas CPA Survey

In 1994, a survey was conducted to determine the number and nature of the citizen academies being conducted in Texas. The earliest academy implemented in Texas was in 1985. The survey indicated that, by the spring of 1994, more than 4,000 Texas citizens had attended such a program and that departmental classes were generally offered two times per year, with 27 students per class. The average academy met once each week for 11 weeks, three hours each session. The purpose, cited by 22 agencies, for conducting a program was the education of the citizens concerning the operations, policies, and procedures of the police department. Another often cited reason was the promotion of communication between the citizens and members of the police agency in an effort to improve relations. Other reasons included dispelling myths and preconceptions that the public may have concerning police work, enlisting the aid of the citizens in the prevention of crime, and promoting support of the police department and the city. Topics taught at the Texas CPAs ranged from traditional police activities such as accident investigation and crime scene investigation to newer, less traditional areas such as victim services, cults, gangs, and police stress and trauma counseling. Some agencies recommended that every police division or unit be discussed and reviewed (Blackwood 1994).

The Texas survey also gathered data about the amount spent annually by police agencies for conducting academies. This amount ranged from no departmental funds to $6,000. The agency that did not spend departmental money charged tuition. The average amount spent by agencies that did not include personnel costs was $1,600. The agencies that included personnel costs averaged $3,500 per year. These agencies reported that personnel costs consumed the largest portion of the program's budget. Several agencies used alternative sources of funding. These sources included alumni associations, citizen contributions, grants, and asset forfeitures (Blackwood 1994).

In addition, the Texas sample also revealed that police departments used a variety of methods to recruit and screen participants. The most popular method for recruitment was by word of mouth, including alumni.

Other methods for recruitment included announcements at community service clubs, neighborhood or city newsletters, flyers at the station or sub-stations, utility billing supplements, and speaking engagements by agency personnel. Requirements for attendance at the academies also varied. Some agencies allowed high school students to attend, while others had a minimum age of 21 years. A criminal history check was required by some of the agencies (Blackwood 1994). A major finding of this survey was that "all respond-ing agencies surveyed recommended that other agencies should implement a CPA, if they haven't already done so" (Blackwood 1994, 7).

Advantages of CPAs

In one study of the effects of a CPA on a large city in Texas, 25 graduates (experimental subjects) and 30 students entering the program (controls) were compared. Overall, compared to controls, the experimental group held more positive opinions of and demonstrated higher levels of satisfaction with the police department in all areas, including response to specific neighborhood problems, overall performance at combating and preventing crime, police image, and police services. The graduates also appeared to have a broader understanding of police work, as well as a greater appreciation and respect for officers. Furthermore, they reported significantly higher levels of involve-ment in crime prevention efforts than controls (Stone and Champeny 2001). Positive findings were also obtained in a study involving the attitudes of 48 attendees who completed a 12-week/36-hour program at a sheriff's depart-ment in the state of Michigan. Based on the analysis of pre- and post test responses, this study found that this particular CPA had a positive impact on the attendees' attitudes toward the police, and on their understanding of police operations, crime, and quality of life issues in their community (Breen and Johnson 2007). There were also positive outcomes in a study that com-pared attitudes using pre- and post tests involving citizen academies in two different cities (Brewster et al. 2005).

According to Aryani et al. (2000, 21), "Citizen police academies represent a vital part of community-oriented policing. CPAs keep the public involved by making them part of the police family ... [and] provide a productive out-let for the mutual sharing of information and concerns in order to further common goals of communities and law enforcement agencies." Generally, citizen academies offer at least two additional positive benefits: (1) citizens gain a better understanding of how their police department works and (2) graduates interested in continuing their involvement in police-related activities may have the option of joining various law enforcement-related volunteer programs such as the CPA Alumni Association, Citizens on Patrol, Community Emergency Response Team, Neighborhood Watch, and VIPS.

Interested citizens bring a wealth of knowledge about their community and, particularly, the problems in their neighborhoods. In this way, agency personnel are able to learn firsthand about the concerns of citizens. Some participants may want to take a more active role in helping to reduce crime by contributing a service or by serving as a volunteer. For example, a bank executive who participated in a CPA offered to include crime prevention messages in monthly statements mailed to depositors (Seelmeyer 1987).

Disadvantages of CPAs

Although citizen academies may have their advantages, they also have their disadvantages. For example, the programs may reach only a small number of residents. Research studies indicate that academies may be held only once or twice a year. Moreover, enrollment may be restricted to only 30 attendees at a time. In addition, the public relations aspects might be overplayed, reducing details about the ability of the criminal justice system to contend with crime and the need for private citizens to engage in array of crime prevention activities. At the same time, the planning for each academy, such as preparing the curriculum and screening applicants, might detract from the time and resources devoted to essential police work. In addition, local liability considerations may limit or eliminate high-interest activities, such as firearms instruction and ride-alongs. Although the expenditures needed to maintain a CPA are supposedly minimal, instruction may be costly if volunteer instructors are unavailable. Individual instruction may be needed for each student while on the firing range.

The Lansing (Michigan) Police Department held its first academy in the spring of 1996. Since then, they have held two CPA sessions each year. A Lansing police officer recruited the initial academy class from Neighborhood Watch coordinators, and the department has advertised subsequent classes in the local paper. Based on a review of the results of an in-house survey of Lansing's existing CPA, Bonello and Schafer (2002, P. 23) concluded: "Reaching out to citizens who are distrustful or skeptical of law enforcement and inviting them to take a closer look at police operations can prove intimidating and even unpleasant, but the rewards for doing so may be worth the effort. For agencies hoping to strengthen community alliances, the challenge for the future is to begin including a broader range of the public in their citizen police academy programs. Every department can identify groups within their community with which they have a history of misunderstandings and conflict. Departments should seek to draw academy participants from this portion of the community."

Police departments also need to maintain citizen interest when the academy ends. This is difficult unless follow-up activities are planned.

A few months after completing the academy, some participants may be disappointed if all they have to show for their efforts are a cap or T-shirt, a certificate, and memories. Departments need to develop meaningful activities after the academy has ended.

Academies could also turn into victims of their own success. Participants could become so overzealous in their concern for justice that they engage in conduct that undermines departmental policies and programs (e.g., establishing a vigilante-type neighborhood patrol organization). Another area of concern is the number of requests for crime prevention speakers and home and business security surveys that academy participation may generate. Although this is not a disadvantage per se, such requests could overburden officers by increasing their workload.

Although these disadvantages are quite real and there may always be some agency personnel who may be resistant to the idea of sharing information or enlisting the aid of citizens in the prevention of crime, the weight of the arguments appear to favor the use of citizen academies (Blackwood 1994; Breen and Johnson 2007; Brewster et al. 2005; Cohn 1996; Stone and Champeny 2001). The assistance of qualified volunteer police can help to eliminate several disadvantages of critical importance.

Overcoming the Disadvantages of CPAs

In the United States, the existence of hundreds of CPAs demonstrates a willingness on the part of local police departments to share information with the general public. However, the weight of the evidence shows that the reach of these classes is limited. The concepts shared during academy sessions, especially those involving crime prevention methods, need to be shared with larger segments of the population. CPAs have been held for over a quarter of a century; new delivery systems should be tried, especially in more populous metropolitan areas. The primary mode of instruction has been face to face. The computer age can extend the reach of useful personal safety information and the importance for citizen cooperation.

However, achieving the support and cooperation of diverse segments of a metropolitan population will require more than an annual course or two. Hybrid academy courses involving online instruction coupled with various hands-on experiences are a better approach to reach the masses. Police codes and critical "insider" information do not have to be shared to provide an effective program. Moreover, to save the expenses associated with the personnel costs of instruction, it would be appropriate for urban and suburban police departments to use their resources to train and certify classes of citizen volunteer police instructors who would then, in turn, become qualified to offer a series of continuous free "academy style" courses to the public.

This would allow all age groups, sooner or later, to learn a variety of self-help skills. Such classes could be delivered in the traditional face to face format as well as using the hybrid model.

Moreover, because graduates of the proposed certification program are expected to become future teachers of CPAs, concern about follow-up activities should be diminished. If a "train the trainer" course for volunteer police is substituted for the existing one or two annual citizen academies in urban areas, the overall purpose of the citizen academies may be multiplied. By offering this instructional training to existing members of volunteer police units, police departments will still be able to maintain close supervision over the content that will be delivered.

The qualified volunteer police instructors will be able to extend the reach of the existing academies in such a way that a new term, such as the "neighborhood police academy," may come into usage. This term emphasizes the importance of people working together for the betterment of the community and seems to be a more accurate designation for the new and broader type of program envisioned here.

By converting various existing CPAs into "train the trainer" courses for qualifying volunteer police officers, many of the current disadvantages would be reduced. For example, the newly certified volunteer instructors would be highly motivated to concentrate on crime prevention topics and less likely to overemphasize public relations. In addition, their services can be used to develop new curriculum guides or to expand and revise current materials for diverse populations. They could also serve to augment the department's personnel resources as crime prevention speakers and home security inspectors.

Finally, volunteer police unit members who receive training for this new mission will help with VIPS program volunteer retention and recruitment because they will be participating in a highly meaningful role and will be in a position to inform others about their work as well as the numerous other roles for volunteers in police service.

Summary

There was a time in American history when the morals of residents were policed by members of the community. Communities were smaller and family attachments strong. No one could be anonymous and punishments were swift. Society is no longer homogeneous, and America's huge metropolitan areas permit many persons to live in relative isolation unless they chose to publish aspects of their lives through social media. Responsibility for community security has shifted from the households on the block to the police station and a variety of other local, state, and federal agencies.

In times of economic decline, the resources of governmental departments become thinned and reliance on alternative resources is of vital importance. Since the attacks of September 11, 2001, there has been resurgence in a variety of existing volunteer organizations concerned with public safety. Moreover, the federal government has helped to stimulate the recruitment of volunteers through expanded Web site information, such as the VIPS program. The Pasadena PD has registered at the VIPS Web site, and a review of its programs may serve to illustrate the many types of opportunities available for neighborhood volunteer service with police agencies throughout the United States. Pasadena PD programs using volunteers include chaplains, CAPP patrol, equestrians, CREDIT, MPU, Pawn Detail, Criminal Investigations Division's Victim Assistance, Records and Traffic sections, general volunteers, and the YAB.

The Pasadena PD and hundreds of other agencies operate citizen academies concerned with law enforcement (e.g., the Federal Bureau of Investigation). The first CPA in the United States was established by the Orlando Police Department in 1985 and was modeled after a British program begun in 1977. Participants usually must pass a criminal and motor vehicle background check and must be fingerprinted. Classes are usually limited to 15–25 participants. They meet one evening a week for approximately three hours. The academies are free and last about 10 weeks. Topics cover an introduction to police operations, patrol, investigation, services, community services, special operations, road safety, criminal law and procedure, and communication. The advantages of a CPA include exposure to new perspectives and better understanding and positive and proactive contact between police and citizens. Potential limitations include possible lawsuits if a participant is killed or injured while attending, resistance among police officers or administrators, lack of resources to sponsor an academy, and the possibility that a graduate will use the information inappropriately.

Graduates of CPAs are not expected to provide any police services, but alumni groups are often established to provide information about further participation in police-related functions. If police departments are interested in reaching out to more community members, a program involving training volunteer police to instruct "neighborhood police academies" is recommended.

Review Questions

1. Who policed the morals of colonial Americans?
2. How do police agencies cope when budgets are reduced?
3. Discuss how the Pasadena PD has attempted to integrate volunteers into its overall operations.
4. Describe two of the Pasadena PD volunteer programs.
5. State at least three purposes of Citizen Police Academies (CPAs).

6. Should community residents who have criminal backgrounds, but are now law-abiding, be eligible to attend CPAs? Discuss.
7. Search online to find at least two types of police volunteer programs involving non-sworn adults that are not listed in this chapter. Present the results of your search.
8. Search online to find out information about a CPA being offered near you. Indicate your findings.
9. List two advantages and two disadvantages of CPAs.
10. Discuss the nature of the author's recommendation regarding the establishment of "neighborhood police academies."

Notes

1. Another association that publishes a newsletter about CPAs is the National Citizens Police Academy Association (NCPAA). The first formal election for NCPAA board members was held in Lombard, Illinois, in 1999. As of April 2012, this organization had a membership of 238 (National CPAA Directory 2012). For additional information about their history, conferences, and other activities, see: http://www.nationalcpaa.org.
2. The history of Ponca City is tied to the history of local American Indian communities, particularly its namesake, the Ponca Tribe of American Indians. They came to the area in 1877 from their traditional homelands in Nebraska and South Dakota. The experience of the Poncas reached a national audience in 1879 when Chief Standing Bear and 66 followers returned to Nebraska to bury his son. In the landmark decision *Standing Bear v. Crook*, Judge Elmer S. Dundy ruled that Indians were entitled to the rights guaranteed to citizens by the Constitution. This case had important repercussions because it opened the judicial system to Native Americans. For an outline of Ponca history see: http://www.poncacity.com/history/ponca_tribe.htm.

References

Aryani, G. A., Garrett, T. D. and Alsabrook, C. L. (2000). The citizen police academy. *The FBI Law Enforcement Bulletin, 69*(5), 16–21.

Blackwood, B. (1994). Citizen police academies. *TELEMASP Monthly Bulletin, 1*(2), 1–8.

Bonello, E. M. and Schafer, J. A. (2002). Citizen police academies: Do they just entertain. *FBI Law Enforcement Bulletin, 71*(11), 19–23.

Breen, M. E. and Johnson, B. R. (2007). Citizen police academies: An analysis of enhanced police–community relations among citizen attendees. *The Police Journal, 80*(3), 246–266.

Brewster, J., Stoloff, M. and Sanders, N. (2005). Effectiveness of citizen police academies in changing the attitudes, beliefs, and behavior of citizen participants. *The American Journal of Criminal Justice, 30*(1), 21–34.

Buffalo Grove. (2012a). Academies. Retrieved May 18, 2012 from http://www.vbg.org/index.aspx?nid = 292

Buffalo Grove. (2012b). Demographics. Retrieved May 18, 2012 from http://www. vbg.org/index.aspx?nid = 142

City of Pasadena. (2013). Pasadena Police Department: Volunteer services. Retrieved September 25, 2013 from http://www.ci.pasadena.ca.us/police/ Volunteer_Mission_Statement/

City of Ponca City. (2012). Community and volunteer involvement. Retrieved May 23, 2012 from http://www.poncacityok.gov/index.aspx?NID = 193

City of Scottsdale. (2011). City of Scottsdale, Parks and Recreation Commission, approved work study session summary minutes, September 7, 2011. Retrieved May 24, 2012 from http://www.scottsdaleaz.gov/Assets/documents/ BoardAgendas/Parks/2011+Minutes/09-07-11_Approved_Work_Study_ Session_Summary_Minutes.pdf

Cohn, E. G. (1996). The citizen police academy: A recipe for improving police-community relations. *Journal of Criminal Justice, 24*(3), 265–271.

Cordero, J. (2011). *Reducing the cost of quality of policing: Making community safety cost effective and sustainable.* NJLM Educational Foundation, Friends of Local Government Services, Vol. 3(1). Trenton, NJ: The Cordero Group.

Economic Downturn. (2011). *The impact of the economic downturn on American police agencies.* Washington, DC: U.S. Department of Justice, Office of Community Oriented Policing Services.

Ferguson, R. E. (1985). The citizen police academy. *FBI Law Enforcement Bulletin, 54*(9), 5–7.

Greenberg, M. A. (1991). Citizen police academies. *FBI Law Enforcement Bulletin, 60*(8), 10–13.

Mayer, A. (2009). Geospatial technology helps East Orange crack down on crime. *Geography & Public Safety, 1*(4), 8–9.

McFarland, C. (2010). *State of America's cities survey on jobs and the economy.* Washington, DC: National League of Cities, Center for Research and Innovation.

National CPAA Directory. (2012). Retrieved May 18, 2012 from http://www. nationalcpaa.org/pdf/MembersList_4_16_12.pdf

Norton, M. B. (1996). *Founding mothers and fathers: Gendered power and the forming of American society.* New York: Alfred A. Knopf.

Pasadena CPA. (2013). Citizen police academy. Retrieved September 26, 2013 from http://www.ci.pasadena.ca.us/police/citizen_police_academy/

Pasadena Facts. (2014). Retrieved January 22, 2014 from http://www.ci.pasadena. ca.us/Pasadena_Facts_and_Statistics/

Pasadena Mounted Unit. (2013). Mounted Volunteers Unit. Retrieved September 26, 2013 from http://www.ci.pasadena.ca.us/police/mounted_volunteers/

Pasadena PD. (2013). VIPS program. Retrieved September 25, 2013 from http:// www.policevolunteers.org/programs/?fa = dis_pro_detail&id = 736

Seelmeyer, J. (1987). A citizen's police academy. *Law and Order, 35*(12), 26–29.

Stone, W. E. and Champeny, S. (2001). Assessing a citizen police academy. *Police Practice and Research, 2*(3), 219–241.

TSA. (2014). Careers. Retrieved March 2, 2014 from http://www.tsa.gov/careers

University of Kentucky PD. (2012). Welcome to the citizen police academy. Retrieved May 21, 2012 from http://www.uky.edu/Police/citizensacademy.html

Walker, S. A. (1998). *Popular justice: A history of American criminal justice* (2nd ed., Rev.). New York: Oxford University Press.

Youth Involvement in Police Work

8

Effective school-to-work transition programs can combat the disillusionment of youths who are struggling to finish high school, making good on the promise that a diploma will lead to a stable and decent-paying job.

—Jon Bright
(1992, 59)

Introduction

Since the 1960s, hundreds of U.S. police agencies have established Law Enforcement Explorer Posts. Today, "over 33,000 Explorers and 8,425 adult volunteers participate in Law Enforcement Exploring. The program highlights include: the National Law Enforcement Exploring Leadership Academies, ride-alongs, career achievement awards, National Law Enforcement Exploring Conferences, and scholarship opportunities" (Exploring 2014). The prototypes for this well-known contemporary youth program were established during the first quarter of the twentieth century when various units of "junior" or "boy police" as well as school boy safety patrols were sponsored by local police departments, public schools, and private schools. The youth photographed in Figure 8.1 were only playacting and did not belong to any "junior police" program in 1900; rather, they wore police costumes to welcome a visit by Rear Admiral William T. Sampson during a weeklong town celebration. However, when and where actual programs existed, they were highly publicized and deemed to be constructive alternatives to an unstructured street life. Such programs were organized in Chicago, Illinois; Berkeley, California; Council Bluffs, Iowa; Cincinnati, Ohio; and New York City, New York. The members of these early youth organizations received instruction in law enforcement and safety topics, thereby inaugurating the first "youth police academies." With the adoption of community policing during the last two decades of the twentieth century, programs embracing the earlier spirit of these efforts began to reemerge (LeConte 2012b). According to Pat Fuller, former chief of the Austin Independent School District (ISD) Police Department, "Our biggest problem is that the schools keep pulling our officers off of the campus to teach more classes. The students may not see it, but we do. And so do the schools—the

Figure 8.1 Maynard, Massachusetts, Merchant's Week, May 14–19, 1900. Each day had a theme. May 16, 1900, was selected as the day to honor a visit by Rear Admiral William T. Sampson, the "Hero of Santiago" in the Spanish-American War. Boys from the town were dressed up in police uniforms to serve as members of his official escort. Other children, both boys and girls, were dressed up as marines. From left to right: Harrison Persons, Douglas Salisbury, Daniel Sullivan, James Ryan, Charles Dyson, and Raymond Veitch.[1] (Used with permission of the Maynard Historical Society.)

junior police academy (JPA) works. It supports a healthy and safe school environment, and we will continue to use it" (Fuller 2012).

The present chapter focuses on the establishment of five prominent youth programs: youth or junior police academies; junior police programs (e.g., Police Athletic Leagues, Explorers, cadets); school safety patrols; police academy magnet schools; and youth courts. In addition, the newest model for the delivery of police education and training for youth that was started in Los Angeles, the Police Orientation and Preparation Program (POPP), is also described. Short-term types of police-sponsored and/or school-based academy programs include: the crime scene investigation camp, the physical training or boot camp model involving at-risk youth, and more generalized programs of instruction with academic units of instruction. The efforts of safety patrollers are devoted to pedestrian safety near school crossings at elementary and middle schools. These safety patrol members may also be assigned to hallways and doorways at times of high levels of hallway traffic during the day. Other types of junior police programs are harder to pin down except to note that they tend to fall within a continuum beginning with the pursuit of recreational goals (e.g., Police Athletic Leagues) to those that perform a limited range of enforcement activities (e.g., crowd control).

The origins and purposes of the various programs are described. Many youth have been brought a step closer to becoming police officers or have been able to focus their studies and narrow their career goals because of their participation in these various types of programs. The topics of liability and insurance as well as youth protection from abuse are also considered. The chapter concludes with an overview of trends and recommendations regarding future developments in the field.

Youth (Junior) Police Academies

The origin of youth (junior) police academies coincided with the advent of junior police in the first two decades of the twentieth century. By the 1930s, most of the early junior or boy police programs were transformed into Police Athletic (or Activities) Leagues (PAL). On occasion, police-related instruction was shared with youngsters. For example, one such mini "junior police academy" was instituted in the late 1940s in Birmingham, Alabama, as a regular feature of the city's recreation program. In 1949, it served 50 children aged 9–13. Various crime prevention demonstrations and investigatory procedures were presented by members of the Birmingham Police Department (Popular Activity 1949). Today, PAL is a national program with a membership exceeding 1.5 million children aged 6–18. More than 300 American law enforcement agencies in some 700 cities are running these programs (Hollywood Community 2013).

A typical example of a modern-day short-term JPA took place during a five-day period in June 2012 on the campus of Washington State Community College (WSCC) in Marietta, Ohio. Its goal was to provide students who are interested in a career in law enforcement or a related field with a hands-on view of the criminal justice system and its procedures. The only eligibility requirements involved a letter of interest and being in a grade from 9 through 12. Online publicity for the academy stated that "the Junior Police Academy is not a disciplinary, recreational, or underprivileged camp but is part of the summer camp program at WSCC" (WSCC 2012). It also indicated that a Level II Academy would be held on the campus the following week that was open to only those students entering grades 9 through 12 who had successfully completed the Level I Academy. Participants were to have the opportunity "to investigate, prepare, and present in mock court a crime that resembles a real life situation in which a 'judge' oversees the courtroom presentation and a jury decides guilt or innocence" (WSCC 2012).

Some communities, such as the village of Buffalo Grove, Illinois, offer both adult and youth academies. The village's junior academy is designed for students who are 12–15 years of age and who either live and/or attend school in Buffalo Grove. Following a national trend, this youth program was held in June after the end of the school year (Buffalo Grove 2012a). In addition to having to sign an injury liability release waiver, applicants were required to grant permission for a law enforcement records check. Participation could be denied to any applicant with a criminal arrest record (Buffalo Grove 2012b).

No doubt the popularity of such short-term academies fostered the creation of an online program known as the "JPA Content Lab." According to posted information on its home page, the site has developed its content in collaboration with an "Advisory Council, members of the law enforcement community and feedback from the cadets themselves" (LeConte 2012a). The site also indicates that "new lessons are currently being field tested in the Austin schools.... Everything here is a work in progress, not only in terms of content, but digital technology as well. We want to know what works with kids and web browsers! ... The information is current and will be updated on a regular basis. We encourage instructors to take full advantage of the program's new digital distribution by checking back from time to time for updates and new multimedia content. New units will be created based on events in the news, so instructor's can provide a timely discussion of the issues that impact youth and our communities" (LeConte 2012a). Titles from its extensive list of free online lessons can be found in Box 8.1.

JPAs can be quite varied. A popular type focuses on the world of the crime scene investigator and is organized as a camp. This format was used by the South Bend (Indiana) Police Department in their weeklong June 2011 program. The campers practiced collecting fingerprints, laying mold on tire tracks, hunting for evidence, taking pictures of mock crime scenes, and digging up DNA samples. Students watched exercises conducted by the police Special Weapons and Tactics (SWAT) team and the K-9 unit. According to South Bend Police Lt. Richard Powers, "the whole idea is to give them a taste of what we do every day in our jobs" (Ferreira 2011).

Another format involves physical training as well as an extended delivery time frame for at-risk youth. This type of academy is conducted by the city of Burlington, North Carolina. It originated in 1996 and currently involves a collaborative effort by the Burlington Police Department, Graham Police Department, Alamance County Sheriff's Department, and the Alamance Burlington School System with a mission intended to provide at-risk middle school-aged juveniles social skills that can make them more productive students and citizens. Academy participants are mentored for the following school year by personnel associated with each participating law enforcement agency (City of Burlington 2012). They are referred to as "cadets" and are selected by law enforcement staff from students recommended by the Alamance Burlington School System. The cadets undergo a structured four-week training program, focusing on

**BOX 8.1   JUNIOR POLICE ACADEMY
CONTENT LAB LESSONS**

Introductory Units:
- Introduction to the Junior Police Academy
- History of Policing
- A Quick Guide to Being a Police Officer
- You're Under Arrest
- Hazards on Patrol
- Do You Have What It Takes?
- Patrolling the Streets

Careers in Law Enforcement:
- Law Enforcement in the United States
- FBI
- Sheriff
- K-9 Unit SWAT
- School Resource Officer
- Bomb Squad
- Secret Service
- Your Place in Law Enforcement
- Civilian Support

Citizens and Law Enforcement:
- Police and the Bill of Rights
- Do We Need Police to Be Happy?

Bullying Units:
- Cyber-Bullying
- Mastering Social Skills
- Reconnecting: Social Skills in the Internet Age
- Stop and Think: Social Survival Skills
- Stop Bullying: Take a Stand!

Technology Units:
- Crime Scene Investigation (CSI)
- The Secret Language of Police
- Police and Technology

Source: https://sites.google.com/site/jpacourse2012/introductory-units/l1

goal setting and self-esteem, conflict resolution and mediation, violence and substance abuse prevention, principles of law and justice, and decision-making skills. The first week of the academy is a 24-hour per day program where the participants and leaders are away from home. All other weeks are conducted at the training center in Haw River, North Carolina

(City of Burlington 2012). The cadets complete a community service project and a high and low ropes confidence course. Drills and physical fitness are used to develop teamwork and to maintain discipline. There is no cost to the cadets and their families for participating in the academy. Community donations are solicited to fund the various needs (food, clothing, etc.) of the academy in the form of cash, goods, and services from businesses, charitable organizations, and private citizens. The program's personnel, facilities, and transportation costs are funded by the agencies involved (City of Burlington 2012).

Avery Montgomery graduated from the Burlington Police Department's JPA in 2006. In July 2011, he returned to the academy as a guest speaker informing the academy cadets about how the academy had helped him make positive changes in his own life. He stressed those lessons from the academy "can help in all aspects of their lives" (Bost 2011).

A more generalized program that is held away from the homes of its participants is the Cadet Lawman Academy. In June 2012, it was held for seven consecutive days in Burns Flat, Oklahoma, at a former air force base. In 2011 and 2012, more than 200 young men and women completed these academies. Candidates for the program must be residents of Oklahoma, rising seniors, and in the top half of their class scholastically. In 1973, two Oklahoma Highway Patrol lieutenants visited Kansas to observe a similar program. It involved mostly classroom work with limited hands-on activities. The Cadet Lawman Academy was started in Oklahoma in 1974 and at that time was cosponsored by the Jaycees and the Oklahoma Highway Patrol—Safety Education Division. Later sponsors includes the Oklahoma State Troopers Association, the Oklahoma Highway Patrol, and the Oklahoma Elks. The current weeklong program includes training in precision driving, traffic and boating law enforcement, firearms instruction, self-defense, and law enforcement history. Activities also include a tour of the state reformatory in Granite, Oklahoma. This is a state prison that opened in 1910 and currently holds medium-level security prisoners. The cadets also participate in other tours and practical exercises (Cadet Lawman 2012). The 41st Cadet Lawman Academy was held in Burns Flat in June 2014.

Junior Police

The rise of junior or youth police academies followed the reemergence of another type of youth program under the sponsorship of law enforcement or school agencies—junior police. The exact origins of junior police organizations may be clouded in time, but they appear to be based on the inclusion of military training as a school activity. For example, Rowbatham (1895) discusses the Rossall Corps of 1862, believed to be the first school in England to establish such a corps among its boys. Various photos of uniformed Rossall Corps members can be found in the four-page *Boy's Own Annual* article dated 1926, written by Captain H. V. Leonard and entitled "The Earliest Public School Volunteer Corps."

Coincidentally, also in the year 1862, the U.S. Congress passed The Morrill Act, which set aside 30,000 acres of public lands for public higher education. The land was then to be sold and the money from the sale of the land was to be put in an endowment fund that would provide support for the "land-grant" colleges in each of the states. Income from the sale of these lands has endowed liberal arts, engineering, agriculture, and military (officer) training at new colleges throughout the United States. The South's secession allowed northern progressives to pass this legislation. Eventually, the schools that were created offered new opportunities for education beyond high school, legislation that members of Congress from the slave-holding states had blocked. "The land-grant has improved the lives of millions of Americans. This was not the case in the early stages. At the time the grants were established, there was a separation of races. In the South, blacks were not allowed to attend the original land-grant institutions. There was a provision for separate but equal facilities, but only Mississippi and Kentucky set up any such institutions. This situation was rectified in 1890 when the Second Morrill Act was passed and expanded the system of grants to include black institutions" (Lightcap 2013). Historically, black land-grant institutions are located in 18 states, the District of Columbia and the U.S. Virgin Islands. (The complete list can be found at: http://www.aplu.org/page.aspx?pid = 1074.)

Virginia Polytechnic Institute and State University (Virginia Tech) was founded on October 1, 1872, as the Virginia Agricultural and Mechanical College (VAMC) in Blacksburg, Virginia. As a land-grant college, military training was mandatory for all able-bodied male students, so the student body was organized into a corps of cadets. A discussion of the establishment of collegiate level Reserve Officer Training Corps (ROTC) and the Junior ROTC is found in Chapter 9.

Junior police programs share many similarities with military schools. For example, in 1925, an advertisement placed in various publications by the Association of Military Colleges and Schools of the United States[2] stated: "The military schools of the country are not conducted primarily for the purpose of making army officers, but to make men. Sound scholarship and true development of the boy physically, mentally, and morally, constitute the fundamental principle of the military school … and carries into his life-work right ideals of citizenship and service" (Figure 8.2).

Figure 8.2 Military Colleges and Schools advertisement, ca. 1925.

Junior police programs also provide opportunities for fostering positive relationships among younger citizens and for promoting activities associated with good citizenship. Various formats have been used in these programs, ranging in emphasis from recreational to enforcement. An example of the recreational type is PAL. At present, in New York City, more than 60,000 youth participate in PAL activities. An enforcement type of program existed in the city of Phoenix, Arizona, in the early 1940s. Only a single traffic police officer was assigned to school crossings. Instead of adult traffic officers, the city relied on a corps of junior police. They received uniforms from local organizations, and their authority to perform traffic duty came from the Phoenix Police Department. They watched school crossings, directed traffic, handed out tickets, and performed other tasks associated with traffic control (Greenberg 2008). Today, the successor organization to the 1940s Phoenix corps of junior police is the Phoenix Police Department's Explorer Post 2906. Established in 1973, members range in age from 14 to 21 (14 years old is acceptable only if the member has graduated from the eighth grade). The Phoenix Explorers have directed off-street traffic and parking, performed crowd control at parades, helped in neighborhood clean-up drives, and display crime prevention materials at local fairs (City of Phoenix 2013).

Historically, the largest municipal junior police program was established by Captain John Sweeney in New York City. In 1914, Sweeney commanded a lower East Side police precinct and created a youth program for boys, aged 11–16.[3] They had uniforms, participated in marching drills, and carried green and white flags. Modeled after the police hierarchy, the junior police inducted boys as patrolmen and promoted them up the ranks to chief inspector. Members attended meetings twice a week where they learned marching drills, participated in track meets and baseball games, enjoyed public swimming pools, and learned first aid, safety, and personal hygiene. At its peak, the program had an enrollment of 6,000 boys. A much smaller number of young women (approximately 50) were selected entirely on the basis of merit to work alongside their male counterparts. They routinely escorted younger children across busy streets, monitored dance halls so that underage girls would not enter, and helped to keep tenement fire escapes clear of debris. By 1917, the junior police had expanded to 32 precincts. Shortly thereafter, the program collapsed when Captain Sweeney retired from the police force and no other leader emerged or was appointed to take his place (Greenberg 2008). The titles of "junior police" or "boy police" are very rarely used anymore. Today, most of these programs use the titles of "Police Explorer" or "police cadet."

Law Enforcement Exploring

The Law Enforcement Exploring program originated within the Exploring Division of the Boy Scouts of America (BSA). As early as 1959, there were Explorer posts specializing in law enforcement in Southern California. In 1976, the Exploring Division of the BSA received a one-year grant from the Law Enforcement Assistance Administration (LEAA) to enhance and promote Law Enforcement Exploring. This grant helped to create the National Law Enforcement Exploring Committee (NLEEC) and led to the appointment of a professional member of the national BSA staff as director of Law Enforcement Exploring. A membership drive was also conducted (Law Enforcement Exploring 2011).

Since 1998, Law Enforcement Explorer programs have been a cooperative venture between Learning for Life (an affiliate of the BSA) and hundreds of police agencies throughout the United States. These programs are designed to give young men and women between the ages of 14 and 21 a chance to find out more about law enforcement careers (Greenberg 2008). In some areas of the country, Explorers may go to an Explorer academy, similar to the junior or youth police academies. These are usually held during consecutive weekends or over weeklong retreats. However, unlike many junior academies, participants are more likely to receive physical training and to learn discipline, emulating regular police academies. Of course, any training and discipline regimen is conducted in an age-appropriate and abbreviated format, and opportunities for social developmental experiences are included in the program. The typical academy always ends with a graduation ceremony where attendance certificates, additional certifications (such as cardiopulmonary resuscitation certification), and other awards are given out. However, because Explorers are participants in an ongoing youth program, their experiences are more likely to have a lasting impact. This is especially true for those Explorer Post members who have the good fortunate to attend one or more of the biennial National Law Enforcement Exploring Conferences. Explorers who attend such a major event not only have the chance to interact with their peers from around the country but to enhance their own relationships with their fellow post members. National conferences are conducted every second year and attended by thousands of Law Enforcement Explorers and adult leaders. Tuition is charged, and space is limited. Young people come together for a week of team and individual competitions, seminars, demonstrations, exhibits, recreation, and fun. The 2012 conference was held at Colorado State University in Fort Collins, and the 2014 conference was held at the Bloomington campus of Indiana University.

The concept and use of the term "Exploring" dates back to at least 1922. Steadily, Law Enforcement Explorer Posts came into being. For example, in 1969, the St. Petersburg Law Enforcement Explorer Post 280 (now Post 980) was established (Figures 8.3 and 8.4). In 1971, young women were admitted

Figure 8.3 Police Explorers Post 980 members engaged in training simulation exercise. (Used with the permission of the St. Petersburg (Florida) Police Department.)

Figure 8.4 Police Explorers Post 980 members. Exploring provides the chance to work directly with police officers, go on ride-alongs, receive police training, meet new friends, and feel good about helping out in the community. (Used with the permission of the St. Petersburg (Florida) Police Department.)

to posts as determined by their chartering organization, and the upper age of Exploring was raised from 17 to 20. In that same year, there were at least 14 active units in the state of Florida with a focus on law enforcement, and a statewide organization was created to plan activities and to publish a newsletter (Folsom 1971). In 1976, members of Explorer Post 280 took a first-place award in a pistol match, competing against 14 other posts (Pistol Team Wins 1976). By the 1990s, girls made up about half of the entire Explorer membership nationwide (Greenberg 2008). By 2009, there were more than 2,000 Law Enforcement Explorer Posts in the United States; these posts accounted for about 35,000 of the group's 145,000 members worldwide (Steinhauer 2009). Various short online videos featuring information about Law Enforcement Exploring are available.[4]

Law Enforcement Explorer Posts have been established from Maine to California as well as in the state of Hawaii and in U.S. territories. Due to the creativity and initiative of police chiefs and mentors, many interesting and useful projects have been developed to engage post members. For example, the Westland Police Department in Michigan has established a "Sober-Up Program." It uses a golf cart with an extra safety break; the cart is marked to look like a Westland police car complete with flashing blue and red emergency lights. Cones, street signs, and various "fatal vision goggles" were also acquired. When worn, the goggles distort the vision of the participant showing them what they would see should they become impaired or intoxicated. A program participant drives the modified golf cart through an obstacle course while wearing the goggles. In this way, the participant and spectators learn what distorted vision does to a person's ability to safely operate a vehicle. The course is run by the Westland Police Explorers, who donate their time to educate community residents, and it has been brought to various community events as well as to the students of John Glenn High School (Westland Police 2012b).

Since 1996, the New York's Broome County Sheriff's Office has sponsored a Law Enforcement Explorer program, Post No. 100. Participant ages range from 14 to 20. In 2007, there were 15 students enrolled in the program.

Its purposes are to introduce youth to law enforcement careers and to the nature of the criminal justice system as well as to promote character development, self-esteem, and citizenship training among Broome County's youth. The program strives to present experiences that are challenging, thought-provoking, and essential to the development of young people interested in law enforcement (Broome County 2007).

The Explorers from Post 100 meet once a week for two hours. During this time, they receive training and instruction on child fingerprinting, traffic enforcement, crime scene investigation, officer survival, shoot/don't shoot, the use of force, the K-9 unit, criminal procedure law, domestic violence, and other topics. The Explorers are issued uniforms purchased with funds from grants, fundraising, and donations. They learn about career opportunities in law enforcement at the local, state, federal, and military levels while analyzing criminal justice college education requirements and visiting law enforcement training academies. They have the opportunity to assist sheriff's deputies in different training exercises, such as alcohol and tobacco stings. The sheriff's detectives partner with Explorers and take them to various business establishments to attempt to purchase cigarettes or alcohol. The purpose is to check these establishments for compliance with local and state laws regarding the sale of alcohol and tobacco products to anyone underage. Explorers are under the direct supervision of the detectives to ensure that problems do not occur. In Broome County, New York, the Endicott, Johnson City, and Vestal police departments have used the sheriff's Explorers to conduct similar investigations in their communities (Broome County 2007). Chapter 2 describes a similar program involving members of the New York City Auxiliary Police Force.

In February 2007, the Post 100 Explorers defended their title in the annual "Explorer Post Mall Show" by taking first-place honors for the eighth consecutive year. Their child fingerprinting exhibit processed more than 175 children. There were K-9 demonstrations as well as defensive tactics and handcuffing procedures. The Explorers also ran a 10-minute video that they produced highlighting the different topics that are covered in the Explorer program (Broome County 2007).

In 2007, the Post 100 Explorers worked more than 85 events including a balloon rally, a winter carnival, various runs, and other community gatherings. They also assisted with the sheriff's summer camp program. Traffic control, security, and child fingerprinting are a large portion of their additional community service activities. In October 2005, the Explorers were introduced to Operation Safe Child, assisting deputies in downloading information into a database and transmitting that information to the Division of Criminal Justice Services (DCJS). This data collection enhances the ability of law enforcement to locate missing or abducted children. By working these events each year, the Explorer program has reduced police overtime expenditures. An important purpose of these hands-on efforts is to help build a better working relationship and understanding between the youth and law enforcement officers. Members can be promoted to the ranks of sergeant and lieutenant after having demonstrated their progress in the program. Several unit members have acted as instructors, teaching search and rescue procedures to local Boy Scout troops, using course outlines and training they received while in the program. These undertakings have contributed to the program's success and have helped many of Broome County's youth come together to learn about law enforcement—how it affects them individually and also their community (Broome County 2007).

Explorer posts have also been established at many fire companies and some ambulance services. An example of the latter is the Henrietta Volunteer Ambulance Service in Upstate New York. The service began in 1963 with just one ambulance and 200 calls and has expanded today to a fleet of 10 vehicles and more than 5,800 calls annually. This Explorer post offers an opportunity for students to learn about the field of emergency medicine, medical procedures, lifesaving skills, and how to react in an emergency. Qualified members are eligible to participate in observation shifts aboard an ambulance (Henrietta Ambulance 2012). A combined four-page *Waterloo Police and Fire Explorer Handbook* contains a succinct list of rules including one that states: "Any misuse of learned tactics will be immediate grounds for termination" (Waterloo Handbook 2012, 1).

In addition, the 15 fire stations of the Aurora (Colorado) Fire Department have a Fire Exploring Program. (Its detailed 36-page *Explorer Program Operations Manual* can be found at: https://www.auroragov.org/cs/groups/public/documents/digitalmedia/002200.pdf.) The city of Aurora[5] has had a Law Enforcement Explorer Post since 1980 (Figures 8.5 and 8.6). Its alumni

Figure 8.5 Aurora Law Enforcement Explorer Post 2024 member serving food at a community service event. The Post has approximately 35 members. (Used with the permission of the Aurora (Colorado) Police Department.)

Figure 8.6 Aurora Law Enforcement Explorer Post 2024 members at a community service event. (Used with the permission of the Aurora (Colorado) Police Department.)

include more than two dozen current members of local, state, and federal law enforcement agencies (Police Explorers 2013). Explorers who excel in the program are eligible for leadership positions in the post. Post leaders plan and organize post functions. Explorers who complete eight hours of service or training each month have the opportunity to ride with a patrol officer and experience police operations in the field firsthand. Moreover, Aurora Post 2024 members who excel in the program are eligible to receive civil service preference points when they apply to become an Aurora police officer. The Aurora Police Explorer Post is NOT a "scared straight" or "second chance" program for juveniles with behavioral problems (Aurora Explorers 2014).

Liability and Medical Insurance for Explorer Post Members and Advisors

Two critical concerns for any agency considering the sponsorship of a Law Enforcement Explorer Post are liability and insurance. Currently, any participating organizations are covered with primary general liability insurance. (A participating organization is defined as its board of directors and/or trustees, its officers and employees, in their official and individual capacity.)

This liability policy is primary except for automobiles or watercraft owned or used by the participating organization. In such cases, the general liability policy provides excess coverage.

If an Exploring volunteer is an employee of the participating organization, he or she is provided with primary liability coverage as long as Learning for Life guidelines are followed. A nonemployee (volunteer, parent, etc.) is provided with excess coverage. Most Explorer advisors (e.g., regular police officers) are employees of the participating partner; therefore, they have primary liability coverage, which covers the organization and its employees. However, it does not cover the youth in an Explorer post.

Accident insurance is the responsibility of individual Explorer posts and its leadership. Many local Exploring councils provide accident insurance to their youth members by collecting a small fee each year. If such an accident policy is not available or not provided, arrangements for assistance should be made through the local Exploring council office (Career Exploring FAQs 2013).

An example of a local Exploring council accident coverage for Learning for Life Explorers and adult volunteer leaders is the secondary "accident and sickness insurance" policy held by the Greater St. Louis Area Council. Their policy only covers individuals registered in the council. It covers them for accidents and sickness (as well as for accidental death and dismemberment) while they are participating in any official Scouting activity or Learning for Life Exploring activity. The council purchases this coverage annually from Health Special Risk. Benefits are in excess of any other insurance covering the individual. Accident medical benefits are limited to $15,000; sickness to $7,500; ambulance to $6,000. A copy of the Health Special Risk's Memorandum of Coverage is required for out-of-council resident camps. In addition, the "Boy Scouts of America general liability policy provides coverage for a bodily injury or property damage claim that is made and arises out of an Official Scouting Activity" (Insurance Information 2011).

Youth Protection Issues

Since October 2009, it has been a felony in Florida to commit a battery[6] on a Law Enforcement Explorer in the line of duty. When the law was initially proposed, it was touted as providing the juvenile Explorers the same legal protection that officers have while on patrol (Wilmath 2008). This law may serve as a model for other states concerned with the safety and protection of their Law Enforcement Explorers.

It is an unpleasant fact that some Explorer post mentors/advisors have been charged with and/or convicted of Explorer member abuse. Learning for Life now requires the completion of a training program before adult volunteers can be assigned to work with youth. Accordingly, the Explorer movement has posted an online series of links under the heading of "Youth Protection Training" that can be accessed at: http://exploring.learningforlife. org/services/resources/youth-protection-training.

The preface to these materials states: "Youth safety is the No. 1 concern of Learning for Life. To increase awareness of the societal problem of child abuse, including sexual abuse, and to create even greater barriers to child abuse than currently exist, Learning for Life has implemented enhanced Youth Protection policies" (Youth Protection 2013). As of June 1, 2010, all registered adult Explorer volunteers, no matter what their position entails, must complete Youth Protection training prior to beginning their volunteer service and show proof of completion of the training. This training must be retaken every two years, and all registered adults in posts participating in summer activities (law enforcement conference, etc.) are required to take the Youth Protection training prior to participating in the event. The instruction can also be provided in a live format at the request of a concerned group. Moreover, every Explorer Post is encouraged to conduct Youth Protection training with all Explorers (youth) once a year using "Youth Protection: Personal Safety Awareness AV-09DVD27" (which can be obtained from a local council office). This visual training covers the topics of sexual harassment, acquaintance rape, Internet safety, and suicide awareness. (The leader discussion guide can be found at: http://www.learningforlife.org/pubs/av/46-506.)

Safety Patrols

By 1902, there were only about 23,000 cars in operation in the United States compared with about 17 million horses, but as many as 50 small motor clubs were already established to assist the pioneering motorists of the day. On March 4, 1902, in Chicago, nine of those clubs joined together to create a national motoring organization known as the American Automobile Association (AAA) (Figure 8.7). Within two decades, the AAA had the wisdom to adopt an existing school safety patrol program—a unique youth organization that quickly spread throughout the nation. It was distinctive because it provided a specific service—namely, pedestrian safety in and around school buildings. The Chicago Motor Club has been widely recognized as the initiator of the first patrol unit to become affiliated with the AAA. Beginning in the early 1920s, a typical patrol consisted of 4–12 boys, depending on the size of the school and the number of hazardous intersections. It was a common sight to see them stopping traffic by raising their hands or stop signs and

Figure 8.7 AAA's fiftieth anniversary commemorative U.S. postage stamp. The AAA school safety patrol was founded in Chicago in 1920 by Charles M. Hayes, president of the Chicago Motor Club, after several children at a school crossing were killed by a speeding car. Horrified by the incident, Hayes pledged to help prevent such a tragedy from happening again. (From http://www.blogtalkradio.com/aaatalkradio/2010/04/19/aaa-school-safety-patrol-1)

then proceeding to escort students across city streets. They wore white "Sam Browne belts"[7] with badges attached to denote ranks. Some had bright colored felt armbands. During inclement weather, poncho-type capes and rain hats were added to the uniform. Patrol members were selected for service based on their good grades and leadership qualities. The AAA also introduced traffic safety education into elementary and junior high schools and pioneered driver education in high schools (AAA 2014).

In 1923, due to the rise of vehicular traffic and concern about pedestrian safety, Police Chief August Vollmer of Berkeley, California, changed the orientation of his "junior police program" from spotting crime to protecting children with the creation of the "Berkeley Traffic Police Reserve" (Greenberg 2008).

Oak Ridge Elementary School was built in 1991 on an 18-acre tract of land in Eagan, Minnesota. Its 30 classrooms on two levels serve nearly 630 students from kindergarten through the fifth grade. The classrooms are designed with one open wall in order to encourage students and staff to make better use of all the resources in the school as well as to promote "a sharing relationship between staff, students, and visitors to our school" (About Oak Ridge 2013). *The Oak Ridge School Safety Patrol Manual* declares that: "The purpose of the safety patrols is to assist in training school children in how to cross streets, to assist school children upon arrival and dismissal, and to protect them from any type of accident" (Patrol Manual 2012). Box 8.2 states several of the rules concerning students assigned to bus patrols.

In 2000, the AAA School Safety Patrols had approximately a half-million participants, and by 2013, this number was estimated to have risen to 600,000 (Chandler 2013). In recent decades, increased traffic and concern about civil liability have diminished the nature of their responsibilities. For the most part, patrols have been confined to sidewalk duty (Greenberg 2008).

Nevertheless, opportunities to engage in lifesaving acts related to school safety still exist, and patrollers have been recognized for heroic actions on a yearly basis. In 1961, U.S. Attorney General Robert F. Kennedy presented lifesaving awards to young AAA safety patrol heroes. Two years later, his brother President John F. Kennedy did the same. In 2011, the AAA honored seven elementary students for their courageous actions that saved the lives of others. The patrollers received AAA Lifesaving Medals in a ceremony at the Rayburn House Office Building. They joined an exclusive group of 399 students who, since 1949, had previously received the medal—the highest honor that can be bestowed on a patroller. Typical actions included stepping into oncoming traffic to pull a fellow student from the path of a distracted driver or preventing an adult from entering a crosswalk as a vehicle approached. Former patrol members include Presidents Jimmy Carter and Bill Clinton, Vice President Joe Biden, as well as several Supreme Court justices, U.S. senators, governors, and U.S. Olympic gold medalists (AAA Honors 2011).

BOX 8.2   BUS PATROL RULES

The bus driver is the person responsible for the safety of both the bus and passengers.

Bus patrols are aides to help with student safety.

The bus driver will establish rules and expectations for his or her bus.

The bus driver is the person in charge of *everything* that happens on his or her bus.

They are the only person on the bus that assigns students to specific seats.

The bus driver will decide how he/she will rotate the duties of front, middle, and back patrol duties.

FRONT PATROL

1. Sits in a front seat and assists with flagging students across the street using proper flagging techniques.
2. Is the first person on and last person off the bus.

MIDDLE PATROL

1. Makes sure all students are seated before the bus starts moving.
2. Assists in keeping the aisle clear.
3. Assists in keeping the bus safe.

BACK PATROL

1. Makes sure all students are seated before the bus starts moving.
2. Assists in keeping the aisle clear.
3. Assists with the use of the emergency door when necessary.
4. Assists in keeping the bus safe.

Source: Patrol Manual, 2012, The Oak Ridge school safety patrol manual, available at: http://learn.district196.org/pluginfile.php?file =%2F156989% 2Fmod_resource%2Fcontent%2F0%2FSafety_Patrol_Manual_2012.pdf

In 1935, a large newspaper photo spread featured the junior police force of Ponca City, Oklahoma. Today, Ponca City has a population of about 25,000, of which more than 2,000 are Native Americans. The Ponca City Police Department sponsors a youth police academy and a citizens police academy. It also provides extra hospitality for foreign visitors. In a citizen exchange program sponsored by the U.S. Chamber of Commerce, a citizen of Zimbabwe attended a session of the citizen police academy (CPA) followed by a tour of the police department (Police Host 2012).

Figure 8.8 Safety patrol members from the St. Hyacinth and St. John the Baptist Schools, Westbrook, Maine, October 27, 1939. (Used with the permission of the Westbrook Historical Society, Westbrook, ME.)

The length of time students served depended on the schools. Some schools selected students to serve for a full year and others changed students on a monthly basis. The job of the safety patrol was to regulate the safe movement of children in the immediate vicinity of a school. At some schools, the duties of the safety patrol also included raising and lowering the flag each day. As school-age leaders in traffic safety, patrols helped teach students about traffic safety on a peer-to-peer basis. They also served as role models to the younger children who looked up to them.

In 1939, some members of the School Boy Patrol at the St. Hyacinth Parish School and St. John the Baptist School in Westbrook, Maine, were responsible for escorting children nearly half a mile in order to assist them in crossing busy streets (Figure 8.8). Today, due to their numbers, safety patrollers are the most visible of the police-related youth organizations. Although escorting youth safely from one street corner to the next is no longer a routine activity, various school districts still permit them to maintain the peace on school buses and to assist younger children getting on and off school buses. In addition, in some schools, selected students continue to help maintain decorum along school hallways and in remote corridors.

Police Academy Magnet Schools

The Los Angeles Police Academy Magnet School Program was established in 1997 as a cooperative effort of the Los Angeles Police Department (LAPD), the Los Angeles Unified School District (LAUSD), and various corporate sponsors. The program was originally implemented at two high schools and later expanded to five more. In 2001, the Mulholland Middle School was added to the program. In 2005, the five schools participating in the program included Monroe, Dorsey, Wilson, San Pedro, and Reseda high schools. The Luther Burbank Middle School's Police Academy Magnet program was begun in 2009. A California Partnership Academy Grant is a major funding source for the daily operation of the Los Angeles Police Academy Magnet School Program. Approximately $40,000 is raised annually, and college scholarships are awarded to deserving graduating senior cadets (LA PAM 2005).

Reseda High School's Police Academy Magnet began in the fall of 1998. The Reseda High School program is designed to be a career pathway to educate students about law enforcement through a rigid course of study involving intense physical training and compulsory community service. An LAPD officer is assigned full-time to teach, counsel, and mentor the students through their police academy experience.

The founder of the Los Angeles Unified School District Board (LAUSD) Police Academy Magnet Schools is Roberta Weintraub (Figure 8.9), an experienced member and past president of the LAUSD. She was concerned about the need for community residents to serve as police officers. In 1995, she enlisted the support of the mayor of Los Angeles, the superintendent of the LAUSD, and the LAPD police chief to establish the Police Academy Magnet Schools. The curriculum emphasizes thematic academics, discipline, community service, physical fitness, and moral and ethical studies (PAMS Founder 2013). Joel Schaeffer was the first Reseda Police Academy Magnet coordinator. He coached football at Reseda High for 23 years and taught in the LAUSD for 40 years. The school named its field after him (Sondheimer 2013). Currently, there are four high schools and two middle schools participating, with approximately 1,200 students. Alise Cayen has been the Police Academy Magnet coordinator at Reseda High School since 2005. She is the person in charge of organizing and producing the PAMS annual commencement ceremony (Alise Cayen, personal communication, January 28, 2014).

Another unique youth program was also inaugurated in Southern California. For more than 50 years, the LAPD has had a distinctive cadet preparation program for youth between 13 and 20 years of age. These LAPD cadet candidates must first complete a 144-hour program that meets on

Figure 8.9 Roberta Weintraub, founder and executive director, Los Angeles Police Academy Magnet Schools.

Saturdays for 18 consecutive weeks. The program is designed to quality them for future participation as an LAPD cadet. (Information about this academy is available at: http://www.lapdcadets.com/about/academy.)

The PAMS concept has spread to other regions. For example, the School for Law Studies, Law Enforcement, Homeland Security and Forensic Sciences was recently established within the Miami-Dade County Public Schools in collaboration with the city of Miami and the Miami Police Department. Students that are accepted into the program have access to forensic science labs, courtroom labs, and computer simulation centers. It is expected that students will have the opportunity to attend dual enrollment programs with Florida International University, the University of Miami, and Miami-Dade Community College (Miami PD 2013).

The Sacramento Police Department has had success with its Criminal Justice Magnet Academy program, which reported an enrollment of 467 at its four high schools during the 2011–2012 school year (Annual Report 2013). Participants are required to perform 50 hours of community service per year, to maintain a specific grooming standard, to wear a provided academy uniform once a week, and to represent the academy in a positive way at all times. The students are also required to maintain an 80% attendance rate and to earn 90% of their credit requirements to qualify (Sacramento PD 2013). According to its *2011–12 Annual Report*, "the Criminal Justice Academy is a partnership between high schools, and public and private organizations that focus on providing knowledge and skills-based education relevant to the work environment high school students may encounter upon graduation. The Criminal Justice Academy offers a school-within-a-school framework, taking students as a group from their freshman year through their senior year. The program is a paramilitary type of academy modeled after the Sacramento Police Department's Police Academy" (Annual Report 2013, 4). In addition, there are opportunities to hold leadership positions such as commanders, captains, lieutenants, sergeants, and corporals. These appointments permit the academy cadets "to learn the complex nature of leadership and the dynamics of human relations. The Sacramento Police Foundation sponsors an annual summer Leadership Camp where cadets learn about integrity, honor, and pride" (Annual Report 2013, 10).

Police Orientation and Preparation Program

Roberta Weintraub, the PAMS founder, has also developed another unique program. Her newest model for the delivery of police education and training for youth is the POPP. It is an exploratory educational experience that places career-bound, law enforcement students in an established LAPD training environment. Currently, classes are held at the LAPD's Ahmanson Recruit Training Center. POPP recruits twelfth-graders and community college students who may satisfy high school diploma requirements and earn four college certificates leading toward an associate's degree in administration of justice. A team of LAPD staff and officers, LAUSD coordinators and consultants, and Los Angeles Community College deans and instructors contribute to the program. For high school students, the program can help them complete the first year of community college by the time they graduate from high school. The program also spans the time from high school to career entry by immersing students in a focused effort. A tutoring service is provided by private funding. All new students must complete a four-week "pre-academy" course, which includes nutrition and physical training, English, and study skill courses, all taught by qualified police officers and high school or college instructors. The program's goals include: providing a rigorous, two-year college curriculum administered by professors that provides high school seniors and college freshman cadets with 15 college units per semester; affording cadets job opportunities in the public and private sector while in school; and offering a curricular foundation that enables cadets to obtain an associate's degree and/or transfer to a four-year university before applying for a wide range of public safety occupations. According to Weintraub, POPP ultimately offers a path to middle-class jobs for children of lower-income families and creates a "home-grown" police force that is made up of members of Los Angeles communities (Torok 2013). (The POPP handbook can be downloaded from the link found at: http://poppartc.com/requirements.)

Youth Courts

The modern youth court concept began in the early 1970s, when a small number of local communities began to experiment with a formalized structure of peer justice. From 1993 to 2008, the number of local youth and teen courts in which volunteer youth help "sentence" their peers has grown from 75 to more than 1,000, according to a report from the Global Issues Resource Center. Approximately 112,000 juvenile cases have been referred to local youth and teen courts. In addition, more than 133,000 volunteers, including youth and adults, have volunteered to help with the disposition of these juvenile cases (Peterson and Beres 2008).

Youth courts are also known as teen courts, peer courts, or student courts. They are juvenile justice programs in which young people are "sentenced" by their peers. Youth courts are established and administered in a wide variety of ways, but most youth courts are used as an alternative sentencing option for first-time offenders aged 11–17 who are charged with misdemeanor nonviolent offenses. In the majority of youth courts, the offender has acknowledged his or her guilt and participates in a youth court voluntarily, rather than going through the more formal, traditional juvenile justice procedures.

BOX 8.3   YOUTH COURT MODELS

The *Adult Judge Model* employs an adult judge to rule on courtroom procedure and to clarify legal terminology. Youth volunteers serve as defense and prosecuting attorneys and as jurors. Young people may also serve as bailiffs and clerks. This is the most common model.

The *Youth Judge Model* is similar to the Adult Judge Model except that a juvenile serves as the judge, usually after a term of service as a youth court attorney.

The *Peer Jury Model* employs a panel of teen jurors who question the youth offender directly. No defense or prosecuting attorney is employed. The judge is usually an adult volunteer.

The *Tribunal Model* has no peer jury. Instead, the prosecuting and defense attorneys present cases to a juvenile judge who determines the sentence.

Youth courts differ from other juvenile justice programs because they involve other young people in the process, especially in determining the offender's sanction. For example, a peer jury may assign an offender to a combination of community service, conflict resolution training, restitution, youth court jury duty, and/or educational workshops. Depending on the model used, young people may serve as jurors, prosecuting attorneys, defense attorneys, bailiffs, clerks, and even judges.

Because youth courts are developed in local communities and by local communities, there is no cookie-cutter approach to the structure of these programs. However, Box 8.3 indicates some common models that youth courts employ.

Regardless of the model employed, most youth courts are based in the juvenile justice system or in a community setting. The most common agencies operating or administering youth court programs are juvenile courts and private nonprofit organizations (29% each). The next most common agencies are law enforcement agencies and juvenile probation departments (17% each). Schools are the operating agencies for about 10% of youth courts, while a variety of other agencies (e.g., city government, the administrative office of the court) are less commonly the operating agency (Peterson and Beres 2008).

Future Directions

There is documentation available indicating that the Police Academy Magnet Schools are achieving their primary goal of increasing the number of high school students who enter college. However, there is much less evidence about the success or long-term value of holding intermittent and relatively brief youth academies. According to Bright (1992, 40), "Young people make a significant contribution to the crime problem both as offenders and victims, and they should be the principal focus of any crime prevention strategy." It is hard to imagine how programs of short duration (e.g., a weeklong summer youth academy) can have desirable and lasting effects when the problems encountered by youth are often compounded by family breakdown, poor schools and housing, the proliferation of drugs and guns, limited employment opportunities, and the social and physical decline of neighborhoods. The four-week Burlington Police Department's JPA appears to be an exception. Although short duration youth academies may or may not have a lasting effect for participants, the practice of having in-house officers, such as school district police officers, to offer such programs on a routine basis should be expanded and evaluated. As Chief Fuller noted: "When an officer stands before a class and presents material that he understands and loves, students respect that. When a student raises his hand and shows genuine curiosity about a profession that he sees depicted a thousand times a day on radio and television, officers return that respect" (Fuller 2012). The Police Academy Magnet Schools appear to represent the optimum type of police-oriented youth program.

Comparable to like the magnet schools, most Explorer posts and Junior ROTC units insist that, to remain affiliated, participants must maintain strict requirements related to their character and academic performance. Consequently, the inclusion of a Law Enforcement Explorer program can strengthen any department's or school district's efforts to resist and prevent crime and disorder among youth. Such programs may also lead to a more congenial relationship between the youth of a community and the police. Police agencies should develop these programs as an integral agency function, and they should draw on the knowledge and skills of current and retired police officers as well as qualified community members. College students over 21 can be recruited to serve as volunteer post advisors under faculty supervision. Through involvement with such programs, youthful participants are bound to become more career focused, empowered, and more concerned about lifelong learning. In addition, police officers, teachers, and adult volunteers will have the satisfaction of knowing that they are participating in a meaningful and needed activity.

For the sake of maintaining interest and enthusiasm for the Explorer movement, individual Explorer units have offered programs beyond the usual activities of training lectures, crowd control, clerical work, dispatch work, ride-alongs, and such community projects as clean-up drives.[8] Occasionally, newsworthy activities have been reported. For example, in May 2009, a controversy erupted when the *New York Times* reported that Explorer programs were engaging in "training thousands of young people in skills used to confront terrorism, illegal immigration and escalating border violence" (Steinhauer 2009). The report indicated that during a simulation exercise, an Explorer group used compressed-air guns, known as Airsoft guns, that fire tiny plastic pellets[9] (Steinhauer 2009). It remains to be seen whether this activity will become widespread. Upon the publication of this particular news report, hundreds of comments were posted on the *New York Times*' online commentary Web site regarding the type of training being provided; the vast majority of these were unfavorable.[10]

The official Web site for the Law Enforcement Explorer program is found at: http://exploring.learningforlife.org/services/career-exploring/law-enforcement. The site provides recent updates about the program. For example, at its October 2010 meeting, the National Law Enforcement Exploring Committee (NLEEC)[11] approved voluntary training certification for Law Enforcement Exploring, effective on January 1, 2011. Each agency or organization that has its basic or advanced training program for Law Enforcement Explorers certified will receive paperwork from the national office signed by the national director for Law Enforcement Exploring and the chairperson of the subcommittee for training certification that designates this fact. Each course presented in a basic or advanced training program must have a written lesson plan that includes a variety of basic information such as the title of the lesson, number of instructional hours, learning objectives, testing procedures, and so on. Such documentation could prove invaluable when seeking high school or college credits (Law Enforcement Training 2012). It is interesting to speculate that the advent of individual Explorer training certification might someday serve as the model or catalyst for the establishment of a national individual police officer training certification (see Lindsay and Greenberg 2013). This type of police training standard would greatly enhance the development of police professionalism. Box 8.4 provides a list of additional recommended activities or projects for Explorer posts.

Larson et al. (2009, 2) concluded that "some of the current methods used to involve citizens in the policing of their communities are: Community Oriented Policing, Problem Oriented Policing, Police Reserves, and Volunteer Citizen Patrol. All of these methods should be used together for services to be delivered in the most effective way." In addition, carefully screened and trained youth should be used to enhance the delivery of a wide array of selected public safety activities. However, in many communities, financing for such services are often lacking, or they are given scant support.

BOX 8.4   NEW ROLES FOR POLICE EXPLORER POSTS

- Assist with new citation approach for juvenile delinquency/status offenses
- Conduct seminars on law and security (active shooter, identity theft, etc.)
- Revitalize School Resource Officer (SRO) and anti-bullying programs
- Monitor/investigate reports of elder abuse
- Provide crime victim services
- Help to coordinate neighborhood watch programs
- Staff storefront locations
- Operate bookmobiles for homebound residents
- Engage in cemetery inspections
- Assist with animal cruelty investigations
- Serve as tutors/assistant coaches in community centers and on playgrounds
- Encourage leaders in minority communities to attend CPAs

Summary

Throughout the nation, there exist a variety of police-sponsored and/or school-based programs involving youth. Generally, these programs are being supervised by police officers, retired military personnel, and/or teachers. This chapter reviewed several types: youth police academies; recreational (e.g., PAL); limited enforcement (e.g., Explorers); magnet school (LA Police Academy Magnet Schools, Sacramento PD Criminal Justice Academy, etc.); and school safety (e.g., AAA Safety Patrollers). The short-term youth police academies are typically held for a week during the summer, and their popularity has contributed to the creation of the "JPA Content Lab," an online program with posted lessons that can be easily accessed by all students, teachers, parents, and counselors.

A new and promising program to bridge the gap between high school and career entry was also described—the POPP. It was founded by Robert a Weintraub, who also founded the LA Police Academy Magnet Schools. In 2011, Weintraub commented about her new initiative: "Here is a high school/college degree program that provides students with an educational program that includes extensive physical training, discipline, plus real and simulated experiences that will enhance a law enforcement career decision" (Weintraub 2011).

During their heyday, the early junior police programs provided opportunities for fostering positive relationships between younger citizens and the police as well as opportunities for practicing values associated with good citizenship. In some cities, these units evolved into Police Athletic Leagues (PAL). Many of these traditions are now being carried out by thousands of members of numerous Law Enforcement Explorer Posts, safety patrollers, and by military-related organizations such as the Junior ROTC. In this way, the early junior police who participated in community projects have served as pathfinders for those contemporary local police agencies and federal services interested in community policing by assisting youth. In some ways, the coincidence of new police-related Explorer units in the 1960s along with the inadequate and oftentimes uncivil response of police during the social upheavals of that period may have encouraged the reforms that took place in later years, such as the "community policing movement" that began in the late 1970s. The former demonstrated the importance of citizen participation in police work, while the latter demonstrated how the absence of citizen participation can lead to citizen abuse. Today, two of the signature policies of "community policing" are having regular officers leave their cars in order to encourage positive contacts with businesses and community residents and seeking possible partnerships with community groups as often as possible.

Short-term youth (junior) police academies have varying emphases. A few basic types of police-sponsored and/or school-based academy programs include: the crime scene investigation camp (e.g., South Bend, Indiana); the physical training or boot camp model involving at-risk youth (e.g., Burlington, as seen in Figure 8.10); and more generalized programs of instruction with academic units of instruction (e.g., the Oklahoma's Cadet Lawman Academy). Programs for at-risk youth tend to exceed the duration of the other types of programs.

Figure 8.10 A past graduating class from the Burlington (North Carolina) Police Department Junior Police Academy. The academy is a nationally recognized at-risk youth program developed in 1996. (Used with the permission of the Burlington Police Department.)

Currently, more than 33,000 Explorers and more than 8,400 adult volunteers participate in Law Enforcement Exploring in the United States. The program highlights include: the National Law Enforcement Exploring Leadership academies, ride-alongs, career achievement awards, National Law Enforcement Exploring conferences, and scholarship opportunities (Westland Police 2012a; AAA 2014). The types and duration of training provided to Law Enforcement Explorers varies from post to post and ranges from a simple orientation class to extensive multilevel academic and practical application-based instructional programs. In some instances, such training has been accepted for high school and/or college academic credit. On at least one occasion, unfavorable publicity was engendered by militaristic role-playing activities. In order to remove some of the uncertainty and inconsistency with respect to such training, a new national training certification program was established in 2011. Its goals are to provide validation and recognition for those Law Enforcement Posts or organizations that provide training programs that meet or exceed minimum standards with respect to curriculum development and content, performance evaluation procedure, record management, and instructor qualifications. Like the CALEA certification program, this youth program certification is voluntary.

The Broome County Sheriff's Law Enforcement Explorer Post Web pages claim that it is one of the most successful Exploring posts in its local area, noting that their curriculum and course outlines have been used as guides by other Explorer posts. It attributes its success rate to continual adult leadership and programs that encourage youth development (Broome County 2007). Continued requests for unit Explorers are indicative of the success of the program. Ultimately, however, the availability of local resources, the integrity of a unit's advisors, and the decisions made by the leadership of the sponsoring agency will determine the quality and effectiveness of a particular youth program.

Throughout the twentieth century, many communities have experimented with programs involving youth in the performance of limited types of police work (e.g., crowd control). In addition, youth in both urban and rural settings have engaged in important roles in the field of pedestrian safety. The AAA safety patrollers were the most ubiquitous of these organizations because they were routinely assigned to traffic and crossing guard duty at the streets adjacent to their elementary and middle schools. They also helped to keep order on school buses, assisted younger children getting on and off school buses, and maintained decorum along school hallways. In several towns and cities, some members of the first wave of junior police groups actually engaged in a limited amount of routine street patrol. The junior police members were trained to perform their assignments by local police agencies. Heroic actions by the safety patrollers still take place when a pedestrian's safety is at risk. One source has estimated that some 600,000 individuals participate in such patrols in 32,000 elementary or middle schools (see Chandler 2013).

The early twentieth-century creation of junior police forces in Berkeley and in New York City and their modern-day Explorer counterparts exemplify the basic aspect of community policing by bringing communities and police closer together. Moreover, by providing additional personnel, they may fill gaps in the public safety net. In some ways, the early junior police who participated in community projects may have served as the pathfinders for those contemporary police who have been, once again, assigned to walk foot patrols around business and residential areas and to ride bicycles so that community problems might be better identified and resolved.

According to John Ellison, a former police chief in West Linn, Oregon, "The promises of community policing are many. They include—strengthening the capacity of communities to resist and prevent crime and social disorder; creating a more harmonious relationship between the police and the public, including some power sharing with respect to police policy making and tactical priorities; restructuring police service delivery by linking it with other municipal services; and reforming the police organization model by creating larger and more complex roles for individual officers" (2006, 12).

Progress in police work with youth involving Explorer posts, JPAs, magnet schools, as well as Drug Abuse Resistance Education (D.A.R.E.), Gang Resistance Education and Training (G.R.E.A.T.), and PAL programs[12] is continuing. These programs demonstrate that frontline full-time police officers, as well as non-sworn adult police volunteers, can play significant roles as educators and mentors of youth. In the late 1990s, the first Police Academy Magnet Schools began to appear. Due to their multiyear nature, they appear to represent a value-added approach to the existing mix of police-oriented youth programs.

Youth programs should be broadened to include other municipal agencies (e.g., schools, hospitals, emergency services, and so on). In addition, many school districts have begun to recognize the value of having students engage in peer mediation, student courts, conflict resolution, teen courts, and similar programs. "Youth courts empower youth to be active participants in community problem solving, and they foster important values, attitudes, and beliefs related to the implementation and execution of the justice system" (Peterson and Beres 2008, 6). It is interesting to note that for several decades in the twentieth century, most efforts aimed at the protection of school children were carried out solely by the students themselves under the watchful eyes of their teachers. Today, this type of activity rarely occurs due to the violent nature of many inner-city schools and concerns over school district liability. Nevertheless, if after appropriate screening and training today's school-age youth were offered more opportunities for undertaking such duties, perhaps they might be better prepared to face life's greater challenges, and our schools might be safer. The selection and training of youth for participation in teen courts in hundreds of communities is a positive step forward because they offer a positive alternative to traditional juvenile justice and school disciplinary procedures.

The following chapter will address several semi-military/homeland security programs involving youth at the federal level, such as Junior ROTC, Civil Air Patrol cadets, and Explorer units sponsored by federal law enforcement agencies. A few federal internship programs are also examined as well as the new Federal Emergency Management Agency (FEMA) Corps.

Review Questions

1. List at least five topics that might be included in a typical short-term junior police academy. Select one topic from this list and explain who might be best qualified to serve as the topic's instructor.
2. Identify several types of activities engaged in by Broome County (New York) Explorer Post members and discuss the appropriateness of having police Explorers participate in alcohol and tobacco stings.
3. Discuss the types of insurance coverage available to individual Explorer posts, their members, and their leadership.
4. The successor organization to the 1940s Phoenix corps of junior police is the police department's Explorer Post 2906. Provide arguments for and against the idea of permitting Post 2906 Explorers to serve as sworn traffic enforcement officers, a practice in which junior police were permitted to participate in the past.
5. Many of the junior police programs discussed in this chapter have or have had a rank structure similar to that of the regular police hierarchy. Provide arguments for and against the use of such a rank structure.
6. Discuss a few of the benefits and possible drawbacks of participating in a Law Enforcement Exploring Program as an adult volunteer or as a student participant.
7. Describe the Westland (MI) Police Department's Explorer Post "Sober-Up Program."
8. Search online to find an article describing a recent incident that led to the AAA Lifesaving Medal being awarded. Summarize these facts. Do you consider the actions worthy of such a medal? Explain your views.
9. Do you believe that it should be a more serious crime to assault a Police Explorer than to assault a person who has no such affiliation? Explain your views.

10. For a number of decades prior to World War II and a few years there-
    after, it was a common sight to observe safety patrol boys and girls
    stopping traffic in order to escort students across streets near school
    buildings. Is there any need to reinstitute this practice? If so, who
    might object? Explain your views.
11. Discuss the pros and cons of organizing short-duration (e.g., a week-
    long summer youth academy) versus longer-term police-affiliated
    youth programs, such as a police magnet school.
12. Examine the list of proposed new roles for Police Explorers found in
    Box 8.4. Do you believe that these roles should or can be performed
    by qualified Police Explorers? Explain your views.

Notes

1. As part of "Merchants Week," boys dressed as police were on hand to escort
   Rear Admiral William T. Sampson (the "Hero of Santiago") when he visited
   Maynard, MA, on May 16, 1900. He was presented with a shuttle from the
   Assabet Mills. (The original photo is in the Maynard Historical Society Archives
   and is reproduced here with permission of the Society.)
2. The Association of Military Colleges and Schools of the United States
   (AMCSUS), formed in 1914, is a nonprofit service organization that, since its
   founding, has served as an advocate for military colleges and schools and has
   acted as a liaison with the Departments of Defense and Education. Currently
   there are nine military colleges and universities, five military junior colleges,
   25 military preparatory (institute) schools, and one associate member school in
   the association (AMCSUS 2012).
3. It is important to note that many police agencies maintain adult auxiliary or
   reserve police programs that involve sworn duties as well as Law Enforcement
   Explorer units that function in a non-sworn capacity; such dual programs can
   be found, for example, in the Manchester Township (NJ) Police Department.
   Another key difference is that the initial age of membership can be as low as 14
   for an Explorer, but auxiliaries are usually 18 or older.
4. Two four-minute slide show videos produced in 2009 and featuring a total of
   44 different photographs of police Explorer posts can be viewed online at: http://
   www.youtube.com/watch?v=WqKGPsbPXsA and at http://www.youtube.com/
   watch?v=1aTfi3Jik-g. A useful nine-minute video that provides a good overview of the variety of activities in which Explorers engage can be found at:
   http://www.youtube.com/watch?v=CBYd4hR62A0.
5. Known as the "Gateway to the Rockies," Aurora sits at an elevation of 5,435
   feet and is adjacent to Denver International Airport. Aurora is about 13 miles
   from Littleton, CO—the site of the April 1999 Columbine High School massacre. In July 2012, James Holmes opened fire in a crowded Aurora movie theater.
   Holmes has pleaded not guilty by reason of insanity to multiple charges of murder and attempted murder. He is accused of killing 12 people and injuring 70
   during a midnight showing of the feature film *The Dark Knight Rises*.

6. Chapter 784.03 of the Florida Statutes defines felony battery as occurring when a person, "Actually and intentionally touches or strikes another person against the will of the other; or intentionally causes bodily harm to another person."

7. "The telltale sign of the safety patrol is the neon belts. The design, with its waist and diagonal shoulder straps, is named for a 19th century British army officer who used the belt to carry his sword. The design has remained but the colors have changed—from white to neon orange to a fluorescent green that the AAA calls 'lectric green'" (Chandler 2013).

8. For example, the Pinellas Park (FL) police and Explorers have volunteered their time to eradicate graffiti from buildings, walls, and fences. On one occasion, they painted over illicit art at 30 locations to eliminate gang-related and so-called "tagger" graffiti. Tagger art is graffiti usually done by nongang individuals (Michalski 2009).

9. The news article focused on the Explorer program in Imperial County, a needy county in Southern California where the local economy appears to be based largely on the criminal justice system. In addition to the sheriff and local police departments, there are two state prisons and a large Border Patrol and immigration enforcement presence (see Steinhauer 2009).

10. One commentator, who was serving on the executive board of the National Capital Area Council, Boy Scouts of America, wrote: "Please readers, understand that there are those of us in the leadership of the Scouting Movement who are as appalled as you are. And we're Scouting's majority by a long mile. Your beef is with the local law enforcement Explorer Post leaders in Imperial County, California, not with the BSA. If you care to study the history and the peculiar sociology of Scouting a little more closely, you will discover that precisely this concern—an encroachment of paramilitary indoctrination—has been eschewed by the Scouts in Britain and the USA ever since Scouting's foundation a hundred years ago" (Pocalyko 2009).

11. The National Association of Law Enforcement Explorers functioned as the principal organization for Law Enforcement Exploring until the formation of the National Law Enforcement Exploring Committee (NLEEC) in 1976. The NLEEC provides advice and guidance on the Exploring program. The committee comprises the directors of several federal law enforcement agencies, various sheriffs and chiefs of police, the provost marshal of the U.S. Army, representatives from allied organizations, and individuals from the private sector who support law enforcement. A national youth representative and a vice national youth representative also serve on the NLEEC (Law Enforcement Exploring 2011).

12. In New York City, PAL evolved from the establishment of junior police, play-street movement, and the Twilight Athletic League (PAL 2012). Founded 1983 in Los Angeles, the Drug Abuse Resistance Education (D.A.R.E.) program is currently a police officer-led series of classroom lessons taught from kindergarten through twelfth grade. "It is now being implemented in 75 percent of our nation's school districts and in more than 43 countries around the world" (DARE 2012). Established in 1991, Gang Resistance Education and Training (G.R.E.A.T.) is also police-instructed, but its curricula for elementary and middle schools focus on youth crime, gang, and violence prevention.

The Federal Law Enforcement Training Center (FLETC) sponsors regional advanced training for G.R.E.A.T. instructors who have taught G.R.E.A.T. for at least one year (GREAT 2012).

References

AAA. (2014). History: A century of service. Retrieved March 3, 2014 from http://newsroom.aaa.com/about-aaa/history/

AAA Honors. (2011). AAA honors seven elementary school students on Capitol Hill with 2011 lifesaving medal for the heroic actions. Retrieved October 2, 2013 from http://newsroom.aaa.com/tag/school-safety-patrol/

About Oak Ridge. (2013). About Oak Ridge elementary. Retrieved October 4, 2013 from http://www.district196.org/or/AboutUs.html

AMCSUS. (2012). Our mission and purposes. Retrieved June 1, 2012 from http://www.amcsus.org/page.cfm?p = 12

Annual Report. (2013). Sacramento Police Department, Criminal Justice Academy, 2011–2012 annual report. Retrieved October 3, 2013 from http://www.sacpd.org/pdf/youth/youthar12.pdf

Aurora Explorers. (2014). What type of activities and benefits are available to explorers? Retrieved January 24, 2014 from http://www.auroraexplorers.com/Postoverview.html

Bost, C. (2011, July 12). Junior police academy returns a better man. Retrieved May 21, 2012 from http://www.thetimesnews.com/common/printer/view.php?db = burlington&id = 45828

Bright, J. (1992). *Crime prevention in America: A British perspective.* Chicago, IL: Office of International Criminal Justice/The University of Illinois at Chicago.

Broome County. (2007). Broome County Sheriff 2007 annual report. Retrieved September 28, 2013 from http://www.gobroomecounty.com/files/sheriff/pdfs/OfficeOfSheriffAnnualReport.pdf

Buffalo Grove. (2012a). Academies. Retrieved May 18, 2012 from http://www.vbg.org/index.aspx?nid = 292

Buffalo Grove. (2012b). Participant liability waiver and hold harmless agreement. Retrieved May 18, 2012 from http://www.vbg.org/DocumentCenter/Home/View/88

Cadet Lawman. (2012). Cadet Lawman Academy. Retrieved May 22, 2012 from http://www.cadetlawman.com/

Career Exploring FAQs. (2013). Retrieved September 27, 2013 from http://exploring.learningforlife.org/contact-us/exploring-faqs/

Chandler, M. A. (2013, September 9). How much do you know about the school safety patrol? Retrieved October 3, 2013 from http://articles.washingtonpost.com/2013-09-09/local/41890468_1_dangerous-student-practices-safety-patrol-patrol-badges

City of Burlington. (2012). Junior police academy. Retrieved May 21, 2012 from http://www.ci.burlington.nc.us/index.aspx?NID = 526

City of Phoenix. (2013). Law enforcement explorer program. Retrieved September 25, 2013 from http://phoenix.gov/police/explor1.html

DARE. (2012). About DARE. Retrieved May 24, 2012 from http://www.dare.com/home/about_dare.asp

Ellison, J. (2006). Community policing: Implementation issues. *FBI Law Enforcement Bulletin, 75*(4), 12.

Exploring. (2014). Law enforcement career exploring. Retrieved March 3, 2014 from http://exploring.learningforlife.org/services/career-exploring/law-enforcement/

Ferreira, C. (2011). Real-world CSI for South Bend teens. Retrieved May 18, 2012 from http://articles.wsbt.com/2011-06-17/south-bend-teens_29672542

Folsom, A. (1971). Youth form state-wide law enforcement organization. *Law and Order, 19*(12), 121, 128.

Fuller, P. (2012). The junior police academy works. Retrieved May 21, 2012 from http://www.juniorpoliceacademy.org/jpa-works/

GREAT. (2012). Welcome to the G.R.E.A.T. web site. Retrieved May 24, 2012 from http://www.great-online.org/

Greenberg, M. A. (2008, April). A short history of junior police. *The Police Chief, 75*(4), 172–180.

Henrietta Ambulance. (2012). Explorer post. Retrieved May 23, 2012 from http://henriettaambulance.org/explorer-post/

Hollywood Community. (2013). Hollywood Community Police Activities League (PAL) program. Retrieved September 24, 2013 from http://www.lapdonline.org/hollywood_community_police_station/content_basic_ view/23690

Insurance Information. (2011). Insurance information for volunteers. Retrieved October 2, 2013 from http://www.stlbsa.org/volunteers/pages/insurance-information-for-volunteers.aspx

LA PAM. (2005). Los Angeles Police Academy Magnet School Program. Retrieved October 3, 2013 from http://www.lacp.org/2005-Articles-Main/YouthPrograms/Report2-MagnetSchools.html

Larson, J., Lewis, V., Day, K. and Kelso, C. (2009). Reducing the cost of crime through reserve police officers and volunteer citizen patrol. *Research in Business and Economics Journal*, (3), 1–8. Retrieved May 29, 2012 from http://www.aabri.com/manuscripts/09316.pdf

Law Enforcement Exploring. (2011, July). Law enforcement exploring: Program and resource guide for adult leaders. Retrieved May 24, 2012 from https://c183757.ssl.cf1.rackcdn.com/wp-content/documents/LEE_Program%20and%20Resource%20Guide_0811.pdf

Law Enforcement Training. (2012). Law enforcement training certification. Retrieved May 23, 2012 from https://c183757.ssl.cf1.rackcdn.com/lawenforcement/Law-Enforcement-Exploring-Training-Certification.pdf

LeConte, K. (2012a). JPA content lab. Retrieved May 18, 2012 from https://sites.google.com/site/jpacourse2012/home

LeConte, K. (2012b). Message from JPA Program Director Kelly LeConte. Retrieved May 21, 2012 from http://www.juniorpoliceacademy.org/what-is-jpa/

Lightcap, B. (2013). *The Morrill act of 1862*. Retrieved October 2, 2013 from http://www3.nd.edu/~rbarger/www7/morrill.html

Lindsay, V. and Greenberg, M.A. (2013). The evolution of the need for establishing a national certification program for criminology/criminal justice majors. *Journal of the Institute and International Studies*, No. 13, 129–139.

Miami PD. (2013). Training center – Magnet high school. Retrieved October 3, 2013 from http://www.miami-police.org/magnet_program.html

Michalski, T. (2009, April 23). Police, explorers conduct 'paint out'. Retrieved May 24, 2012 from http://www.tbnweekly.com/pubs/pinellas_park_beacon/content_articles/042309_par-06.txt

PAL. (2012). Police athletic league of New York City: History. Retrieved May 24, 2012 from http://www.palnyc.org/800-PAL-4KIDS/History.aspx

PAMS Founder. (2013). Retrieved October 3, 2013 from http://resedapoliceacademy-magnet.com/pams-founder/

Patrol Manual. (2012). The Oak Ridge school safety patrol manual. Retrieved October 4, 2013 from http://learn.district196.org/pluginfile.php?file =%2F156989%2Fmod_resource%2Fcontent%2F0%2FSafety_Patrol_Manual_2012.pdf

Peterson, S. B. and Beres, J. (2008). *The first report to the nation on youth courts and teen courts.* Cleveland, OH: Global Issues Resource Center.

Pistol Team Wins. (1976, February 27). Pistol teams wins in pistol match. *St. Petersburg Independent*, p. 5-B.

Pocalyko, M. (2009, May 14). Online post no.423. Retrieved October 6, 2013 from http://community.nytimes.com/comments/www.nytimes.com/2009/05/14/us/14explorers.html?sort = oldest

Police Explorers. (2013). Aurora Police Department explorer post 2024. Retrieved September 28, 2013 from https://www.auroragov.org/LivingHere/YouthResources/PoliceExplorers/index.htm

Police Host. (2012). Police host exchange visitor. *City News*, p. 4.

Popular Activity. (1949). *Popular activity of the Birmingham recreation program is the Junior Police Academy .... (photo caption).* Free Press, Birmingham, UK, p. 10.

Rowbatham, J. F. (1895). *The history of Rossall School* (1st ed.), Manchester, UK: John Heywood.

Sacramento PD. (2013). Criminal Justice Magnet Academy. Retrieved October 3, 2013 from http://www.sacpd.org/getinvolved/student/magnet/

Sondheimer, E. (2013, January 14). Football: Ex-Reseda coach Joel Schaeffer dies. Retrieved October 3, 2013 from http://latimesblogs.latimes.com/varsitytimes-insider/2013/01/football-ex-reseda-coach-joel-schaeffer-dies.html

Steinhauer, J. (2009, May 14). Scouts train to fight terrorists, and more. *New York Times*, p. A1.

Torok, R. (2013, May 1). Turning teens into police officers. Retrieved January 25, 2014 from http://www.jewishjournal.com/los_angeles/item/turning_teens_into_police_officers

Waterloo Handbook. (2012). Waterloo Police, S.A.E.S.A. Explorers handbook. Retrieved May 23, 2012 from http://www.docstoc.com/docs/23703765/Waterloo-Police-Explorers-Handbook

Weintraub, R. (2011, July 14). A Note from our founder, Roberta Weintraub. Retrieved January 25, 2014 from http://poppartc.com/2011/07/a-note-from-our-founder-roberta-weintraub/

Westland Police. (2012a). About us: Westland police explorers. Retrieved May 26, 2012 from http://www.westlandpoliceexplorers.com/index.php?option = com_content&view = article&id = 47&Itemid = 53

Westland Police. (2012b). The sober up program. Retrieved May 26, 2012 from http://www.westlandpoliceexplorers.com/index.php?option=com_content&view=article&id=52&Itemid=58

Wilmath, K. (2008, December 24). Police explorer's bravery inspires bill. *Tampa Bay Times*. Retrieved May 24, 2012 from http://www.tampabay.com/news/article947749.ece

WSCC. (2012). Junior Police Academy. Retrieved May 18, 2012 http://www.wscc.edu/programs-and-certificates/public-service/public-safety-academies/junior-police-academy.html

Youth Protection. (2013). Youth protection training. Retrieved September 27, 2013 from http://exploring.learningforlife.org/services/resources/youth-protection-training/

Youth Involvement in Public Safety and Security at the Federal Level

9

We cannot always build the future for our youth, but we can build our youth for the future.

—Franklin Delano Roosevelt
Address at the University of Pennsylvania, September 20, 1940

Introduction

Adult volunteer participation in law enforcement is found at all governmental levels, but it is mostly a local endeavor. At the federal level, there exist a variety of obvious roles such as: voting in national elections, calling emergency federal "hotlines," serving on federal juries, and participating in interest groups to influence federal policy. Other roles also exist. For example, citizen participation in identifying and reporting potential and alleged violations of various federal regulatory laws, such as bringing citizen lawsuits in the federal district courts against polluters for violations of environmental laws. The Internal Revenue Service has had a citizen reward program for many years. Also known as the "whistle-blower program," it offers informants rewards of up to 30% of any fines and unpaid taxes recouped by the government. Other federal agencies have similar programs, and awards can be in the million-dollar range (see Kocieniewski 2012). However, citizen participation also includes mainstream organizations concerned with public safety, disaster relief, and homeland security, such as the Federal Emergency Management Agency (FEMA), the U.S. Coast Guard Auxiliary, and the Civil Air Patrol.

Of course, young people under the age of 18 cannot vote or sit on juries and are unlikely to possess the type of information necessary to benefit from the various bounty programs conducted by federal agencies. Nevertheless, as we have seen in Chapter 8, youth and young adults still have other significant opportunities to contribute to the field of law enforcement at the local level. Moreover, there exist several national and federal programs for involving youth in the field of public safety and security. The most well-known examples are: Senior (college level) Reserve Officers' Training Corps (ROTC) units, Junior ROTC units, U.S. Navy Sea Cadets,[1] and the Civil Air Patrol Cadet Program.

Although numerous operational similarities exist, it would be a mistake to assume that the current mix of federal law enforcement related youth programs has been simply modeled after the local and state Police Explorer programs of the past half century (discussed in Chapter 8) because other factors must be considered. For example, for nearly 100 years, the federal government has been directly involved in youth education and occupational preparation, primarily due to the need for preparedness in the area of national defense. During the 1920s and 1930s, aside from the Civilian Conservation Corps (CCC),[2] the most well-known (but now forgotten) example of such a program was the Citizens' Military Training Camp (CMTC) program introduced by Major General Leonard Wood in 1913.

Today, the most manifest and enduring examples of federal law enforcement or military-related youth initiatives are: Senior (college level) ROTC units, Junior ROTC units, U.S. Navy Sea Cadets, and the Civil Air Patrol Cadet Program. In 2012, a partnership between FEMA (a division within the U.S. Department of Homeland Security) and the Corporation for National and Community Service (CNCS) formed the FEMA Corps for young people aged 18–24. In addition, a frequently asked question at the FEMA Web site is whether young people under 18 can participate in the Community Emergency Response Team (CERT) program. This is considered a local decision. Someone under 18 should be with a parent or have permission to attend. Some communities have reached out specifically to young people. Florida's Winter Springs High School offers the training to high school students. CERT is a great way to address the community service requirements for high school students, and it provides students with useful skills. According to the FEMA Web page, CERT also fits nicely with training given to Boy and Girl Scouts and to the Civil Air patrol.

In addition to the foregoing list of organizations, there are a variety of federal Law Enforcement Explorer Leadership academies as well as more than two dozen Explorer Posts sponsored by the U.S. Customs and Border Protection service. A few features of the civilian military training camps of past generations have appeared again in these modern-day programs. Apparently, each arose out of concern for the future well-being of youth. Several programs also address the need to prepare thousands of young people for future careers related to homeland security. This chapter considers many of the leading federal initiatives for youth in public safety activities as well as information regarding the availability of federal internship opportunities.

The Citizens' Military Training Camps

Military training camps for civilians were established just prior to World War I. In 1913, under the direction of Major General Leonard Wood, two "vacation camps" were held for students from educational institutions in

Monterey, California, and Gettysburg, Pennsylvania. The men who attended these camps paid their own expenses. Four camps were held in 1914, and five camps were offered in 1915. A 1916 amendment to the National Defense Act led to the establishment of 12 camps, with the federal government covering the expenses associated with each camp. By 1921, the camp programs gained a permanent status when the CMTC program was created under the 1920 National Defense Act (Citizens' Military Training 2013). It could be considered a "youth" program because participants could be as young as 17. The CMTC program ended in 1941. The purpose of CMTCs was to train young men (approximately 17–30 years old) of good character for 30 day summer periods of time in order to promote citizenship, patriotism, and Americanism, as well as to benefit the young men individually and to instill in them a sense of obligation to the country through physical, athletic, and military training. Those interested filed an application, which included a medical fitness statement and a certificate of good moral character signed by a prominent citizen such as a member of the clergy, a current or former officer of the armed forces, or a schoolteacher (War Department 1925).

Initially, the program consisted of three training levels (Red, White, and Blue), and in 1923, an advanced Red level course was added. In time, the courses were simply identified as: Basic, Red, White, and Blue. There was no obligation to join the regular service, but opportunities did exist to do so. The government paid all expenses including transportation to and from the camps, as well as paying for all food, clothing, housing, and medical care (War Department 1925).

Instruction was given over a four-year period with each course conducted for a month during the summer. The usual age of participation in the first or basic course was between 17 and 24. By 1924, the total number of civilian trainees had passed the 30,000 level (Citizens' Military Training 2013). National Guard, organized reserves and, later, ROTC personnel could also take the advanced training levels in order to increase their rank (War Department 1925).

Camp Meade (renamed Fort Meade in 1929) belonged to the III Corps area. It was named for Maj. Gen. George Gordon Meade, whose victory at the Battle of Gettysburg proved a major factor in turning the tide of the Civil War in favor of the North. The largest number of CMTC participants in the III Corps area, which included men from Pennsylvania, Maryland, Virginia, and the District of Columbia, trained at Camp Meade, Maryland. In 1923, about 4,000 attended Camp Meade, and the number remained high in 1940 at approximately 3,000. Participants at Camp Meade had facilities such as a theater, swimming pool, and library (War Department 1925). The Army Tank School was originally located at Fort Meade after World War I. It became a training center during

World War II, its ranges and other facilities used by more than 200 units and approximately 3.5 million men between 1942 and 1946 (Fort Meade History 2013).

College Level ROTC Units

Members of college level ROTC units engage in most of the same activities as regular college students. For example, they earn a four-year academic degree and learn to think and reason at the college level. However, at the same time, they learn leadership skills and have experiences that will qualify them to become commissioned officers in the particular military unit (e.g., Army, Air Force, Navy, and Marines) located on their campus. ROTC is taken for elective credit and, depending upon the student's major, may count as a minor in military science. The modern Army Reserve Officers' Training Corps was created by the National Defense Act of 1916. This program commissioned its first class of lieutenants after World War I. The concept behind ROTC, however, had its roots in military training that began taking place in civilian colleges and universities as early as 1819 with the founding of the American Literary, Scientific and Military Academy at Norwich, Vermont (today's Norwich University). Thereafter, various other military schools were established, including the civilian land-grant colleges, which came after the Civil War and required military training to be part of their curriculum (History of ROTC 2013). In 1887, the Marian Military Institute (MMI) was established in Alabama. The school evolved over the years and it traces its organization in the year 1842. It is considered the oldest military junior college in the nation. An ROTC program was introduced at MMI in 1916.

The Naval Reserve Officer Training Corps (NROTC) at the Berkeley campus of the University of California is among the oldest ROTC units in the country. One of the original six ROTC units created, NROTC Berkeley was originally headed by Chester W. Nimitz, the famous World War II fleet admiral. Since then, NROTC Berkeley has been training college students in the disciplines of leadership, physical fitness, and military sciences. Over the years, the addition of such institutional affiliates as the California Maritime Academy, University of California Davis, and Stanford University has increased the number of officers the unit has commissioned into the Navy and Marine Corps. Today, the unit has four officers, two civilian staff members, and 60–70 midshipmen (NROTC Berkeley 2013).

Currently, ROTC college programs are offered at more than 1,000 colleges and universities across the United States. Unlike other service branches, the Coast Guard has a different format for preparing officer candidates who are still undergraduate college students at certain approved colleges and institutions. The age qualification ranges from 19 through 27. It is called the College

Student Pre-Commissioning Initiative (CSPI) program.[3] Following college graduation, CSPI students attend the 17-week officer candidate school (OCS) in New London, Connecticut. Upon successful completion of OCS, graduates receive a commission as an ensign (O-1) and an assignment in one of the Coast Guard missions, including (but not limited to) marine safety and prevention, contingency planning, law enforcement and incident management, vessel navigation and safety, search and rescue coordination, and icebreaking. Information about this program is available at: http://www.ocoastguard.com/cspi.

FEMA Corps

In 2012, the Department of Homeland Security's FEMA and the CNCS partnered to establish the FEMA Corps. The unit is limited to a maximum of 1,600 members within the AmeriCorps National Civilian Community Corps (NCCC), and its activities are solely devoted to disaster preparedness, response, and recovery (FEMA Corps 2013). A relatively new program, its goals include: the enhancement of the federal government's disaster capabilities; increasing the reliability and diversity of the disaster workforce; promoting an ethic of service; expanding education and economic opportunity for young people; and achieving significant cost savings. On a yearly basis, the program is expected to see a savings of approximately $60 million (FEMA Corps 2013).

FEMA Corps is a full-time residential service program for individuals aged 18–24. FEMA Corps members are assigned to one of five NCCC campuses (located in Denver, Colorado; Sacramento, California; Perry Point, Maryland; Vicksburg, Mississippi; and Vinton, Iowa). This program has been established to augment FEMA's existing workforce. FEMA also has a cadre of reservists that FEMA continues to call upon (FAQs 2013). Volunteers work directly with disaster survivors, support disaster recovery centers, and share disaster preparedness and mitigation information with the public (FEMA Corps 2013).

FEMA Corps members serve full-time for a 10-month term with an option to extend for a second year. Members serve in teams of 8–12 persons and are assigned to projects throughout the region served by their campus; they also travel to complete service projects throughout those regions. To be considered for FEMA Corps, candidates must first apply to AmeriCorps NCCC. The program is open to all U.S. citizens between the ages of 18 and 24. Members are given a living allowance of approximately $4,000 for 10 months of service; housing; meals; limited medical benefits; if needed, up to $400 a month for child care; and member uniforms, and members become eligible for the Segal AmeriCorps Education Award upon successful completion of the program (FEMA Corps 2013).

Junior ROTC Units

In a variety of ways, the Junior ROTC units resemble the style of the junior police organizations, magnet schools, junior police academies, and military training camps previously reviewed. The Army Junior Reserve Officers' Training Corps (JROTC) also came into being with the passage of the National Defense Act of 1916. Under the provisions of this federal law, high schools were able to obtain a loan of federal military equipment, and students were able to receive instruction from active duty military personnel. In 1964, the ROTC Revitalization Act opened up JROTC to the other military services and replaced most of the active duty instructors with retirees who worked for and were cost shared by the schools. Title 10 of the U.S. Code declares that "the purpose of Junior Reserve Officers' Training Corps is to instill in students in United States secondary educational institutions the value of citizenship, service to the United States, personal responsibility, and a sense of accomplishment" (U.S. Army 2014). Leavenworth High School in Kansas claims the distinction of having the first official JROTC program in the United States. The school's official JROTC program has been in existence since 1917; however, it had a military science and tactics program as far back as 1897 (Lewis 2012).

In 1996, there were more than 2,400 JROTC programs nationwide. By 1999, the number of programs exceeded 2,600 with more than 400,000 participants (Hanser and Robyn 2000). In Hawaii, 29 public and private schools had JROTC programs in 1996. Kamehameha School established the first JROTC unit in Hawaii in 1916, followed by Punahou School in 1918. McKinley was Hawaii's first public school unit (in 1921) followed by Roosevelt (in 1938). Common curriculum topics include military history, science, and current affairs. Students can also participate on the rifle and drill teams; attend military balls; be part of the adventure training team, color guard, and honor guard; attend summer camps and field trips; and complete various community service projects. Activities are selected for self-esteem and leadership development (Kakesako 1996). See Box 9.1 for a list of JROTC program objectives compiled by the Jackson Public Schools in Mississippi.

Francis Lewis High School is located in Queens, one of the five boroughs comprising New York City. It is the city's second largest high school and arguably one of the nation's most diverse. With nearly 4,600 students enrolled, the school has nearly double the capacity for which it was designed more than 40 years ago. There are so many students that two school day sessions are held, with the first starting just after 7 a.m. and the second ending just before 7 p.m. There are no lockers due to lack of space; students must carry necessary books and materials throughout the day. With almost 700 cadets, Francis Lewis High School's JROTC program,

> **BOX 9.1   OBJECTIVES OF JROTC PROGRAMS**
>
> Awareness of the rights and responsibilities of citizenship
> Preparation to be good leaders; willingness to show initiative and take charge
> Ability to think logically and communicate effectively with others, orally and in writing
> Commitment to improving physical fitness
> Commitment to living drug free
> Improved self-discipline and positive self-motivation
> Awareness of the historical perspective of the military services
> Awareness of the importance of teamwork
> Development of core character traits and values for successful living
> Greater self-awareness of strengths and weaknesses
> Awareness of the problem solving/decision-making process for resolving issues
> Fostering adaptability and confidence
> Preparation for successful living upon graduation from high school
>
> *Source:* http://www.jackson.k12.ms.us/content.aspx?url=/page/447

begun in 1994, is the largest in the country and recently won a national drill team competition. According to retired First Sgt. Richard Gogarty, Francis Lewis' senior army instructor: "The biggest mistake I ever made was underestimating kids.... You let them run with something, and they'll get it done" (Arel 2009). Most Francis Lewis cadets will go on to college. In fact, since 2003, 20 of them have been accepted to the U.S. Military Academy at West Point. Besides drill teams, the program also has male and female Raider squads (a sport similar to Ranger Challenge in Senior ROTC), an honor guard, a drum corps, and a choir. On any given day, some 300 students stay after school to participate in JROTC extracurricular activities. But for the overwhelming majority of students, their ROTC experience ends with graduation. This is because many are not American citizens; due to their alien status, they are not eligible to receive Senior ROTC scholarships (Arel 2009).

Junior RTOC cadets also get involved in community activities and may, on a rare occasion, earn a small salary due to a grant opportunity. For example, students in Aztec High School's Army JROTC program in Farmington, New Mexico, have begun using a $75,000 grant from the New Mexico Youth Conservation Corps to maintain and improve the nearby

Aztec Ruins National Monument while also learning skills and earning pay. Cadets work to replace pipes, build fences, grow gardens, remove invasive species, help with archaeological digs, and complete any other projects needed to preserve the monument. Selected students who participate in the program earn $2,000 to $3,000 as employees of the National Park Service (NMJROTC Unit 2012).

Civil Air Patrol Cadets

Another federal program that predates the establishment of Law Enforcement Explorers posts is the Civil Air Patrol Cadet Program. Civil Air Patrol came into being in December 1941 as a civilian arm of the Army Air Force. It provided valuable war-related services, from hunting for German submarines off the coast to locating downed military pilots. It also supervised an extensive cadet program that provided military and aviation training to teenagers (see Figure 9.1 photo). The Civil Air Patrol guarded our coastlines against enemy infiltrators and U-boat attacks. After World War II, the Civil Air Patrol's contributions were recognized when Congress made this organization an official civilian auxiliary of the U.S. Air Force.

Although there are many youth-oriented programs in the United States today, Civil Air Patrol's cadet program is unique in that it uses aviation as its cornerstone. Thousands of young people aged 12 through 21 are introduced to aviation through Civil Air Patrol's cadet program. Young people are allowed to progress at their own pace through a 16-step program including aerospace education, leadership training, physical fitness, and moral leadership. Cadets compete for academic scholarships to further their studies in fields such as engineering, science, aircraft mechanics, aerospace medicine, meteorology, as well as many others. Those cadets who earn cadet officer status may enter the air force as an airman first class (E3) rather than an airman basic (E1) (CAP 2012). There are approximately 24,000 cadets of whom about 20% are female (see Cadets 2010).

Figure 9.1 Civil Air Patrol Cadet Walter Spangenberg, a high school student, is seen in this photo at Stevens Airport in Frederick, Maryland, ca. 1943. (Courtesy of Library of Congress, Prints and Photographic Div.)

Figure 9.2 CBP Explorers from Post 4701 (JFK Airport, New York, New York) and Post 4601 (Newark, New Jersey) pose at the New York City Marathon on November 1, 2009.

Customs and Border Protection Explorer Posts

Today, more than 700 Explorers serve in Customs and Border Protection (CBP), a branch of the U.S. Department of Homeland Security. CBP appears to be the largest Law Enforcement Explorer Program in the federal government, having 28 posts, primarily in Texas, Arizona, and California at various ports of entry and at Border Patrol sectors. Routine activities include assisting with passenger processing and crowd control at airports and seaports, observing and assisting with surveillance operations, observing vessel searches, and taking field trips (CBP Explorer Program 2007). Some CBP Explorers have also participated as "crash victims" at simulated crash scenes during first responder drills (CBP Explorer Program 2008).

Some federally sponsored Explorers have engaged in other unusual activities. For example, the CBP Post 4701 (JFK Airport, New York, New York) and CBP Post 4601 (Newark, New Jersey) helped provide security at the start of the 2009 New York City Marathon (as seen in Figure 9.2). The New York City Marathon had more than 40,000 runners from all over the world. The Explorers' job was to control the starting line until the 26.2-mile race began. To start their job, the Explorers arrived at the runner's check-in area in Ft. Wadsworth, Staten Island, at 4:30 a.m. Their first assignment was to keep all runners in their designated areas prior to relocation at the starting area. The runners are started in staggered groups with the elite runners in the first group. The Explorers formed a human chain across the starting line to hold the runners in place. Five seconds before the start, members of the chain must run to the sides of the road in order to get out of the way of the runners (CBP Explorer Program 2009).

National Law Enforcement Exploring Leadership Academy

The idea for the creation of federal leadership academies for Law Enforcement Explorers was first conceived by a Federal Bureau of Investigation (FBI) supervisory special agent who developed a curriculum for the program. The first National Law Enforcement Exploring Leadership Academy was conducted in

1985 at the FBI Academy in Quantico, Virginia. This FBI-sponsored National Law Enforcement Exploring Leadership Academy served as the model for similar local, regional, state, and federal agency sponsored Explorer academies. The National Law Enforcement Exploring Leadership Academy is considered a leading program. It is offered on a biennial schedule, hosted by various federal law enforcement agencies. The academy offers selected Explorers the opportunity to learn leadership skills (team building, how to motivate others, etc.). The academies also include historical, ceremonial, and recreational activities. In addition, the U.S. Drug Enforcement Administration (DEA), FBI, U.S. Marshals Service, and the Secret Service have hosted academies in the Washington, DC area, and the U.S. Military Police has hosted an academy in Ft. Leonard Wood, Missouri. The week-long federal academies are conducted during the summer when a National Law Enforcement Explorer Conference is not being held. The first biennial National Academy was held in 1979 at Michigan State University. Information about the leadership academies is posted on the Law Enforcement Exploring section of the Learning for Life Web site approximately one year prior to the event (Law Enforcement Exploring 2011, 13).

In July 2005, the DEA conducted a Law Enforcement Explorer Leadership Program at the DEA Training Academy in Quantico. Thirty Law Enforcement Explorers, aged 15–20, who had expressed serious interest in pursuing a career in federal law enforcement, attended the program. Training took place in the classroom and in the field using practical and team-building training scenarios. The students also experienced a "day in the life" of a DEA special agent, which included instruction in firearms, physical fitness, defensive tactics, and a team-building obstacle course. At the conclusion of the program, the Explorers received a graduation certificate and a video detailing their week-long experiences (DEA 2014). In order to attend a leadership program, youth usually submit an application consisting of all high school and college transcripts, letters of recommendation, and a detailed essay.

Currently attending college, Samantha Faro-Petersen of Winthrop, Massachusetts, is representative of the type of student selected to attend one of these academies. In 2011, she attended the National Law Enforcement Explorer FBI Leadership Academy after graduating from Pope John XXIII High School. In March 2012, she was selected as the "Explorer of the Year" at Winthrop Police Explorer Post 99. As a lieutenant at the post, she organized the biweekly meetings and helped to run the post's activities, including assisting with fundraising efforts for trips to the national conference (Domelowicz 2012).

FBI Field Office Initiatives for Youth

The Criminal Justice Information Services (CJIS) Division of the FBI includes an extensive "Community Outreach Program." It is a nationwide initiative that connects local FBI offices with their communities. The program employs civilian community outreach specialists who coordinate programs and lead teams of volunteers from the FBI that provide meaningful services to communities throughout the nation. The overall program is designed to improve the FBI's understanding of the communities they serve and the threats these communities face. A large number of its outreach activities involve youth and school presentations. Programs have been presented on a variety of topics, including Hardest Working Student Award, Junior Special Agent Program, Student's Academy, Stranger Danger, Internet Safety, Cultural Awareness, K-9 Demonstration, and the Students Who Achieve Today (SWAT) Team.

The "Stranger Danger" presentation educates area youth about staying safe and provides practical information to prevent abduction, child abuse, and Internet stalking. In West Virginia, for "Cultural Awareness" purposes, FBI staff present a February Black History Month program to area schools. The program includes a choir of FBI employees who sing traditional and historical African American music. Choir members discuss the songs with the children to further cultivate cultural awareness. The "Student's Academy" is a 12-week course that gives students at high schools an inside view of the FBI. The "SWAT Team" serves as a catalyst to involve area high school students in projects such as child identification fingerprinting, producing public service announcements, creating drug and alcohol awareness posters, distributing child identification kits, and serving as ushers or escorts at FBI ceremonies (FBI, Community Outreach 2013).

The "Junior Special Agent Program" provides a biweekly overview of FBI and CJIS Division programs for fourth- and fifth-grade students that include lessons on civic duty. Students who complete the program are presented with a Junior Special Agent badge and credentials by the assistant director of the CJIS Division during a graduation ceremony. In 2012, more than 150 fourth- and fifth-grade students at Harms Elementary School in southwest Detroit completed the "FBI Junior Special Agent Program." Andrew G. Arena, Special Agent-in-Charge of the Detroit Division, said to the students: "You can be whatever you want to be. I'm from this neighborhood and this is what I've achieved" (Detroit Public Schools 2012). During the training sessions, the students learned about how law enforcement works and how they can make a difference in the community. Topics included bullying avoidance, self-defense, physical fitness, and the duties of the FBI (Detroit Public Schools 2012).

Other FBI initiatives involving youth have included additional educational programs. For example, in July 2013, a one-day FBI Baltimore Field Office Teen Academy Program for high school students aged 14–18 was offered to provide a firsthand look at law enforcement as a career choice. The competitively selected students learned about major investigations and participated in a variety of "hands-on" exercises that illustrated the duties and responsibilities of the FBI. Prospective attendees had to be residents of Delaware or Maryland, have a grade point average (GPA) of at least 2.5, provide a school reference, answer an essay question, and submit a completed application form (Teen Academy 2013).

An earlier illustration of FBI community outreach involved the FBI's Challenge Program held at the Police Fire Academy of Santa Teresa High School in San Jose, California. Goals of the program included reducing the risk of youth involvement in gang activities and drug abuse. The High School Police Fire Academy was established in 1988 as a "magnet" program to draw students from all areas of San Jose who expressed an interest in a public safety career. The FBI Challenge Program began in February 1994 as a supplement to the existing high school academy program. Staff members from the Police Fire Academy and the FBI developed an instructional program designed to motivate, encourage, and challenge students to excel, not only academically but also in their personal lives. FBI volunteers conducted presentations to help the students better understand the FBI's law enforcement role. They served as positive role models in discouraging student involvement in youth gangs and illicit drugs. Twice monthly training sessions (50 minutes in duration) covered a variety of topics including the history of the FBI and its jurisdiction, the importance of completing high school and staying out of trouble, positive alternatives to gangs and drug use, the uses and importance of fingerprints for law enforcement, the training required for agents, how to take fingerprints, the FBI's role in child abduction cases, and cultural diversity in law enforcement. The students at the Police Fire Academy are known as "cadets" and perform more than 5,000 hours of community service each year, involving such activities as event security, graffiti cleanup, park trail building and cleanup, assistance at domestic violence and child abuse conferences, recycling, and so on. (Smith and Stapleton 1995).

There at least two FBI-sponsored Explorer Posts. Post 2060 is affiliated with the New York field Office. The Edwin C. Shanahan Memorial Post 1920 is sponsored by the Chicago field office as a community outreach activity but is not a part of the FBI. The post is named to honor the memory of Special Agent Shanahan who was born and raised in Chicago and began his service with the FBI in 1920. Five years later, he became the first FBI agent in the United States to be killed in the line of duty. It is a registered 501(c)(3) organization and Illinois nonprofit charitable organization, assisting youths in their communities. Activities in the post are carried out in collaboration with local law enforcement agencies to give students hands-on exercises. Post goals involve instilling self-confidence and developing leadership abilities among the participating students. The post educates the students in learning segments. Seven learning sessions were completed in the first semester that began in August 2012. Six additional sessions are taught in the second semester, leading up to graduation. Topics of instruction include an introduction to the FBI selection process, the history and organization of the FBI, legal principles, basics of investigations, counterintelligence, evidence response and collection, interviewing and interrogations, and weapons familiarization. FBI personnel volunteer their time to conduct all sessions and are assisted by the post's layperson board of directors (Chicago FBI Explorers 2014).

Youth Programs in American Territories

The United States possesses five major overseas areas namely, Puerto Rico, the U.S. Virgin Islands in the Caribbean, American Samoa, Guam, and the Northern Mariana Islands in the Pacific (see Figure 9.3). Those born in the major territories and commonwealths, except for American Samoa, possess U.S. citizenship. American citizens residing in the territories and common-wealths have many of the same rights and responsibilities as citizens residing in the United States; however, they are generally exempt from federal income tax, may not vote for president, and have only nonvoting representation

Figure 9.3 In 2009, the United States Mint released proof quarter images depicting themes honoring the District of Columbia and five U.S. territories—Guam, American Samoa, U.S. Virgin Islands, the Commonwealth of Puerto Rico, and the Northern Mariana Islands.

in the U.S. Congress. American Samoa, Guam, and the Virgin Islands are all territories of the United States. Washington, D.C., and the Northern Mariana Islands are commonwealths. Puerto Rico was once a territory but is now a commonwealth. American Samoans are considered U.S. nationals not citizens. They can elect one nonvoting delegate to the U.S. House of Representatives, who is permitted to cast votes on amendments to a bill but not on its final passage. The 580,000 U.S. citizens living in Washington, D.C., have one nonvoting delegate in Congress, but they can vote for president due to the ratification of the 23rd Amendment of the U.S. Constitution, sending three members to the Electoral College (Rubin 2014).

Two CBP Explorer Posts from the Caribbean participated in the week-long 2006 National Law Enforcement Exploring Leadership Academy conference held at Northern Arizona University in Flagstaff, Arizona. The two participating posts were San Juan Post 818 and U.S. Virgin Islands Post 5101. CBPs Puerto Rico Explorers Post 818 sent 18 Explorers and U.S. Virgin Islands Post 5101 sent seven Explorers to participate in the hostage negotiation, emergency field first aid, pistol, bomb search, crime prevention, shoot/don't shoot, and white-collar crime competitions. Members of CBP Explorer Posts in Puerto Rico and the U.S. Virgin Islands have attended 10 National Law Enforcement Explorer Conferences since 1988. There have been at least seven Explorer Posts in Puerto Rico. At least two of these posts had themes other than border protection; for example, the Ponce, Puerto Rico, post focused on fire and emergency services. Explorer Post 156 in Carolina, Puerto Rico, was the first military aviation Exploring Post in the United States (Explorer Posts 2006).

Federal Internships for College Students

There are also numerous internship opportunities throughout the federal government. However, many of the positions involve stiff competition and require early application. These are mainly available to college students at the undergraduate and graduate levels. (To access internship opportunities and information within the federal government for undergraduate, graduate, and law students, visit the links indicated at the federal government Web page: http://answers.usa.gov/system/templates/selfservice/USAGov/#!portal/1012/article/3800/Government20Internships.)

There are a variety of agencies offering internship opportunities, including the Consumer Product Safety Commission, the Department of Homeland Security, the Smithsonian Institution, the Peace Corps, the Internal Revenue Service, the Department of Justice, and the Administrative Office of the U.S. Courts. The Administrative Office of the U.S. Courts supports the mission of the federal courts to provide equal justice under the law. It accepts interns throughout the year in many of its program offices and recruits students with career goals and interests in court administration and management, information technology, human resources, budget and finance, law, criminal justice, legislative and public affairs, and education and training.

The mission of the DEA is to identify, target, investigate, disrupt, and dismantle the international, national, state, and local drug trafficking organizations that are having the most significant impact in the United States. They are committed to investigating and prosecuting major drug law violators in the United States and all over the world. The DEA currently accepts college students in volunteer (nonpaid) internships throughout the year in many of their domestic offices, which are located throughout the United States. Student volunteers may work up to six months with the DEA to gain experience in clerical and administrative support positions that involve activities such as organizing nondrug evidence, answering telephones, or performing research projects. Students are required to be enrolled at least half-time in college and in good academic standing in order to participate in the program (Watt 2010).

The special agents of the U.S. Naval Crime Investigative Service (NCIS) "are among the most adept and resourceful law enforcement professionals anywhere. Never restricted to a narrow specialty, even relatively junior agents are expected to handle a wide variety of criminal, counterterrorism, and counterintelligence matters with equal skill. Special Agents travel the globe and may even be stationed aboard ship" (Careers at NCIS 2013). The NCIS encourages college juniors, seniors, and graduate students who are interested in a criminal justice career to apply for an internship with an NCIS field office. The NCIS internship is an unpaid, hands-on opportunity, designed to provide education-related work assignments for students. The NCIS seeks individuals who possess strong academic credentials, outstanding character, and a high degree of motivation. Those candidates who exhibit excellent research, analytical, and communication skills are considered, regardless of academic major. Internship candidates who reside in or who attend the universities located within the respective field office geographic area of operations are afforded priority consideration in the selection process (NCIS Honors 2013). A 50-page guide to the NCIS Honors Intern Program with descriptions of dozens of field office opportunities is available online at: http://www.ncis.navy.mil/Careers/Interns/Pages/default.aspx.

The mission of NCIS is to investigate and defeat criminal, terrorist, and foreign intelligence threats to the United States Navy and Marine Corps—ashore, afloat, and in cyberspace. It is the federal law enforcement agency charged with conducting investigations of felony-level offenses affecting the Navy and Marine Corps—that is, crimes punishable by confinement for more than one year. The NCIS is comprised of some 2,400 personnel in more than 40 countries around the globe. The organization is roughly 90% civilian, and its cadre of federal agents—about half its total personnel—is 98% civilian (NCIS Honors 2013).

For many years, the FBI has sponsored a robust summer intern program for high-achieving college students; in 2014, however, budgetary restrictions affected the FBI's ability to staff the internship programs. Consequently, in 2014, the Bureau suspended the FBI Honors Internship Program, the FBI Volunteer Internship Program, and the Cyber Internship Program. Interested students will need to keep informed about the availability of these and all federal internship opportunities by periodically examining agency Web sites (see FBI Internships 2013). A selected list of potential internship opportunities with federal intelligence agencies and law enforcement agencies is included in Appendix D.

Summary

The present chapter has described a range of federal initiatives for involving youth in public safety and security. In particular, Junior and Senior ROTC units offer valuable leadership skills training and may qualify individuals to become commissioned officers in a branch of the armed forces. In addition, the Civil Air Patrol Cadet Program also includes opportunities for educational and career advancement. Opportunities for participation in the new FEMA Corps exist that can provide service members with one or more years of hands-on experience in the field of emergency management. Various living allowances and educational stipends are paid to FEMA Corps and senior ROTC participants.

In addition, college students at the undergraduate and graduate levels can apply for a wide variety of federal agency internships. However, many of the positions involve stiff competition and require early application. For example, the NCIS encourages college juniors, seniors, and graduate students who are interested in a criminal justice career to apply for an internship with an NCIS field office.

Although the concept of "community policing" is generally associated with local law enforcement, the broad reach of federal criminal statutes and their enforcement extends into local communities. Thus, federal law enforcement agencies have every reason to be concerned about community youth and to establish and maintain youth programs. Federal agencies and agents who work with youths are promoting public safety and the quality of community life.

At the federal level, the achievement of the promises of community policing may be enhanced through junior police units such as Police Explorers and related public safety programs. By involving young people, any federal department strengthens its abilities to resist and prevent crime and disorder. The mere addition of such a program supports more congenial relationships among the youths of a community, the local police, and special agents federal. All law enforcement agencies should develop these programs as an integral agency function, and they should draw on the knowledge and skills of individual federal officers and agents. Through involvement with such programs, individual officers are bound to become more committed, empowered, and analytical within their own professional careers. However, due to major concerns about the threat posed by terrorists, there is a potential for federal law enforcement agencies to exploit their community outreach programs for intelligence gathering purposes.

Review Questions

1. Identify at least four youth programs at the federal level that are concerned with public safety and security.
2. State the purpose of the Citizens' Military Training Camp (CMTC) program. Search online to identify any similar program that might still be in existence.
3. List the areas of study and training involved in the NROTC Berkeley program.
4. Indicate three roles performed by FEMA Corps members.
5. List at least five JROTC program objectives compiled by the Jackson Public Schools in Mississippi and discuss their relevance for building self-esteem and leadership skills.
6. Many students in the Army JROTC program at Francis Lewis High School (Queens, New York) are not American citizens; due to their alien status, they are not eligible to receive Senior ROTC scholarships after they graduate. Discuss the pros and cons of this policy.
7. The FBI has conducted a variety of community outreach programs involving youth. Discuss why the FBI considers these to be important initiatives.
8. The American Civil Liberties Union (ACLU) has commented that on some occasions "it appears FBI agents are improperly exploiting the goodwill established through its community outreach programs as a method of gaining access to community members for investigative purposes" (see German 2013). Conduct online research to ascertain the validity or invalidity of this commentary.
9. Search online to find at least one federal agency that interests you. Describe the nature and qualifications of any internships available for college students.

Notes

1. Sea Cadet organizations exist in most of the maritime nations of the world. In 1958, at the request of the U.S. Navy, the Navy League of the United States established the Naval Sea Cadet Corps (NSCC) for American youth aged 13–17. The program is designed for youth who have a desire to learn about the Navy, Marine Corps, Coast Guard, and Merchant Marines. "Sea Cadets are authorized by the Secretary of the Navy to wear Navy uniforms appropriately marked with the Sea Cadet Corps insignia. The objectives of the Sea Cadet program are to introduce youth to naval life, to develop in them a sense of pride, patriotism, courage, self-reliance, and to maintain an environment free of drugs and gangs" (Sea Cadets 2013). In addition, a junior version of the Sea Cadet program is also conducted for youth in the age range of 11–14. This is also a Navy League program. It is designed to introduce young people to maritime and military life and to prepare them for later entrance into the NSCC (Navy League 2013).

2. Formed in March 1933, the Civilian Conservation Corps, was one of the first New Deal programs. It was a public works project intended to promote environmental conservation and to build good citizens through vigorous, disciplined outdoor labor. President Franklin Roosevelt believed that this civilian "tree army" would relieve the rural unemployed and keep youth "off the city street corners." The CCC operated under the supervision of the U.S. Army. Camp commanders had disciplinary powers and corpsmen were required to address superiors as "sir." By September 1935, more than 500,000 young men had lived in CCC camps, most staying from six months to a year. In all, nearly three million young men participated in the CCC and more than 800 parks were built (see Foner and Garraty 1991).

3. CSPI is a scholarship and leadership training program for future Coast Guard officers. Enrolled students must adhere to high standards of performance and conduct in order to maintain their scholarship status. In this way, the program is similar to ROTC. However, unlike the typical ROTC program, CSPI students are actually active duty enlisted members of the Coast Guard with full pay and benefits—until completion of OCS, when they receive a commission as an officer. An important requirement is sophomore or junior undergraduate status or having been accepted for enrollment in a bachelor degree program at an accredited college or university designated as a minority institution. Links to the institutions that satisfy this educational requirement are found at: http://www.gocoastguard.com/find-your-career/officer-opportunities/programs/college-student-pre-commissioning-initiative-(scholarship-program).

References

Arel, S. (2009). Big-city JROTC is model program. Retrieved May 22, 2012 from http://armyrotc.wordpress.com/2009/12/02/big-city-jrotc-is-model-program/

Cadets. (2010, April 8). Cadets by the numbers. Retrieved May 24, 2012 from http://www.capmembers.com/file.cfm/media/blogs/documents/Stats_C091196AC47C8.pdf

CAP. (2012). Cadet programs. Retrieved May 24, 2012 from http://www.gocivilairpatrol. com/about/civil_air_patrols_three_primary_missions/cadet_p rograms.cfm

Careers at NCIS. (2013). Retrieved October 10, 2013 from http://www.ncis.navy.mil/ Careers/Pages/default.aspx

CBP Explorer Program. (2007, September 21). Be an explorer. Retrieved May 24, 2012 from http://www.cbp.gov/xp/cgov/careers/explorer_program/explorer.xml

CBP Explorer Program. (2008, October 28). CBP explorers and officers survive disaster drill 'plane crash'. Retrieved May 24, 2012 from http://www.cbp.gov/xp/ cgov/careers/explorer_program/expl_news/drill_plane_crash.xml

CBP Explorer Program. (2009, November 16). Explorers help to provide security at the start of the 2009 New York City Marathon. Retrieved May 24, 2012 from http://www.cbp.gov/xp/cgov/careers/explorer_program/expl_news/ny_ marathon.xml

Chicago FBI Explorers. (2014). Chicago FBI Explorers: About. Retrieved March 4, 2014 from http://www.facebook.com/Chicagoexplorerpost1920/info

Citizens' Military Training. (2013). Citizens' Military Training Camp. Retrieved October 7, 2013 from http://1-22infantry.org/history/cmtcpartone.htm

DEA (2014). Law enforcement explorers. Retrieved June 27, 2014 from http://www. justice.gov/dea/ops/Training/Community.shtml

Detroit Public Schools. (2012, February 3). FBI hosts graduation ceremony for 'FBI junior special agents' -1st program of its kind in Southwest Detroit. Retrieved September 24, 2013 from http://detroitk12.org/content/2012/02/03/fbi-hosts-graduation-ceremony-for-f bi-junior-special-agents1st-program-of-its-kind-in-southwest-detroit/

Domelowicz, J. (2012, March 16). Three-year veteran Faro-Petersen named 2011 Explorer of the Year. *Winthrop Transcript*. Retrieved May 24, 2012 from http:// www.winthroptra nscript.com/2012/03/16/three-year-veteran-faro-petersen-named-2011-explorer-of-the- year/

Explorer Posts. (2006, July 6). Explorers Posts 818 and 5101 represent the Caribbean. Retrieved October 8, 2013 from http://cbp.gov/archived/xp/cgov/newsroom/ news_releases/archives/2006_news_releases/ 072006/07062006.xml.html

FAQs. (2013). Frequently asked questions (FAQs). Retrieved October 9, 2013 from http://www.nationalservice.gov/about/frequently-asked-questions-faqs#12454

FBI, Community Outreach. (2013). Retrieved October 10, 2013 from http://www.fbi. gov/about- us/cjis/community-outreach

FBI Internships. (2013). Retrieved October 12, 2013 from http://www.fbijobs.gov/ 2.asp

FEMA Corps. (2013). Retrieved October 9, 2013 from http://www.nationalservice. gov/programs/americorps/fema-corps

Foner, E. and Garraty, J. A. (1991). *The reader's companion to American history*. New York: Houghton Mifflin Harcourt.

Fort Meade History. (2013). Retrieved October 7, 2013 from http://www.ftmeade. army.mil/pages/history/history.html

German, M. (2013, February 15). Is the FBI's community outreach program a Trojan horse? Retrieved October 10, 2013 from http://www.aclu.org/blog/ national-security/fbis- community-outreach-program-trojan-horse

Hanser, L. M. and Robyn, A. E. (2000). *Implementing high school JROTC career academies*. Santa Monica, CA: RAND.

History of ROTC. (2013). History of ROTC beginning. Retrieved October 2, 2013 from http://www.hsu.edu/interior4.aspx?id = 2996

Kakesako, G. K. (1996). Snap and polish. Retrieved May 22, 2012 from http://archives.starbulletin.com/96/12/10/news/story1.html

Kocieniewski, D. (2012, September 12). Whistle-blower awarded $104 million by I.R.S. *New York Times*, p. A1.

Law Enforcement Exploring. (2011, July). Law Enforcement Exploring: Program and resource guide for adult leaders. Retrieved May 24, 2012 from http://c183757.ssl.cf1.rackcdn.com/wp- content/documents/LEE_Program%20and%20Resource%20Guide_0811.pdf

Lewis, P. (2012). Our history: The first JROTC unit. Retrieved May 22, 2012 from http://www.usd453.org/gen/usd453_generated_pages/Our_History__The_First_JROTC_ *Unit_m1208.html*

Navy League. (2013). Navy League Cadets – Age 11–14. Retrieved September 24, 2013 from http://www.seacadets.org/public/programs/nlcc/

NCIS Honors. (2013). NCIS Honors Intern Program. Retrieved October 9, 2013 from http://www.ncis.navy.mil/Careers/Interns/Documents/NCIS%20Honors%20Intern%20Program%20June%202013.pdf

N.M. JROTC Unit. (2012, February). N.M. JROTC unit lands $75,000 grant for spring project. *The Cadet, 3*(1), 2.

NROTC Berkeley (2013). Naval Reserve Officers Training Corps, UC Berkeley. Retrieved October 9, 2013 from http://navyrotc.berkeley.edu/

Rubin, J. (2014). Can American Samoans vote? Retrieved January 23, 2014 from http://www.slate.com/articles/news_and_politics/explainer/2008/01/canamerican_samoan svote.html

Sea Cadets. (2013) Sea Cadets – Ages 13 – 17. Retrieved September 30, 2013 from http://www.seacadets.org/public/programs/nscc/

Smith, W. E. and Stapleton, M. E. (1995). FBI challenge program: Inspiring youth to a law enforcement career. *FBI Law Enforcement Bulletin, 64*(9), 1–5.

Teen Academy. (2013). Baltimore FBI Field Office Teen Academy flyer. Retrieved September 24, 2013 from http://www.youth202.org/sites/default/files/Teen%20Academy%20brochure%20new.pdf

U.S. Army. (2014). U.S. Army Junior ROTC: History. Retrieved June 27, 2014 from http://www.cadetcommand.army.mil/jrotc-history.aspx

War Department. (1925). Album of photographs of Citizen Military Training Camp, Camp Meade, Maryland, 1925 – 1925, scope and content. Retrieved October 7, 2013 from http://research.archives.gov/description/542449

Watt, M. (2010). Internship opportunities within the federal government. Retrieved October 8, 2013 from http://gwired.gwu.edu/career/merlin-cgi/p/downloadFile/d/24559/n/off/other/1/name/FedInternship_Opportunities_20101pdf/

Legal Issues and Volunteer Police

10

> The police are the public and the public are the police; the police being only members of the public who are paid to give full time attention to duties which are incumbent on every citizen in the interests of community welfare and existence.

—**Sir Robert Peel**

During his service as home secretary, Sir Robert Peel (1788–1850) introduced a number of important reforms to British criminal law. His changes to the penal code system resulted in fewer crimes carrying a death penalty sentence and the provision of educational programs for inmates. In the criminal justice field, he is most often remembered as the "founder of modern policing" (Nazemi 2013). In 1829, Peel was successful in establishing the Metropolitan Police of London. His achievement helped him become prime minister of England in 1835. The initial force had over a thousand officers and was studied throughout the century as a new approach to crime fighting. In time, after the passing of the County Police Act in 1839, its style was duplicated in the London Boroughs and then into the counties and towns.

Many characteristics of Peel's police were adopted in the United States. Peel proclaimed that "The police are the public and the public are the police." (Commissioner Bratton's Blog 2014) One of the major tenets of this understanding was the recognition that police must secure the willing cooperation of the public in voluntary observation of the law, and a vital way to accomplish this support was by constantly demonstrating absolute impartiality in the enforcement of the law and in the delivery of services. These tenets form an important part of modern-day police efforts. Both sworn volunteer police (i.e., those possessing peace officer status) and non-sworn police volunteers may best contribute to the safety of the public by following Peel's tenets. Peel established the Metropolitan Police based on several major principles or tenets. In many communities throughout the world, these principles are cited as the basic foundation for current law enforcement organizations and community policing (see Box 10.1).

Police officers and their volunteer counterparts or aides not only need to be familiar with Peel's tenets but also with many other regulations and laws. There are a huge number of principles, rules, court decisions, and statutes that program administrators and volunteer police and police volunteers need to know. Some changes in state law can be expected from time to time.

255

BOX 10.1   PEEL'S PRINCIPLES FOR POLICING

1. The basic mission for which the police exist is to prevent crime and disorder.
2. The ability of the police to perform their duties is dependent upon public approval of police actions.
3. Police must secure the willing cooperation of the public in voluntary observance of the law to be able to secure and maintain the respect of the public.
4. The degree of cooperation of the public that can be secured diminishes proportionately to the necessity of the use of physical force.
5. Police seek and preserve public favor not by catering to the public opinion but by constantly demonstrating absolute impartial service to the law.
6. Police use physical force to the extent necessary to secure observance of the law or to restore order only when the exercise of persuasion, advice, and warning is found to be insufficient.
7. Police, at all times, should maintain a relationship with the public that gives reality to the historic tradition that the police are the public and the public are the police; the police being only members of the public who are paid to give full-time attention to duties which are incumbent on every citizen in the interests of community welfare and existence.
8. Police should always direct their action strictly toward their functions and never appear to usurp the powers of the judiciary.
9. The test of police efficiency is the absence of crime and disorder, not the visible evidence of police action in dealing with it.

Source: http://lacp.org/2009-Articles-Main/062609-Peels9Principals-SandyNazemi.htm

For example, in 2012, a new state law in Oregon became effective relating to the status of reserve police officers. The law includes reserve officers within the definitions of "peace officer" and "police officer" for certain purposes (see House Bill 3153, 76th oregon legislative assembly—2011 Regular Session). In Illinois, a rule change by the Law Enforcement and Standards Training Board was implemented in 2006. It requires that all municipal governments (and law enforcement agencies) that exercise their option to create an auxiliary police unit in the state of Illinois shall provide the Illinois Law Enforcement and Standards Training Board with a copy of their local ordinance. Moreover, the rules requires that the "Ordinance shall explicitly indicate whether auxiliary officers are designated as having conservator of the peace powers. In the case of municipalities which create auxiliary police units by ordinance, but explicitly state (within the ordinance) that officers are not to exercise 'conservator of the peace' powers, then all auxiliary officers so designated shall be required to complete the 40-Hour Mandatory Firearms Training Course before being permitted to carry a firearm…. Auxiliary police officers with conservator of the peace powers will be directed to attend the 400-Hour Basic Law Enforcement Officer Training Course at a certified State academy" (Statement of Policy 2006).

This chapter highlights several legal concepts and laws that are crucial for the achievement of the basic police mission of preventing crime and disorder as well as the successful fulfillment of the numerous tasks associated with being a volunteer law enforcement officer. It deals, especially, with those liability issues that may arise when private citizens take on volunteer policing roles. The Federal Emergency Management Agency's (FEMA) *The Citizen Corps Volunteer Liability Guide* is briefly reviewed. The materials in this chapter and those available in the *Volunteer Liability Guide* are offered for general information purposes only. They do not constitute legal advice, and the user is encouraged to seek out state-specific counsel from a qualified attorney before taking any action.

Overview of the Law

The U.S. government, the governments of each of the 50 states, and their many subdivisions have established rights and responsibilities through a system of laws. Laws are considered a system because they come from more than one source and they work together. A basic understanding of this system helps one understand the laws that may affect volunteer police liability. The components of the legal system include the following:

- Constitutions outline the principles of a government and provide a foundation for its exercise of powers. Federal and state governments have constitutions.
- Statutes are codes of laws that are enacted by the elected members of the legislatures of federal, state, territorial, tribal, and local governments.
- Regulations are rules adopted by government agencies to implement statutes.
- Common law or case law is a body of legal principles derived from the decisions of federal and state courts in individual lawsuits, which factor into deciding the outcome of later cases.

All of these components of the law affect one another, and they all affect emergency or police volunteers. Courts interpret constitutions, statutes, and regulations when deciding cases before them. Legislatures that do not like a court decision may pass a statute that could produce different results in future cases. Agencies revise regulations to conform to new statutes or to comply with court decisions. Complete research of a legal issue looks at all these components of the law and how they interact (FEMA 2014).

Status and Authority

There are about 15,000 municipal or local police departments and about another 3,500 county, state, and federal law enforcement agencies in the United States. The municipal agencies may also include a variety of specialized groups such as school and transit police forces. No other nation in the world has ever had as many different types of police departments as the United States; a fact that means no two police agencies in America are structured alike or function in the same way (Inciardi 2000). Therefore, agency responsibilities, patrol policies, technology, departmental rules, and a wide range of other practices will vary from agency to agency and from state to state. The same pattern holds true for volunteer police units.

The city of Waltham, Massachusetts, is 8.5 miles from Boston and occupies about 13 square miles. The city is home to Brandeis University and Bentley University, which have a combined full-time enrollment of approximately 10,000 students (Waltham, MA, 2013).

Its population is about 62,000. Approximately 45% of the adult population who are over the age 25 has a bachelor's degree or higher. The median household income is about $68,000, and about 10% of the population is below the poverty level (U.S. Census Data 2013). The area is known for its cotton mills and famous pocket watches. It is safer than 48% of the cities in the United States (Crime Rates 2013), and in 2011 had 174 full-time police department employees, of whom 147 were police officers.

Early in 2011, the following notice concerning auxiliary police appeared at the bottom of the city of Waltham's Web page: "February 1, 2011—Effective immediately the Waltham Police Department will not be accepting applications for the position of Auxiliary Police Officer. There will be NO First Tuesday of the Month Recruiting Meeting until further notice. Please check back with this website periodically" (Auxiliary Police Department 2011). What had happened to cause this announcement?

The events leading to the unit's demobilization were a shoplifting arrest and a 2011 lawsuit by the alleged shoplifter for use of excessive force, false arrest, and false imprisonment. The suit was filed against two Waltham City police officers and one auxiliary officer. Eventually, the lawsuit was settled.

At the time, however, an issue arose over the liability coverage for the city's auxiliary police force when the private firm handling legal matters for the Waltham Police Department refused to represent the volunteer auxiliary officer. Subsequently, the police chief ordered the suspension of all activities by the 14-member auxiliary police force.

All is now well. The auxiliary unit is functioning as in the past, and the city maintains an attractive Web site to encourage recruitment. Waltham reinstated its volunteer force in the fall of 2013 after obtaining a new insurance policy for its auxiliary program and after amending its local ordinances, which had not previously included the term "auxiliary police officers" (Sherman 2013; see Figure 10.1). Waltham's auxiliaries are not designated as peace officers, and they are not permitted to carry firearms (Sherman 2013). Throughout the year, they patrol and provide traffic support for road and bicycle races, parades, and other community events. Training requirements include the completion of the 120-hour Massachusetts Reserve Intermittent Police Academy within two years of appointment. This training takes place at the Waltham Police Department. Officers receive annual training and certification in cardiopulmonary resuscitation (CPR), the Red Cross First Responder course, handcuffing, use of force, defensive tactics, the use of over-the-counter pepper spray, and expandable batons (Waltham Auxiliary Police 2013).

A related case involved the reserve police force in Fort Worth, Texas. The city suspended the program in March 2011 when questions arose about whether the city council had properly approved each reserve officer.

Figure 10.1 Russ Malone administering oath of office to eight Waltham (Massachusetts) Auxiliary Police Officers in 2013. The Waltham Auxiliary Police Department is a non-sworn, unarmed, volunteer organization of men and women between the ages of 21 and 70 that are committed to the safety and well-being of the citizens of Waltham. (Courtesy of Robert G. Logan, photographer, and used with permission of Russ Malone, City Clerk and Clerk of the Waltham City Council.)

Another question arose regarding whether a city with civil service for police could maintain a reserve force. The Texas attorney general determined that the city could maintain a reserve force that does not take a civil service examination. The opinion states that "The statute authorizing reserve police forces presumes the coexistence of reserve and 'regular police'" and "We have not found, nor has any briefing submitted to this office purported to find, any Texas case that has stated or implied that reserves must comply with civil service requirements" (Opinion No. GA-0893, November 22, 2011). Subsequently, a new general order for police reserves was drafted, and the reserves were permitted to resume operations. The reserve program has been made a part of the patrol division, rather than in a separate division. In addition, a no-rank system was devised, other than probationary reserve officers and reserve officers. Fort Worth reserve officers can work a minimum of 15 hours a month and up to 20 hours per week. A minimum of 560 hours training is required to become a reserve officer (Reserve LEO News 2013).

Fort Worth police reserve officers are sworn law enforcement officers and must become certified by the Texas Commission on Law Enforcement Officer Standards and Education. This is accomplished through course attendance from 6 p.m. to 10 p.m. Monday through Thursday for a period of 20 weeks. While on duty, these volunteer police possess the same authority as peace officers. They are usually assigned to the patrol division and assist regular patrol officers in the performance of their duties. A normal work assignment usually is six hours, once a week. Requirements for membership include a high school diploma or General Educational Development (GED) certificate and 12 semester hours of college; 21 years of age at time of certification; weight standards based on an individual's percentage of body fat; vision correctable to 20/20 with no color vision deficiency; and a valid Texas driver's license. Moreover, applicants must pass a physical fitness test, a medical exam, an extensive background check, a polygraph examination, and a psychological examination. Before acceptance, all applicant credentials are reviewed by the Police Personnel Review Board (Fort Worth Police 2013). The original draft of the new 2012 General Order for Fort Worth police reserves includes the following statement about carrying a service firearm: "Reserve officers may carry their department-issued service weapon only for the period of time the Reservist is actually on duty and discharging the official functions of a duly constituted peace officer as authorized by the Chief of Police. When off-duty, Reserve Officers are encouraged to report breaches of the peace or on-view felonies for response by an on-duty officer. Reserve Officers should be mindful that any law enforcement action taken by them while off duty may be considered by a court of law to be action taken by a civilian" (Fort Worth Police Department, General Order, Section 217.06 D).

The temporary suspensions of the volunteer police units in Waltham and Fort Worth involved very basic issues regarding the nature of their legal status and authority. An important related concept is "jurisdiction." Jurisdiction generally refers to a specific geographical area. In the field of criminal justice, it has a wider meaning—the right or authority of a justice agency to act in regard to a particular subject matter, territory, or person. A city's police may not patrol or answer calls for service outside the city's boundaries unless cooperative agreements with those other jurisdictions have been developed or assistance has been requested by a neighboring agency due to a specific incident. In addition, various states specifically authorize municipal police officers to exercise police powers outside the territorial limits of their municipality under specified circumstances such as fresh pursuit or when summoned by another officer. Thus, absent such special agreements, or under circumstances identified by statutes, a local law enforcement officer possesses no more authority to act than a private citizen when acting outside his or her jurisdiction (Florida Attorney General 1989). Police who are appointed by statewide agencies typically possess statewide jurisdiction. Several states have statewide volunteer police units. For a discussion concerning these units, see Chapter 5.

Sovereign Immunity and the Public Duty Doctrine

Historically, the doctrine of sovereign immunity shielded municipalities from tort liability. The source of the doctrine is thought to be rooted in the English theory that "The king can do no wrong." This has been interpreted to mean that the sovereign, be it national, state, or local, was completely immune from all tort liability unless the sovereign gave consent. As far back as the thirteenth century, "Applications to the king in council or in person were occasionally made and redress afforded" and "it was possible to obtain relief against a sheriff and bailiff in the administrative court known as the exchequer..." (Borchard 1926, 21). In addition, "Edward I (1239–1307), the so-called English Justinian, introduced a regular course of procedure for bringing claims against the king" (Borchard 1926, 23). As a general rule, the doctrine of sovereign immunity prohibits all suits against the United States unless it has given consent (e.g., see *Cohens v. Virginia*, 19 U.S. 264 [1821]; *Library of Congress v. Shaw*, 478 U.S. 310 [1986]; *Block v. North Dakota*, 461 U.S. 273 [1983].)

Although the doctrine of sovereign immunity has been abolished in many jurisdictions, courts are still very reluctant to impose liability on a municipality for its failure to provide adequate police protection. The general rule in such cases is that a municipality owes police protection to the general public but owes no duty to any particular individual (e.g., see *Brutomesso v. Las Vegas Metro. Police Dept.*, 591 P. 2d 254, 1979; *Doe v. Hendricks*, 590 P.2d 647, 1979; *Schuster v. City of New York*, 154 N.E.2d 534, 1958).

Absent a "special duty" to a particular individual, a municipality is not liable for its failure to provide adequate police protection (see also *Riss v. City of New York*, 22 N.Y. 2d 579, 240 N.E.2d 860, 1968).

In the West Virginia Supreme Court of Appeals case of *Gloria Allen v. Greenbrier County Sheriff's Dept. and Greenbrier County Commission* (decided June 28, 2013), the court affirmed the granting of summary judgment for respondents stating that the public duty doctrine barred a petitioner's negligence claim. In discussing the public duty doctrine, the court stated that "The duty to... provide police protection runs ordinarily to all citizens and is to protect the safety and well-being of the public at large; therefore, absent a special duty to the plaintiff(s), no liability attaches to a municipal... police department's failure to provide adequate... police protection" (see the 1999 opinion in *Rhodes v. Putnam County. Sheriff's Dept.*, 530 S.E.2d 452, 455, 1999; quoting the 1991 opinion in *Randall v. Fairmont City Police Dept.*, 412 S.E.2d 737, 747–748).

In West Virginia, the four requirements necessary to establish such a "special duty" or "special relationship" exception are codified in W. Va. Code § 29–12–5 as follows: "(1) An assumption by the state governmental entity, through promises or actions, of an affirmative duty to act on behalf of the party who was injured; (2) knowledge on the part of the state governmental entity's agents that inaction could lead to harm; (3) some form of direct contact between the state governmental entity's agents and the injured party; and (4) that party's justifiable reliance on the state governmental entity's affirmative undertaking."

All members of the public and those who volunteer to assist the police need to know about the principle called the "public duty doctrine." A community's understanding of this doctrine should serve to reinforce the selfless nature of police work as well as the remarkable civic benefits conferred by those persons who would undertake police responsibilities without monetary compensation. Surely, the average police officer and volunteer considers every person as well as the public at large to be worthy of his or her response. It would be quite an unusual case for such officers to refrain from helping others by proclaiming otherwise. Nevertheless, there is a public duty doctrine, which holds that the government and its representatives have no duty to any specific person (absent a special relationship) but have duties to the public at large.

There have been other cases where the courts have affirmed this principle. One of the first cases to address this issue was *South v. Maryland*, 59 U.S. 396 (1856). In this case, the Supreme Court found that a sheriff or public officer could only be found personally liable if they failed to provide protection to someone they had entered into a special agreement to protect. But they found no recorded case in American or English law where an officer was subject to personal liability for failure to protect an individual from injury to their property or person. From this case the "public duty doctrine" was formed. In *Warren v. District of Columbia,* (444 A.2d. 1, D.C. Ct. of Ap. 1981), the District of Columbia Court of Appeals, in a four to three vote, stated that official police personnel and the government employing them owe no duty to victims of criminal acts and thus are not liable for a failure to provide adequate police protection unless a special relationship exists.

In the case of *Castle Rock v. Gonzales,* 545 U.S. 748 (2005), the U.S. Supreme Court found that Jessica Gonzales did not have a constitutional right to police protection even in the presence of a restraining order. By a vote of seven to two, the court ruled that Gonzales had no right to sue her town under 42 U.S.C. § 1983 and her local police department for failing to protect her and her children from her estranged husband. Her husband murdered the woman's three children. In the hours before her children were found dead in her husband's car, Gonzales had contacted the police department on five occasions to ask for assistance.

In a related case, *DeShaney v. Winnebago County Dept. of Social Service, et al.,* 489 U.S. 189 (1989), the petitioner sued respondents claiming that their failure to act to protect him deprived him of his liberty in violation of the due process clause of the Fourteenth Amendment to the U.S. Constitution. By a vote of six to three, the U.S. Supreme Court held that a state government agency's failure to prevent child abuse by a custodial parent did not violate the child's right to liberty under the due process clause of the Fourteenth Amendment. In this case, the petitioner was Joshua DeShaney. He was beaten and permanently injured by his father, with whom he lived as a result of a divorce decree. Respondents were social workers and other local officials who received complaints that petitioner was being abused by his father; they had reason to believe that this was happening but nonetheless did not act to remove the petitioner from his father's custody. The opinion, by Chief Justice William Rehnquist, held that the due process clause protects against state action only and because it was Randy DeShaney, the child's father, who abused Joshua, the Winnebago County Department of Social Services (DSS), a state actor, was not responsible. Rehnquist's opinion stated that although the DSS's failure to act may have made it liable for a tort under Wisconsin state law, the Fourteenth Amendment does not transform every tort by a state actor into a violation of constitutional rights. The court left open the possibility that the act of creating a Department of Social Services to investigate and respond to allegations of child abuse may have meant that Winnebago County assumed a duty to prevent what Randy DeShaney did to Joshua DeShaney, and that any failure to fulfill that duty may have constituted a tort.[1]

Torts and Negligence Law

No one desires to be the respondent in a lawsuit. Volunteer police who have devoted months undergoing training and who have had years of service want to be assured that all of this effort will not be squandered due to a legal action. Volunteers and their supervisors can diminish this risk by undergoing proper training in accordance with their assigned positions and state standards. With regard to emergency situations, established plans such as the incident command system[2] should be used. At every training opportunity, volunteers need to understand the scope of their duties and how these should best be carried out in a variety of situations. When in the field, long detailed documentation would not be expected in emergencies, but maintaining a journal or notes could prove helpful in the event of a lawsuit. Moreover, awareness of basic tort law principles may help concerned volunteers avoid the types of conduct that could result in a legal action.

A "tort" is an action that harms another. It is often referred to as a "civil wrong" for which a lawsuit can be started. It occurs when a person acts, or fails to act, without right and as a result another is harmed. Torts involve civil actions for personal injuries or property damage rather than a criminal action or a contractual claim.

The law of torts can be found in statutes, court decisions, and constitutional provisions; it applies to government entities, individual citizens, and businesses. It protects individual and business interests from harm and provides a means for those harmed by another to seek compensation for their loss.

Tort liability claims also provide a basis for distributing losses to those who are responsible for the harm. Tort law provides a systematic means for analyzing and resolving liability claims, while protecting the interests of the person injured and the governmental jurisdiction. Torts encompass a very broad area of the law including such categories of law as intentional acts that harm others, negligence, and strict liability cases. Intentional acts that harm others include trespass, assault and battery, intentional infliction of emotional distress, defamation, and invasion of privacy. Negligence involves unintentional acts or omissions that cause harm to another. A person has a duty to exercise that degree of care, skill, and diligence that a reasonable or prudent person would exercise under similar circumstances. This rule, as applied to governmental entities, must be understood in terms of the essential elements of negligence. The elements include the duty owed to conform to a defined standard of care, a breach of that duty, damages, and causation.[3] Strict liability is liability without fault and relates to situations where one is held responsible for the consequences of his/her actions or omissions, regardless of fault or exercise of due care. Strict liability was first applied in cases involving abnormally dangerous activities such as blasting but has achieved significantly broader application in the law of product liability and workers' compensation (Oleck 1982).

Immunity and Indemnification in Claims of Negligence

When authorized volunteers respond in a disaster emergency, immunity may be available to them. For example, the use of auxiliary police units in New York State "has been ... found to be proper for such activities as patrolling the streets [and] unprotected public parks in ... the late hours..." (Collins 1981, 629). While performing such activities, the individual member and the municipality are immune from liability for torts committed during the performance of authorized drills (Collins 1981). The key factor to ensuring that volunteers are protected during disasters for possible negligent actions is that they are formally appointed by the emergency management agency or other governmental entity. The volunteer thus becomes a "public actor" rather than a private citizen offering aid. In addition to formally appointing or authorizing the volunteer, the public agency should provide training and guidance to volunteers so as to minimize harm to citizens. A failure to formally appoint the volunteer to assist in a disaster response means that the various forms of "governmental immunity" do not apply to the actions of the volunteer and other standards of care may apply. This protection, however, does not apply where the actor intentionally harms another. In addition, governmental immunity does not apply to criminal conduct.

Governmental immunity is a special form of immunity recognized for some activities of public agencies in more than a dozen states. These laws make a distinction between governmental functions, which are traditionally performed by the government, and those functions that are proprietary in nature or that are performed traditionally by the private sector. Under the governmental function theory, core governmental functions—such as public safety, firefighting, police activities, health and building inspections, as well as the collection of taxes—are mandated responsibilities that can be performed only by governmental units. Because of the unique role that these essential governmental functions have in the community, public agencies and employees enjoy immunity from claims of negligence under state law. Each state that recognizes governmental immunity defines what is a governmental function (Pine, n.d; Pine 2013).

Proprietary functions, however, have no special immunity attached to the activity. Proprietary activities may be performed by either a public or private organization. Public actors or volunteers do not enjoy immunity when performing proprietary activities (Pine, n.d; Pine 2013).

Other state immunity statutes may be beneficial to volunteers who respond in disasters as long as they are acting on behalf of the public authority. A critical element of these provisions involves the defining of an "emergency." If the emergency activity is not included in the definition of "emergency," then the immunity provision does not apply. These immunity provisions extend protection to negligent acts but not to actions for gross negligence or intentional or willful actions intended to harm another. Gross negligence is more than mere thoughtlessness, inattention, or a mere mistake resulting from inexperience or confusion.

The concept of "indemnification" involves protection against personal financial loss for the actions of governmental employees and volunteers. Official representatives of a governmental unit (volunteers) who are named individually in a tort action are generally entitled to protection against personal financial loss or indemnification. (In the present discussion, "indemnification" refers to the payment of any settlement or judgment for a negligent act.) This may apply to both attorney's fees and judgments that might be awarded. Almost all states recognize that the governmental unit is liable for the negligent acts or omissions of its agents (volunteers) or employees who are acting within the scope of their duties as public employees. The employee in this context includes not only paid staff but also volunteers. Elected officials who receive no pay and volunteers would be included in this definition of employee. The liability for the employee's actions is passed on to the governmental unit as employer, under a theory generally known as "vicarious liability." However, most state indemnification statutes provide that, where the employee (or volunteer) acted with malice or the employee's actions were outside the scope of the job, no defense is provided nor shall any judgment be paid (Pine, n.d; Pine 2013).

The Volunteer Protection Act 42 USCA §§ 14501-14505 (1997)

Beginning in the mid-1980s, suits against volunteers grew in number and attracted the attention of national media. At about the same time, the insurance picture for volunteers and nonprofit organizations darkened. Premiums rose dramatically, coverage exclusions increased, and several types of coverage became unavailable. Due to substantially higher insurance premiums, some nonprofit organizations cut back on services (Public Entity Risk Institute 1999).

In response, Congress enacted the Volunteer Protection Act of 1997 (VPA) in order to encourage volunteerism by reducing the possibility of litigation brought against volunteers. The federal statute sought to make available statutory immunity to increase the labor pool for voluntary organizations.

In particular, punitive damages may not be awarded against a volunteer acting within the scope of his/her responsibilities to a nonprofit organization, even when harm is caused due to an act or omission of the volunteer on behalf of the organization or entity. A variety of conditions qualify this immunity.[4] For example, the immunity does not attach to the volunteer's organization. The VPA does not exempt volunteers from liability for any harm caused while driving a motor vehicle. This exclusion is important because research indicates that half the claims involving emergency response organizations arise from vehicle accidents (Pine, n.d; Pine 2013).

The VPA only applies to 501(c)(3) organizations and governmental entities. In addition, the VPA does not prevent a nonprofit from bringing an action against a volunteer. Despite the existence of the VPA, many volunteers remain *fully liable* for any harm they cause, and all volunteers remain liable for some actions (Public Entity Risk Institute 1999). In general, the limitations on the liability of a volunteer under this act do not apply to any misconduct that: (a) constitutes a crime of violence (as that term is defined in section 16 of title 18, United States Code) or act of international terrorism (as that term is defined in section 2331 of title 18) for which the defendant has been convicted in any court; (b) constitutes a hate crime (as that term is used in the Hate Crime Statistics Act (28 U.S.C. 534 note); (c) involves a sexual offense, as defined by applicable state law, for which the defendant has been convicted in any court; (d) involves misconduct for which the defendant has been found to have violated a federal or state civil rights law; or (e) where the defendant was under the influence (as determined pursuant to applicable state law) of intoxicating alcohol or any drug at the time of the misconduct.

Volunteer immunity laws may provide volunteers with some protection, but they are not complete solutions. Many persons in the nonprofit sector mistakenly believe that volunteer protection statutes provide volunteers (including directors and officers) with complete protection from civil liability. A second mistaken belief is that volunteer immunity laws provide protection from liability for the nonprofit entity. Belief in either of these myths could lead to potentially disastrous consequences. For this reason, volunteer immunity laws should be understood by both the volunteer and the organization. Other risk management mechanisms, including insurance, should be in place to fill the gaps and to provide peace of mind. The bottom line appears to be that if certain conditions are satisfied, volunteers may be protected from claims of negligence, but they are not protected against claims of gross negligence. Thus, if a lawsuit contains an allegation of gross negligence against a volunteer, the volunteer must defend against the action and will typically incur defense costs in doing so.

The frequency of employment practices claims, which include claims of discrimination, harassment, retaliation, and wrongful termination, has grown substantially since the early 1990s. In fact, employment practices claims are the most common type of claims brought against nonprofits. The cause of these allegations may be the result of the actions of an organization's volunteers or its employees. Volunteer administrators, managers, supervisors, and board members cannot rely on federal and state volunteer immunity laws for protection against these lawsuits because such statutes do not provide immunity from federal civil rights laws, which are the basis of most employment practices claims (CNA 2011).

Liability in New York State: A Case Study

Volunteer police authority and liability issues can vary from state to state. During the 1950s, in counties and cities throughout New York, units of auxiliary police were organized under the various local community civil defense units, which were each headed by a local volunteer director. Currently, there are approximately 60 volunteer police units in New York. "Today, auxiliary police officers wear uniforms almost identical to regular police, drive police cars which look almost identical to regular police cars and which are equipped with the same emergency lights, sirens, and police radios. Auxiliary police officers usually carry police batons (a potentially deadly weapon) and handcuffs. ... departments have begun to outfit auxiliary police officers with bullet resistant vests. Some police departments permit auxiliary police officers to carry mace and guns when they receive the same training as regular police officers.... In some counties, auxiliary police perform duties such as issuing summonses for handicap parking violations, checking vacation homes, participating in emergency rescues, riding as second man in patrol cars, and performing administrative work for police departments" (Franckel 2013).

Auxiliary police were organized in New York State pursuant to the New York State Defense Emergency Act 1951 (the Act) and NYS CPL 2.10:26 (designation of peace officer) and CPL 2.20 (powers of peace officers), which came about as a result of the federal Civil Defense Act of 1950. At the time, there was substantial federal and state concern about a nuclear attack by the Soviet Union. A comprehensive plan was needed to ensure the safety and survival of the citizens of New York in the event of an anticipated or actual nuclear attack.

The Act defines auxiliary police, auxiliary firemen, bomb squads, radiological units, rescue squads, emergency medical units, monitoring and decontamination squads, and all other similar forces having duties and responsibilities in connection with civil defense as "volunteer agencies." The Act imposes, upon virtually every county in the state, the obligation to recruit, train, equip, and discharge auxiliary police officers. The Act also provides worker's compensation coverage and immunity (see Article 9 § 113) for negligent acts only when auxiliary police officers are performing duties "relating to civil defense, including but not limited to activities pursuant thereto, in preparation for anticipated attack, during attack, or following attack or false warning thereof, or in connection with an authorized drill or test."

In regard to the authorized scope of auxiliary police duties, these volunteer police were given the authority to perform duties only during specifically limited instances related to the fear of an enemy attack. The Act states that the "local legislative body of any county, town, city, or village may by resolution confer or authorize the conferring upon members of the auxiliary police the powers of peace officers, subject to such restrictions as such body shall impose, and subject to the provisions of subdivision twenty-six of section 2.10 and section 2.20 of the criminal procedure law" (see Article 8 § 105). CPL § 2.10:26 provides the restrictions that auxiliary police officers shall have the power of peace officers set forth in CPL § 2.20 only during a period of imminent or actual attack by enemy forces and during drills authorized under § 29-b of Article 2-B of the executive law, providing for the use of civil defense forces in disasters. In addition, other than directing traffic during official drills (see Criminal Procedure Law, § 2.10:26), there is no statutory authority that permits auxiliary police officers to conduct specific activities. Nevertheless, at present, "Auxiliary Police are trained and extensively utilized by police departments for a myriad of activities far outside of the original intent, scope, and authorization of the New York State Defense Emergency Act" (Franckel 2013).

The expansion of duties was acknowledged in *Fitzgibbon v. County of Nassau, et al.*, 541 N.Y.S.2d 845 147 A.D.2d 40 (N.Y.A.D. 2 Dept., 1989): "It is clear that the contemporary functions of auxiliary police units have evolved beyond those contemplated by the framers of the Act ... there is little question that auxiliary police units have been principally deployed in order to assist law enforcement personnel in combating the threat of crime from within, and less so as the statutorily envisaged civilian reserve to be mobilized in preparation for the perceived threat of external invasion or natural disaster." In addition, in *People v. Rosario*, 78 N.Y.2d 583, 585 N.E.2d 766, 578 N.Y.S.2d 454 (1991), the New State Court of Appeals (the state's highest court) ruled that the "fellow officer" rule (which entitles police officers and police agencies to pass along probable cause from one police officer to another) applied to auxiliary police.[5] Under the rule, a police officer is entitled to assume the reliability of information obtained from a radio bulletin, telephone, or teletype alert and to make a warrantless arrest based upon that information, when the source of the information is a "fellow police officer" or police department. If the probable cause existed prior to being transmitted to the arresting officer, then the arresting officer has probable cause to make the arrest.

However, there is a serious risk of liability exposure for acts of negligence in New York State. In *Fitzgibbon v. County of Nassau, et al.*, (1989), the plaintiff David Fitzgibbon Jr. was crossing a street in Massapequa Park, Nassau County, at approximately 11:00 p.m., when he was struck and injured by a marked RMP (radio motor patrol car) owned by the defendant Nassau Auxiliary Police Unit 316 and operated by the defendant Auxiliary Police Officer (APO) Frank Dennis Jr. APO Dennis was in uniform and on patrol at the time of the accident. The plaintiff alleged that APO Dennis operated the patrol car in a negligent manner and that he had done so with the "consent and permission" of the defendant, the county of Nassau. The defendants moved for summary judgment to dismiss the plaintiff's complaint, arguing that the New York State Defense Emergency Act conferred complete immunity with regard to any claim premised upon APO Dennis's alleged negligence because the functions performed were part of a statutory civil defense "drill" or training exercise to which the immunity provision of the Act applied. It was also alleged that the defendant county of Nassau was negligent in its supervision of Officer Dennis and vicariously liable for his conduct under the doctrine of *respondeat superior*. Interestingly, in an effort to avoid liability, the defendant Nassau County also argued that it did not direct, maintain, or control the auxiliary unit's activities and, accordingly, was not responsible to the plaintiff under the doctrine. The Supreme Court (the lower trial court) denied the respective motions of the defendants, thereby precluding the granting of summary judgment to dismiss the plaintiff's complaint. The court also found that questions of fact existed with respect to the county's vicarious liability for Dennis's alleged negligence. The defendants appealed this decision to the appellate division, which upheld the decision, ruling that APO Dennis's patrol was a routine patrol and not a "drill" or training exercise entitling the defendants, including APO Dennis, to immunity. The justices of the appellate division finalized their decision by stating "It must be concluded that the activities in question are not among those to which the shield of immunity was intended to apply."[6]

Thus, in New York State (absent any local immunity law), contemporary volunteer auxiliary police officers appear to perform their routine patrols beyond the scope of the state's Emergency Defense Law as well as the federal VPA. The lack of legal authority creates a myriad of legal issues, one of which is liability for negligent acts. In New York State, lack of appropriate legal authority could also result in loss of eligibility for the workers' compensation benefits (see Franckel 2013).

It is important that volunteer police in all jurisdictions of the United States carefully review the scope of their authority in relation to the duties they perform, so that in the event of alleged negligent actions they can obtain the benefits associated with the applicable state and federal immunity and indemnification statutes.

The Law Enforcement Officers Safety Act of 2004

This federal statute and its subsequent amendments concern a peace officer's ability to carry a concealed weapon off-duty throughout the United States. In this regard, it supersedes most state law, local ordinances, and local policy restricting carrying off-duty. However, it does not exempt such officers from federal laws, which regulate firearms on aircraft and federal property. Moreover, all officers must still obey local prohibitions or restrictions against the carrying of concealed weapons on (1) private property if the owner imposes such restrictions and (2) state or public property, such as courthouses or a public park. In addition, an officer is still subject to his or her employing agency's policies and conditions of employment. The agency can develop a policy to dictate what the standards are for employees of that agency that carry firearms (e.g., qualification standards). An agency, it appears, is not free to develop a policy about how it will implement the provisions of this act relative to other law enforcement officers (California Attorney General 2013). Useful information about the Law Enforcement Officers Safety Act (LEOSA) for persons who are about to retire or who are retired can be found at: http://www.dhs.gov/xlibrary/assets/foia/mgmt_instruction_257_01_001_law_enforcement_officers_safety_act.pdf.

LEOSA and its amendments have generated much commentary, and case law is developing on this topic. Despite its 2010 amendments, LEOSA and related laws remain an issue subject to interpretation. When an individual is considering membership in a particular volunteer police unit, it is quite appropriate to inquire if the sponsoring agency meets the standards that will qualify its volunteer police members for the benefits of this law. According to an opinion of the attorney general of the state of California, all active reserve officers will be authorized to carry, "If they meet the criteria of the Act (active). Retired reserves are not likely to qualify—they need to have non-forfeitable retirement rights. Most don't" (California Attorney General 2013).

In order to be considered a qualified law enforcement officer for the benefits of this act to apply, the following criteria must be met. The officer must be "an employee of a governmental agency who (1) is authorized by law to engage in or supervise the prevention, detection, investigation, or prosecution of, or the incarceration of any person for any violation of law, and has statutory powers of arrest; (2) is authorized by the agency to carry a firearm; (3) is not the subject of any disciplinary action by the agency; (4) meets standards, if any, established by the agency which require the employee to regularly qualify in the use of a firearm; (5) is not under the influence of alcohol or another intoxicating or hallucinatory drug or substance; and (6) is not prohibited by Federal law from receiving a firearm" (see title 18, United States Code, § 926B).

As long as individuals meet the criteria set forth in LEOSA, they will be protected from the carry permit requirements of other jurisdictions. This consideration occurred in a courtroom, when for the first time, a New York City trial judge was asked to consider the applicability of LEOSA. It involved the arrest of an elected part-time constable from Pennsylvania, conceded to be a constable by the prosecution, who was arrested in New York City for carrying a concealed firearm without a license. The issue in this case was whether by virtue of his status as a law enforcement officer, the defendant was entitled to carry his weapon across state lines without having a gun permit. A hearing was held to determine the merits of the defendant's motion to dismiss the case. The sole witness was the defendant. The court's opinion reviewed the elements of the LEOSA requirements and determined that the defendant satisfied the necessary criteria. He therefore came within the protections of LEOSA, and the grand jury indictment was dismissed ending the case unless the prosecution should appeal. The 14-page decision by New York County Supreme Court Justice Arnold A. Zweibel in the case of *People v. Rodriguez* (2006) can be found at: http://www.handgunlaw.us/documents/agopinions/ NYCtLEOSARulingPeoplevsRodriguez.PDF.

In 2011, after several similar cases of U.S. Coast Guard (USCG) officers getting into conflicts with this law, the Coast Guard issued its own LEOSA policy. The new Coast Guard policy defines who is a qualified law enforcement officer with respect to only certain uniformed active duty, reserve Coast Guard members, and special agents of the Coast Guard Investigative Service (CGIS). The policy specifically states that "Civilian members of the USCG and members of the Auxiliary are not covered by the LEOSA unless they are CGIS special agents or otherwise meet the LEOSA definition of 'qualified law enforcement officer.'" Perhaps, some of the problems in the past could have been cleared up if that policy had already been in existence. (The full text of the USCG policy is available at: http://www.uscg.mil/ announcements/alcoast/549-10_alcoast.txt.)

In view of the current restrictions placed on the activities of Coast Guard Auxiliary members, it is not surprising that the Coast Guard LEOSA policy has excluded members of the Coast Guard Auxiliary. However, eligibility under LEOSA is still possible for those volunteer police who have law enforcement responsibilities and who satisfy all of its other provisions, such as possessing the appropriate identification.

Within the 2013 National Defense Authorization Act, an amendment was added to the required LEOSA identification (ID) card language. The amendment mandates that qualified law enforcement officers must carry a photographic ID that "identifies the employee as a police or law enforcement officer of the agency," and that qualified retired law enforcement officers carry a photographic ID "that identifies the person has having been employed as a police or law enforcement officer." The LEOSA does "not bestow either an explicit right to obtain the required photographic ID or a federal remedy for an agency's failure to issue one" (Baranowski 2013). Thus, to be in full compliance with the amended Act, concerned individuals will be dependent upon their agency's cooperation with respect to the issuance of the necessary ID.

A person carrying an ID card designating them as an "auxiliary or reserve police officer" does not automatically mean that they are a qualified law enforcement officer in their jurisdiction or for the purposes of LEOSA. In some jurisdictions, a police or sheriff's department may have an auxiliary or reserve program, but their assignments may be quite limited to directing traffic at fairs, helping with searches for lost children, lending a hand at disasters, and so on (e.g., see aforementioned information about Waltham's auxiliary police). In various jurisdictions, volunteers may be qualified to carry firearms, but they do not have arrest authority. On the contrary, there are many departments that have authorized volunteers to serve as part-time peace officers or police officers and that offer them the same or equivalent training as full-time paid officers (e.g., see Fort Worth reserve police information presented earlier).

Any person interested in volunteer police work should ascertain the nature of their authority and legal status because state laws will vary in their definitions of such terms as auxiliary or reserve (see Chapter 4). Furthermore, active and retired qualified law enforcement officers (including members of reserve police units) should fully educate themselves on the firearm laws of any jurisdiction in which they are traveling and should strive to always be in compliance with the various laws because their knowledge is what will ultimately protect them. Finally, police administrators and other officials concerned with public safety and volunteer programs need to think realistically and carefully about the activities to be included in their programs. They need to design preservice training that considers real-life situations. The lives of citizens could be placed unnecessarily at risk by poorly conceived strategies.

Volunteer Liability Guide

The Citizen Corps Volunteer Liability Guide (CCVLG) is a FEMA publication available online at: http://www.ready.gov/guides. It provides an overview of liability concerns and suggests approaches to address these concerns. Liability refers to the legal responsibility for one's acts or omissions and includes such matters as legally imposed payment of damages for personal injury or property damage, penalties for practicing a profession or trade without the required license or permit, compensation for lost income and medical expenses of an injured volunteer, and damages for breach of contract. The topic of liability is a significant concern and a potential barrier to volunteer involvement in volunteer policing and other programs involving the delivery of emergency services. To offer guidance in this area, FEMA funded the nonprofit Public Entity Risk Institute (PERI) to develop the 100-page guide. The following three paragraphs contain excerpts from this guide to illustrate its contents.

> Liability and liability protection for emergency volunteers (volunteers in preparedness planning, emergency response, and disaster mitigation and recovery) are usually matters of state law. These laws differ significantly: some states provide much better emergency volunteer liability protection than others. In addition to appearing inequitable, these differences create a barrier to interstate mutual aid. Organizations that manage volunteers are reluctant to respond to a disaster in another state if their volunteers' licenses will not be recognized, or if they will have less liability protection and fewer Workers' Compensation benefits than are offered in their home state. The complexity, uncertainty, and lack of parity between states leaves many advocating a comprehensive federal solution, but Congress has not acted, despite a flurry of bills introduced in Congress in 2005 and 2006. (FEMA 2014, 3)
>
> State statutes, case law, and regulations all affect emergency volunteer liability protection. Most states' statutes and regulations are available online, but finding them can be difficult for someone unfamiliar with legal research. States organize their statutes and regulations differently, so there is no single place to look. A statute's or regulation's meaning is also affected by case law, which can be difficult to find and interpret. Bringing these diverse sources of law together with confidence usually requires a legal professional. (FEMA 2014, 6)
>
> The three types of liability are civil liability, injury benefits for emergency volunteers, and penalties for breach of licensing and certification requirements.... There are four major types of civil liability (also known as tort liability): a) negligent acts or omissions; b) intentional acts; c) liability for the acts of others; and d) strict liability. (FEMA 2014, 10)

The CCVLG consists of the following resources: *Citizen Corps Volunteer Liability Manual*; Glossary of Terms; Volunteer Liability Checklists; Links to State Statutory and Legislative Web sites; How-To Guide on Finding Bills and Statutes Online; References, and Additional Resources. About half of this manual or guideline consists of its appendices. They include the following: a glossary of terms that are used in the manual and are important to the understanding of liability issues; volunteer liability checklists that contain a series of questions to lead the reader through an investigation of the protection provided to emergency volunteers in their states; links to state statutory, legislative, and emergency management agency websites; a description of how to search for state laws online; additional resources of potential interest to users of the CCVLG; and examples of approaches used in different states. (FEMA 2014)

Commission on Accreditation for Law Enforcement Agencies Standards

The Commission on Accreditation for Law Enforcement Agencies, Inc. (CALEA®), was established in 1979 by the International Association of Chiefs of Police, the National Organization of Black Law Enforcement Executives, the National Sheriffs' Association, and the Police Executive Research Forum as an independent accrediting authority. Accreditation by this organization is a highly prized recognition of law enforcement professional excellence. To achieve "accredited" status, an agency must comply with hundreds of "best practice" standards established by CALEA for the operation of police organizations. CALEA sends an assessment team to examine all aspects of a department's policies and procedures, management, operations, and support services. Participation in the CALEA process is voluntary, but it is important because it can provide some assurance that the accredited police department is rated highly by its peers based on compliance with national standards and that it will be maintaining compliance with the identified standards by reporting annually to CALEA. As of 2008, fewer than 4% of law enforcement agencies had completed this process (Fresno Police Department 2008).

"Agencies that seek accreditation are required to comply only with those standards that are specifically applicable to them. Applicability is based on two factors: an agency's size and the functions it performs. Applicable standards are categorized as mandatory or other-than-mandatory. Agencies must comply with all applicable mandatory standards and at least 80% of applicable other-than-mandatory standards. If an agency cannot comply with a standard because of legislation, labor agreements, court orders, or case law, waivers can be sought from the Commission" (CALEA 2013).

In Kansas, the Ottawa Police Department's quest to achieve national accreditation had the unexpected consequence of causing the disbanding of its four-officer reserve unit in 2013. As part of the accreditation process, CALEA standards specify that every member of the reserve force must complete the same training as a full-time certified police officer. Certification requires 576 hours of training at the Kansas Law Enforcement Training Center in Hutchinson, in addition to 40 hours of annual training to maintain certification. All officers who wear a department's uniform, carry a gun, and are authorized to make arrests must undergo the same training, regardless of whether the officer is full-time or reserve. The reserve officers declined to pursue the more than 500 hours of academy training due to the time commitment that would have been required. An arrangement was made to have the four reserve officers join the county's sheriff's reserves unit and one reserve officer pursued that option (Carder 2013).

As previously discussed at some length in Chapter 5, CALEA standards greatly impacted the volunteer police program within the Connecticut State Police. In response to the nation's entry into World War II, the Connecticut State Police organized an auxiliary program and assigned their 1,200 volunteers to guard bridges and installations vital to defense against possible sabotage. Auxiliary officers are still doing their job today but as a much smaller unit. No one has been added to state trooper auxiliary ranks since 1988. The stated reasons for this freeze on recruitment was that the new training adopted by both the state and CALEA had now reached more than 800 hours, making it unlikely that volunteers would be able to attend and that the state authorities would bear the cost of this training. Nevertheless, when the new training hours became mandatory, existing auxiliary trooper members were permitted to remain. In 1995, there was a list of 900 people waiting for openings, and the force had been reduced to 130 members. At that time, auxiliary troopers patrolled highways and helped disabled motorists, directed traffic at accidents, did courier work for barracks, and backed up troopers. They had no arrest powers and did not respond to alarms. They did carry firearms but only for self-defense as they drove in marked state cruisers (Leukhardt 1995). Today there are less than 50 auxiliary troopers in the program; as they "retire," they are not replaced, and eventually, the program will cease to exist. When volunteers turn 70, they have the option of serving as administrative aides. They do not wear a uniform or carry a gun.[7]

World War II also spurred such Connecticut municipalities as Milford, New Britain, Hartford, New Haven, Bridgeport, Waterbury, and Stamford to create similar programs. However, when state training requirements were passed in 1982 for anyone doing police work, these units were disbanded. The new state law required all municipal police officers to be trained and certified. At that time, the cost of running a 560-hour police academy was deemed to be excessive for the purpose of only certifying their part-time officers. Before the new laws, many auxiliary officers carried guns and could make arrests. The Milford force had part-time members until the mid-1990s, but the stringent certification standards and the expense of providing that training led to its demise. Because most of the volunteers had other full-time jobs, making them complete a police academy program did not seem practical. An alternative was devised to spread the volunteer police training over time—namely, three nights a week over three years. Most of those trained men and women have since retired, and the few remaining are often retired police officers who have kept up their certification (Juliano 2011).

In Connecticut, there is no distinction between full-time and part-time officers with regard to their certification. "Certification is the formal acknowledgement that a police officer has met the minimum, entry level requirements and basic training requirements of the Council and is thus authorized to exercise the authority of a police officer. Certification is awarded after the minimum entry level requirements have been met and basic training requirements have been completed, and is valid for a period not to exceed 3 years" (Klein 2013). According to William E. Klein, the certification officer for the Police Officer Standards and Training Council (POST) in Connecticut, although the era of the auxiliary cop is ending, in its place has emerged a more professional and better trained police force (Juliano 2011).

This trend is also illustrated by new training requirements in the state of Illinois. Due to insurance coverage needs, on December 31, 2011, Illinois instituted a 400-hour mandatory basic law enforcement training course for volunteer police that matched what regular officers attended. Milan (Illinois) Police Chief Mark Beckwith said that these new training rules for auxiliary police forced the disbanding of his city's auxiliary unit. This unit was active for 42 years and worked unselfishly during times of floods, windstorms, snowstorms, parades, concerts, and city events. "The unit was truly community policing in every sense of the word," according to Beckwith (Geyer 2012).

In the foregoing jurisdictions and in many others, higher training standards have affected the status of volunteer police units. Many units have simply folded, while others have attempted to offer long periods of part-time instruction in order to keep their members in compliance with the new higher standards. However, if existing state laws permit, a wide range of organizations have sought to preserve their units by making clear distinctions between levels or types of volunteer service. For example, in Wenham, auxiliary and reserve police units were reorganized in 2006 in consideration of the accreditation standards (Waters 2008). In New Britain (Connecticut), a new designation for volunteer police without arrest authority was created—community service officer (CSO). (It is also known as "the Police Reserve program.") The CSOs do not perform law enforcement duties nor do they have the power of arrest, but they do perform functions that are also the responsibility of sworn officers. Some examples of CSO duties are: assistance at accident scenes; completing reports in noncriminal cases; assisting in searches; providing transportation to stranded motorists; patrolling school grounds; and standing by at alarms. As with other types of volunteer police units, CSOs enable police officers to have more time to devote to law enforcement and public safety matters. The CSOs are deployed in pairs during the evening hours, and the volunteers receive no salary. Their uniforms are distinctive in order not be confused with those of regular officers, and volunteer safety is a paramount concern. At its Web page, the online posted materials end with these civic-minded words: "This program is an excellent opportunity for those interested in a career in law enforcement to gain valuable experience and for service-oriented individuals to contribute to the community" (Wardell 2013).

Thus, the higher training standards can be either a hindrance or a stimulus for organizing volunteer police units. Much will depend upon the discretion of police administrators and other public officials tasked with police oversight responsibilities. Moreover, there is a wide range of new activities for volunteer police to engage in (e.g., see Chapters 11 and 12). The reader is also referred to this book's Epilogue for suggestions about how to approach the need to upgrade or institute a volunteer police unit. The CALEA standards for volunteer police are set forth in Appendix A.

Summary

In colonial America, a constable-watch system was imported from England. In this approach to policing, the people were, in fact, the police. Watch participation was a compulsory duty for the community's male population. However, over time it became a common practice for wealthier and disinterested citizens to pay for a watch replacement, which led to overall poor policing. The system broke down when Boston and other cities deployed the most elderly citizens and occasionally sentenced minor offenders to serve on the watch. The success of the new approach to policing begun in London in 1829 eliminated the constable-watch system in England and later in the United States. Irrespective of the disappointing practices of a bygone era, citizens who are recruited and trained by police agencies for volunteer positions in contemporary society embody the highest ideals of civic participation and concern for community safety.

Police officers and their volunteer counterparts or aides should familiarize themselves with police history including the classic tenets composed by Sir Robert Peel, who organized London's Metropolitan Police. His list of law enforcement standards is highly applicable today. In addition, there exist a huge number of legal principles to be concerned about. These include local ordinances, peace officer standards and training requirements, departmental rules and regulations, case law, and state and federal statutes.

Many of these legal principles are not well known; for example, as a general rule, the government owes a duty to protect their citizens as a whole but to individuals only if a special relationship can be proven. According to the rule set forth by the U.S. Supreme Court in the 1989 *DeShaney* case, nothing in the language of the Fourteenth Amendment's due process clause requires a state to protect the life, liberty, and property of its citizens against invasion by private actors. The clause is phrased as a limitation on the state's power to act, not as a guarantee of certain minimal levels of safety and security. In order to supplement the governmental agents assigned to protect the public, volunteers are a vital resource, especially in emergency situations. Properly managed, they can play critical roles in crisis situations, and they can do much to prevent crises from taking place.

Some municipalities have had problems arise concerning liability coverage and the legal status of their volunteer police. For more than three decades, Waltham's auxiliary police had been providing safety at a host of civic functions such as parades and festivals, but the entire force was demobilized for more than a year after the attorney representing the police agency refused to represent an auxiliary member sued for false arrest. In the city of Fort Worth, the volunteer force was suspended due to concern about whether proper documentation existed indicating that reserve appointments had been approved by the city council. Although these forces were eventually reinstated, other communities may no longer be accepting applications for volunteer police positions because of uncertainties over liability and related matters. In recent years, the advent of CALEA standards has led to the permanent disbanding of various volunteer units.

Any number of legal issues may arise in connection with the utilization of volunteer resources. In order to bring an action for the negligence of a governmental entity, such as a governmental employee (or authorized volunteer), it must be proved that there was a breach of a specific duty involving the exercise of a degree of care, skill, and diligence that a reasonable or prudent person would have exercised under similar circumstances. Additional elements, such as damages and causation must also be shown.

The concept of "indemnification" involves protection against personal financial loss for the actions of governmental employees and volunteers. However, the governmental entity may not be liable for an employee's (or volunteer's) actions if the employee acted outside the scope of his or her duties, acted with an intent to harm (malice) or the intent to harm another, or if the actions were with reckless disregard for the rights of others. Role-playing exercises and drills help to reveal the gray areas where employees and volunteers do not understand their jobs. The risks of civil liability can be reduced by proper training.

The Volunteer Protection Act of 1997 (VPA) sought to reduce the personal liability of volunteers so long as certain conditions were satisfied. The statute provides that no volunteer of a nonprofit organization or governmental entity shall be liable for harm caused by an act or omission of the volunteer on behalf of the organization or entity if the volunteer was acting within the scope of the volunteer's responsibilities in the nonprofit organization or governmental entity at the time of the act of omission; if appropriate or required, the volunteer was properly licensed, certified, or authorized by the appropriate authorities for the activities or practice in the State; the harm was not caused by willful or criminal misconduct or gross negligence, and so forth; or the harm was not caused by the volunteer operating a motor vehicle, vessel, aircraft, or other vehicle for which the state requires the operator or the owner of the vehicle, craft, or vessel to possess an operator's license or maintain insurance. Clearly, the successful deployment of volunteers in today's world requires an appropriate combination of volunteer oversight, government protections, risk management processes and procedures (e.g., completion of necessary training programs and certifications), and insurance coverage. FEMA's CCVLG provides an overview of liability concerns and suggests approaches to address these concerns. It also deals with the methods and procedures for risk assessment.

The Law Enforcement Officers Safety Act of 2004 (LEOSA) is important because with certain limitations and conditions, LEOSA exempts qualified active or retired law enforcement officers ("retirees") from most state and local laws that prohibit the carriage of concealed firearms. However, many potential candidates for its benefits, both regular and reserve police, may not yet be familiar with the law. Despite its 2010 and 2013 amendments, understanding LEOSA and related laws seems to be subject to some interpretation. Active and retired law enforcement officers should fully educate themselves on the firearm laws of any jurisdiction in which they are traveling and should strive to always be in compliance with the various laws because their knowledge is what will ultimately protect them. Volunteer and regular law enforcement officers carry concealed firearms for one major purpose—the protection of human life. Given the nature of our litigious society, off-duty officers or retirees should be especially concerned about the potential or actual use of their firearms. A shooting incident becomes a lot more complicated if a court determines that an individual was in illegal possession of the weapon used in the case.

Review Questions

1. One of Sir Robert Peel's principles is that the police should demonstrate "absolute impartial service to the law." In 2013, a federal court ruled that the New York City Police Department's stop-and-frisk policy violated the civil rights of minorities. Find out more information about stop and frisk and discuss whether such laws or their exercise violate this principle.

2. In Illinois, auxiliary police officers with "conservator of the peace powers" are required to attend the 400-hour Basic Law Enforcement Officer Training Course at a certified state academy. Waltham, Massachusetts, requires a 120-hour training program for its auxiliary members, and in Fort Worth, a minimum of 560 hours training is required to become a reserve officer. What, if any, justifications can be given for the disparity in these training requirements?

3. Both the Fort Worth and Waltham volunteer police were suspended. Do you believe these suspensions were warranted? Discuss your reasoning.

4. Explain why jurisdiction is important for both regular and volunteer police.
5. Explain the "public duty doctrine" and discuss why it may be of great interest to the general public as well as volunteer police.
6. Find *Castle Rock v. Gonzales*, 545 U.S. 748 (2005) online and carefully review the court's opinion. If you were a member of the court, explain how you would have voted and state your reasons.
7. Provide at least three examples of torts.
8. Define "negligence."
9. Identify at least one factor to ensure that volunteers are protected for possible negligent actions during their response in disasters.
10. Congress enacted the Volunteer Protection Act of 1997 (VPA) in order to encourage volunteerism by reducing the possibility of litigation brought against volunteers. List at least three conditions that will render VPA benefits inapplicable to a volunteer.
11. Discuss the significance of the opinion by New York County Supreme Court Justice Arnold A. Zweibel in the case of *People v. Rodriguez* (2006).
12. Discuss how CALEA and higher state training standards have affected volunteer police units.
13. Dr. Peter Moskos received his PhD in Sociology from Harvard University. He is a former Baltimore City police officer and currently is an associate professor at John Jay College of Criminal Justice. Professor Moskos has stated that Sir Robert Peel is often mistakenly credited with having authored the "Nine Principles of Policing." Who should be credited? For more information, go to: http://www.copinthehood.com/2011/09/principles-that-never-were.html

Notes

1. The 1989 *DeShaney* decision remains a subject of contention. It has prompted a large literature, including at least one book (Lynne Curry's *The DeShaney Case: Child Abuse, Family Rights and the Dilemma of State Intervention*, University of Kansas Press 2007) and many law review articles. Lower courts have cited it hundreds of times. No doubt the severity of Joshua DeShaney's injuries when he was four years old prompted this interest. Joshua was beaten so severely that he fell into a life-threatening coma. Emergency brain surgery revealed a series of hemorrhages caused by traumatic injuries to the head inflicted over a long period of time. Joshua did not die, but he suffered brain damage so severe that he was expected to spend the rest of his life confined to an institution for the profoundly retarded. Randy DeShaney was subsequently tried and convicted of child abuse. For information about Curry's book see: http://www.kansaspress.ku.edu/curdes.html.

2. Training materials for the incident command system (ICS) are provided by FEMA. The system is a standardized on-scene all-hazards concept that allows users to adopt an integrated organizational structure to match the complexities and demands of single or multiple incidents without being hindered by jurisdictional boundaries. The system helps ensure the safety of responders and others, achieve tactical objectives, and efficiently use resources. ICS is used by all levels of government—federal, state, tribal, and local—as well as by many nongovernmental organizations and the private sector. FEMA's Emergency Management Institute (EMI) offers more than 40 independent study courses concerned with ICS and related topics. These are self-paced, no-cost courses designed for people who have emergency management responsibilities and for the general public. (To obtain more information go to: http://www.fema.gov/incident-command-system.)

3. A duty maybe based upon a specific statute, judicial decisions, or found in a governmental rule. Such a duty requires a person to use a reasonable degree of attention, perception, memory, knowledge, intelligence, and judgment in his or her actions. Statutory duties include traffic codes, motor vehicle maintenance codes, workplace safety requirements, park construction and maintenance standards, environmental regulations, or inspection requirements. A "duty breach" is a failure to conform to that standard of care or a failure to carry out the duty. "Damages" refers to the actual loss or damage to the injured party. The "causation" element of negligence is the requirement that there must be a connection between the acts of the governmental employee, official, or agency body and injury to a third party, and the loss must be related to the act of the government representative. All negligence cases have these elements in common, and absence of proof of any one element will defeat a finding of liability (Pine, n.d.).

4. The VPA provides protection to nonprofit and government volunteers if: (1) the volunteer was acting within the scope of his or her responsibility; (2) the volunteer was properly licensed, certified, or authorized to engage in the activity or practice; (3) the harm was not caused by willful, criminal, or reckless misconduct, gross negligence, or conscious, flagrant indifference to the rights or safety of the individual harmed by the volunteer; and (4) the harm was not caused by the operation of a motor vehicle, aircraft, or other vehicle for which an operator's license or insurance is required by the state.

5. In *People v. Rosario*, a New York City Auxiliary Police Officer, while on routine patrol, received a radio transmission about a murder suspect and, upon spotting the murder suspect, advised a regular police officer who then made the arrest. The arrest, made by a regular police officer, was based upon information obtained from an auxiliary police officer who obtained the information from a radio transmission from the New York City Police Department. It should be noted that New York City Auxiliary Police use the same police radios as the regular police and receive the same radio transmissions. The New York State Court of Appeals ruled that the auxiliary police officer received extensive training, which was sufficient to pass along probable cause under the "fellow officer" rule and decided that the lack of peace officer status did not prevent the rule from applying to a New York City Auxiliary Police Officer.

6. Auxiliary police officers in Nassau County now have the protection of the Nassau County Charter § 2105(b) page 160, which provides: "Volunteer workers

shall be county employees for the purpose of receiving benefits pursuant to the workers' compensation law and shall be indemnified, defended, and held harmless by the county against any claim, demand, suit, or judgment for property damages, personal injury, including death, and any other liability which may be assessed against volunteer workers by reason of alleged negligence or other act committed by volunteer workers who were acting in the discharge of their duties within the scope of their employment or authorized volunteer duties." According to Franckel (2013), auxiliary police officers working in Nassau County, while on a function not authorized by New York's Defense Emergency Act, should currently have the protection of the Nassau County charter as a volunteer worker (barring the county filing for bankruptcy).

7. Since 1922, 21 troopers and auxiliary troopers of the Connecticut State Police Department have died for the state of Connecticut and its citizens during the performance of their duties. On May 25, 1994, Auxiliary Trooper Phillip A. Mingione of Milford was struck and killed on I-91 in the town of North Haven. Auxiliary Mingione had stopped and was standing outside his vehicle when a passing motorist lost control of her car and struck Auxiliary Mingione. On November 13, 1992, Auxiliary Trooper Edward W. Truelove stopped for a disabled motorist in the truck climbing lane of I-84 in Cheshire. After directing the driver and passenger to safety on the far side of the guardrail, Auxiliary Truelove radioed for a tow truck and attempted to safeguard the scene with his strobe lights. Several minutes later, an interstate truck driver drove into the rear end of the cruiser and Auxiliary Truelove was killed in the crash. If not for his concern about the occupants of the broken down car and his orders to move off the roadway, they too might have died (CSPAAA 2014).

References

Auxiliary Police Department. (2011). Recruiting. Retrieved October 26, 2013 http://www.city.waltham.ma.us/auxiliary-police-department

Baranowski, J. (2013). LEOSA welcomes the military by requiring new identification card language for all. Retrieved October 26, 2013 http://le.nra.org/leosa/leosa-welcomes-the- military.aspx

Borchard, E. M. (1926). Governmental responsibility in tort, IV. *Yale Law Journal, 36*(1), 1–41.

CALEA. (2013). Law enforcement program: The standards. Retrieved November 1, 2013 from http://www.calea.org/content/law-enforcement-program-standards

California Attorney General. (2013). HR 218 – Law Enforcement Officers Safety Act (LEOSA)—Issues. Retrieved October 26, 2013 from http://ag.ca.gov/firearms/forms/pdf/leosiss.pdf

Carder, D. (2013, October 30). Police disband reserve force. Retrieved October 31, 2013 from http://ottawaherald.com/news/103113reserve

CNA. (2011). The myth of volunteer immunity. Retrieved October 22, 2013 from https://www.cnapro.com/pdf/Myths%20of%20Volunteer%20Immunity%2012012-11.pdf

Collins, H. C. (1981). Municipal liability for torts committed by volunteer anticrime groups. *Fordham Urban Law Journal, 10*(4), 595–631.

Commissioner Bratton's Blog. (2014, March 6). Peel's nine principles of policing. Retrieved June 27, 2014 from http://www.nyc.gov/html/nypd/html/administration/commissioners_corner.shtml

Crime rates. (2013). Crime rates for Waltham, MA. Retrieved October 26, 2013 from http://www.neighborhoodscout.com/ma/waltham/crime/

CSPAAA. (2014). Honor Roll Photos. Retrieved June 27, 2014 from https://www.cspaaa.com/honor_roll/list.asp

DeShaney v. Winnebago County Department of Social Services, 489 US 189, 109 S. Ct. 998, 103 L. Ed. 2d 249 - Supreme Court, 1989.

FEMA. (2014). *Citizen corps volunteer liability guide.* Washington, DC: Community Preparedness Division, Federal Emergency Management Agency.

Florida Attorney General. (1989, September 15). Florida Attorney General advisory legal opinion – AGO 89-62: Officer's duty to provide aid to ill or injured. Retrieved October 29, 2013 from http://www.myfloridalegal.com/ago.nsf/Opinions/85E4F114E318503185256570006E05B3

Fort Worth Police. (2013). Reserve division. Retrieved October 28, 2013 from http://www.fortworthpd.com/divisions/reserve-division.aspx

Franckel, P. L. (2013). Auxiliary police authority and liability for negligence. Retrieved October 1, 2013 from http://www.hurt911.org/articles/auxiliary_police_liability.html

Fresno Police Department. (2008). CALEA accreditation. Retrieved October 31, 2013 from http://www.fresno.gov/Government/DepartmentDirectory/Police/AboutFresnoPD/CALEAAccreditation.htm

Geyer, T. (2012, January 8). Illinois rules force many cities to drop auxiliary police units. Retrieved October 31, 2013 from http://qctimes.com/news/local/illinois-rules-force-many-cities-to-drop-auxiliary-police-units/article_59f88ec8-3a7a-11e1-983f-0019bb2963f4.html

Inciardi, J. (2000). *Elements of criminal justice* (2nd ed.). New York (NY): Oxford University Press.

Juliano, F. (2011, March 5). Higher training standards, costs mean fewer part-time police. Retrieved November 1, 2013 from http://www.ctpost.com/local/article/Higher-training-standards-costs-mean-fewer-1043894.php#

Klein, W. E. (2013). *Frequently asked questions.* Police Officer Standards and Training Council. Retrieved November 1, 2013 from http://www.ct.gov/post/cwp/view.asp?a = 2058&q = 291946

Leukhardt, B. (1995, February 19). A city calls auxiliary police back to duty. Retrieved November 1, 2013 from http://articles.courant.com/1995-02-19/news/9502190210_1_auxiliary-professional-police-citizens-and-police

Nazemi, S. (2013). Sir Robert Peel's nine principals of policing. Retrieved October 20, 2013 from http://lacp.org/2009-Articles-Main/062609-Peels9Principals-Sandy-Nazemi.htm

Oleck, H. L. (1982). *Oleck's tort law practice manual.* Englewood Cliffs, NJ: Prentice-Hall.

Opinion No. GA-0893. (2011, November 22). Texas Attorney General Opinion No. GA-0893 Re: Whether a city that has adopted civil service rules for its police officers under chapter 143 of the Local Government Code may authorize a reserve police force. Retrieved October 28, 2013 from https://www.oag.state.tx.us/opinions/opinions/50abbott/op/2011/htm/ga-0893.htm

Pine, J. C. (n.d.). *Catastrophe readiness and response course; Session 5: Political and legal issues'*. Emergency Management Institute, FEMA, pp. 27–33. Forthcoming. Retrieved October 21, 2013 from www.training.fema.gov/.../catastrophe/Session%205%20Legal%20Issues...

Pine, J. C. (2013). Political and legal issues. In R. Bissell (Ed.), *Preparedness and response for catastrophic disasters* (pp. 77–108). Boca Raton, FL: CRC Press, Taylor and Francis Group.

Public Entity Risk Institute. (1999). Understanding the volunteer protection act. Retrieved October 22, 2013 from http://www.riskinstitute.org/peri/index.php?option = com_bookmarks&task = detail&id = 584

Reserve LEO News. (2013). Fort worth to resume reserve police officer program. Retrieved October 26, 2013 from http://www.vleoa.org/

Sherman, E. (2013, June 22). Waltham auxiliary police officers could return. Retrieved October 26, 2013 from http://www.wickedlocal.com/waltham/news/x1220217363/Waltham-auxiliary-police-officers-could-return

Statement of Policy. (2006, October 11). *Statement of policy auxiliary police officers*. Illinois Law Enforcement and Standards Training Board. Retrieved October 26, 2013 from http://www.ptb.state.il.us/pdf/auxiliary.pdf

U.S. Census Data. (2013). Waltham, MA. Retrieved October 26, 2013 from http://quickfacts.census.gov/qfd/states/25/2572600.html

Waltham Auxiliary Police. (2013). The Waltham Auxiliary Police Department is currently seeking qualified applicants. Retrieved October 26, 2013 from http://www.city.waltham.ma.us/police-department/pages/auxiliary-police

Waltham, MA. (2013). Retrieved October 26, 2012 from http://www.city-data.com/city/Waltham-Massachusetts.html

Wardell, J. (2013). CSO program. Retrieved November 1, 2013 from http://www.newbritainpolice.org/cso-program

Waters, W. (2008, March 15). Wenham police department to be restructured. Retrieved October 31, 2013 from http://www.wickedlocal.com/hamilton/news/x563308331

Volunteer Police and the Prevention of Human Trafficking

11

It ought to concern every person, because it is a debasement of our common humanity. It ought to concern every community, because it tears at our social fabric. It ought to concern every business, because it distorts markets. It ought to concern every nation, because it endangers public health and fuels violence and organized crime. I'm talking about the injustice, the outrage, of human trafficking, which must be called by its true name—modern slavery.

—President Barack Obama[1]

In the 1990s, Kathleen Barry (1995) estimated that the number of women and children trafficked worldwide for prostitution was approaching the numbers associated with the African slave trade of the 1700s. Approximately 150 years ago, the Thirteenth Amendment of the U.S. Constitution was adopted, banning slavery and involuntary servitude. Nevertheless, according to combined figures from the U.S. Justice, Labor, and State Departments, more than 100,000 people are presently being forced into servitude in the United States. Every year, human traffickers generate billions of dollars in profits by victimizing millions of people worldwide. Human trafficking is considered to be one of the fastest growing criminal industries in the world (Polaris Project 2013d).

This chapter considers the important role that volunteer police and other concerned individuals may play in the prevention of human trafficking and worker exploitation. It indicates the various types of existing human slavery (contract, chattel, etc.) and describes a citizen's role in the prevention of human trafficking. Victims of trafficking often do not speak the language of their new country and may in fact be illegal immigrants who fear deportation. Minors are especially vulnerable to exploitation and several states have begun to recognize this problem through the passage of "Safe Harbor" legislation. For example, in 2008, New York enacted the Safe Harbor for Exploited Children Act, which recognizes that children in prostitution are not criminals or delinquents but victims of child sex trafficking and child sexual abuse that need specialized services. In addition, in 2010, the Texas Supreme Court declared that child victims of prostitution should be provided counseling, rehabilitation, and services instead of being placed in a detention system that is ill-suited to their needs.[2]

The U.S. Department of State's Office to Monitor and Combat Trafficking in Persons is the country's leading agency with respect to a worldwide effort to reduce human trafficking. The Trafficking Victims Protection Act of 2000[3] (TVPA) is the nation's primary statute for combating this phenomenon, which has a variety of forms including forced labor, sex trafficking, bonded labor, debt bondage, involuntary domestic servitude, forced child labor, child soldiers, and child sex trafficking. "The Office has responsibility for bilateral and multilateral diplomacy, targeted foreign assistance, and public engagement on this issue of modern slavery and partners with foreign governments and civil society to develop and implement effective counter-trafficking strategies" (U.S. Department of State 2013a). Under the Trafficking Victims Protection Act of 2000, the phrases "trafficking in persons" or "human trafficking" have been used as umbrella terms for activities involved when one person obtains or holds another person in compelled service. Human trafficking is the acquisition of people by improper means such as force, fraud, or deception, with the aim of exploiting them (UNODC 2013b).

The United Nations Office on Drugs and Crime (UNODC) undertakes regional and transnational initiatives that seek to strengthen the rule of law, stability, and development. It targets the world's most vulnerable regions where the convergence of drugs, crime, corruption, and terrorism threatens regional and global security. It also tries to cope with organized crime and human trafficking, including the smuggling of migrants. Smuggling of migrants involves the procurement, for financial or other material benefit, of illegal entry for a person into a country of which that person is not a national or resident (UNODC 2013b). Such crimes are high on the international agenda because they pose major threats to security, which undermines human progress and challenges democracy. Virtually every country in the world is affected by these crimes. The challenge for all countries is to target the criminals who exploit desperate people and to protect and assist victims of trafficking and smuggled migrants, many of whom endure unimaginable hardships in their quest for a better life (UNODC 2013b).

The UNODC recognizes that the resources available to deal with these threats are minute compared to the suffering these threats instill (UNODC 2010). According to Yury Fedotov, the UNODC's executive director, human trafficking is a crime with millions of victims that stretches around the globe, although much of it remains hidden. "We are dealing with a crime of the 21st Century: adaptive, cynical, sophisticated; existing in developed and developing countries alike.... We need more sharing of best practices, greater mutual legal assistance, more joint operations across borders, national strategies on human trafficking linked to regional and international approaches, as well as the cooperation of key stakeholders such as civil society, the private sector and the media" (UNODC 2013a).

In 2014, as the February date for America's biggest sports event—the Super Bowl—was approaching, New Jersey's law enforcers redoubled their efforts to reduce the threat of sex trafficking. Many believe the state's sprawling highway system, its proximity to New York City, and its diverse population make it an attractive base of operations for traffickers. Consequently, New Jersey officials have trained law enforcement personnel, hospitality workers (e.g., hotel and nightclub employees), high school students, airport employees, and others in identifying the signs of trafficking. Local houses of worship are notifying congregants of warning signs, and truckers are being trained to look for people—mostly women but also men—who may be held against their will. To be prosecuted, sex trafficking must involve—unlike prostitution—not only a buyer and seller of sex but also a pimp or trafficker controlling the transaction, according to the New Jersey Attorney General's Office. In Arizona, where the 2015 Super Bowl will take place, Senator John McCain's wife, Cindy, has been speaking out, calling the Super Bowl the "largest human-trafficking venue on the planet" (Zezima 2014).

This chapter considers the definitions, cases, and types of human trafficking. It also addresses whether volunteer police in the United States should be considered stakeholders in the global fight against human trafficking and modern-day slavery. Arguments justifying this point of view can be based on the potential and significant roles volunteer police may undertake—for example, obtaining the cooperation of ordinary citizens, addressing the needs of victims, enforcing the laws designed to halt trafficking, protecting human rights, and providing other essential resources for the prevention of human trafficking and related crimes. In addition, various kinds of initiatives designed to facilitate the work of existing local volunteer police organizations are considered. The importance of federal assistance in harnessing the energies and talents of volunteer police is addressed as well as the form such assistance might take. Appendix E provides a brief annotated list of books and online videos concerning human trafficking.

Definitions

The U.S. government considers trafficking in persons to include all of the criminal conduct involved in forced labor and sex trafficking, essentially the conduct involved in reducing or holding someone in compelled service. Under the Trafficking Victims Protection Act of 2000 and its amendments and consistent with the United Nations *Protocol to Prevent, Suppress, and Punish Trafficking in Persons, Especially Women and Children* (hereinafter referred to as the Palermo Protocol),[4] individuals may be trafficking victims regardless of whether they once consented, participated in a crime as a direct result of being trafficked, were transported into the exploitative situation, or were simply born into a state of servitude. Despite a term that seems to connote movement, at the heart of the phenomenon of trafficking in persons are the many forms of enslavement, not the activities involved in international transportation (U.S. Department of State 2013b).[5]

Within the United Nations, the Office of the High Commissioner for Human Rights (OHCHR) is mandated to promote and protect the enjoyment and full realization by all people of all rights established in the Charter of the United Nations and in international human rights laws and treaties. A 2002 report entitled *Recommended Principles and Guidelines on Human Rights and Human Trafficking* was prepared by the OHCHR. The report was developed in order to provide practical, rights-based policy guidance on the prevention of trafficking and on the protection of victims of trafficking. The OHCHR report recommended that nations and—where appropriate— intergovernmental and nongovernmental organizations consider adopting and consistently using the internationally agreed upon definition of trafficking contained in the Palermo Protocol.

Under Article 3(a), the Palermo Protocol defines trafficking in persons as: "The recruitment, transportation, transfer, harboring, or receipt of persons, by means of the threat or use of force or other forms of coercion, of abduction, of fraud, of deception, of the abuse of power or of a position of vulnerability or of the giving or receiving of payments or benefits to achieve the consent of a person having control over another person for the purpose of exploitation. Exploitation shall include, at a minimum, the exploitation of the prostitution of others or other forms of sexual exploitation, forced labor or services, slavery or practices similar to slavery, servitude, or the removal of organs." Article 3(b) states the consent of a victim of trafficking in persons to the intended exploitation set forth in subparagraph (a) of this article shall be irrelevant where any of the means set forth in subparagraph (a) have been used. Article 3(c) of the Protocol further states that the recruitment, transportation, transfer, harboring, or receipt of a child for the purpose of exploitation shall be considered "trafficking in persons" even if this does not involve any of the means set forth here.

Article 3(b) indicates that the consent of the victim is irrelevant. It should be understood that the consent of the victim at any stage of the trafficking process is irrelevant. Just as legally a person cannot consent to slavery; neither can a victim consent to trafficking. "Exploitation, rather than coercion, is the operative concept in this definition. A definition of trafficking, based on a human rights framework, should protect all who are trafficked, drawing no distinctions between deserving and undeserving victims of trafficking, that is those who can prove they were forced and those who cannot. Any definition based on the victim's consent places the burden of proof on the victim and offers a loophole for traffickers to use the alleged consent of the victim in their own defense" (Hynes and Raymond 2002, 198–199).

The Polaris Project: Hotline, Advocacy, Services, Training

Founded in February 2002 by two Brown University graduates, Katherine Chon and Derek Ellerman, the "Polaris Project is a leading organization in the global fight against human trafficking and modern-day slavery. Named after the North Star 'Polaris' that guided slaves to freedom along the Underground Railroad, Polaris Project is transforming the way that individuals and communities respond to human trafficking, in the United States and globally. By successfully pushing for stronger federal and state laws, operating the National Human Trafficking Resource Center hotline (1–888–373–7888), conducting trainings, and providing vital services to victims of trafficking, Polaris Project creates long-term solutions that move our society closer to a world without slavery" (Polaris Project 2013a). Law enforcement officers, service providers, and other key first responders have used the Polaris Project for valuable training on how to recognize the signs of trafficking.[6]

Human trafficking is a form of modern-day slavery where people profit from the control and exploitation of others. As defined under U.S. federal law, victims of human trafficking include children involved in the sex trade, adults aged 18 or over who are coerced or deceived into commercial sex acts, and anyone forced into different forms of "labor or services," such as domestic workers held in a home, or farm workers forced to labor against their will. The factors that each of these situations has in common are elements of force, fraud, or coercion that are used to control people. This ability to control may then be used to induce someone into commercial sex acts, labor, or services. Numerous people in the field have summed up the concept of human trafficking as "compelled service" (Polaris Project 2013d).

Labor trafficking occurs in diverse contexts that encompass all forms of labor or services. Common places where forced labor has been found in the United States range from domestic servitude and small-scale "mom and pop" labor operations to more large-scale operations such as farms and factories. Certain brokers that supply labor to multinational corporations have also been identified as an emerging type of labor traffickers. Sex trafficking includes commercial sexual exploitation of children (CSEC), as well as every instance where an adult is in the sex trade as the result of force, fraud, or coercion. Sex trafficking occurs in street prostitution, online escort services, residential brothels, and brothels disguised as massage businesses. Under U.S. and international law, commercially sexually exploited children found in the sex trade are considered to be victims of trafficking, even if no force or coercion is present. Victims of human trafficking in the United States include American citizens or foreign nationals, adults or minors, and men or women. Foreign-born victims in the United States may be either documented or undocumented (Polaris Project 2013d).

Figure 11.1 National Human Trafficking Resource Center hotline call specialists are available 24 hours a day, 7 days a week, 365 days a year to take reports from anywhere in the country related to potential trafficking victims, suspicious behaviors, and/or locations where trafficking is suspected to occur. All reports are confidential. Interpreters are available. (From http://www.polarisproject.org/what-we-do/national-human-trafficking-hotline/report-a-tip)

Because human trafficking is considered to be one of the fastest growing criminal industries, the U.S. government and academic researchers are currently working on an annual estimate of the total number of trafficked persons in the United States. With 100,000 children estimated to be in the sex trade in the United States each year, it is clear that the total number of human trafficking victims in this country reaches into the hundreds of thousands when estimates of both adults and minors as well as sex and labor trafficking are aggregated (Polaris Project 2013d). The Polaris Project focuses on the day-to-day needs of the victims of human trafficking as well as the creation of long-term solutions that affect systemic and social change. For both of these purposes, in 2012, Polaris Project launched Vision 2020 to expand their impact on a global scale. One aspect of this initiative is to build on the work of the National Human Trafficking Resource Center (NHTRC) hotline (Figure 11.1) by identifying and connecting globally with human trafficking hotlines in order to develop a more coordinated and data-driven response to modern-day slavery. In addition, training and technical assistance may be offered to support the creation and expansion of hotlines in target countries (Polaris Project 2013c).

Trafficking in Persons Worker Exploitation Task Force

Within the U.S. Department of Justice, the Trafficking in Persons Worker Exploitation Task Force (TPWETF) seeks to prevent trafficking in persons and worker exploitation throughout the United States and to investigate and prosecute cases when such violations occur. The Task Force is chaired by the Assistant Attorney General for Civil Rights and the Solicitor of Labor. Other Department of Justice participants in this national effort include: the Federal Bureau of Investigation (FBI), the Immigration and Naturalization Service (INS), the Executive Office for United States Attorneys, the Justice Department's Criminal Division, and the Office of Victims of Crime and the Violence against Women Office. The TPWETF also works in coordination with the Department of Labor, the Department of State, the Equal Employment Opportunity Commission, and various U.S. Attorneys' offices across the country (U.S. Department of Justice 2013).

The Criminal Section of the Civil Rights Division has primary enforcement responsibility for America's involuntary servitude and peonage statutes and plays an active role as a leading member of the TPWETF. The Criminal Section's attorneys conduct grand jury investigations and prosecute cases. The section works closely with the FBI, the INS, and the 94 U.S. Attorneys Offices to ensure that allegations of trafficking and slavery are investigated. Since the creation of the TPWETF, the number of open slavery investigations in the section has tripled (U.S. Department of Justice 2013). The rise in such cases may be due to an increase in the smuggling of immigrants. When immigrants enter the United States illegally, they have an increased risk of being exploited by criminals because they may be indebted to them. A Rutgers University study of 300 smuggled Chinese immigrants found that many of them had been tortured before paying off their debts (Gordy 2000). The Criminal Section also works with victim/witness coordinators from the FBI, INS, U.S. Attorneys' Offices, and the Executive Office for United States Attorneys to assist victims of trafficking in receiving health care, housing, and other protections. Since 2000, the TPWETF has operated a Complaint Line at 1–888–428–7581 (weekdays, 9 a.m. to 5 p.m. EST) for anyone to report suspected instances of trafficking or worker exploitation. A TPWETF Complaint Line call is toll-free and offers foreign language translation services in most languages as well as text telephone (TTY) (U.S. Department of Justice 2013). TTY is also sometimes called a telecommunication device for the deaf or TDD. However, TTY is the more widely accepted term as it is used by many people not just people who are deaf (see http://www.abouttty.com).

Cases and Types of Human Trafficking

Slavery can be found in almost every country. Its various forms can include contract slavery (the individual initially agrees to engage in work but discovers upon arrival usually in a foreign land that they are powerless to leave); debt bondage (where an individual ostensibly works to pay off a debt, but in reality, the obligation is not permitted to end); and chattel slavery (where an individual is kept in permanent servitude as a result of being captured, born, or sold into it) (Bales 1999). According to Bales (1999, 26), "Much modern slavery is hidden behind a mask of fraudulent labor contracts." For example, it has been estimated that there may be as many as 1,000 domestic slaves in London. The discovery of such cases is often hampered because a contract for hire can be produced to delay the detection of the reality of the situation by honest officials or to provide a justification for dishonest ones to simply walk away. Many of these workers will be told how and what they must answer if questioned by the officials of the host country (Bales 1999).

In 1999, a conviction for "conspiring to enslave" 14 women was obtained by the U.S. Justice Department. The women had been forced to work as prostitutes in a network of nine brothels in several southern states (see the story of Rosa later in this chapter). In 1993, a conviction was obtained in a case involving U.S. citizens who were employed as migrant laborers but were forced to sleep in a single room and work in the fields patrolled by a guard armed with a machete.

In 2001, Got, a four-year-old Thai boy, was detained by immigration officials in California. He had been rented by his heroin-addicted mother to serve as a decoy for a ring engaged in the smuggling of prostitutes from Thailand to the United States. At the time of his detention, doctors discovered that he suffered from a serious case of chicken pox complicated by his HIV-positive status. Got was hospitalized and officials began deportation proceedings for his return to Thailand "where it was likely that his use as a disguise for illegal entry by Thai prostitutes would continue" (Barone 2003, 580). Fortunately, his deportation was stopped and he was issued a temporary visa (T visa) in accordance with the terms of a new federal statute—The Trafficking Victims Protection Act of 2000.

Another example of modern-day slavery concerns the case of Mende Nazer who was kidnapped when she was 12 years old from her home in the Nuba Mountains region of Sudan. Until her escape eight years later, Nazer tended to the needs of the family she was sold to. She washed their clothes, cooked their meals, cleaned their home, and cared for their children. When she did not comply with the wishes of the family, they beat her. At the time of her escape, she was living in London, having been passed along to another family. It has been estimated that more than 11,000 southern Sudanese have been abducted during the past two decades (Winter 2004).

A fourth illustration of a modern-day form of slavery involves Rosa, a 13-year-old girl who came to the United States from Mexico. She had been promised employment in a Texas restaurant but instead was taken to a rural area in Florida where she was compelled to work in a brothel after being gang raped. After six months in captivity, she was able to escape with two other young girls (Lederer 2004). The story of Rosa and information about the latest governmental efforts to combat trafficking can be found at the U.S. Department of State's Web site (http://www.state.gov). The story of Rosa is presented in detail at: http://2001-2009.state.gov/tip/rls/rm/2005/48309. htm Each of the foregoing cases involved various aspects of contract, chattel, and debt bondage.

In another instance, Russian women were recruited and imported into the United States as folk dancers. Instead, they were forced to work as exotic dancers. The women were not free to leave their employment, were threatened with violence if they attempted to escape, and had their travel documents and return airline tickets confiscated by their employer. The women were forced to turn over their earnings to their captors. This case began as a contract arrangement but quickly became a case involving deceit and coercion. Debt bondage was used in another case when Mexican farm workers were smuggled into the United States, then held, and forced to work for their captors to pay off their smuggling fees. Fees were usually $5,000 or more, and the victims were held by threats of violence. According to the victims, they were smuggled into the United States in a van; during the three-day trip, they were not allowed to leave the van for bathroom breaks or for food. The youngest victim was 13 years of age (U.S. Department of Justice 2013). Human trafficking can be said to exist, whether or not victims initially went voluntarily or consented, because it is what happens to victims along the pipeline of activity through force, fraud, and coercion that signifies cases of modern-day slavery (Lederer 2004; LILYA 4-EVER 2004).

The training information provided by New Jersey officials in preparation for the 2014 Super Bowl noted that human trafficking may involve a local woman forced into sex work by a man she initially thought had romantic intentions or a woman from another country whose family is threatened. The indications may be a woman who appears not to be in control, who looks frightened, and who may exhibit signs of physical abuse. Victims are often runaways, the impoverished, abuse victims, or those living in the country illegally (Zezima 2014). Box 11.1 provides a summary of a 2010 United Nations report on human trafficking.

Trafficking Victims Protection Act of 2000

The Trafficking Victims Protection Act of 2000 (TVPA) has three purposes: (1) to prevent trafficking; (2) to punish traffickers; and (3) to protect victims. The statute provides for a T visa (capped at 5,000 per year for victims of trafficking) and the alternative U visa for victims of certain crimes. However, these visas are contingent on the applicant agreeing to provide investigative

**BOX 11.1   GLOBAL REPORT ON TRAFFICKING
IN PERSONS: KEY FINDINGS**

- The most commonly reported purpose of human trafficking is sexual exploitation (79%), followed by forced labor (18%), but many types of trafficking may be underreported, in part because they are largely "invisible"—including forced or bonded labor, domestic servitude and forced marriage, organ removal, and exploitation of children for begging, the sex trade, and warfare.
- Women comprise by far the largest portion of trafficking victims (80%–84%).
- The number of convictions of traffickers is increasing but not proportionately to the growing awareness (and, probably, size) of the problem.
- Most trade in humans occurs at the national or regional level, though interregional trafficking is also common.
- A growing number of countries are taking steps to address human trafficking, but there are still many, especially in Africa, that lack the necessary legal instruments to do so.

Source: UNODC, 2010, UNODC: Promoting health, security and justice, 2010 annual report. Available at: http://www.unodc.org/documents/frontpage/UNODC_Annual_Report_2010_LowRes.pdf

and prosecutorial assistance against the traffickers or other alleged criminals. The purpose of the U visa is to give victims of certain crimes temporary legal status and work eligibility in the United States for up to four years.[7] The U visa is a nonimmigrant visa, and only 10,000 U visas may be issued every fiscal year. Family members may also be included on the petition including spouses, children, unmarried sisters and brothers under 18, mothers, fathers, as well as stepparents and adoptive parents. An approved T or U visa petition will automatically grant the applicant work eligibility in the United States (U-Visa 2013). An essential difference with respect to these two types of visas is that U visas are awarded to people who have suffered substantial physical or mental abuse as a result of having been a victim of specified criminal activity.[8]

The TVPA also created an interagency Task Force on Trafficking in Persons (see earlier) to study and combat trafficking as well as increased penalties for those found guilty of trafficking. The law also created the Office to Combat and Monitor Trafficking in Persons in order to assist victims in the United States and in foreign countries through the provision of necessary services (shelter, medical care, etc.). This office is required to prepare an annual report about the status of trafficking in persons throughout the world. The statute was adopted in response to the need for reforms to deal with the problem of human trafficking. For example, one study found many drawbacks in the prosecution of involuntary servitude cases. "The cases are complicated and difficult to put together, they fall into the purview of a number of agencies, and it's not always clear who has responsibility.... Victims frequently wind up treated like criminals themselves, detained and deported to the countries from which they were seeking to escape in the first place" (Fighting the Slave Trade 2000, 25). In 1988, the "involuntary servitude" statutes had been narrowly defined by the U.S. Supreme Court (see, e.g., *U.S. v. Kominski* 487 U.S. 931). The court's legal definition did not extend to modern-day traffickers' practices of using blackmail, coercion, and fraud.

Volunteer Police Roles

Since World War II, many opportunities have existed to foster a public safety role for concerned citizens. The present era is no exception. Concerned individuals as well as volunteer police can directly contribute to the ideal contained in Article I of the *Universal Declaration of Human Rights* (1948) that "Human beings are born free and equal in dignity and rights."

Federal and state governments can do more to help victims and to deter traffickers. In particular, the federal government could implement a series of initiatives designed to facilitate the work of existing local volunteer police units and several related agencies on the federal level. For example, the federal government can establish volunteer police units in order to assist various federal agencies with the use of new hotlines and the enforcement of the laws designed to protect foreign workers from exploitation. It would be quite worthwhile for the federal government to appoint a representative from the volunteer police community to become a member of the TPWETF. This individual could make recommendations about how to harness the energies and talents of the more than 200,000 volunteer police in the United States (U.S. Department of Justice 2011).

Since 2004, the International Association of Chiefs of Police (IACP) has seen a vast increase in the number of volunteers that are being used by law enforcement agencies to perform police duties (U.S. Department of Justice 2011, 25). Figure 11.2 illustrates this trend. Many U.S. police agencies have some type of volunteer worker. They may be police reserves, auxiliaries, administrative aides, Community Emergency Response Team (CERT) members, or serving in other capacties.[9] These units comprise an important part of today's world of law enforcement and should be considered an essential resource in the protection of human rights and in the enforcement of laws concerned with the prevention of human trafficking. A critical need in this

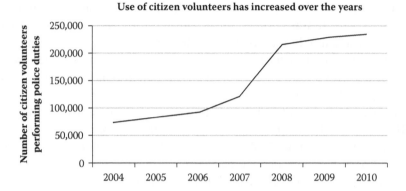

Figure 11.2 Police volunteer numbers and trends. (From U.S. Department of Justice, The impact of the economic downturn on American police agencies, U.S. Department of Justice, Office of Community Oriented Policing Services, Washington, DC, 2011.)

regard involves appropriate training. This could be done through the establishment of an auxiliary police training division at one or more of the national or regional law enforcement training centers. The centers could teach leadership development, appropriate reporting techniques, how to handle drug and smuggling offenders, crime prevention, and surveillance skills. The course of study could also be made available to the volunteer members of the National Park Service, Civil Air Patrol, U.S. Coast Guard Auxiliary, and other groups with more limited policing responsibilities. Thus, volunteers in the field of policing could be sent for extra training in much the same way as the National FBI Academy provides extra training for local police officials.

Financial support for the supervision and in-service training of local volunteer police units could be augmented by the federal government. A program could be established through congressional action modeled on the Defense Department's original "Troops to Teachers Program." This program has helped to place several thousand veterans from all branches of the armed forces into positions within local school districts. Significantly, for each veteran who qualified by October 1, 1995, school districts received an incentive grant of up to $50,000 to help pay their salaries during a five-year period. More than 31,000 persons retire each year from the military, many of them relatively young (Hewitt and Siew 1998). Just as some of them have become schoolteachers, others could draw upon their military training and help to train and supervise new volunteer police personnel.

Police and volunteer police could also be joined by other community professionals and members of concerned groups and organizations. Generally, these additional human resources: (1) will know the nature of the human trafficking problem and working together may develop new ways to help reduce this problem; (2) may help to disseminate information regarding the purpose of the

T and U visas for victims of human trafficking and related crimes; and (3) help to inform the public about the existence of the Worker Exploitation Task Force Complaint Line. Moreover, the proliferation of nongovernmental organizations (NGOs) dedicated to the protection of human rights (e.g., Amnesty International and Human Rights Watch) may also provide concerned citizens with opportunities to counter the trade in humans. Some have referred to recent developments as a "rights revolution" (Ignatieff 2000; Power 2001; Sellars 2002). However, as Cmiel (2004, 131) indicates "more human rights NGOs do not necessarily mean that fewer people are being detained or tortured."

The principal congressional sponsor of the Trafficking Victims Protection Act of 2000 was Christopher H. Smith of New Jersey. In a speech delivered on the floor of the U.S. House of Representatives in 2001, Congressman Smith concluded: "What we need to make this law work are 'true believers' who will spare no effort to mobilize the resources and the prestige of the United States government to implement this important Act and shut down this terrible industry, which routinely and grossly violates the most fundamental human rights of the world's most vulnerable people" (Smith 2001). "New Jersey has a huge trafficking problem," said Smith, co-chairman of the House anti-human trafficking caucus. "One Super Bowl after another after another has shown itself to be one of the largest events in the world where the cruelty of human trafficking goes on for several weeks" (in Zezima 2014). No single agency can solve this complex social problem, which has numerous global aspects. A combined community-police effort is needed to address this difficult problem.

Volunteer Crime Prevention Specialists

In recent decades, the field of crime prevention has become a specialization among police departments. Police officers attend additional training in this field to earn qualifications from a variety of associations and state governments.[10] Volunteer police are also welcome to attend these training programs. In general, crime prevention is a field that recognizes that public safety must no longer remain the exclusive domain of the criminal justice system; rather, it should be pursued through a network of other state institutions and nongovernmental organizations. Most importantly, the prevention of crime requires the proactive participation of communities and individual citizens, in partnership with police, other government agencies, local businesses, neighborhood groups, schools, and any other partner with a stake in the community.

In 1972, the National Crime Prevention Institute (NCPI) defined "crime prevention" as "the anticipation, recognition, and appraisal of a crime risk and the initiative of some action to remove it." (NCPI 1978, 1). In 1990, the National Crime Prevention Council[11] developed a supplemental and more practically oriented definition: "Crime prevention is a pattern of attitudes and behaviors directed at reducing the threat of crime and enhancing the sense of safety and security, to positively influence the quality of life in our society, and to develop environments where crime cannot flourish." One rationale underlying crime prevention is that "the cops, courts, and corrections approach" has been unable to cope with the actual quantity of crime. Furthermore, this punitive approach fails to address the opportunities and the root causes that give rise to criminal behavior.

An important aspect of crime prevention is teaching about its definitions and then putting together an appropriate response based on the problem to be addressed. Education appears to be an important tool to prevent some forms of trafficking. If children and adults are aware of the stories that traffickers tell, and recognize the patterns of traffickers, this might decrease some trafficking. A counter-trafficking program in Romania works with school-age children, educating the children on the risks of trafficking. It appears to be having some success. However, educating people on the risks of trafficking helps only in situations where children are not initially taken by force (Brusca 2011). The huge but rather demobilized force of U.S. volunteer police should become more knowledgeable about the problem, and specialists should be trained from among their ranks to educate the general public about anti-trafficking laws, the state of their enforcement, and the patterns of traffickers. America's lead in this regard could spur other police departments throughout the world to include their volunteer police in a similar effort. In this way, more forces might be mobilized to decrease the success of traffickers.

Albemarle is a 726-square-mile county located in the state of Virginia. As of 2012, Albemarle County's population was about 102,000. Its county seat is Charlottesville, and its police force celebrated its thirtieth anniversary in 2012. Col. Steven Sellers, Albemarle County's police chief, says human trafficking can involve many forms of extortion. Sex trafficking, which falls under the umbrella of human trafficking, can be tied to underage sex acts, child pornography, and—most commonly—prostitution. Both types are occurring in Albemarle County, according to Col. Sellers, and the victims are primarily foreign nationals. Human trafficking is one of the least understood crimes, and Col. Sellers has indicated that more police training is needed to better distinguish it from other issues (Newsplex.com 2013). "In order for traffickers to be caught and prosecuted, the victims must be found, but the extreme fear among the victims makes this crime much more difficult to uncover. Many times a person is held for years before they either escape, die, or are let go. Consequently, the traffickers have many years to continue in the buying and selling of individuals. This issue is even more pronounced for children, who just by the nature of their age are at a disadvantage. The opportunity to be heard or rescued is diminished as often a child is either constantly held captive, is escorted by an adult at all times or is coerced into not speaking up" (Brusca 2011, 15).

Targeting human trafficking is a challenge for officers because it can be a quick moving underground business, but Col. Sellers recognizes that the problem needs to be a priority for police departments (Newsplex.com 2013). Moreover, law enforcement agencies are often the first responders at trafficking situations (Clawson et al. 2006; Wilson et al. 2006) and are more likely to encounter perpetrators of human trafficking than federal agencies (De Baca and Tisi 2002). "Another difficulty is getting victims to come forward against their traffickers. There is the fear of retaliation, the fear of being punished for the crimes committed while enslaved, or the fear of being ostracized after telling their story" (Brusca 2011, 17).

Coincidentally, Chief Sellers is in the process of establishing an auxiliary force.[12] In addition to having selected volunteers serve as specialists in the field of crime prevention, volunteer police can play significant roles in manning key checkpoints (e.g., rest stops) along major highways and at transportation hubs to distribute informational flyers for travelers to be alert for possible traffickers and their victims. Depending on their level of training, they could also be called upon to assist in aided cases as well as crimes in progress.

Nongovernmental Prevention Efforts

The Salvation Army was founded in London, England, in 1865, by the husband and wife team of Catherine and William Booth. The Booths went against Victorian conventions and took their ministry to the streets of London's east side where they reached out to the destitute and desperate. Their efforts included direct interventions to help women and girls involved in organized sexual exploitation. The Salvation Army has opened homes to protect and shelter them.[13] In 2010, Anne's House became the first long-term, residential program in the Chicago area for young women and girls who were victims of sex trafficking. The program offers comprehensive residential services to sex trafficking victims and was established to address the limited number of shelters and services available for this unique population (Anne's House 2013).

In the United Kingdom, the Salvation Army's effort to help women and girls in prostitution has included the opening of many rescue homes. In a different era, it also has played a volunteer role in the field of law enforcement. The Salvation Army participated in the planning and execution of an undercover investigation into the trafficking of young girls for prostitution. A detailed account of this role was published in July 1885 by the *Pall Mall Gazette* in a series of articles called "The Maiden Tribute of Modern Babylon." The series created enough fervor to foment public opinion in support of the Criminal Law Amendment Act of 1885, a measure passed in the United Kingdom that raised the age of consent from 13 to 16 (although reformers sought 18). The Salvation Army's advocacy efforts were a major catalyst in the bill's passage. More than a century later, in the United States and abroad, the Salvation Army is part of a revived movement for the abolition of sex trafficking and other forms of commercial sexual exploitation (Salvation Army 2013b).

The Department of Homeland Security (DHS) has teamed up with Western Union to combat human trafficking. Western Union has agreed to provide multilingual training and awareness materials to select Western Union locations in the southwest border region and other areas across the United States. Working with the DHS, Western Union plans to use training and awareness materials developed by the DHS Blue Campaign to educate agents who regularly interact with the public on potential indicators of human trafficking and on how to identify victims. In the past, Western Union and the Western Union Foundation have worked with and supported several U.S. global organizations combating human trafficking (Pankratz 2013).

Redlight Traffic is a 501(c)(3) organization under the Seattle Kiwanis Memorial Fund established in 1947. In 2013, Redlight Traffic launched a first-of-its-kind app for iPhones and Androids that funnels citizens' anonymous tips on suspected prostitution activities to law enforcement through a secure Web site that can only be accessed by police officers. The aims of the new app include teaching citizens how to identify signs of sex trafficking; giving citizens an easy way to do something about the problem; and providing law enforcement with data that can potentially help officers rescue victims and build criminal cases against pimps and men who pay for sex. Through the app, citizens will be able to report their suspicions, upload photos and GPS locations, and provide information on a business, vehicle, or person—whether that person is a suspected prostitute, pimp, or buyer. Officers are then able to search and review individual reports and view a map of all reported incidents in an area (Green 2013). (More information is available from: http://www.redlighttraffic.org/app.)

Banks and credit card companies can play a crucial role in shutting down human traffickers by flagging the electronic fingerprints they leave behind, according to Manhattan District Attorney (DA) Cyrus Vance. An estimated 14,000 to 17,000 people are smuggled into the United States each year and forced to work as domestic servants, laborers, or in the sex trade, according to estimates from the DA's office. Human trafficking is a global business worth $32 billion a year, according to the U.S. State Department. The International Labor Organization estimates that nearly 21 million people worldwide are victims of slavery or forced labor. Almost half are thought to be trafficked, either across borders or within their own countries. The Manhattan DA's office and the Thomson Reuters Foundation are coordinating the efforts of a working group set up by the banks. U.S. and European financial institutions already have a regulatory duty to report suspected illegal activity, but there have been few efforts to leverage methods used to spot money laundering, extremist violence, and other crimes to hone in on human trafficking. The first bank to do so was JPMorgan Chase, and it has developed a model for monitoring transactions and partnering with law enforcement (McGurty 2013).

Summary

Under the TVPA, the phrases "trafficking in persons" or "human trafficking" have been used as umbrella terms for activities involved when one person obtains or holds another person in compelled service. The TVPA describes this compelled service using a number of different terms: involuntary servitude, slavery, debt bondage, and forced labor. The TVPA uses definitions drawn from and correlated with the United Nations *Protocol to Prevent, Suppress, and Punish Trafficking in Persons, Especially Women and Children* (the Palermo Protocol).

The document entitled *Recommended Principles and Guidelines on Human Rights and Human Trafficking* published in 2002 by the OHCHR was developed in order to provide practical, rights-based policy guidance on the prevention of trafficking and on the protection of victims of trafficking. The purpose of the OHCHR is to promote and facilitate the integration of a human rights perspective into national, regional, and international anti-trafficking laws, policies, and interventions. The *Principles and Guidelines* serve as a framework and reference point for the work of OHCHR on this issue. The term "trafficking," as used in the *Principles and Guidelines*, is taken from the Palermo Protocol and refers to the recruitment, transportation, transfer, harboring, or receipt of persons, by means of the threat or use of force or other forms of coercion, of abduction, of fraud, of deception, of the abuse of power, or of a position of vulnerability or of the giving or receiving of payments or benefits to achieve the consent of a person having control over another person, for the purpose of exploitation. Exploitation includes, at a minimum, the exploitation of the prostitution of others or other forms of sexual exploitation, forced labor or services, slavery or practices similar to slavery, servitude, or the removal of organs. This critical definition comes from the *Protocol to Prevent, Suppress and Punish Trafficking in Persons, Especially Women and Children, Supplementing the United Nations Convention against Transnational Organized Crime*, Article 3(a), also known as the Palermo Protocol.

The Polaris Project is a leading organization in the global fight against human trafficking and modern-day slavery. Its activities involve operating a national hotline, legislative advocacy, victim services, and trainings on how to recognize the signs of trafficking. Under U.S. and international law, commercially sexually exploited children found in the sex trade are considered to be victims of trafficking, even if no force or coercion is present. Victims of human trafficking in the United States include U.S. citizens or foreign nationals, adults or minors, and men or women. Foreign-born victims in the United States may be either documented or undocumented. Every year, human traffickers generate billions of dollars in profits by victimizing millions of people around the world and in the United States. Human trafficking is considered to be one of the fastest growing criminal industries in the world. Law enforcement officers, service providers, and other key first responders have been able to benefit from the training provided by the Polaris Project on how to recognize the signs of trafficking (Polaris Project 2013d).

Efforts to curtail the exploitation of individuals have also been undertaken by a variety of nongovernmental organizations including the Salvation Army, Western Union, the Redlight Traffic organization, and the Thomson Reuters Foundation. For example, working with DHS, Western Union plans to use training and awareness materials developed by the DHS Blue Campaign to educate agents who regularly interact with the public on potential indicators of human trafficking and on how to identify victims.

Federal and state governments can do more to help victims and deter traffickers. In particular, the federal government could implement a series of initiatives designed to facilitate the work of existing local volunteer police units and related agencies on the federal level. For example, the federal government can establish volunteer police training courses to instruct qualified volunteers about how best to protect foreign workers from exploitation. A critical need exists for volunteer police to have appropriate training so that they can be assigned to engage in such activities as speaking to groups about the signs of trafficking; educating people who may be at risk of victimization; addressing the needs of victims; enforcing the variety of laws concerned with human trafficking; and protecting human rights. There is also a need to mobilize volunteer police for law enforcement supporting roles at the time of large sporting events such as the Super Bowl. The existence of more than 200,000 police volunteers makes them important stakeholders in the field of public safety.

Review Questions

1. List at least five types of human trafficking.
2. Identify stakeholders who could work together in order to address the problem of human trafficking.
3. Do you consider volunteer police to be important stakeholders in efforts to cope with human trafficking? Discuss.
4. The definition of human trafficking established by the Palermo Protocol indicates that victim consent to trafficking must be

considered irrelevant. Discuss why this clause was included in this international agreement to prevent and suppress human trafficking.

5. Provide at least three ways that the Polaris Project seeks to create long-term solutions in the global fight against human trafficking and modern-day slavery.

6. Indicate at least three of the venues where sex trafficking may take place.

7. State two functions of the Trafficking in Persons Worker Exploitation Task Force.

8. List the three purposes of the Trafficking Victims Protection Act of 2000.

9. What agreement with the U.S. government do victims seeking either T or U visas have to make as part of the visa application process?

10. Identify two initiatives involving volunteer police that might be undertaken by the federal government to deter and suppress human trafficking.

11. Do you believe volunteer police force members would be interested in serving as crime prevention specialists to educate the public about human trafficking deterrence and enforcement? Discuss.

12. Explain why it may be difficult to identify and find victims of human trafficking.

13. Chief Sellers is in the process of establishing an auxiliary police force. What arguments would you make to him about the advantages and disadvantages of using his new volunteer police unit to combat human trafficking?

14. Present three of the benefits or aims of the Redlight Traffic new app program.

15. There are scant statistics and much debate over how much sex trafficking increases during a Super Bowl or other large sporting event, but it has been enough of a concern to prompt New Jersey and previous Super Bowl host cities to pay attention to it. What assignments, if any, do you think volunteer police could undertake to reduce any sex trafficking activity at the time of the Super Bowl?

Notes

1. Source of President Obama's quote: U.S. State Department, Office to Monitor and Combat Trafficking in Persons Web page. Retrieved December 29, 2013, http://www.state.gov/j/tip/index.htm.

2. In 2010, the Texas Supreme Court ruled that children involved in prostitution are victims not criminals (see In Matter of B.W., June 18, 2010, No. 08-1044). In this case, a 13-year-old girl flagged down the car of an undercover officer and offered to engage in oral sex for $20. She was arrested for prostitution.

The trial court (Family Court) found her guilty of a Class B misdemeanor of prostitution, and she received a sentence of 18 months' probation. The Court of Appeals affirmed the judgment, and the case was appealed. The Supreme Court of Texas reversed the Court of Appeals by a 6–3 decision. The court cited a variety of reason for its decision including the finding that because a 13-year-old child cannot consent to sex as a matter of law, the 13-year-old in this case cannot be prosecuted as a prostitute. The Supreme Court argued that children below the age of 14 cannot understand the significance of agreeing to sex and, therefore, could not satisfy the "knowing" requirement of the statute. The Court cited longstanding common law, Texas statutes, and numerous cases. "The notion that an underage child cannot legally consent to sex is of longstanding origin and derives from common law." The court also reasoned that treating child prostitutes as victims rather than criminals will also undermine the ability of pimps to play on the child's fear of police, removing a powerful tool pimps use to assert control. (The full text of the opinion can be found online at: http://caselaw.findlaw.com/tx-supreme-court/1527849.html.)

3. The Trafficking Victims Protection Act of 2000 (TVPA) was created to combat traffickers through punishment and also to protect trafficking victims. Its protections include new types of visas for victims of trafficking (T visas) and violence (U visas), which allow victims to stay in the United States from three years to permanent residency in exchange for investigative and prosecutorial assistance against traffickers. "Through the TVPA, new crimes were created around trafficking, which will make prosecution possible. Protection for victims comes through the visas, prevention of trafficking comes through establishing programs for increasing job skills, increasing education for children, and offering grants to international organizations who employ women" (Brusca 2011, 16).

4. The Palermo Protocol is an international treaty developed in Palermo, Italy, by member states of the United Nations in December 2000 for the purpose of undertaking a comprehensive international approach to prevent and combat trafficking in persons, especially women and children, including measures to prevent such trafficking, to punish the traffickers, and to protect the victims of such trafficking and the internationally recognized human rights of such victims. It supplements the United Nations Convention against Transnational Organized Crime and it is to be interpreted together with this Convention. The protocol entered into force on December 25, 2003, and by the end of 2009, 117 states had signed and 133 states were party to the protocol. In addition, a second agreement was also developed entitled the *Protocol Against Smuggling of Migrants by Land, Sea, and Air*. An online copy of the first Protocol can be found at: http://www.osce.org/odihr/19223. It is 12 pages in length. Ten years after the Palermo Protocol's adoption, Brusca (2011) addressed its strengths and weaknesses. "Even with the Palermo Protocol and the states' domestic anti-trafficking laws in place, only one to two percent of trafficked individuals are rescued. When the trafficked person is a child, the chance for rescue before extensive damage has been done is slim due to the vulnerable nature of a child" (Brusca 2011, 9–10).

5. The term "traffickers" is used in the 2002 OHCHR report entitled *Recommended Principles and Guidelines on Human Rights and Human Trafficking*. It is used to refer to recruiters; transporters; those who exercise control over trafficked persons;

those who transfer and/or maintain trafficked persons in exploitative situations; those involved in related crimes; and those who profit either directly or indirectly from trafficking, its component acts, and related offences (OHCHR 2002).

6. The organization's founders, Katherine Chon and Derek Ellerman, read a newspaper article describing the horrific conditions of a brothel located near their college apartments. The brothel had been disguised as a massage business. But inside the building, police officers had found six Asian women with cigarette burns on their arms being held in a situation of debt bondage. "This was like slavery," were the words of the officer who handled the investigation. Together, they developed a vision for an organization where everyday people could come together to overcome the contemporary forms of slavery. The day after graduation, they packed up a U-Haul truck and relocated to Washington, D.C., to launch the Polaris Project's first office on Capitol Hill. Their strategy "was grounded in an analysis of human trafficking as a market-based phenomenon driven by two primary factors: low-risk and high-profit. They believed then, as they do today, that modern-day slavery can be eliminated by reaching a tipping point where human trafficking becomes a high-risk, low-profit endeavor.... Early on, they launched an innovative victim outreach program to uncover trafficking locations, directly target trafficking networks, identify victims and connect them to services. As the organization grew, staff members worked with coalition partners to help pass landmark bills through Congress and groundbreaking legislation in 48 states that protect victims and punish perpetrators. In 2007, Polaris Project expanded the National Human Trafficking Resource Center to operate as a national anti-slavery lifeline" (Polaris Project 2013b).

7. However, extensions are available upon documentation by a certifying agency that the foreign national's presence in the United States is required to assist in the investigation or prosecution of the qualifying criminal activity. Certifying agencies can be federal, state, or local law enforcement agencies, prosecutors, judges, or other authorities that investigate or prosecute criminal activity. Other agencies such as child protective services, the Equal Employment Opportunity Commission, and the Department of Labor also qualify as certifying agencies because they have criminal investigative jurisdiction within their respective areas of expertise. Moreover, an individual who has held U nonimmigrant status might eventually apply for a Green Card (permanent residence). For this to occur, the individual must have been physically present in the United States for a continuous period of at least three years since the date of admission as a U nonimmigrant and the individual must not have unreasonably refused to provide assistance to law enforcement since receiving a U nonimmigrant visa (U.S. Citizen and Immigration Services 2013).

8. Qualifying criminal activity is defined as being an activity involving one or more activities that violate U.S. criminal law, including blackmail, domestic violence, extortion, false imprisonment, rape, torture, and other related crimes (U.S. Citizen and Immigration Services 2013).

9. Bartels (2014, 8) has determined that volunteers in policing carry out the following types of administrative roles: "Working on the police newsletter, answering phones, acting as a greeter at the front desk, assisting with photography, performing data entry, or being assigned as a clerk in the records department

or property room." Such administrative duties were carried out by volunteers in 152 out of a sample of 300 police departments. The sample was randomly generated at: http://www.random.org from a list of 22,446 registered programs provided by the Volunteers in Policing program (Bartels 2014).

10. Crime prevention practitioner certifications are awarded by a variety of governmental and organizational entities and include the National Crime Prevention Association's National Crime Prevention Specialist certification; Florida Office of the Attorney General's Crime Prevention Practitioner designation; New York State Crime Prevention Coalition's Crime Prevention Specialist certification; Ohio Crime Prevention Association's Certified Crime Prevention Specialist program; Texas Crime Prevention Association's Certified Crime Prevention Specialist program; Virginia Department of Criminal Justice Services Crime Prevention Specialist designation; ASIS International's Certified Protection Practitioner (CPP) program; International Society of Crime Prevention Practitioner's Crime Prevention Specialist certification; and Fox Valley Technical College's Crime Prevention Professional, Practitioner, or Specialist programs.

11. A very useful PowerPoint (PPT) presentation (44 slides) on the subject of crime prevention, which includes the definitions provided here, can be found at: http://www.slideshare.net/NCPC/crime-prevention-history-and-theory-presentation. The PPT's content can be adapted for a variety of community groups. It is a production of the National Crime Prevention Council. The council has also placed several other PPT programs on the Internet. In the late 1970s, the leaders of 19 organizations began to work together and developed the National Citizens' Crime Prevention Campaign. This effort was expanded into an additional entity known as the Crime Prevention Coalition of America. In 1982, the coalition group founded the National Crime Prevention Council (NCPC) to manage the campaign, administer the coalition, and promote crime prevention through trainings, technical assistance, and publications (NCPC 2013).

12. The Albemarle County Police Department has a VIPS program that contributed more than 1,700 hours to the department in 2012. Volunteers in the house check program supplement officers by providing safety checks on vacant homes. Two police chaplains have also been integrated into the department's wellness program, providing services for the mind, body, and spirit. Future plans involve gaining authorization from the board of supervisors to formally establish an auxiliary police officer (APO) program. APOs are certified police officers who volunteer their time to support the mission of the agency. APOs undergo the same rigorous appointment and training standards as paid police officers. "APOs will be tasked with assisting in traffic safety efforts, crime prevention tasks, select enforcement assignments, and administrative tasks. The APO program will support the department's efforts to build capacity", and the citizen involvement will help to "enhance the safety of the community" (ACPD 2012, p. 20).

13. By 1887, rescue homes were introduced to America. The first was opened in New York. Within seven years, 15 homes were operating across the United States. These homes were primarily for destitute women. Many who came were young expectant mothers. A Salvation Army Web site states: "It should be understood that The Salvation Army never served as an adoption agency. Mothers were referred to an adoption agency of their choice and worked with

these agencies independently of The Salvation Army Booth Maternity Homes" (Salvation Army 2013a). In recent times, there has been criticism of the past practices of these homes in Canada. In particular, the question of whether forced adoptions had taken place was raised. In response, the Salvation Army has indicated that these "homes were operational during a time when there was a tremendous social stigma attached to being an unwed mother" and began an internal review of the subject (Carlson 2012). On the contrary, during recent years, the Salvation Army has established an "Initiative against Sexual Trafficking" (IAST) to educate persons desiring to become better informed about human trafficking and the current efforts to contend with such exploitation and the dehumanization of human beings. Information can be found at: http://iast.net.

References

ACPD. (2012). *Albemarle County Police Department 2012 annual report.* Retrieved December 30, 2013 from http://www.albemarle.org/upload/images/forms_center/departments/Police/forms/2012% 20Annual%20Report%20.pdf

Anne's House. (2013). Anne's House: A residential program for trafficking victims. Retrieved December 30, 2013 from http://s147851.gridserver.com/annes-house-a-residential-program-for-trafficking-victims/

Bales, K. (1999). *Disposable people: New slavery in the global economy.* Berkeley: University of California Press.

Barone, T. (2003). Note & Comment: The Trafficking Victims Protection Act of 2000: Defining the problem and creating a solution. *Temple International and Comparative Law Journal, 17*(Fall), 579–594.

Barry, K. (1995). *The prostitution of sexuality: The global exploitation of women.* New York: New York University Press.

Bartels, E. C. (2014). *Volunteer police in the United States: Programs, challenges, and legal aspects.* Heidelberg, Germany: Springer.

Brusca, C. S. (2011, Summer). Palermo Protocol: The first ten years after adoption. *Global Security Studies, 2*(3), 1–20.

Carlson, K. B. (2012, March 13). Coerced adoption: Salvation Army launches review of maternity homes that housed unwed mothers. Retrieved January 3, 2014 from http://news.nationalpost.com/2012/03/13/coerced-adoption-salvation-army-launches-review-of-maternity-homes-that-housed-unwed-mothers/

Clawson, H. J., Dutch, N. and Cummings, M. (2006, October). *Law Enforcement Response to Human Trafficking and Implications for Victims: Current Practices and Lessons Learned.* Fairfax, VA: Caliber, An ICF International Company. Retrieved June 28, 2014 from https://www.ncjrs.gov/pdffiles1/nij/grants/216547.pdf

Cmiel, K. (2004). Review essay: The recent history of human rights. *American Historical Review, 109*(1), 117–135.

De Baca, L. and Tisi, A. (2002, August). Working together to stop modern day slavery. *Police Chief, 69*(8), 78–80.

Fighting the Slave Trade. (2000, April 17). *The Washington Post National Weekly Edition* p. 25.

Gordy, M. (2000, February 20). A call to fight forced labor. *Parade*, pp. 4–5.

Green, S. J. (2013, October 30). Sex-trafficking app to tip off police. *Seattle Times*. Retrieved from http://seattletimes.com/html/localnews/2022158566_sextraffickingapp2xml.html

Hewitt, B. and Siew, W. (1998, November 23). In the trenches. *People Weekly, 50*(19), 143–144.

Hynes, H. P. and Raymond, J. G. (2002). Put in harm's way: The neglected health consequences of sex trafficking in the United States. In J. Silliman and A. Bhattacharjee (Eds.), *Policing the national body: Sex, race, and criminalization* (pp. 197–229). Cambridge, MA: South End.

Ignatieff, M. (2000). *The rights revolution*. Toronto: Anansi Press.

Lederer, L. (2004). Trafficking in persons: A modern-day form of slavery. Retrieved February 29, 2004 from http://www.state.gov/g/tip/rls/rm/2002/14325.htm

LILYA 4-EVER. (2004). LILYA 4-EVER: A film by Lukas Moodysson examining the tragic realities and horrors of trafficking in humans. Presentation at the Secretary's Open Forum, Washington, DC. Retrieved February 29, 2004 from http://www. State.gov/s/p/of/proc/22337pf.htm

McGurty, F. (2013, April 25). Banks can help to stop human trafficking. Retrieved January 2, 2013 from http://www.reuters.com/article/2013/04/25/us-banks-trafficking-idUSBRE93O1FU20130425

NCPC. (2013). History. Retrieved December 30, 2013 from http://www.ncpc.org/about/history

NCPI. (1978). *The practice of crime prevention, Volume 1: Understanding crime.* Lexington, KY: The National Crime Prevention Institute Press.

Newsplex.com. (2013, November 4). Police: Human sex trafficking a growing problem. Retrieved December 27, 2013 from http://www.newsplex.com/home/headlines/230611621.html

OHCHR. (2002). *Recommended principles and guidelines on human rights and human trafficking*. Retrieved December 29, 2013 from http://www.ohchr.org/Documents/Publications/Traffickingen.pdf

Pankratz, H. (2013, November 6). Western Union and Homeland Security team up to combat human trafficking. *Denver Post*. Retrieved December 27, 2013 from http://www.denverpost.com/breakingnews/ci_24469238/western-union-amp-homeland-security-team-up-combat

Polaris Project. (2013a). About Polaris Project. Retrieved December 30, 2013 from http://www.polarisproject.org/about-us/overview

Polaris Project. (2013b). Founding story. Retrieved December 30, 2013 from http://www.polarisproject.org/about-us/overview/founding-story

Polaris Project. (2013c). Global programs. Retrieved December 30, 2013 from http://www.polarisproject.org/what-we-do/global-programs

Polaris Project. (2013d). Human trafficking. Retrieved December 28, 2013 from http://www.polarisproject.org/human-trafficking/overview

Power, J. (2001). *Like water on stone: The story of Amnesty International*. Boston, MA: Allen Lane.

Salvation Army. (2013a). Additional services: Salvation Army maternity homes: History. Retrieved January 3, 2014 from http://www.use.salvationarmy.org/use/www_usn20.nsf/vw-text-dynamic-arrays/F74D62E42552DA77852579A3007B4147

Salvation Army. (2013b). Combating human trafficking. Retrieved December 30, 2013 from http://salvationarmyusa.org/usn/combating-human-trafficking

Sellars, K. (2002). *The rise and rise of human rights*. Stroud, Gloucestershire, UK: Sutton Publishing.

Smith, C. H. (2001). Fighting the scourge of trafficking in women and children. *Congressional Record, 147*(163): 2179–2180.

UNODC. (2010). UNODC: Promoting health, security and justice. 2010 annual report. Retrieved December 27, 2013 from http://www.unodc.org/documents/frontpage/UNODC_Annual_Report_2010_LowRes.pdf

UNODC. (2013a). General Assembly reviews efforts to combat human trafficking. Retrieved December 27, 2013 from http://www.unodc.org/unodc/en/frontpage/2013/May/general-assembly-reviews-efforts-to-combat-human-trafficking.html?ref = fs1

UNODC. (2013b). UNODC on human trafficking and migrant smuggling. Retrieved December 27, 2013 form http://www.unodc.org/unodc/en/human-trafficking/index.html?ref = menuside

U.S. Citizen and Immigration Services. (2013). Questions & Answers: Victims of criminal activity, U nonimmigrant status. Retrieved December 30, 2013 from http://www.uscis.gov/humanitarian/victims-human-trafficking-other-crimes/victims-criminal-activity-u-nonimmigrant-status/questions-answers-victims-criminal-activity-u-nonimmigrant-status

U.S. Department of Justice. (2011, October). *The impact of the economic downturn on American police agencies*. Washington, DC: U.S. Department of Justice, Office of Community Oriented Policing Services.

U.S. Department of Justice. (2013). Civil Rights Division: Trafficking in Persons and Worker Exploitation Task Force. Retrieved December 31, 2013 from http://www.parentsinaction.net/english/Complaints/Human_Trafficking_Complaint_USDOJ.htm

U.S. Department of State. (2013a). Office to Monitor and Combat Trafficking in Persons. Retrieved December 19, 2013 from http://www.state.gov/j/tip/index.htm

U.S. Department of State. (2013b). What is modern slavery? Retrieved December 29, 2013 from http://www.state.gov/j/tip/what/

U-Visa. (2013). U Visa for immigrants who are victims of crimes. Retrieved December 31, 2013 from http://www.usimmigrationsupport.org/visa-u.html

Wilson, D., Walsh, W. and Kleuber, S. (2006, May). Trafficking in human beings: Training and services among US law enforcement agencies. *Police Practice and Research, 7*(2), 149–160.

Winter, J. (2004). BBC News: My life as a modern-day slave. Retrieved February 29, 2004 from http://newsvote.bbc.co.uk/mpapps/pagetools/print/news.bbc.uk/2/hi/africa/3430305.stm

Zezima, K. (2014, January 6). NJ works to curb sex trafficking before super bowl. Retrieved January 7, 2014 from http://www.philly.com/philly/news/new_jersey/20140106_ap_9c1854ad76b74a4996aba69147ac3e6b.html?c=r

The Future of Volunteer Police

12

How wonderful it is that nobody need wait a single moment before starting to improve the world.

—Anne Frank Haimowitz 2014

Background

The opening quote is attributed to Anne Frank, a victim of the Holocaust. Her famous diary was first published in Dutch in 1947 under the title *Het Achterhuis* (*The Secret House*) by her father, Otto Frank, who survived the concentration camps. Her diary provides an account of a teenager living in hiding with seven others in fear for their lives in occupied Holland during World War II. Anne Frank died in 1945, just before her sixteenth birthday, in the Bergen-Belsen concentration camp (BBC News 2014). President John F. Kennedy discussed Anne Frank in a 1961 speech. He said: "Of all the multitudes who throughout history have spoken for human dignity in times of great suffering and loss, no voice is more compelling than that of Anne Frank" (David 2013). Information about various Holocaust memorials and historic sites in Amsterdam can be found at: http://www.kennesaw.edu/holocaustmemorials/amsterdam.shtml.

The present work has consistently urged the use of volunteer police for the betterment of society, but as we consider the future of volunteer policing, it is prudent to consider the past. The Nazis, for a time, deployed volunteer police. After Adolf Hitler was appointed chancellor of Germany in 1933, he called upon elements of the Nazi party to act as auxiliary police. The *Schutzstaffel* or SS, initially Hitler's bodyguards, and the *Sturmabteilung* or SA, the street fighters or storm troopers of the Nazi party, were extended official police authority, further increasing the power of the Nazi party in German society (SS Police State 2014). Thus, as we look toward the future, a word of caution is in order. Volunteer police have not always been used to enhance democratic principles or righteous purposes.

In the United States, the merit selection of local and state police took hold during the first third of the twentieth century up until this time and in various eras, American law and order was kept by a variety of local residents, including: clergymen; militia members; vigilantes; temporarily mobilized posse members; self-appointed or compulsory serving slave patrollers and watch members (especially, during the 1700s to 1865); elected mayors, sheriffs, constables, and justices of the peace; private detectives and guards; and police and correctional officers who were often selected as a result of simple payoffs and the existence of the "spoils system." The "spoils system" arose during the administration of President Andrew Jackson (1829–1837). It was widely used for the selection of paid governmental employees until laws were passed for the establishment of civil service commissions for the merit selection of governmental employees at the federal, state, and local levels. Throughout the nineteenth century, appointments to police ranks were dependent upon "loyalty to the party that was most victorious in the most recent election." For example, New York City's police officers "were subject to immediate removal upon the failure of their party to win reelection" (Johnson et al. 2008, 221).

In the 1800s and early 1900s, there also existed a wide range of voluntary organizations including anti-horse thief protection societies, law and order leagues, and ethnically based welfare agencies. Later, in some communities, this diverse mix was supplemented by part-time peace officers known as "auxiliary or reserve police." World War II, as well as the Korean and Cold War eras, gave rise to a new generation of volunteer police groups under the banner of "civil defense auxiliary police." A large part of this book has considered the activities of volunteer police that have taken place during the post–World War II era.[1]

This chapter reviews a few of the current or emerging trends for citizens willing to undertake the duties of part-time volunteer police in the United States. Several new roles are just emerging and were selected because of their potential for reducing crime and disorder. For example, volunteer police can be called upon to help with school safety, homelessness, and the prevention of human trafficking (see Chapter 11). They can also assist with crime prevention educational programs like Drug Abuse Resistance Education (D.A.R.E.), Gang Resistance Education and Training (G.R.E.A.T.), or conflict resolution classes (see VIPS in a School Setting 2010). New state training guidelines require volunteer police who are peace officers to complete many more hours of training. In some jurisdictions, this has led to the phasing out of volunteer police units. In addition, due to the limited availability of municipal financial resources, more and more states are encouraging local police candidates to pay for their own police training.

Current Trends in Volunteer Policing

Since the early 1980s, when the concept of community policing began to spread, the role of volunteers in policing has been expanding. Today, it is not unusual to find community residents volunteering their time to work as sworn or non-sworn uniformed auxiliary or reserve officers; police administrative assistants; amateur radio operators; search and rescue team members; mounted patrol members; chaplains; computer specialists; crime lab assistants; crime prevention aides; maintenance assistants; translators; citizen patrol members; youth service workers; and in investigatory support assignments. Reserve police are "becoming widely accepted in tactical units across the country.... Reserves who are physicians, nurses, or trained EMS personnel in their full-time positions volunteer to serve on tactical units" (Wolf and Russo 2005, 27). In the formation of their tactical teams, various police departments have called upon such medical and EMS career personnel to join as part-time law enforcement officers. Throughout the United States and in many countries within the British Commonwealth, volunteers have become an integral part of community support for the police because they provide additional resources without extra costs.

The role of volunteer police chaplains is particularly important because they have been involved in, but not limited to, counseling peace officers and their families; counseling members of other city departments and their families; visiting sick or injured employees; responding to major incidents and cases involving serious injury to an employee or community member; providing assistance to victims and their families; speaking to civic and public groups; participating in patrols; performing crisis intervention; and providing input on community issues and problems.

Unarmed, but uniformed, citizens who engage in citizen patrol units often in vehicles with an amber light bar and marked with the words "volunteer patrol" have become quite popular in many towns in the Sun Belt, particularly within the states of Florida, Arizona, and California. Their duties have included neighborhood watch patrol; vacation house checks; document delivery; transportation details; traffic control; school patrol; assisting with DUI/license check points; and parking enforcement. Their police vehicles are equipped with a radio for communications with police dispatchers. Retirees from northern states oftentimes fill the volunteer ranks of these southern citizen patrol units. Since the 1960s, the Sun Belt (as seen in Figure 12.1) has been one of the most important growth regions in the United States (Briney 2009).

Figure 12.1 This map provides an outline of the states most commonly included in the definition of the Sun Belt, which stretches from South Carolina and Florida in the East to California in the West.

In communities throughout America, volunteers have also participated in various mounted units. They assist in areas where crowd control is important, but they are also available for ceremonial functions in color guard formation. Communities may have both reserve and/or unsworn civilian mounted units. In previous chapters, information about such units in New York City and Maryland has been highlighted. The city of Arcadia, California, is an upper-middle class community of approximately 60,000 people who live in an area located 20 miles east of Los Angeles. At one time, it had both a sworn reserve established in 1997 and a civilian mounted volunteer patrol program established in 2003. However, within a few years, the latter unit was disbanded. Its regular (salaried) mounted and reserve officers patrol a horse trail that runs the entire length of the city and the Santa Anita Race Track. The track is considered by many to be the finest facility of its type in the country (City of Arcadia 2013b). Recently, the city of Arcadia decided that all of its reserve police officers would become paid part-time employees (City of Arcadia 2013a).

Another important trend in the field of volunteer police has been the establishment of Law Enforcement Explorer Posts for youth in the 14–20 age group. Exploring as a youth movement can be traced to the 1920s and posts specifically associated with police departments began to emerge in the 1960s and 1970s under the direction of the Boy Scouts of America.[2] They are very common today, and their activities have kept pace with new technologies. Local, regional, and national junior police academy programs have been organized. Merit selection may be used by some of these academies because of limited space and personnel resources. In general, post participants must maintain good moral character and at least average grade work. When not engaged in training exercises, many Law Enforcement Explorers have opportunities to practice their skills by providing security, crowd, and traffic control at community events. The youth involved in such career exploration posts must register with the Learning for Life Corporation. Law Enforcement Exploring programs are based on five areas of emphasis: career opportunities, life skills, citizenship, character education, and leadership experience. (For more information, go to: http://www. learningforlife.org.)

Individual Explorer posts can specialize in a variety of career skills. The Learning for Life Web site states that "at a time when drugs and gangs are ravaging many of our schools and communities, Learning for Life programs can be a catalyst to help stop this trend."

Police departments and school districts have also initiated other types of youth programs including peer mediation, student courts, conflict resolution, and antibullying programs. It is interesting to note that for several decades in the twentieth century, most efforts aimed at the protection of schoolchildren traveling by foot to and from school and within school corridors were carried out by the students themselves under the watchful eyes of their teachers. Today, this type of activity rarely occurs due to concerns over school district liability. Perhaps, if after appropriate screening and training, today's school-age children (especially, those over age 14) were offered more opportunities for undertaking such duties, they might be better prepared to face life's greater challenges and our schools might be safer.

In 2013, the International Association of Chiefs of Police (IACP) conducted a study of those programs that had registered with the Volunteers in Police Service (VIPS) program. The study was supported by a grant awarded by the Bureau of Justice Assistance (BJA) within the U.S. Department of Justice. Program managers of established VIPS programs were asked to gather and share information on promising approaches, programmatic challenges, and resource needs. Responses were collected from 226 of these law enforcement volunteer program managers.

When asked if their agency had expanded or limited the duties volunteers can perform as a result of fiscal issues, 31% of respondents in the IACP study indicated that they had expanded volunteer duties. This was an increase over the 2009 VIPS Program Analysis when just 20% indicated an increase in volunteer duties. The most common volunteer activities were administrative duties (71%); community outreach/crime prevention (65%); citizen patrols (63%); emergency preparedness/response (48%); chaplain services (45%); and volunteer program administration (42%). The use of volunteers in investigations increased from 16% in 2009 to 27% in 2013. Other advanced and skill-based volunteer duties respondents reported included: research, technology, translation/interpretation, code or parking enforcement, crime analysis, fleet maintenance, and subpoena or warrant services (VIPS Program Analysis 2013).

Violence Prevention in School Settings

According to the Centers for Disease Control and Prevention, "Violence is a serious public health problem in the United States. From infants to the elderly, it affects people in all stages of life. In 2010, over 16,250 people were victims of homicide and over 38,360 took their own life" (Violence Prevention 2013). In the United States, an estimated 50 million students are enrolled in pre-kindergarten through twelfth grade. Another 15 million students attend colleges and universities across the country. School violence is youth violence (bullying, fighting, weapon use, punching, slapping, kicking, etc.) that occurs on school property, on the way to or from school or school-sponsored events or during a school-sponsored event (About School Violence 2013). This section highlights recommendations and reasons for the use of volunteer police in school settings.

In 2013, the state of Utah reached a high plateau that was unusual for a small state with just 2.86 million residents. In that year, more than a half million people were holding a Utah permit to carry concealed firearms, but the largest share of those permits went to people who were living outside of Utah. The split was 62% to 38%. The main reason appeared to be that Utah's permit was recognized by more states than other permits, allowing for easier interstate travel by Utah permit holders with guns (Davidson 2013)—perhaps a fortunate opportunity for all these individuals. On the contrary, the proliferation of guns and permit holders could be a potential threat for many others. The availability of guns may be especially threatening to those children living in neighborhoods where they "can't attend class without fear of being recruited by gangs; where they can't enjoy afterschool activities without putting their lives at risk" (Rice 2013).

However, according to James Alan Fox, murders including guns are not increasing, at least with respect to mass killings in America. Much more common than public shootings are "family annihilations, where a guy kills his wife, children, and himself" (Welch and Hoyer 2013). Fox is a professor of criminology at Northeastern University and coeditor of the book, *Extreme Killing: Understanding Serial and Mass Murder.*[3] Nevertheless, incidents of deadly violence continue to take place in public and private spaces. Shoppers in malls, workers in offices, and especially schoolchildren in their schools are the potential victims. Gun control measures have been stalled on the federal level. Gun control advocates are now trying to build political support at the local level to compete with the National Rifle Association. For example, one organization, Moms Demand Action for Gun Sense in America, mounted a successful campaign during the summer of 2013 to pressure Starbucks into banning guns from its cafés and was hoping to have similar support from McDonald's (Epstein 2013). These advocates are prepared to take one little step at a time.

The need for better solutions for violent crime control is of paramount importance. It is likely that advocates for more law enforcement, self-defense measures, and/or stricter gun regulation will continue their discussions for years to come. While this debate rages, school districts and police agencies are forming new partnerships to ensure safer schools. Moreover, there is a growing recognition that school safety is a shared responsibility among schools, law enforcement, and the community. This understanding has led to a role for volunteer police.

This role is addressed in several sections of a resource document published by the VIPS program. The VIPS program is a partnership between the IACP and the BJA within the Office of Justice Programs, U.S. Department of Justice. The 19-page document provides information specific to law enforcement volunteer efforts in elementary, middle, and high school settings. In concise words, the guide states: "Community volunteers play important roles in implementing and maintaining school-based public safety programs. Their presence in and around schools enhances public safety and allows law enforcement agencies to focus on policing and enforcement functions. Volunteer tasks may include monitoring crosswalks while students are on their way to and from school, registering and tracking school visitors, patrolling school building and grounds during and after school hours, and assisting at special events. Parents, school neighbors, and students can volunteer to accomplish these tasks and build stronger relationships between law enforcement and the school community" (VIPS in a School Setting 2010). Moreover, it recommends that "Reserve police officers are a valuable resource to the community and the police department and are increasingly being called upon to help bolster safety and security in schools. Reserve or auxiliary police officers are highly trained community volunteers who often wear the same uniform and perform the same duties as regular police officers but are unpaid and work part-time. Reserves undergo thorough background checks and most are required to attend an accredited law enforcement academy to obtain proper police certification.... Volunteer officers may respond to calls for service regarding accidents, emergencies, crimes, threats, altercations, and/or requests for aid within the schools.... They can also assist with crime prevention educational programs like D.A.R.E. (Drug Abuse Resistance Education), G.R.E.A.T. (Gang Resistance Education And Training), or conflict resolution classes" (VIPS in a School Setting 2010). The IACP VIPS program has posted numerous resources for establishing police volunteer units on school campuses.[4]

In 2004, an unsworn local VIPS program volunteer teamed up with a school resource officer (SRO) at a Modesto, California, elementary school. The elementary school was in a low-income, high minority, and highly transient neighborhood. They initiated a truancy intervention program patterned after the local sheriff's department's program. The goal of the program was to increase daily attendance and reduce tardiness through parental contact. Working one morning a week, armed with a telephone, a list of absentees, and two thermometers with disposable mouthpieces, they visited the various homes of the absent students. The parents of many of the children were surprised to find a representative from the police department standing at their door asking why their child was not at school. The surprises only continued for those parents who claimed their child had a fever, and the thermometer reading showed 98.6. Other excuses ranged from a lack of clothing, to lice infection, to not being able to get up on time. As a direct result of their efforts, unexcused absences as well as excused absences were decreased by a third (Volunteer Profiles 2013).

Since the Sandy Hook Elementary School massacre in Newtown, Connecticut, in December 2012, many school districts and state governments have been searching for ways to protect their students. One of the most popular decisions has been to hire more SROs. Nationwide, there are about 10,000 such officers assigned to schools from kindergarten through twelfth grade. In 2013, the U.S. Department of Justice awarded $46.5 million to fund 370 additional SROs. SROs are selected from the ranks of local and state police agencies and are assigned to work at local schools on a full-time schedule. However, paid officers may only be one option. In 2013, the North Carolina State Legislature created a Volunteer School Safety Resource Program.[5] The idea was being looked into by officials with the Winston-Salem/Forsyth County Schools. Only individuals with prior law enforcement or military experience would be eligible to volunteer for the program, and they would be required to update or renew their law enforcement training and be certified by the state's Criminal Justice Education and Training Standards Commission as having met the educational and firearms proficiency standards (Herron 2013).

However, in a response to the North Carolina initiative, one commentator noted that there is evidence that in certain instances SROs might escalate adolescent behavior into criminal behavior and that paid SROs do not receive enough training. Consequently, there is no reason to believe that volunteer officers will be better trained than their salaried counterparts (Hill 2013). An SRO carries out some of the functions of a guidance counselor or social worker, such as mentoring or advising, but with arresting authority and a license to carry a weapon in schools. In a national assessment of SRO programs, SROs reported that they spend approximately 20 hours per week on law enforcement activities, 10 hours on advising and mentoring, 5 hours on teaching (e.g., G.R.E.A.T. or D.A.R.E. programming), and another 6 or 7 hours on other activities (Finn and McDevitt 2005). It appears that academic research is limited related to the effectiveness of SROs or law enforcement at keeping schools safe. In Alabama, a study during the 1994–1996 school years indicated that the presence of SROs decreased school violence and disciplinary actions between school years (Johnson 1999). In November 2011, the Justice Policy Institute issued a 43-page report about SROs and recommended that they and other law enforcement officers be removed from schools stating: "School safety can be addressed without on-site SROs. And although there is some evidence that SROs can play a positive role as counselors and mentors in schools, these roles can be better filled by people primarily trained in these areas" (Petteruti 2011, 31).[6]

In addition, junior police programs should be enlisted in new efforts to reduce bullying. Bullying has progressed from attacks in the hallway or on a bus to attacks that can occur anytime due to texting, e-mails, YouTube, and social media such as Facebook, Twitter, LinkedIn, and so forth. A variety of measures concerning school safety have already been implemented to reduce bullying and harassment in schools, but if additional human resources were made available, perhaps more students might benefit.[7] As previously indicated in Chapter 8, supervisors of youth programs should be carefully vetted to reduce any risk of abuse.

Active Shooter and Carjacking Response and Prevention

Law enforcement agencies should take full advantage of such programs as auxiliary/reserve police and Law Enforcement Explorer Posts to fulfill the need for supplemental human resources. Qualified members of these volunteer police programs can be certified to conduct a variety of programs to educate the public with respect to personal safety. In an age of widespread availability of firearms, the promotion of personal safety in public spaces is akin to learning how to swim. Instruction is needed for basic survival. Two areas of critical concern are carjacking and the active shooter.

Carjacking involves stealing a car by force. It is a very serious and sometimes traumatic form of auto theft. It is also a crime of opportunity that can threaten an individual's personal safety. Most local and state criminal codes do not define "carjacking." It is reported as either auto theft or armed robbery. This means that no solid statistics exist on time, place, and victims. Though a carjacking can occur at any time, a sizable share appears to take place during the late night hours (LAPD 2013). The U.S. Department of State's Bureau of Diplomatic Security has declared that "Carjacking has become one of the most prevalent crimes in many parts of the world. Most carjacking occurs for the sole purpose of taking the car; it is a crime without a political agenda and does not specifically target Americans" (U.S. Department of State 2002). Individuals can learn to protect themselves by becoming familiar with the methods, ruses, and locations commonly used by carjackers. (The Bureau of Diplomatic Security has produced a two-page flyer on avoiding carjacking that is available at: http://www.state.gov/documents/organization/19697.pdf.)

Explorer post members can be enlisted to place carjacking prevention fliers or brochures in the waiting rooms of auto dealer service departments, repair shops, and gas stations. An active Law Enforcement Explorer Post was established in 1999 at the California Highway Patrol (CHP) office in Visalia. The Explorer program has provided young men and women with an opportunity to see the inner workings of the CHP and to make lifelong friendships. Through the program, participants attend weekly meetings and training sessions, work in the CHP office, ride along with patrol officers, participate in community events, and attend Explorer competitions that are held throughout the state. Activities have included participating in a DUI checkpoint by working the line and standing with officers as they talked with drivers and handing out DUI checkpoint information. When individuals were arrested and had to have their vehicles towed, Explorers assisted in filling out vehicle storage forms and citations. Periodically, Visalia Explorers also assist the agency with its "active shooter" training. Explorers play the role of both victims and suspects and engage officers in "paintball" type shooting scenarios (CHP 2013).

Although an active shooter incident is unpredictable and is usually a rapidly evolving event, procedures have been developed to enhance public safety. (See the video produced by the city of Houston at: http://www.youtube.com/user/RunHideFight.) Qualified volunteer police officers and senior volunteer police and Explorers can deliver presentations designed to increase chances of survival in an active shooter event.

Professionalism and Volunteer Police: Training and Accreditation

Volunteer police unit members, especially those of the sworn (i.e., peace officer) category, must comply with the most current training standards and other qualifications established by their state's Peace Officer Standards and Training (POST) Commission. This has been a matter of serious concern among regular police agencies and their volunteer police participants. Noncompliance with such standards can result in the termination of the concerned auxiliary and reserve volunteer member. However, it is the existence of a second set of standards that has resulted in the disbanding of one or more volunteer police units. The additional standards were developed by the Commission on Accreditation for Law Enforcement Agencies, Inc. (CALEA). Those police agencies interested in achieving recognition through national accreditation must comply with CALEA. CALEA, created in 1979, is a private, nonprofit organization that serves as the main accreditation source for law enforcement agencies across the United States. Significantly, CALEA has separate standards regarding auxiliaries and reserves. Appendix A provides a copy of the latest available standards. For example, CALEA Standard 16.4.1 requires that agencies seeking the commission's national accreditation must have a written directive that establishes and describes the agency's auxiliary program that includes a statement that auxiliaries are not sworn officers and a description of the duties of auxiliaries, including their role and scope in authority. Standard 16.4.3 states that "If auxiliaries wear uniforms, the uniforms clearly distinguish them from sworn officers." As part of the accreditation process, the CALEA standards also specify that every member of a volunteer or paid reserve force must complete the same training as a full-time certified police officer. Only 4% of the 18,000 non-federal law enforcement agencies in the United States have earned CALEA accreditation (Carder 2013).

In several jurisdictions (Kansas City, Connecticut State Police, etc.), new training standards and accreditation issues have been used as the principal justifications for phasing out the use of existing volunteer police units. Police administrators have stated that they either do not have the financial resources to provide the volunteer training and/or doubt that volunteers will be willing to devote themselves to the longer training requirements. The Ottawa (Kansas) Police Department has an authorized strength of 27 full-time paid officers, and it had a reserve unit consisting of four volunteer police officers. The reserve officers assisted with staffing special events, working during certain holidays and when other staffing needs arose. Uniforms, some equipment, and training were provided (City of Ottawa 2013). However, according to Dennis Butler, the Ottawa police chief, the standards set forth for CALEA accreditation caused the elimination of Ottawa's reserve force when the reserve officers declined to pursue the same training as full-time certified police officers (more than 500 hours of academy training). Chief Butler remarked: "They have other careers and other jobs, and it just didn't make sense for them, given their situations. They provided us with a tremendous amount of support.... We certainly appreciate all they have done for the department" (Carder 2013). Nevertheless, the discontinuance of this reserve unit still left opportunities for the public to participate in the police department's unsworn VIPS program.

Although only a relatively small number of agencies have achieved CALEA recognition and the process for accreditation can take as long as three years to complete, the CALEA standards can provide a benchmark for agencies to aspire to whether or not they are ready to begin the application process. The standards pertaining to auxiliaries and reserves appear to represent a reasonable attempt to assure quality. Surely, police agencies that strive to follow them are moving higher on a scale of professionalism. Clearly, when followed, the standards also raise the status of the concerned volunteer police groups. Carte and Carte (1975) have authored a book about the history of August Vollmer, the principal architect of the professional model of policing. The authors identified at least six attributes in Vollmer's model of police professionalism: (1) rigorous training; (2) dedication; (3) use of the latest science and technology; (4) community involvement; (5) high standards of conduct; and (6) separation from politics.

The development of accreditation standards is an important benefit for the American public. According to these professional standards, if police agencies desire to have their police volunteers assume full police duties, they must train them in the same manner as regular police. This type of training is greatly needed not only for the improvements it can mean for the delivery of police services but also because it can aid and equip the next generation of police officers with a foundation they would not otherwise have had. Across the country, many young adults are joining reserve or auxiliary forces as well as Law Enforcement Explorer posts to learn about police careers. They are sharing their experiences via the social media and other online services. At the same time, agency contact persons are registering with the VIPS program online directory and posting information about their volunteers on their own agency Web sites. These efforts are contributing to a greater public awareness about volunteer police opportunities and helping to foster the selection of new members. In these ways, agencies are better able to draw upon the vast talents and energies of the American citizenry and helping to promote such basic democratic attributes as consensus building, community participation in government, and equality of opportunity.

Immigration and Border Security

In 2013, there was widespread agreement in the United States that America's immigration system was broken. Too many employers were hiring undocumented workers, and it was estimated that 11 million people were living in the United States without appropriate documentation. President Obama proposed a plan that would continue efforts to secure America's borders as well as provide undocumented immigrants with a legal way to earn citizenship. His plan included requiring background checks, paying taxes and a penalty, going to the back of the line, and learning English. His plan was also designed to stop businesses from exploiting the system by knowingly hiring undocumented workers by establishing a reliable way to verify that their employees possess the necessary legal immigration status. An aspect of his enforcement approach was the goal of improving partnerships with border communities and law enforcement as well as creating tough criminal penalties for trafficking in passports and immigration documents and schemes to defraud (White House 2013).

The second largest unit of volunteer police in America is made up of the various posses administered by the Maricopa County (Arizona) Sheriff's Office. It has approximately 3,000 members and its activities and initiatives are routinely touted by the county's long-serving sheriff—Joe Arpaio. In November 2010, in a special ceremony, he swore in 56 new posse members added to address the issue of illegal aliens. The event was highly publicized because the actor Lou Ferrigno was among the new volunteers. Posse members also include the actors Steven Seagal and Peter Lupus. According to Sheriff Arpaio: "Law enforcement budgets are being cut and agencies are losing personnel and yet the battle to stop illegal immigration must continue. Arizona is the busiest port of entry for people being smuggled in from Mexico, Latin and South America. So asking for the public's help in this endeavor makes sense, especially given the success the posses have experienced over the years" (Seper 2010).

During the 2010 swearing-in ceremony, Sheriff Arpaio candidly remarked that he did not expect that the trio of actors would be available for duty anytime soon. He noted that both Seagal and Ferrigno were busy actors and also held other volunteer police positions. At that time, Seagal had been a volunteer deputy with the Jefferson Parish County Sheriff's Office in Louisiana for more than 20 years, and Ferrigno was serving as a reserve deputy with the Los Angeles County Sheriff's Office.[8] Arpaio stated: "But they can be instrumental in heightening public awareness of the immigration issue and encouraging others to join the posse's effort to help reduce the flow of illegal immigrants into our communities" (Seper 2010).

Three years later, following the tragedy at Sandy Hook Elementary School, Sheriff Arpaio began sending his county's armed volunteer posse members to patrol the schools in Phoenix after receiving instruction provided by Steven Seagal. A training simulation exercise involving three armed intruders (portrayed by law enforcement officers) was held, and Seagal conducted training on hand-to-hand defense techniques, drawing upon his martial arts experience (Chasmar 2013).

Although the protection of schoolchildren requires a high level of vigilance and preparation, dealing with the problem of undocumented immigrants within the United States need not always have to be a punitive undertaking. Volunteer police can be recruited to assist persons who may be in need of English language proficiency as well as information about the customs and norms of the United States. An important aspect of this educational program would be to inform immigrants who may be undocumented that they can seek help from law enforcement, emergency shelters, as well as obtain legal assistance without the fear of deportation. This assistance may be needed because of elder abuse, child abuse, domestic violence, sexual assault, human trafficking, or other violent crimes. In order to receive such assistance, victims must cooperate with the prosecution (see the Violence Against Women Act of 1994 and its 2000 and 2005 amendments). Volunteer police of the unsworn variety might be appropriate for this task. Such multilingual volunteers can be recruited for this purpose, thereby helping to establish a more positive relationship between the police and this vulnerable segment of the population.

It may be that the U.S. border is the weakest link in the nation's chain of security. If that is the case, civilians with expertise in the areas of security training, tactics, and planning should be welcomed. Southern border states are particularly at risk because of their proximity to the notorious drug cartels and gangs operating in Central and South America. Members of the general public, all police officers, and police volunteers should be aware of the U.S. State Department's Consular Information Program, which informs the public of conditions abroad that may affect their safety and security. (Country specific information, travel alerts, and travel warnings are vital parts of this program and can be found online at: http://travel.state.gov/content/passports/english/alertswarnings.html.) Alerts concern short-term events that travelers should know about, such as an outbreak of H1N1 or evidence of an elevated risk of terrorist attacks. When these short-term events are over, the alert is cancelled. Warnings are issued to urge travelers that they should very carefully reconsider plans to travel to a particular country. Examples of reasons for issuing such a warning might include unstable government, civil war, ongoing intense crime or violence, or frequent terrorist attacks (U.S. Department of State 2013b). A travel warning is also issued when the U.S. government's ability to assist American citizens is constrained due to the closure of an embassy or a consulate or because of a drawdown of its staff. As of December 17, 2013, there were 34 countries included on the travel warning list. In the Western Hemisphere, the countries included Mexico, El Salvador, Honduras, Colombia, and Venezuela (U.S. Department of State 2013a). In the posted travel warning regarding the security situation in Mexico, information on security conditions is provided for specific regions of Mexico. This particularization is provided because millions of U.S. citizens safely visit Mexico each year for study, tourism, and business, including more than 150,000 who cross the border every day. Nevertheless, the warning states that "Carjacking and highway robbery are serious problems in many parts of the border region, and U.S. citizens have been murdered in such incidents" (U.S. State Department 2013c).

Chapter 6 provides details about a proposal for the establishment of a U.S. Border Patrol Auxiliary (BPA). The plan concerns a professional organization of auxiliary members working side-by-side with Border Patrol agents in support of the Border Patrol's mission. This volunteer police force would be screened to ensure they have the traits essential to maintain the high standards of the U.S. Border Patrol. The proponents of the plan have emphasized that the first step to controlling the influx of criminal activity and illegal immigration into the United States involves a secure border. Because the Border Patrol is a proven deterrent to illegal immigrants and criminals along the border, the deployment of the auxiliary force can serve as a force-multiplier that increases the agency's operational capability throughout the full range of its responsibilities (see Hall et al. 2007). Significantly, the use of a federal volunteer unit should also mean that there will be less need to rely on local police volunteers, such as Sheriff Arpaio's posse members.

Homelessness and Volunteer Police[9]

Like many undocumented aliens, the homeless population is especially vulnerable to becoming crime victims. Homeless teens may engage in sex for items they need to survive. Homelessness can involve a continuous cycle of response by law enforcement personnel. In wintertime, it can be a life-and-death matter as police try to deal with complaints about transients camping near buildings and in parks. Moreover, the problem can be compounded when interest groups raise concerns about the rights of those transients who want to be left alone or to be who they are. Some police agencies have resorted to transporting the homeless out of their area, a practice known as "dumping." According to the National Coalition for the Homeless (2009), families with children are among the fastest growing segments of the homeless population. Moreover, approximately half of all women and children experiencing homelessness are fleeing domestic violence. Volunteer police can play a strategic role in dealing with the homeless population. Because their volunteer ranks often consist of middle-aged adults, they represent a cross-section of the occupations found in a community. These roots place them in a unique position to engage in the necessary collaboration and pooling of resources essential for working with the homeless.

According to San Bernardino (California) Police Chief Robert Handy, "It's difficult to keep up with … we deal with chronic homelessness and offer them services but many don't want services. They want that lifestyle. There's a lot of mental illness or criminal backgrounds with the homeless" (Nolan and Emerson 2013a). Chief Handy also commented that his resources were limited in contending with the city's homeless population (Nolan and Emerson 2013a). Although limited, city resources and social services across San Bernardino County are available to the homeless and the working poor, who need a range of services, from transitional housing to food banks. However, Tom Hernandez, the county's homeless services program manager, estimated that more than 30% of homeless people are not aware of the services that are available to them. "Criminal backgrounds, mental illness and substance abuse, relationship issues, physical and developmental disabilities, the economic downturn, all find a part in the different stories of homelessness" (Nolan and Emerson 2013b).

Police Chief Gregory Veitch (Saratoga Springs, New York) has stated: "Police officers do not, however, have the legal authority to require an individual to receive any services offered through government programs, nonprofit organizations, or private entities. The challenge of dealing with the homeless population in any locality is a community issue and one that the local police department has only a small part in addressing" (Veitch 2013). In recent years, Saratoga Springs and other U.S. cities have established Code Blue alert programs, but only after the deaths of homeless persons were discovered due to weather-related conditions.[10] Volunteer police along with clergy and social service professionals can form teams in an emergency effort to shelter homeless persons during cold and stormy nights.

Homelessness is an extremely complex social problem that impacts the quality of life in every community. There are no easy solutions. Many homeless are on the street because of substance abuse, mental illness, or both.

Sometimes the disorder issues associated with homelessness are criminal in nature but difficult to enforce. Volunteer police can be qualified and trained to assist communities in providing better service to this "at-risk" population. They can participate and even lead "homeless outreach teams." Such a team has been established in San Diego and consists of police officers, county health and human services specialists, and psychiatric clinicians from a private nonprofit organization (San Diego PD 2013). In addition, to working as part of these teams, volunteer police can also be assigned to meet with individuals or groups that are experiencing problems dealing with the homeless. Various police agencies have posted information that is relevant for this purpose; for example, the Monterey police and San Diego Police Department have prepared a useful set of tips that can be discussed with concerned persons. In addition, specialized units of volunteer police could be recruited and trained to serve as "community center resource officers." Such auxiliary police units could be used to assist existing staff with security at local homeless shelters, soup kitchens, and daytime neighborhood drop-in centers. Perhaps with such additional personnel, these centers could also provide empowerment classes and other structured programming for homeless persons and families.

It is important to note that homelessness does not always indicate a police problem. There have been instances when people in such circumstances have aided the police. In September 2013, for example, Glen James, a panhandler and shelter resident, discovered a backpack at the South Bay shopping plaza in Boston. The bag had $2,400 in cash and nearly $40,000 in traveler's checks along with a passport and personal papers belonging to a student from China. James immediately flagged down police, who in short order returned the bag to its owner. For his actions, James received a citation at Boston police headquarters, where Police Commissioner Edward F. Davis praised his "extraordinary show of character and honesty" (Schworm 2013). Moreover, there have been instances when members of the homeless population have gone to the aid of overpowered police officers. This occurred in San Francisco in 2013 when Ryan Raso was the only person in a small crowd who rescued a female police officer who was being choked and beaten by a suspect. At that moment, the suspect, a larger woman, was reaching for the officer's service firearm. In 2012, Charles Alexander, a former gang leader and homeless man, "saved a Dallas police officer who was being pummeled by a suspect said to be high on drugs" (Dicker 2013).

Reserve Officers Training Corps Police Cadets

In 1908, the first police academy was opened in Berkeley, California, when August Vollmer realized that many officers lacked the skills necessary to solve crimes. For the greater part of the twentieth century, the emphasis on police training has not been on academic work but rather on physical training and experience. However, a college education is beginning to emerge as one of the most valuable assets a police officer can have, especially if there is an interest in promotion and advancement (Armstrong and Polk 2002). Warren (1999) indicates that it is important for law enforcement agencies to partner with organizations such as colleges and professional organizations in order to ensure a quality training program. He points out that there is also an increased need for training that is focused on police ethics, cultural diversity, and methods of stress adaptation.

In the United Kingdom, due to economic conditions, there has been a shifting of some police training responsibilities from the police service to colleges and universities as well as recommendations to do a lot more in this regard (Neyroud 2011). It is a way of shifting the cost of training onto individuals rather than onto the government. However, "this trend is in full swing in many U.S. states, where individuals pay their own way to attend the basic police academy and then go in search of police employment" (Cordner and Shain 2011, 282). At some college campuses, this training takes place in a separate facility or in a section of a building somewhat removed from the academic department. Some colleges will grant academic credit for the completion of basic police schools or academies in the form of elective credits that may be applied for a current or future degree.[11] Significantly, the offering of any such academic credit is discouraged by the degree certification requirements of the Academy of Criminal Justice Sciences.[12] Perhaps a more integrated and rigorous approach to police education might be more acceptable to future planners who are charged with judging the quality of academic programs. A model for this approach is addressed here.

ROTC stands for "Reserve Officer Training Corps." Most branches of the U.S. armed forces sponsor both junior and senior level ROTC programs at selected American high schools and colleges. An adaptation of this program would involve a college undergraduate undertaking police training while still a student and then graduating with a college degree and a certification as a sworn volunteer police officer. Such a program would require an agreement between the participating colleges and the sponsoring law enforcement agencies. It is not an entirely new idea. In the early 1970s, Indiana University developed an on-the-job paid student cadet program to enhance the quality of its university security force. It was a three-year program that led to cadets having full police authority including the carrying of firearms. At the end of the students' junior year, the program required completion of an eight-week summer session involving advanced police training (Delaney 1973). Over the years, police departments in various cities have embraced the idea of recruiting paid cadets who must maintain satisfactory grades and complete their degree programs to remain in good standing. For several decades, the New York City Police Department has had a cadet program for city residents with at least 45 credits and a 2.0 Grade Point Average (GPA). The program provides tuition assistance (up to $20,000), an hourly wage, flexible work hours during the school year, and full-time summer employment. Students must earn a minimum of 12 credits each semester and be enrolled in a four-year degree program at an accredited college within New York City, Nassau, or Westchester counties (NYPD Cadets 2013).

The proposed program would not detract from any of the requirements of an undergraduate degree program or limit student activities but would be an enhancement to any program by giving it a distinctive career focus. The proposed program would be offered as an optional choice (track) within an existing bachelor's degree program. Additional benefits would include improving academic competence and performance (especially communication skills) and increasing the leadership abilities of participants.

A key focus of the program would be fostering the development of very useful career-building skills and experiences. Students would serve a two- to three-year internship with the sponsoring law enforcement agency and participate in a variety of community public safety events as reserve cadets. They would be required to pass background checks, appear in uniform, and have their own command structure. Each of these elements is a fundamental requirement in most public safety agencies.

The field service (cadet) aspects of the program would be supervised by members of the sponsoring agency. This would include the necessary instruction for becoming "certified reserve officers." An office for the personnel involved in the program would be maintained on the college campus. Good academic standing would be a prerequisite for continuous participation. Students in the program would learn to work as a team and develop an *esprit de corps*—two essential attributes for criminal justice career success.

In essence, the program would have many "ROTC" features, the main difference being that its "commissioned" graduates would have had actual volunteer police reserve experience. Having developed a solid record of work in the field of public safety along with good references, students would be much more employable. Moreover, they would have a much better understanding of the occupation and be prepared to deal with the stresses of police work.

One program that comes close to this model exists at the University of Central Florida (UCF) in association with the Orange County Sheriff's Office. It is career track internship program in which college seniors majoring in criminal justice are given the opportunity "to participate in two semesters of job-shadowing with deputies in varying roles with the agency, including road patrol, aviation, marine patrol, communications, evidence, and court services…. Interns in this program, called Law Enforcement Officer Training Corps Cadets, report to a reserve officer, who in turn reports to a full-time sheriff's office volunteer services commander and to human resources personnel for background information. One large advantage to this program is that the curriculum devised by the reserve officer internship coordinator is designed with the university program in mind. This is possible because the reserve officer is a criminal justice faculty member of the university, and attempts to create the necessary link between the practice and theory that students report to be missing in other types of internship experiences" (Wolf and Russo 2005). Although the UCF program is unlike the proposed program because it does not include a requirement that the college students engage in the extensive training necessary to become reserve or regular police officers by the time of their graduation from college, students in the UCF program have the option of attending a law enforcement academy after graduation. Most of the students who complete the UCF program and the academy go into full-time law enforcement positions with either the sheriff's office or a local police agency and some become reserves[13] (personal communication from Ross Wolf, January 2, 2013).

There are a number of college programs in the United States where credit for police academy attendance is incorporated into a four-year degree program in criminal justice, enabling graduates to become eligible for police employment upon graduation. For example, at Alvernia University in Reading, Pennsylvania, criminal justice majors may graduate with a Reading Police Academy certification. The academy is located on the university's campus. The basic training course as prescribed by Pennsylvania Act 120 is designed to provide students with the initial skills necessary to begin their police careers. The Act 120 course is required training for all Pennsylvania municipal police officers. Two types of students attend the academy. The first are newly hired police officers enrolled to satisfy the requirements of Act 120. The second are preservice students who have not yet been hired by a police department. The preservice students are taking the course in the hopes of enhancing their chances of police employment. To be accepted into the academy, applicants must pass physical fitness tests, a criminal background check, and a psychological exam. The course consists of 820 hours and is completed in a 20-week program. Alvernia students have the option of attending the Reading Police Academy and are eligible to apply for the academy during their junior year in order to attend during the first semester of their senior year. The students start the academy in July and are in training at the academy until December. This allows them to obtain Act 120 certification as part of their four-year degree without extended time or expense (Reading Police Academy 2013).

East Texas Baptist University (ETBU)[14] is located in Marshall, Texas, a city of 25,000, 150 miles east of Dallas. Students at ETBU can complete a four-year university degree and be eligible to test for a basic Texas peace officer's license without the need for additional police academy training. The ETBU program was approved by the Texas Commission on Law Enforcement (TCOLE) in December 2013 to serve as an academic alternative peace officer basic training provider. In the past, students who graduated from ETBU with either a bachelor of science or bachelor of arts degree in criminal justice had to continue their training for licensure by attending a certified law enforcement academy elsewhere. The criminal justice program at ETBU had to demonstrate the ability and the commitment to meet all of the standards for law enforcement training and education within the state of Texas. The program was designed to exceed state requirements in several areas, including classroom contact hours, internship requirements, and physical fitness and skills training. Prior to acceptance into the program, students must pass the same background, medical, and psychological exams required for any officer entering a department or training program (ETBU 2013a). Significantly, the completion of this program will also make students eligible for part-time paid or unpaid reserve officer appointments. However, neither the Alvernia University nor the ETBU program mentions the possibility of a reserve police officer opportunity in their online posted materials.

The merging of police training with the curriculums of college and university degree programs appears to be a possible trend in the making, but it must be cautioned that "Higher education can be quite an intransigent institution in its own right, so one should not approach it naively when looking for better models for police education and training" (Cordner and Shain 2011, 283).

Prerogatives of Police Chiefs

Over the course of the history of volunteer policing in America, critical decisions regarding the creation or continuation of volunteer police units have taken place due to the actions initiated by police leaders. For example, in 1918, the reorganization of the New York City's Home Defense League into regiments and brigades of a mobile reserve police force to aid the regular police in disasters or other emergencies was initially proposed by New York City's Police Commissioner Enright. In 1942, New York City's Mayor La Guardia established an auxiliary police program that he entitled "the City Patrol Corps." In 1976, Sanford D. Garelik, the head of the New York City Transit Authority Police Force, created the city's first volunteer auxiliary transit police unit to reduce crime in the subways. In 1988, the Columbus (Ohio) Auxiliary Police Force became the "Columbus Police Reserve" at the behest of Police Chief James G. Jackson and other city leaders (Greenberg 2005). In 2013, the Albemarle County (Virginia) Auxiliary Police unit was initiated by the county's police chief. Conversely, such units have also been abolished by police administrators. In the early 1990s, the city of New Brunswick (New Jersey) ended its auxiliary program but revised it in 2012 (Kratovil and del Rosario 2012). The Chattanooga (Tennessee) Police Department abolished its reserve program in 2000 when the department applied for accreditation from CALEA. The announced reasons for its termination had to do with the finances and time frames needed for satisfying the new standards for training of volunteer police officers if accreditation guidelines were to be met (Gregory 2007).

Using volunteers to help supplement sworn staff is a possible way for law enforcement agencies to continue to enhance public safety. Volunteer police can provide communities with another layer of protection and are an ideal way to enhance civic engagement for uplifting the quality of life. However, the encouragement of partnerships between the public and police are often tied to the decisions made by key law enforcement officials. In a 2003 study conducted at Eastern Michigan University, Madison Heights Police Department Sgt. Stephen Worton concluded: "As a continuation of the community policing programs of the early to mid-1990s, police volunteerism leads to a furthering of trust between a law enforcement agency and the community it serves. The drawbacks of police volunteers are minor: liability can be minimized by proper selection and training, and negative perceptions from sworn officers will eventually diminish as volunteers prove their worth and continue to express their respect for their police officers. Agencies both large and small, rural and urban, are well served by volunteers" (Worton 2003, 21).

The Need for an American Institute of Volunteer Police

This work has covered a large number of citizen-based and police-sponsored initiatives in the field of volunteer policing. However, although there are some national and state-level membership associations involving active and/ or retired volunteer police,[15] there are very few scholars engaged in volunteer police research and there is no government-sponsored entity to encourage the research necessary to discern the full potential of the volunteer police movement in the United States.

The existence of the IACP VIPS Web-based directory and related resources was a huge beginning, but more effort is needed. The IACP VIPS program, which had relied on voluntary registration, included listings and brief descriptions of auxiliary and reserve police units; citizen patrols; search and rescue units; Community Emergency Response Team (CERT) units; mounted posses; Law Enforcement Explorer Posts; local, state, and federal citizen police academy alumni associations; volunteer and unsworn police administrative units; and so forth. However, it is quite another task to determine through carefully designed studies how such volunteers are actually contributing to greater public safety and to make recommendations for their success in the future.

The establishment of an American Institute of Volunteer Police can greatly enhance the future of volunteer police by considering new initiatives for their deployment as well as the quality of their education and training.

In addition, such an institute can examine how citizen participation in the field of law enforcement affects the practices and development of community policing, human rights, and the rule of law. In the field of public safety, the stakes are often high because a life or lives will depend upon the initial performance of first responders.

Summary

Volunteer police are serving throughout the United States. Many are in sworn positions with full law enforcement authority, but a large segment also engage in administrative roles, search and rescue units, medical teams, and citizen patrols. Citizen patrols composed of seniors are quite common in the nation's Sun Belt region. Moreover, since the events of September 11, there appears to have been a spurt in the establishment of Law Enforcement Explorer Posts, especially with respect to their sponsorship by federal agencies. Chapter 9 reviewed the variety of programs for youth initiated by federal agencies.

In 2013, a new state law authorizing volunteer safety resource officer programs in North Carolina public schools was passed. It came as a direct response to the fears generated about school safety after the Sandy Hook Elementary School tragedy and in consideration of older incidents. Under the law, a local school board can enter into an agreement with a sheriff or police chief to provide security at schools by assigning volunteer school safety resource officers. The law requires that volunteer SROs have prior experience as law enforcement officers or as military police officers. The volunteers can make arrests and carry weapons on school property when carrying out official duties. The law provides immunity from liability claims for good-faith actions taken by the volunteers while performing their duties. Also under the law, volunteer SROs must receive training on social and cognitive development of elementary, middle, and high school children; meet selection standards established by the sheriff or police chief; work under supervision of the sheriff, police chief, or their designee; and meet the same educational and firearms proficiency standards required of special deputy sheriffs or special law enforcement officers. North Carolina's new law was among the many actions taken nationwide by state and local governments to address school safety.

In addition, it would be worthwhile for any community to consider having volunteer police work on "truancy intervention teams." Such an initiative was undertaken in 2004, when an unsworn VIPS program volunteer teamed up with a SRO at a Modesto, California, elementary school. A VIPS program recommendation is that reserve police officers can be a valuable resource for school safety and security. They can also assist with crime prevention educational programs.

In Arizona, after the Sandy Hook Elementary School massacre, Maricopa County Sheriff Joe Arpaio directed members of his volunteer police posse (the second largest in the United States) to begin patrols of Phoenix area schools. In past years, he has recruited posses to not only contend with illegal immigration concerns but also reduce the dangers of drug cartel violence spilling across southern border states. In order to accomplish such demanding assignments, the importance of the CALEA standards for auxiliaries and reserves assume prominence. According to these professional standards, if police agencies desire to have their volunteers undertake more complex police duties, they must train them in the same manner as regular police.

Several additional ideas regarding the mobilization of volunteer police were discussed in this chapter. These concerned carjacking, active shooter incidents, immigration, border security, and homelessness. Such future recommendations included the creation of a "Border Patrol Auxiliary" (BPA) to protect the integrity of America's borders. BPA volunteers would be selected and screened to ensure they have the characteristics essential to maintain the high standards of the U.S. Border Patrol. Other recommendations involved having qualified volunteer police: (1) deliver presentations designed to increase chances of survival in an active shooter event or carjacking; (2) assist immigrants in need of English language proficiency and knowledge about America's laws and customs; and (3) lead "homeless outreach teams." In particular, volunteer police can reduce the stress of undocumented immigrant crime victims about deportation matters, and they can participate—along with clergy and social service professionals—to form teams in an emergency effort to shelter homeless persons during cold and stormy nights.

Looking toward the future, two other recommendations were discussed for the advancement of police professionalism: (1) using an ROTC style undergraduate education model to encourage careers in law enforcement and (2) establishing an American Institute of Volunteer Police to encourage the research necessary to bring to fruition the full potential of the volunteer police movement.

The activities proposed here are designed to reduce and deter crime. When there exists only limited resources to supplement ongoing efforts or to initiate new programs, the use of qualified volunteer police should be considered. Each of these new possibilities requires imagination—a characteristic that Drucker (1990, 113) warns can become suppressed in volunteer organizations: "Non-profits are prone to become inward-looking. People are so convinced that they are doing the right thing, and are so committed to their cause, that they see the institution as an end in itself. But that's a bureaucracy. Soon people in the organization no longer ask: Does it service our mission? They ask: Does it fit our rules? And that not only inhibits performance, it destroys vision and dedication." Governmental organizations are prone to the same type of inertia; perhaps, they tend to stagnate even more.

In 2013, the IACP asked program managers of established VIPS programs to gather and share information about their programs and needs. A key finding of their study was that volunteers continue to take on additional duties in law enforcement volunteer programs. Recruiting new volunteer police and qualifying existing members to perform new missions should always require that some level of research be performed. A wise police chief demands evidence of success before initiating a new program. This can be satisfied through the use of Herman Goldstein's "scanning, analysis, response, and assessment" (S.A.R.A) model[16] and case studies of existing volunteer organizations and programs. A major goal of this book has been to explore the current and past operations of such initiatives and to reveal existing trends and the potential for future undertakings.

Ultimately, the present work has attempted to answer the question: Who are American volunteer police? They are the men, the women, and even the children who have committed their extra time to the delivery of services associated with public safety. They represent all racial, ethnic, and religious segments of American society. As long as their ranks are strong and they adhere to democratic principles of equality and fairness, there should be sufficient resources and elasticity to cope with the social control and criminal justice issues of the future.

Review Questions

1. Identify at least four types of school violence.
2. Describe how a volunteer police officer might assist in a truancy prevention program.
3. Discuss the advantages and disadvantages of having a volunteer school resource officer program.
4. State how volunteer police and Law Enforcement Explorers can help prevent carjacking and reduce the risks associated with an active shooter incident.
5. Identify the CALEA standard that may have the greatest impact on the longevity of various volunteer police units and explain why this is so.
6. There are at least six attributes in August Vollmer's model of police professionalism. Discuss how the establishment of a volunteer police program may help foster two or more of these attributes.
7. The documentary film *Bully* has been shown in schools across America in an effort to stop the problem at its source. A 40-page guide for using this film is available at: http://www.facinghistory.org/for-educators/educator-resources. Read at least the first few pages of this guide and identify from the information presented how some

young students may respond when viewing this film. To access this resource a login is required.

8. Read page 34 of the study guide for the film *Bully*. Based on its content, discuss how Lee Hirsch, the film's director, was able to obtain permission to film inside schools, particularly in Sioux City.

9. In January 2013, after Sheriff Arpaio announced his intent to have Steven Seagal serve as a self-defense instructor, the Arizona House Minority Leader called the plan to use movie actor Seagal as an instructor "ludicrous." Discuss the pros and cons of involving celebrities in efforts to control and prevent crime.

10. Discuss how the use of volunteer police to aid the homeless may diminish the police practice known as "dumping."

11. Discuss the pros and cons of using an ROTC college cadet model to provide volunteer and/or regular police education and training.

12. Explain how the Alvernia University and East Texas Baptist University police track degree programs differ from the University of Central Florida's Law Enforcement Officer Training Corps program.

13. Can you think of any areas or needs in the field of public safety that volunteer police can fulfill? Describe these areas and indicate the type of education and training that might be needed to fulfill such roles.

14. Based on your understanding of the nature of volunteer police programs, provide at least three advantages and three disadvantages for relying on a volunteer program to augment police services.

Notes

1. Readers are encouraged to review the following works concerning volunteer police history in order to obtain a fuller understanding of the rise of contemporary volunteer police units in the United States: Greenberg (1984, 2005); and Bartels (2013). Greenberg (1984) explores the origins of the two major types of citizen volunteer police—auxiliary and reserve. The first section of this work is devoted to the early origins of policing and the remainder presents a case study of the use of volunteer police in New York City. Greenberg (2005) builds upon the former work by chronicling the nature and purpose of volunteer police units in America since 1620. In particular, the history of volunteer policing (using a robust definition of the concept) is interwoven with the nation's past in order to consider the possibilities for a safer and more secure future. It also includes details regarding homeland security efforts and various citizen emergency response groups, such as the Civil Air Patrol, U.S. Coast Guard Auxiliary, Community Emergency Response Teams, and fire units. In 44 pages, Bartels (2013) covers an overview of volunteer police in the United States, including training programs, requirements, and qualifications; the nature and implications of the "Stand Your Ground" law and the "Good Samaritan" law; cases of police volunteers killed or seriously injured on duty; and a comparative analysis of volunteer programs worldwide.

2. For an informative review of the history and activities of junior police, see Chapters 8 and 9. An informative 10-minute promotional video for the July 14–19, 2014, National Law Enforcement Exploring Conference held at Indiana University is posted at: http://www.youtube.com/watch?v=9DwqiXKOaj0&feature=c4-overview&list=UUkpz2qX3Oiag3pvI-0WL9iQ.

3. In 2012, a second edition of this work co-edited by James Alan Fox and Jack Levin was published by Sage. It is filled with contemporary and classic case studies illustrating the many violent expressions of power, revenge, terror, greed, and loyalty. The book examines the theories of criminal behavior and applies them to many well-known and lesser-known multiple homicide cases from around the world. The work considers the commonalities and variations among multiple murders; addresses the characteristics of killers and their victims; and, in the concluding chapter, discusses the special concerns of multiple murder victims and their survivors.

4. On March 31, 2014, IACP closed down the former VIPS website, http://www.policevolunteers.org, and transitioned VIPS resources to a newly redesigned IACP website whose homepage is http:// www.theiacp.org/VIPS. Perhaps, the most valuable set of resources ever compiled involving the management of citizen participation in police work can now be found at http://www.theiacp.org/VIPSResources. This IACP Web page provides links to hundreds of useful planning documents. These posted materials can readily be adapted for establishing specialized volunteer police units to assist school districts. For example, there are links to: the 10-page Baltimore County (MD) Police Department "Auxiliary Unit Standard Operating Procedures"; the 11-page General Order regarding the operation of the Waynesboro (VA) Police Reserve Unit; and the 21-page procedures and guidelines of the Longview (WA) Auxiliary/Reserve Police Program. These specific resource links are found under the "Policies and Procedures" section on the Web page. Of course, there exist many other valuable online resources dealing with crime prevention, such as *Best Practices of Youth Violence Prevention: A Sourcebook for Community Action*, a study by Thornton et al. (2002). Their research examines the effectiveness of specific violence prevention practices in four key areas: parents and families; home visiting; social and conflict resolution skills; and mentoring. It is a June 2002 publication of the National Center for Injury Prevention and Control of the Centers for Disease Control and Prevention, Atlanta, GA. It can be downloaded in English or Spanish using the various links found at: http://www.cdc.gov/violenceprevention/pub/yv_bestpractices.html.

5. The law creating the Volunteer School Safety Resource Program is entitled the "Gold Star Officer Program/School Volunteer." The North Carolina statute: (1) defines volunteer school safety resource officer as a person who volunteers as a school safety resource officer in a program developed by a sheriff or chief of police; (2) provides that school safety resource officers may carry a weapon on school property providing that they are engaged in official duties; (3) provides that a local board of education may enter an agreement with the sheriff or chief of police to provide security at schools by assigning volunteer school safety resource officers; (4) authorizes sheriffs or chiefs of police to establish volunteer school safety resource officer programs by recruiting nonsalaried special deputies or special law enforcement officers to serve as school safety resource officers

in public schools; (5) requires that volunteers in the program must have prior experience as either a law enforcement officer or as a military police officer; (6) requires that a program volunteer must receive training on research into the social and cognitive development of elementary, middle and high school children; (7) requires that the volunteer must meet the selection standards and any additional criteria established by the sheriff or chief of police; (8) provides that a volunteer must report to the sheriff or chief of police and work under the direction and supervision of the sheriff or chief of police or their designee; (9) requires that a volunteer must update or renew their law enforcement training and be certified by the North Carolina Sheriffs' Education and Training Standards Commission or the North Carolina Criminal Justice Education and Training Standards Commission as meeting the educational and firearms proficiency standards required of persons serving as a special deputy sheriff or special law enforcement officer but is not required to meet the physical standards required for certification but must have a standard medical exam to ensure a volunteer is in good health; (10) authorizes a volunteer to have the power of arrest while performing the duties of a volunteer school safety resource officer; (11) provides that there is no liability on the part of and no cause of action may arise against a volunteer school safety resource officer, the Sheriff or Chief of Police or employees supervising, or the public school system or its employees for any good-faith action during the performance of their duties; and (12) provides that the assets of the State and Local Governmental Law-Enforcement Officers' Separate Insurance Plan may be used to pay the employer health insurance contributions on behalf of state law enforcement officers" (North Carolina Sheriffs'Association 2013, 3–4). Numbers were added for clarification purposes.

6. Among the alternatives to a police presence in schools, the Justice Policy Institute recommends the creation of "graduated responses to student behavior that take into account the circumstances of the case … to limit the referrals to the juvenile justice system, suspensions and expulsions by establishing a rubric and system for meting out discipline. This could also include developing an agreed upon discipline code that makes it clear what is an arrestable offense and what is not. Ideally, jurisdictions should aim for zero referrals from schools to the justice system" (Petteruti 2011, 32).

7. In 2010, a study conducted by http://bullying.org showed that: 15% of students have missed school out of fear of being bullied; 71% of students reported bullying as an ongoing problem at their school; and 54% of students have witnessed physical abuse take place at the hand of another student (Coster 2012). The documentary film entitled *Bully* premiered in 2012. It was directed by Lee Hirsch and filming began in the fall of 2009, shortly after two 11-year-old boys—one from Massachusetts and one from Georgia—committed suicide following prolonged harassment at school. Hirsch spent the rest of that academic year in a handful of schools across the country, following five students and families. He wanted to understand how bullying is handled and how it is approached within the walls of the school building. Among the victims featured are a 12-year-old boy who sustains regular taunts, jabs, and punches from classmates; a 16-year-old one-time basketball star who became a town outcast after coming out as a lesbian; and a 14-year-old girl jailed for wielding a gun on her school bus to protect herself from bullying. The film also follows two families dealing with the

aftermath of teen suicide (Rappaport 2012). *Bully* has been shown in schools across America in an effort to stop the problem at its source. Recently, the Ohio School District screened the film for all 9,000 of its students as a teaching tool to reach out to both bullies and their victims (Coster 2012). A guide for using this film is available at: http://safeschools.facinghistory.org. In order to view this guide, a brief online registration form must be completed.

8. Actor Steven Seagal's volunteer experiences as a Jefferson Parish Sheriff's Office deputy were filmed in the reality series "Steven Seagal: Lawman" on the A&E cable network. Steven Seagal, who has played no-nonsense tough guys in dozens of movies, has also been sworn in as a sheriff's deputy in Doña Ana County in Southern New Mexico. This took place in January 2013 when Seagal was 60 years old and more than a year after Seagal was named a part-time deputy in sparsely populated Hudspeth County in West Texas. Hudspeth County, which is east of El Paso, is best known for the drug busts of Willie Nelson, Snoop Dogg, and other celebrities at a Border Patrol checkpoint in Sierra Blanca. At the time of Seagal's swearing-in, a Doña Ana County sheriff's spokeswoman said that Seagal is a reserve officer. According to New Mexico law, he can carry out police work only while with a commissioned peace officer. She said Seagal is expected to take part in border security training in the coming months (Borunda 2013).

9. According to the Stewart B. McKinney Act, 42 U.S.C. § 11301, et seq. (1994), a person is considered homeless who "lacks a fixed, regular, and adequate nighttime residence; and ... has a primary night time residency that is: (A) a supervised publicly or privately operated shelter designed to provide temporary living accommodations ... (B) An institution that provides a temporary residence for individuals intended to be institutionalized, or (C) a public or private place not designed for, or ordinarily used as, a regular sleeping accommodation for human beings." The term "homeless individual" does not include any individual imprisoned or otherwise detained pursuant to an act of Congress or a state law.

10. In many communities, authorities may declare a "Code Blue" alert during periods of extreme cold weather. The response to such an alert is to trigger a multiagency effort to reduce hypothermia deaths during the winter months by protecting the homeless, seniors, and other vulnerable populations. Typically, first-responders, trained volunteers, and one-to-one mentors form a team to spread the word about the Code Blue program. The success of such an initiative depends upon transporting, housing, and communicating with those in need of shelter. Volunteer police can perform each of these roles. They can be invaluable extra hands by assisting in the community centers and temporary shelters that will be occupied for the duration of Code Blue emergencies. According to Bridgeton, New Jersey's mayor, Albert B. Kelly, "We really need volunteers just to be present to help some of our most vulnerable citizens ... the work itself is not hard, but it's work that is good and decent and worthy of our best efforts" (Kov 2013). Center directors are less likely to get "burned out" or overwhelmed by working multiple overnight shifts to keep their centers open if volunteers, such as auxiliary or reserve police, are available for center work. In the city of Baltimore, officials announce a Code Blue day for the following weather-related events: when temperatures are expected to be below 25° with winds of 15 miles per hour or higher; when temperatures are less than 20°; or during other periods of intense winter weather (Scharper 2010).

11. A few examples of state-approved law enforcement academies housed on various college campuses that may be open to qualified members of the public include Stark State College in North Canton, OH; Yuba College in Marysville, CA; Alvernia University in Reading, PA; and Niagara University in Lewiston, NY.

12. To be certified by the Academy of Criminal Justice Sciences (ACJS), the institution must provide evidence demonstrating that the program is in compliance with all requirements of the certification standards. The standards were adopted in 2005. Standard D.3 of the "Certification Standards for College/University Criminal Justice Baccalaureate Degree Programs" states: "Only credit from institutions that are accredited by their regional higher education accrediting body is accepted for transfer into an undergraduate criminal justice program. No academic credit is awarded by the criminal justice program for life experience or for military, police academy, or other professional training." For further information, contact: ACJS Academic Review Committee Chair, Dr. Gerald Bayens. e-mail: gerald.bayens@washburn.edu.

13. At the time of the preparation of this book, Dr. Ross Wolf, associate professor of criminal justice and associate dean for academic affairs and technology at the College of Health and Public Affairs, University of Central Florida (UCF), was serving as a reserve chief in the Orange County Sheriff's Office Reserves and as the coordinator for the Law Enforcement Officer Training Corps for that agency. The training and qualifications to become a reserve deputy are the same as that of a full-time deputy. Many former members of the reserve unit have become full-time sheriff's office employees. Wolf has traveled to Hong Kong and Singapore to conduct research on volunteer policing and to share his knowledge of American volunteer law enforcement. UCF students have studied volunteer policing in England during study abroad programs. (Dr. Ross Wolf can be contacted via e-mail at: ross.wolf@ocfl.net.)

14. East Texas Baptist University (ETBU), affiliated with the Baptist General Convention of Texas, is a private, Christian university of liberal arts and sciences. ETBU was founded as the College of Marshall in 1912. It became East Texas Baptist College in 1944. ETBU is accredited by the Southern Association of Colleges and Schools Commission on Colleges to award baccalaureate and master's degrees. Enrollment is approximately 1,200 students and more than 85% of full-time faculty members have earned doctorates or terminal degrees (ETBU 2013b).

15. The following information about several national and statewide volunteer police associations is entirely based on their respective Web site postings. *The Reserve Law Officers Association of America* was founded in 1970 to serve the needs of volunteer peace officers. It is a tax exempt nonprofit fraternal organization, and it offers insurance for line of duty injuries. *The Volunteer Law Enforcement Officer Alliance* strives to assist in the formation, expansion, and training of state, county, and city volunteer law enforcement units and to promote awareness of the role of the volunteer officer in providing for the safety of the citizens of their communities. Membership also includes an insurance plan while performing any and all law enforcement, emergency response, and criminal justice duties while working in any full-time, part-time, auxiliary, and reserve volunteer capacity. It was incorporated, as a not for profit corporation, in the state of Florida in 2009. *The Massachusetts Volunteer Law Enforcement Officer Association* (MA-VLEOA)

seeks to promote the ideals, goals, general welfare, and professionalism of the volunteer law enforcement officers of the Commonwealth of Massachusetts. The MA-VLEOA has established a scholarship to honor the memory of Massachusetts Institute of Technology Officer Sean Collier who was murdered in the line of duty on April 18, 2013. Officer Collier started his law enforcement career as an auxiliary officer in Somerville, MA. The Sean Collier Scholarship will provide reserve academy tuition assistance to members of the MA-VLEOA. *The California Reserve Peace Officers Association* (CRPOA) membership is open to anyone who is involved in or supportive of law enforcement. CRPOA serves the entire law enforcement community through organizational networking, education, legal services, and medical benefits. Annual training conferences are held. It works closely with the California State Legislature on bills where volunteers are involved. *The New York State Association of Auxiliary Police, Inc.* (NYSAAP), is a type A not for profit trade association incorporated in 1973 as the New York State Auxiliary Police Association, Inc. In 2001, it was reorganized under its current name to represent members of uniformed volunteers in law enforcement, primarily auxiliary police in New York State. It works closely with the New York State Legislature on bills concerning volunteer police work and benefits.

16. Herman Goldstein's S.A.R.A. model involves scanning, analysis, response, and assessment. The first step is to identify the problem and scan the community so that you understand the underlying dynamics that can inform your response. The next step is to analyze the pressure points where intervention can make a positive difference. In the response phase, all the data collected from the previous steps can be used to build in a series of assessments that can allow you to make course corrections along the way.

References

About School Violence. (2013). Retrieved December 16, 2013 from http://www.cdc.gov/violenceprevention/youthviolence/schoolviolence/index.html

Armstrong, D. and Polk, O. E. (2002). College for cops: The fast track for success. *Journal of the Institute of Justice and International Studies, 17*(5), 24–26.

Bartels, E. C. (2013). *Volunteer police in the United States: Programs, challenges, and legal aspects.* Heidelberg, Germany: Springer.

BBC News. (2014). 1952: Anne Frank published in English. Retrieved March 4, 2014 from http://news.bbc.co.uk/onthisday/hi/dates/stories/april/30/newsid_3715000/3715435.stm

Borunda, D. (2013, January 24). Actor Steven Seagal sworn in as Doña Ana County sheriff's deputy. *El Paso Times.* Retrieved December 19, 2013 from http://www.elpasotimes.com/newupdated/ci_22435057/actor-steven-seagal-sworn-do-ana-county-sheriffs

Briney, A. (2009). Sunbelt. Retrieved December 15, 2013 from http://geography.about.com/od/specificplacesofinterest/a/sunbelt.htm

Carder, D. (2013, October 30). Police disband reserve force. *Ottawa Herald.* Retrieved October 31, 2013 from http://ottawaherald.com/news/103113reserve

Carte, G. and Carte, E. (1975). *Police reform in the United States: The era of August Vollmer*, 1905–1932. Berkeley, CA: University of California Press.

Chasmar, J. (2013, February 10). Sheriff Joe Arpaio, actor Steven Seagal train posses to guard schools. *The Washington Times*. Retrieved December 19, 2013 from http://www.washingtontimes.com/news/2013/feb/10/sheriff-joe-arpaio-actor-steven-seagal-train-posse/

CHP. (2013). Visalia Explorer Post 480. Retrieved December 24, 2013 http://www.chp.ca.gov/recruiting/explorers_visalia.html

City of Arcadia. (2013a) City of Arcadia, CA: Volunteer programs. Retrieved December 15, 2013 from http://www.ci.arcadia.ca.us/home/index.asp?page = 1560

City of Arcadia. (2013b). Information on the Arcadia Mounted Enforcement Team. Retrieved December 15, 2013 from http://www.ci.arcadia.ca.us/home/index.asp?page = 1612

City of Ottawa. (2013). Police programs. Retrieved December 18, 2013 from http://www.ottawaks.gov/Departments/Police/Programs/tabid/146/Default.aspx

Cordner, G. and Shain, C. (2011, August). Editorial: The changing landscape of police education and training. *Police Practice & Research, 12*(4), 281–285.

Coster, J. (2012, May 22). Increase in bullying affecting youth. Retrieved May 26, 2012 from http://my.hsj.org/Schools/Newspaper/tabid/100/view/frontpage/articleid/528821/newspaperid/3334/Increase_in_bullying_affecting_youth.aspx

David, J. A. (2013, April 1). C.S. Lewis Daily: A tribute to Anne Frank. Retrieved March 4, 2014 from http://johnadavid.wordpress.com/2013/04/01/c-s-lewis-daily-a-tribute-to-anne-frank/

Davidson, L. (2013, December 7). Permits for concealed guns: Utah hits 500K. *The Salt Lake Tribune*. Retrieved December 16, 2013 from http://www.sltrib.com/sltrib/politics/57214669-90/utah-permits-permit-gun.html.csp?page = 2

Delaney, M. J. (1973). *Indiana University Police Academy Cadet Program evaluation: Police technical assistance report*. Arlington, VA: Westinghouse Justice Institute.

Dicker, R. (2013, September 3). Ryan Raso, homeless man, saves female police office. *The Huffington Post*. Retrieved December 20, 2013 from http://www.huffingtonpost.com/2013/09/03/ryan-raso-homeless-man_n_3860450.html

Drucker, P. F. (1990). *Managing the nonprofit organization: Principles and practices*. New York, NY: HarperCollins.

Epstein, R. J. (2013). Gun control battle moves to main street. Retrieved December 16, 2013 from http://www.politico.com/story/2013/12/gun-control-efforts-101153.html?hp = f1

ETBU. (2013a). ETBU gets approval for peace officer training. Retrieved December 22, 2013 from http://www.marshallnewsmessenger.com/news/etbu-gets-approval-for-peace-officer-training/article_9f2ba857-d034-5122-8d05-78a3f191a1f6.html

ETBU. (2013b). History. Retrieved December 22, 2013 from http://www.etbu.edu/about/glance/

Finn, P. and McDevitt, J. (2005). *National assessment of school resource officer programs: Final project report*. Washington, DC: National Institute of Justice.

Greenberg, M. A. (1984). *Auxiliary police: The citizens approach to public safety*. Westport, CT: Greenwood Press.

Greenberg, M. A. (2005). *Citizens defending America: From colonial times to the age of terrorism*. Pittsburgh, PA: University of Pittsburgh Press.

Gregory, L. (2007, October 14). Backups in reserve. *Chattanooga Times Free Press*. Retrieved January 19, 2014 from http://www.timesfreepress.com/news/2007/oct/14/Backups-in-reserve/

Haimowitz, M. (2014). We didn't wait a single moment. Retrieved June 28, 2014 from http://jewishpalmbeach.org/community/feature/we_didnt_wait_a_single_moment/

Hall, C., Schauerman, G., Ewing, R. and Brandner, B. (2007, May 5). *Securing the borders: Creation of the Border Patrol Auxiliary*. Master's thesis. National Security Program, Kennedy School of Government, Harvard University. Retrieved October 10. 2013 from http://www.dtic.mil/dtic/tr/fulltext/u2/a476945.pdf

Herron, A. (2013, August 23). Armed volunteers could find place in local schools. *Winston- Salem Journal*. Retrieved December 12, 2013 from http://www.journalnow.com/news/local/article_62e5a9f2-0c57-11e3-8a16-001a4bcf6878.html?mode = jqm

Hill, C. (2013, July 14). The problem of volunteer school resource officers. Retrieved December 12, 2013 from http://pulse.ncpolicywatch.org/2013/07/24/the-problem-of-volunteer-school-resource-officers/

Johnson, H. A., Travers, N. T. and Jones, M. (2008). *History of criminal justice* (4th ed.). Newark, NJ: LexisNexis Group.

Johnson, I. M. (1999). School violence: The effectiveness of a school resource officer program in a southern city. *Journal of Criminal Justice, 27*, 173–192.

Kov, D. J. (2013, December 17). Bridgeton's Code Blue program shaping up. Retrieved December 22, 2013 from http://www.thedailyjournal.com/article/20131217/NEWS01/312170013/B-ton-s-Code-Blue-program-shaping-up

Kratovil, C. and del Rosario, A. (2012, July 28). City resurrects auxiliary police program with 7 volunteers. Retrieved January 19, 2014 from http://newbrunswicktoday.com/article/city-resurrects-auxiliary-police-program-7-volunteers

LAPD. (2013). Carjacking. Retrieved December 17, 2013 from http://www.lapdonline.org/crime_prevention/content_basic_view/1368

National Coalition for the Homeless. (2009, July). Who is homeless? Retrieved December 19, 2013 from http://www.nationalhomeless.org/factsheets/who.html

Neyroud, P. (2011). *Review of police leadership and training*. London: Home Office.

Nolan, M. and Emerson, S. (2013a, August 18). Dealing with the homeless: Lessons in success, failure. Retrieved December 18, 2013 from http://www.sbsun.com/social- affairs/20130818/dealing-with-the-homeless-lessons-in-success-failure

Nolan, M. and Emerson, S. (2013b, August 17). San Bernardino County poised to help the homeless. Retrieved December 18, 2013 from http://www.sbsun.com/social-affairs/20130817/san-bernardino-county-poised-to-help-the-homeless

North Carolina Sheriffs' Association. (2013, July 22). Special Legislative Report. *Weekly Legislative Report*. Retrieved December 12, 2013 from http://www.ncsheriffs.org/Weekly%20Legislative%20Report/2013/NCSA%20Weekly%20Legislative%20Report-2013.07.22.pdf

NYPD Cadets. (2013). Retrieved December 26, 2013 from http://www.nypdcadets.com/

Petteruti, A. (2011, November). *Education under arrest: The case against police in schools*. Washington, DC: Justice Policy Institute.

Rappaport, J. (2012). Interview with Director Lee Hirsch: Bullying impacts who we are as a nation. Retrieved May 22, 2012 from http://safeschools.facinghistory.org/content/interview-director-lee-hirsch-bullying-impacts-who-we-are-nation

Reading Police Academy. (2013). Retrieved December 23, 2013 from http://www.readingpa.gov/content/reading-police-academy

Rice, C. (2013, December 3). Beyond Newtown: The larger tragedy of guns and kids. Retrieved December 16, 2013 from http://www.thecrimereport.org/archive/2013-12-beyond- newtown-the-larger-tragedy-of-guns-and-kids

San Diego PD. (2013). Prevention tips: Dealing with homeless people. Retrieved December 18, 2013 from http://www.sandiego.gov/police/services/prevention/tips/homeless.shtml

Scharper, J. (2010, December 14). City declares 'Code Blue' conditions. *The Baltimore Sun*. Retrieved December 22, 2013 from http://articles.baltimoresun.com/keyword/code-blue

Schworm, P. (2013, September 16). Police honor homeless man's good deed. *The Boston Globe*. Retrieved December 19, 2013 from http://www.bostonglobe.com/metro/2013/09/16/glen-james-homeless-man-who-returned-bag-cash-honored-boston-police/yUZjfKiELlXDURjhQwQ23O/story.html

Seper, J. (2010, November 17). Arizona sheriff Arpaio forms armed 'immigration posse' with Hollywood actors. *The Washington Times*. Retrieved December 18, 2013 from http://www.washingtontimes.com/news/2010/nov/17/arizona-sheriff-arpaio-forms-armed-immigration-pos/

SS Police State. (2014). SS and SA become auxiliary police units. Retrieved March 4, 2014 from http://www.ushmm.org/outreach/en/article.php?ModuleId = 10007675

Thornton, T. N., Craft, C. A., Dahlberg, L. L., Lynch, B. S. and Baer, K. (2002). *Best practices of youth violence prevention: A sourcebook for community action (Rev.)*. Atlanta, GA: Centers for Disease Control and Prevention, National Center for Injury Prevention and Control.

U.S. Department of State. (2002). Carjacking: Don't be a victim. Retrieved December 17, 2013 from http://www.state.gov/m/ds/rls/rpt/19782.htm

U.S. Department of State. (2013a). Current travel warnings. Retrieved December 19, 2013 from http://travel.state.gov/travel/cis_pa_tw/tw/tw_1764.html

U.S. Department of State. (2013b). International travel. Retrieved December 19, 2013 from http://travel.state.gov/travel/

U.S. Department of State. (2013c). Travel warning: Mexico, July 12, 2013. Retrieved December 19, 2013 from http://travel.state.gov/travel/cis_pa_tw/tw/tw_6033.html

Veitch, G. (2013, December 12). Letter to the editor. *Saratoga Wire*. Retrieved December 18, 2013 from http://www.saratogawire.com/article/1780/131216-police-homeless/

Violence Prevention. (2013). Retrieved December 16, 2013 from http://www.cdc.gov/ViolencePrevention/

VIPS Program Analysis. (2013). 2013 Volunteers in Police Service program analysis of registered volunteer law enforcement programs. Retrieved January 18, 2014 from http://www.policevolunteers.org/files/2013_Analysis_Results_Report.pdf

Volunteer Profiles. (2013). Herb Hamby: Modesto, California, Police Department. Retrieved December 12, 2013 from http://www.policevolunteers.org/vips_action/?fa = volunteer_profiles

Warren, G. A. (1999). *Police academy training for 21st century law enforcement*. Dover, DE: Delaware Law Enforcement Institute.

Welch, W. M. and Hoyer, M. (2013, December 15). 30 mass killings, 137 victims: A typical year. *USA Today*. Retrieved December 16, 2013 from http://www.usa-today.com/story/news/nation/2013/12/15/mass-killings-main/3821897/

White House. (2013). Immigration: Creating an immigration system for the 21st century. Retrieved December 18, 2013 from http://www.whitehouse.gov/issues/immigration

Wolf, R. and Russo, C. (2005). Utilizing reserves: Getting the most from your volunteers. *Campus Law Enforcement Journal, 35*(3), 24–28.

Worton, S. (2003, September). *Volunteers in police work: A study of the benefits to law enforcement agencies. An applied research project submitted as part of the School of Police Staff and Command Program.* Eastern Michigan University. Retrieved January 20, 2014 from http://www.emich.edu/cerns/downloads/papers/PoliceStaff/Police%20Personnel%20(e.g.,%20Selection,%20%20Promotion)/Volunteers%20in%20Police%20Work.pdf

Epilogue

Readers of this book may want to know more about volunteer policing, how to improve an existing program, or even how to start a volunteer police unit. The acquisition and study of some basic reading materials are essential, including the following works: Everett M. King's *The Auxiliary Police Unit* (Charles C. Thomas, 1960), 215 pages; Elizabeth C. Bartels' *Volunteer Police in the United States* (Springer, 2014), 44 pages; Ross Wolf and Carol Jones' Volunteer Police: Choosing to serve (CRC Press, 2015); and the Federal Emergency Management Agency's *The Citizen Corps Volunteer Liability Guide*, 100 pages.

King's book, although quite outdated, presents a well-ordered guide covering nearly every aspect of organizing a functional unit and is invaluable for an administrator planning such an institution. A special order, 230-page paperback edition of this work became available in May 2012. (It is published by Literary Licensing, LLC.) Bartels' book is available in both e-book and softcover formats. It can serve as an overview of the challenges facing volunteer policing units. It also contains examples of international volunteer police programs to provide recommendations and best practices. FEMA's guide provides an overview of liability concerns and suggests approaches to address these concerns. It is a free publication available at: http://www.ready. gov/guides. The material in this guide is offered for general information purposes only. It does not provide legal advice, and the user is encouraged to seek out state-specific counsel from a qualified attorney before taking any action. Chapter 10 contains additional information about the guide.

In 1993, Richard Weinblatt's 250-page book—*Reserve Law Enforcement in the United States: A National Study of State, County, and City Standards Concerning the Training & Numbers of Non-full-time Police and Sheriff's Personnel was published*. It provides an overview of the numbers, training standards, and rules governing full-time, part-time, and volunteer law enforcement officers in the United States based on research conducted prior to 1993. Dr. Weinblatt is the dean of the School of Public and Social Services and the School of Education at Ivy Tech Community College based in Indianapolis. Additional information about his background and publications is available at: http://www.thecopdoc.com/index.html.

The next step in preparation for a new volunteer police program or for updating an existing program is to engage in networking with other concerned persons. The annual training conference of the California Reserve

Peace Officers Association (CRPOA) is highly recommended. In August 2013, the CRPOA held a four-day training conference in San Jose with more than 300 reserve officers and coordinators in attendance. Topics covered included building searches, understanding street gangs, identity theft, crimes against children, search and seizure, and officer safety. The conference also included an eight-hour Reserve Coordinator Introduction class for newer reserve coordinators that was followed the next day by a four-hour Reserve Coordinator Update class for experienced coordinators. Nearly 50 attendees participated in the two classes, which provided information and discussions on reserve training, reserve levels, selection standards, training requirements, and recruitment. The CRPOA's 2014 annual conference was held in San Diego. CRPOA's training programs are open to volunteers in policing, search and rescue members, and reserve and full-time peace officers. The knowledge gained by conference attendance is useful to persons not only from California but from other states as well (C. Adams, personal communication, January 29, 2014).

Finally, concerned readers should routinely refer to the newly revised Web pages of the IACP VIPS program which can be found at http://www. theiacp.org/VIPS. The site contains hundreds of useful documents dealing with the management of citizens who have volunteered to participate in crime prevention programs, such as volunteer police. This important Web resource includes examples of volunteer program manuals; position descriptions; and screening, waiver, and confidentiality forms. Many of these documents should be of special interest to new program developers as well as the coordinators and members of existing units of volunteer police.

Appendix A:
The Commission on Accreditation for Law Enforcement Agencies Reserve and Auxiliary Police Standards

Appendix A contains sections 16.3 and 16.4 from the *Standards for Law Enforcement Agencies* along with the manual's definition of "reserve" and "auxiliary." The Commission on Accreditation for Law Enforcement Agencies, Inc. (CALEA®), is the registered copyright holder and publisher of this information. The material is from *Standards for Law Enforcement Agencies*, ©2006, update 5.17 from August 2013. All rights are reserved. Permission has been granted to reprint these standards and definitions.

Reserve

A sworn officer, armed or unarmed, who works less than full time, with or without compensation, and who, by their assigned function or as implied by their uniform, performs duties associated with those of a police officer.

Auxiliary

A non-sworn, unarmed, uniformed or non-uniformed, affiliate whose duties contribute to the mission of the agency in a support capacity. Included are police volunteers, law enforcement cadets, law enforcement explorers, senior citizen groups, and other volunteers. Excluded are part-time paid employees of the agency and reserve officers.

16.3.1 Program Description

A written directive establishes and describes the agency's reserve officer program.

> **Commentary:** Terminology describing reserve officers can vary from jurisdiction to jurisdiction and for the purpose of this manual,

the glossary term will be used. Reserve officers generally assist full-time sworn personnel in the day-to-day delivery of law enforcement services and for emergencies, consistent with applicable law. To accomplish these tasks, they may require law enforcement powers equivalent to those of full-time officers. The directive should describe the duties and responsibilities of reserve officers, define their authority and discretion in carrying out their duties, including any limitations or restrictions to this authority, and delineate the amount of supervision they are to receive.

Commission Interpretation (November 16, 2001). The Commission acknowledges that some agencies utilize reserve officers who do not meet the definition of an "employee." For example, some agencies utilize volunteer reserve officers and the absence of wages or salary excludes them from the definition. For the purpose of this Standards Manual, all reserve officers shall be considered "employees" when applying standards dealing with performance evaluations. Procedures and forms used for evaluating the performance of the agency's reserve officers may be the same as those used for full-time sworn officers or they may differ significantly, based on distinctions made in the role, scope of authority, or responsibilities of the reserve officer.

16.3.2 Selection Criteria

Excluding the educational requirements for reserve officers, the selection criteria for reserves relating to knowledge, skills, and abilities are the same as that for full-time officers.

Commentary: Experience, physical condition, and other job-related selection criteria applicable to full-time officers apply equally to reserves. The process of selection may be different from that of full-time officers, but the criteria are the same, with the exception of educational requirements which are addressed in 16.3.9. —Change Notice 5.7 (November 20, 2009)

16.3.3 Entry Level Training

The agency requires all sworn reserve officers to complete a recruit academy training program comparable to that required in standard 33.4.1, prior to any routine assignment in any capacity in which the reserve officer is allowed to carry a weapon or is in a position to make an arrest, except as part of a formal field training program required in standard 33.4.3. If the agency restricts or prohibits reserves from performing specific functions, topics related to those functions may be omitted from the curriculum.

> **Commentary:** The intent of this standard is to ensure that reserve officers receive training equal to that required of full-time officers in those areas of assigned duties and responsibilities. The training should be the same as that received by full-time officers or an equivalent, parallel course that meets the requirements of standard 33.4.1. The subject matter in the training program should over topics related to assigned duties and responsibilities to the same extent that full-time officers are trained to perform like functions. Training hours and schedule may vary to accommodate the reserve schedule and the course duration may be extended.
>
> If a comparable recruit-training program for reserves exists in the state, successful completion of this program may fulfill the requirements of this standard.

> **Commission Interpretation (March 14, 2008):** If the reserve officer state certification training does not include critical task training identified by CALEA for the responsibilities performed by the reserve officer, such training must be delivered. Those critical tasks include: Community Interaction; Introduction to Basic Law; Post Crime Considerations; Introduction to Traffic; Field Activities; Use of Force; First Aid for Criminal Justice Officers; Law Enforcement Vehicle Operations; and Personnel. Further information regarding critical tasks may be found on the CALEA website.

16.3.4 Uniforms and Equipment

Uniforms and equipment for reserve officers are the same as those for full-time officers who perform such functions.

> **Commentary:** Equipment and uniforms for reserve officers, except for insignia, patches, or badges, should not be distinguishable from those of full-time officers. However, quantity of uniforms and equipment may be reduced to reflect the level of activity of reserve officers. The purchase of equipment/uniforms may be the responsibility of the reserve officer.

16.3.5 In-Service Training

Reserve officers receive in-service training equivalent to that statutorily required for full time officers performing such functions.

> **Commentary:** None.

16.3.6 Use of Force Training & Firearms Proficiency

Reserve officers are trained in use of force policy(ies) and tested for weapons proficiency with the same frequency as full-time officers in accordance with standard 1.3.11.

> **Commentary:** Reserve officers' schedules may not permit participation in regularly scheduled weapons training. They should qualify either as a part of the regularly scheduled program or in a special reserve qualifications program. Qualifying standards and scores for reserve officers should be Identical to those for regular officers.

16.3.7 Bonding/Liability Protection

Reserve officers are bonded and/or provided with public liability protection equal to that provided to full-time officers.

> **Commentary:** The protection attached to the functions of full-time officers should be provided to reserve officers.

16.3.8 Performance Evaluations

A written directive requires performance evaluations for reserve officers be conducted in accordance with the standards in (Chapter 35 Performance Evaluation).

> **Commentary:** None.

16.3.9 Educational Requirements

Reserve officers possess high school equivalency diplomas and meet all state educational requirements at the time of sworn appointment.

> **Commentary:** Education is an important attribute for both full-time officers and reserve officers. Careful consideration should be given to the function and responsibilities of reserve officers before establishing educational criteria that differ from that of full-time officers.
> —Change Notice 5.7 (November 20, 2009)

16.4.1 Program Description

A written directive establishes and describes the agency's auxiliary program, to include:

> a. *a statement that auxiliaries are not sworn officers; and*
> b. *a description of the duties of auxiliaries, including their role and scope of authority.*

Commentary: Auxiliaries are not commissioned as law enforcement officers and do not have the authority to make a full custody arrest. Auxiliaries may be assigned to law enforcement–related community service functions. They can also be used as a resource in emergencies and large-scale special events. Generally, they receive significantly less training than sworn officers or full-time employees. However, if the agency chooses to involve them in various activities to assist in the day-to-day delivery of law enforcement services, it should ensure that their duties do not require the status of a sworn officer, their level of training is adjusted according to the scope of their authority, and that unauthorized weapons or equipment are not carried in the performance of their duties.

16.4.2 Training

Auxiliaries receive training in those authorized and assigned duties.

Commentary: Auxiliaries may provide services to support any law enforcement duties not requiring sworn officer status. However, if the agency chooses to use them, auxiliaries should receive training appropriate to the duties anticipated.

16.4.3 Uniforms

If auxiliaries wear uniforms, the uniforms clearly distinguish them from sworn officers.

Commentary: To have an auxiliary appear to be a regularly sworn officer can be hazardous to the auxiliary, confusing to the public, and a potential detriment to the image of the agency. Unless the auxiliary is clearly distinguishable from the sworn officer, members of the community may expect assistance in situations for which the auxiliary is not trained or empowered to act. Purchase of the uniform may be the responsibility of the auxiliary, **compliance may be OBSERVED**.

Appendix B: Modern Era National Service Time Line

1960s	**Retired Senior Volunteer Program (RSVP); Foster Grandparent Program; Senior Companion Program**
	Demonstration projects launched for these three programs to demonstrate the effectiveness of the service model and to engage older Americans in a range of service activities.
1964	**VISTA (Volunteers in Service to America)**
	Created by President Lyndon B. Johnson as a part of the "War on Poverty."
1970s	**Senior Service Programs + Peace Corps + VISTA = The ACTION Agency**
1973	**Domestic Volunteer Service Act of 1973**
	RSVP, Foster Grandparent Program, and Senior Companion Program become authorized through this act.
1989	**Points of Light Foundation**
	President George H.W. Bush creates the Office of National Service in the White House and the Points of Light Foundation to foster volunteering.
1990	**National and Community Service Act of 1990**
	Signed by President Bush, the legislation authorizes grants to schools to support service-learning through Serve America and demonstration grants. Learn and Serve America is created.
1992	**AmeriCorps National Civilian Community Corps (NCCC) created**
1993	**Corporation for National and Community Service created**
	AmeriCorps created; Senior Corps incorporates the three senior-focused programs: Foster Grandparents, Senior Companions, and RSVP.
1994	**King Holiday and Service Act of 1994**
	Congress establishes MLK Day as a national day of service.
2002	**2002 State of the Union Address**
	After 9/11, President George W. Bush asks all Americans to devote two years or 4,000 hours to volunteer service during their lifetimes.
2006	**President's Higher Education Community Service Honor Roll**
	Launched by CNCS to honor the nation's top college and universities for their commitment to community service, civic engagement, and service learning.
2007	**First Annual AmeriCorps Week**
	Officially launched in May 2007.
2009	**Edward M. Kennedy Serve America Act signed**
	April 21, 2009: President Barack Obama signs bipartisan law to expand and strengthen national service programs.
2009	**First Annual September 11th Day of Service and Remembrance**

Continued

2010	**Social Innovation Fund launched**
	Ensures that high-impact nonprofits are able to attract the resources they need to grow and improve the economic, education, and health prospects of low-income communities.
2011	**5-Year Strategic Plan**
	The plan details specific objectives, strategies, and performance measures, which determine how CNCS will evaluate success over the next five years.
2012	**FEMA Corps launched**
	An innovative new partnership designed to strengthen the nation's ability to respond to and recover from disasters while expanding career opportunities for young people.

Source: http://www.nationalservice.gov/about/who-we-are/our-history/national-service-timeline

Appendix C: Preventing Terrorist Attacks

How You Can Help

This is a message that bears repeating, no matter where you live in the world: Your assistance is needed in preventing terrorist acts.

It is a fact that certain kinds of activities can indicate terrorist plans that are in the works, especially when they occur at or near high-profile sites or places where large numbers of people gather—such as government buildings, military facilities, utilities, bus or train stations, and major public events. If you see or know about suspicious activities, such as the ones listed below, please report them immediately to the proper authorities. In the United States, that means your closest Joint Terrorist Task Force, located in an FBI field office. In other countries, that means your closest law enforcement/counterterrorism agency.

Surveillance: Are you aware of anyone video recording or monitoring activities, taking notes, using cameras, maps, binoculars, and so on, near key facilities/events?

Suspicious Questioning: Are you aware of anyone attempting to gain information in person, by phone, mail, email, and so on, regarding a key facility or people who work there?

Tests of Security: Are you aware of any attempts to penetrate or test physical security or procedures at a key facility/event?

Acquiring Supplies: Are you aware of anyone attempting to improperly acquire explosives, weapons, ammunition, dangerous chemicals, uniforms, badges, flight manuals, access cards or identification for a key facility/event or to legally obtain items under suspicious circumstances that could be used in a terrorist attack?

Suspicious Persons: Are you aware of anyone who does not appear to belong in the workplace, neighborhood, business establishment, or near a key facility/event?

"Dry Runs": Have you observed any behavior that appears to be preparation for a terrorist act, such as mapping out routes, playing out scenarios with other people, monitoring key facilities/events, timing traffic lights or traffic flow, or other suspicious activities?

Deploying Assets: Have you observed abandoned vehicles, stockpiling of suspicious materials, or persons being deployed near a key facility/event?

If you answered yes to any of the above ... if you have observed any suspicious activity that may relate to terrorism ... again, please contact the Joint Terrorist Task Force or law enforcement/counterterrorism agency closest to you immediately. Your tip could save the lives of innocent people, just like you and yours.

Source: https://www.fbi.gov/about-us/investigate/terrorism/help-prevent-terrorist-attacks

Appendix D: Selected Government Internship Opportunities with Federal Government Intelligence Agencies and Law Enforcement Agencies

Agency Name	Opportunity	Web Sites
Central Intelligence Agency www.cia.gov	Undergraduate student internships or undergraduate co-ops, and graduate studies programs are available.	https://www.cia.gov/careers/ student-opportunities/ index.html
Department of Energy, Office of Intelligence and Counterintelligence www.energy.gov	**The DOE Scholars Program:** For students or recent college graduates.	http://orise.orau.gov/ doescholars
Department of Homeland Security, Intelligence and Analysis www.dhs.gov	**Secretary's Honors Program (SHP):** For exceptional recent graduates.	http://www.dhs.gov/ secretarys-honors-program
	CBP Explorer Program: For young men and women aged 14 through 21 who assist the border patrol law enforcement mission.	http://www.cbp.gov/careers/ outreach-programs/youth/ explorer-program
	Student Internship and Training Opportunities and Job Opportunities for Recent Graduates	http://www.dhs.gov/ student-opportunities-0 http://www.dhs.gov/ job-opportunities-recent- graduates
	DHS Education Programs: A 10-week summer research experience for undergraduate students majoring in DHS-related science, technology, engineering and mathematics (HS-STEM) disciplines.	http://www.orau.gov/ dhseducation/

Continued

Agency Name	Opportunity	Web Sites
Department of State, Intelligence and Research www.state.gov	**Student Programs:** U.S. Department of State Internship Program and Pathways Programs. The U.S. Department of State offers two programs: one for high school, undergraduates; and another for graduate and postgraduate students who are interested in working in a foreign affairs environment.	http://careers.state.gov/ intern
Department of Treasury, Office of Intelligence and Analysis www.treasury.gov	**Pathways Programs:** Developed by the Office of Personnel Management (OPM) to reform the student hiring programs across the government. There are three main hiring options: Internship Program, Recent Graduate Program, and the Presidential Management Fellows (PMF) Program	http://www.treasury.gov/ careers/Pages/ pathways-programs.aspx
Defense Intelligence Agency www.dia.mil	**Academic Semester Internship Program:** For full-time undergraduate seniors and graduate students **Cooperative Education Program:** Opportunity to gain valuable work experience. **National Intelligence Scholars Program:** For the most well-qualified college graduates.	http://www.dia.mil/careers/ students/
Drug Enforcement Administration www.justice.gov/dea	Students must be able to meet all DEA employment requirements. For information on student employment opportunities, call 202-307-4088.	http://www.justice.gov/dea/ careers/student-entry-level. shtml
Federal Bureau of Investigation www.fbi.gov	**Honors Internship Program:** FBI paid student internship opportunity.	https://www.fbijobs.gov/231. asp
	Volunteer Internship Program (non paid): For undergraduates (junior or senior), graduates, or post doctorate students.	https://www.fbijobs.gov/239. asp
	Laboratory Division's Visiting Scientist Program: Students, postgraduates, and university faculty are eligible to apply for this FBI program.	https://www.fbijobs.gov/242. asp

Continued

Agency Name	Opportunity	Web Sites
National Security Agency www.nsa.gov	**NSA internships:** Various types including co-op, scholarships, and work study for undergraduates and graduate students.	http://www.nsa.gov/careers/opportunities_4_u/students/undergraduate/index.shtml http://www.nsa.gov/careers/opportunities_4_u/students/graduate/index.shtml

Source: Adapted from http://www.umuc.edu/students/support/careerservices/jobsearch/internships/upload/Federal-Government-Student-Internship.pdf

Appendix E: Human Trafficking—A Brief Annotated Bibliography

Books

Aronowitz, A. A. (2013). *Human Trafficking, Human Misery*. Lanham, MD: Scarecrow Press. 304 pp. Paperback book.

> The book takes a victim-oriented approach to examine the criminals and criminal organizations that traffic in and exploit their victims. The author focuses on the different groups of victims and the various forms of and markets for trafficking, many of which remain overlooked including organ trafficking, child soldiers, mail-order brides, and adoption, as well as the use of the Internet in trafficking.

Bales, K. and Soodalter, R. (2009). *The Slave Next Door: Human Trafficking and Slavery in America Today*. Berkeley, CA: University of California Press. 320 pp. Hardcover book.

> This work contains information about modern-day slaves, slaveholders, and traffickers as well as from experts, counselors, law enforcement officers, rescue and support groups, and others. It explores what private citizens can do to subdue this horrific crime.

DeStefano, A. M. (2008). *The War on Human Trafficking: U.S. Policy Assessed*. New Brunswick, NJ: Rutgers University Press. 208 pp. Paperback book.

> This book considers cases involving the forced labor of immigrants and details the events leading up to the creation of the Trafficking Victims Protection Act of 2000, the federal law that first addressed the phenomenon of human trafficking. The author assesses the effectiveness of the 2000 law and its progeny, showing the difficulties encountered by federal prosecutors in building criminal cases against traffickers.

Gallagher, A. T. (2012). *The International Law of Human Trafficking*. Cambridge, UK: Cambridge University Press. 596 pp. Paperback book.

> This book by a leading international legal authority on the issue presents the key norms of international human rights law, transnational criminal law, refugee law, and international criminal law, in the process identifying and explaining the major legal obligations of states with respect to preventing trafficking, protecting and supporting victims, and prosecuting perpetrators.

Powell, C. and Burroughs, D. (2011). *Not in My Town: Exposing and Ending Human Trafficking and Modern Day Slavery*. Birmingham, AL: New Hope Publishers. 192 pp. Paperback book.

> This work includes a DVD dealing with human trafficking, sex exploitation, forced labor, and agricultural slavers. Cases from U.S. cities as well as from Amsterdam, India, Cambodia, and other regions are reviewed. (To hear an 18-minute interview with coauthor Charles Powell, go to: http://www.newhopedigital.com/2012/09/charles-powell-not-in-my-town.)

Simon, R. J. and Hepburn, S. (2013). *Human Trafficking Around the World: Hidden in Plain Sight*. New York: Columbia University Press. 552 pp. Paperback book.

> The authors recount the lives of victims during and after their experience with trafficking, and they follow the activities of traffickers before capture and their outcomes after sentencing. Each chapter centers on the trafficking practices and anti-trafficking measures of a single country, 24 in all. This study points out those most vulnerable in each nation and the specific cultural, economic, environmental, and geopolitical factors that contribute to each nation's trafficking issues. The authors set forth clear policy recommendations to combat trafficking.

Videos

Human Trafficking in the U.S. (2013, September 23). 2 hrs. 49 min.

> This C-SPAN coverage is of a hearing held before the U.S. Senate Committee on Homeland Security and Government Affairs. Federal, state, local, and tribal officials testified on their efforts to combat human trafficking within the United States. The State Department reported that nearly 20,000 people were trafficked to the United States for prostitution, domestic servitude, and other related crimes. Among the issues addressed in the hearing were the causes of human trafficking, identifying victims, intervention and treatment of victims, and the impact on local communities. (View online at: http://www.c-spanvideo.org/program/Traffickingint.)

Affected for Life (2014). 24 min. approx.

> Produced by the United Nations Office on Drugs and Crime (UNODC), this is a training and awareness-raising video on human trafficking. The film is targeted at prosecutors, judges, law enforcement officers, and other specialized audiences, and it illustrates the elements and different forms of human trafficking. The film is available in full-length with abbreviated versions in Arabic, English, French, Russian, and Spanish. The UNODC has enlisted the help of prominent personalities from the worlds of art, music, film, sports, and literature to highlight key issues and to draw attention to UNODC activities in the fight against illicit drugs and international crime. These goodwill ambassadors include Mira Sorvino (actress), Nicolas Cage (actor), Ross Bleckner (artist), Christopher Kennedy Lawford (activist), and Shahid Afridi (cricket star/athlete). (View online at: http://www.unodc.org/unodc/en/human-trafficking/video-and-audio-on-human-trafficking-and-migrant-smuggling.html?ref = menuside#training_film.)

Victim, Survivor, Leader: Empowering CSE and Trafficked Youth (2013, October 16).
39 min. approx.

Rachel Lloyd, who has spent 15 years as the CEO of Girls Educational and Mentoring Services (GEMS), discusses direct services to survivors of commercial sexual exploitation and trafficking. Her talk highlights GEMS' groundbreaking "Victim, Survivor, Leader model," and she explores the stages of healing for victims of trafficking and the core principles for providing services at each stage. Lloyd is a nationally recognized expert on the issue of child sex trafficking in the United States and played a key role in the successful passage of New York State's groundbreaking Safe Harbor Act for Sexually Exploited Youth, the first law in the country to end the prosecution of child victims of sex trafficking. Her trailblazing advocacy is the subject of the critically acclaimed documentary *Very Young Girls* (Showtime 2007) and her memoir *Girls Like Us* (Harper Collins 2011). (View online at: http://www.youtube.com/watch?v=jGy9MxEOxX0.)

Index